ILLUSTRATOR CS5

for Windows and Macintosh
Visual QuickStart Guide

Elaine Weinmann
Peter Lourekas

Peachpit Press

For Simona

Visual QuickStart Guide
Illustrator CS5 for Windows and Macintosh
Elaine Weinmann and Peter Lourekas

Peachpit Press
1249 Eighth Street
Berkeley, CA 94710
510/524-2178
510/524-2221 (fax)

Find us on the Web at: www.peachpit.com
To report errors, please send a note to errata@peachpit.com
Peachpit Press is a division of Pearson Education

ISBN-13: 978-0-321-70661-4

ISBN-10:   0-321-70661-7

9 8 7 6 5 4 3 2 1

Printed and bound in the United States of America

Acknowledgments

We're grateful to many people for their individual contributions to this book.

Nancy Aldrich-Ruenzel, publisher of Peachpit Press, has enthusiastically supported our projects for over a decade.

Susan Rimerman, our editor, keeps the many wheels in motion for us at Peachpit.

Victor Gavenda, longtime editor at Peachpit, tech edited this book in Windows with cleverness and wit.

Production editor Lisa Brazieal gave us speedy answers to our production questions and did an expert job of spearheading the prepress production before sending our files off to RR Donnelley for printing.

Many other Peachpit Press staff members do important work, such as Nancy Davis, editor-in-chief; Gary-Paul Prince, PTG tradeshow and conventions manager; Keasley Jones, business manager; and Glenn Bisignani, marketing manager.

Illustrator pro artists Harry Campbell, Celia Johnson, Chris Lyons, and Daniel Pelavin kindly permitted us to reproduce some of their work (see pages 425–431). We know it will be a source of inspiration to our readers. (For their contact information, see page 432.)

Elaine Soares, photo research manager, and Lee Scher, photo research coordinator, of the Image Resource Center at Pearson Education, the parent company of Peachpit Press, quickly procured the stock graphics from Shutterstock.com that we requested.

As book packagers, we know that no book is complete without some final polishing. Rebecca Pepper, copy editor, scoured our pages for errors with great care and made intelligent corrections.

Steve Rath generated the index and Scout Festa did the final round of proofreading.

This book would have no reason for being without the software that is its subject matter. We commend Adobe Systems, Inc. for making significant improvements to what was already a great product. We thank the Adobe Illustrator CS5 team, and in particular David Macy, senior product manager for Adobe Illustrator, Harpreet Singh, project lead of the Adobe prerelease program, and Silas Lepcha, now a quality engineer.

And finally, we're blessed with loyal friends and family, who are understanding when we're in deadline mode, give our lives some semblance of balance, and are present for us to love and enjoy even more when we reemerge.

Elaine Weinmann and Peter Lourekas

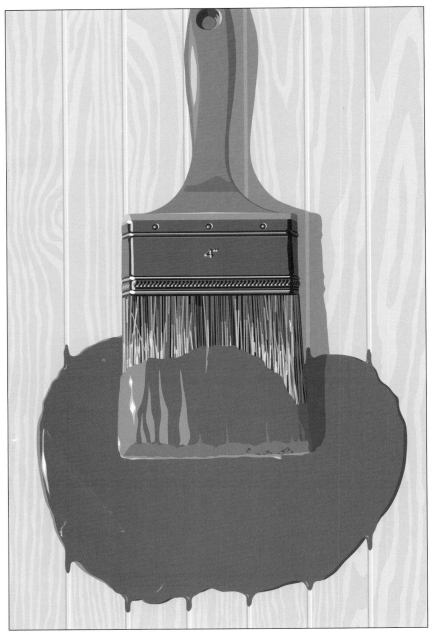

©Chris Lyons

Chapters at a glance

CONTENTS

★ Indicates topics in which new or improved (Illustrator CS5) features are covered

Contents

10 Fill & Stroke

11 Transform

12 Reshape

13 Layers

14 Appearances

15 Effects

©Chris Lyons

REGISTER THIS BOOK!

Purchasing this book entitles you to more than just a couple of pounds of paper. If you register the book with Peachpit Press, you're also entitled to download copies of many of the illustrations used in the book, which you can use to practice with as you follow the step-by-step tutorials. To get started, follow this link: www.peachpit.com/illustratorcs5vqs. This takes you to the book's page at the Peachpit Press website. Once there, click Register your book to log in to your account at peachpit.com. If you don't already have an account, it takes just a few seconds to create one, and it's free!

After logging in, you'll need to enter the book's ISBN code, which you'll find on the back cover. Next you'll be asked a security question to access the illustrations. The answer is found in the book. Click Submit, and you're in! You'll be taken to a list of your registered books. Find *Illustrator CS5 Visual QuickStart Guide* on the list, and click Access to protected content to get to the download page.

Please note that the illustrations are low-resolution (not suitable for printing), and they are copyrighted by their owners, who have watermarked them to discourage unauthorized reproduction. They are for your personal use only, not for distribution.

Of course, you're not restricted to using the downloadable illustrations. For any given set of instructions, you can substitute an illustration of your own or choose a different one from the assortment offered.

In this chapter, we'll show you how to get up and running in Adobe Illustrator. After learning how to launch the program, you'll learn how to create a new document; preview, open, and create document templates; create and modify multiple artboards; save and close your document; and quit/exit Illustrator.

Launching Illustrator

To create a document after launching Illustrator, see page 3.

To launch Illustrator in Macintosh:

Do one of the following:

On the startup drive, open the Applications > Adobe Illustrator CS5 folder, then double-click the Adobe Illustrator CS5 application icon.

Click the Illustrator application icon in the Dock.**A** (To create an icon, drag the application icon from the application folder to the Dock.)

To launch Illustrator by opening a file, double-click an Illustrator file icon or drag an Illustrator file icon over the application icon in the Dock.

➤ By default, a welcome screen opens when Illustrator launches.**B** You can check Don't Show Again to prevent it from appearing upon relaunch. To redisplay it at any time, choose Help > Welcome Screen.

A Click the Adobe Illustrator CS5 application icon in the Dock.

1

IN THIS CHAPTER

Ai
ADOBE ILLUSTRATOR CS5

Open a Recent Item
- Pool table.eps
- Pool table.ai
- art for website.ai
- Brochure cover.pdf
- Brochure cover.ai
- Open...

Create New
- Print Document...
- Web Document...
- Mobile and Devices Document...
- Video and Film Document...
- Basic CMYK Document...
- Basic RGB Document...
- From Template...

- Getting Started »
- New Features »
- Resources »
- Illustrator Exchange »

- Don't show again

B This is the welcome screen for Illustrator.

To create a document after launching Illustrator, see the following page.

To launch Illustrator in Windows:

Do one of the following:

Open Computer, then double-click the icon for the hard drive in which Illustrator is installed. The default location is [Local Disk] (C:). Follow the path Program Files (x86)\Adobe\Adobe Illustrator CS5. Double-click the Adobe Illustrator CS5 icon.

Double-click an Illustrator file icon to launch Illustrator and open that file. **A**

Click the Start button on the taskbar, choose All Programs, then click Adobe Illustrator CS5. **B**

➤ By default, a welcome screen opens when Illustrator launches. **C** You can check Don't Show Again if you want to prevent it from appearing upon relaunch. To redisplay it at any time, choose Help > Welcome Screen.

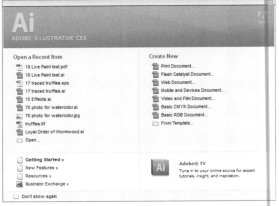

A *Double-click an Illustrator file to open it and launch Illustrator. The documents shown above were created and saved in Illustrator, in several different file formats.*

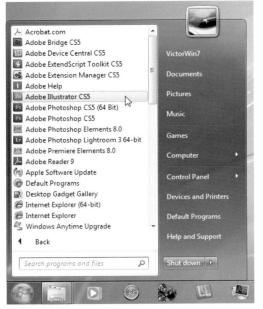

B *Click the Start button, then locate and click the Adobe Illustrator CS5 application.*

C *This is the welcome screen for Adobe Illustrator CS5 in Windows.*

Creating a new document

To create a new document:

1. Do either of the following:

   Choose File > **New** (Cmd-N/Ctrl-N).

   If the Adobe Illustrator CS5 welcome screen is displaying, on the right side under Create New, click **Print Document** or **Web Document**.

2. The New Document dialog opens.**A** Type a **Name** for the new document.

3. From the **New Document Profile** menu, choose a preset for the medium in which you plan to output the file.

4. Each artboard in a document defines a separate printable area. For now, create only one artboard by leaving the **Number of Artboards** value at 1 (at this setting, the Grid, Layout, Spacing, and Column options aren't accessible).

5. Do either of the following:

   From the **Size** menu, choose a size preset.

   Choose a measurement unit from the Units menu (for Web output, use Pixels), then enter custom **Width** and **Height** values.

6. For the document **Orientation**, click the Portrait 📄 or Landscape 📄 button.

7. The **Bleed** values control the width of the print area for items that extend beyond the artboard. Ask your print shop what values to enter. Note: You can either enter them now in this dialog or later in the File > Document Setup or Print dialog.

8. If the Advanced options aren't displaying, click the arrowhead, then do the following:

   Choose a **Color Mode** for the document: CMYK for print output, or RGB for video or Web output.

   Choose a resolution for **Raster Effects**, depending on your output requirements (effects are discussed in Chapter 15). For high-end print output, choose High (300 ppi).

   If you chose the Video And Film document profile, choose a **Transparency Grid** option.

   Leave the **Preview Mode** setting as Default.

   For Web output, to have the horizontal and vertical segments of objects align to the pixel grid so they look as crisp as possible, check **Align New Objects to Pixel Grid**. ★

9. Click OK. A new document window opens.

A In the New Document dialog, type a name, then choose either a preset or custom settings.

Using templates

A template is an Illustrator document that opens automatically as an unsaved copy. Illustrator supplies some industry-standard templates that can be used as a starting point for creating custom projects. They contain artboards, crop marks, objects, styles, symbols, custom swatches, and more. You can get an inkling of what the templates look like via the previews in Bridge (see the steps below). If you're new to Illustrator, this is also a good way to get an idea of what the program can do. On the following page, we'll show you how to open a normal Illustrator document as a template and how to create a custom template.

To preview and open an Illustrator template:

1. Launch Bridge by clicking the Go to Bridge button **Br** at the top left corner of the Application bar.

2. Click the Folders tab in the left panel. In the Mac OS, navigate to and open the Adobe Illustrator CS5/Cool Extras/en_US/Templates folder; in Windows, navigate to and open Program Files (x86)\Adobe\Adobe Illustrator CS5\ Cool Extras\en_US\Templates. Double-click any of the folders in the Templates folder (and any subfolders, if necessary), then browse through any templates that interest you. **A**

3. Double-click a template file. A copy of it opens as a new, untitled document — content, specifications, and all. **B** The original file is left intact.

4. Save the new file (see page 13).

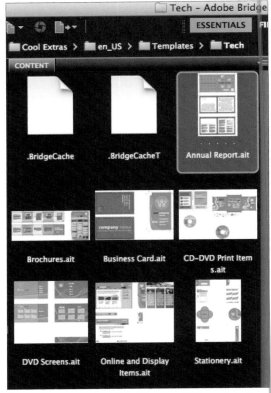

A You can preview the Adobe Illustrator CS5 templates in Bridge.

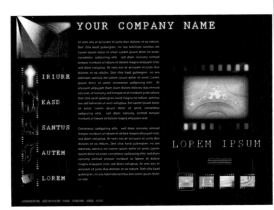

B This template for a website is in the Film subfolder.

You're not limited to using the templates that ship with Illustrator. One alternative is to open any existing Illustrator file as an untitled, unsaved document.

To open an existing Illustrator file as an untitled document:

1. Do either of the following:

   Choose File > **New from Template** (Cmd-Shift-N/Ctrl-Shift-N).

   Under Create New on the Adobe Illustrator CS5 welcome screen, click **From Template**.

2. The New from Template dialog opens. Locate and select an existing Illustrator file, then click **New** to open the file as an untitled document.

3. If the Font Problems dialog or a missing profile alert dialog appears, see the sidebar on page 63.

4. Save the new file (see page 13).

You can also save your own Illustrator files as templates. Regardless of what kind of project you're working on — CD label, business card, book cover, Web graphic, package design, etc. — you will find templates to be great timesavers.

When setting up a file to be saved as a template, you can choose document settings, layout aids such as guides, and multiple artboards, and you can also incorporate such Illustrator features as brushes, swatches, symbols, graphic styles, and, of course, path and type objects. Note: You'll probably want to revisit these instructions later, when you're better acquainted with Illustrator and have created some artwork.

To create a document template:

1. Create a new file or open an existing file.

2. Do any of the following — or anything else you can think of that might be useful to save in your template:

   Create Illustrator objects, such as paths and type.

   Create solid-color, gradient, or pattern swatches; brushes; graphic styles; character and paragraph styles; symbols; etc. — and delete any that won't be needed. You could also load or drag and drop those elements into the current document from another Illustrator document.

   Choose specifications for one or more artboards.

   Set the zoom level.

   Create ruler or object guides, choose ruler units (see page 382), and choose View menu options.

   Create and save custom views.

   Choose default settings for tools.

   Create layers and choose Layers panel options.

   Create crop or trim marks.

   Create transparency flattener, tracing, PDF, and print presets.

   Create text boxes containing instructions for users of the template.

3. Choose File > **Save as Template**. In the dialog, enter a name, keep the default location for templates (the folder that we listed in step 2 on the facing page) or choose a folder, and keep the format as Illustrator Template (ait). Click Save.

THE ANATOMY OF AN ILLUSTRATOR DOCUMENT

To export or print artwork from Illustrator, it must be on an artboard (see the next page). To compare the currently active artboard to the paper size for the currently chosen printer, choose View > Fit Artboard in Window or press Cmd-0/Ctrl-0 (zero), then choose View > Show Print Tiling (the page size can be larger than the artboard size). To display the artboard boundaries if they are hidden, choose View > Show Artboards (Cmd-Shift-H/Ctrl-Shift-H). To learn more about the Illustrator workspace, see Chapter 3.

The following information is listed in the title bar: the current document name, zoom level, color mode (CMYK or RGB), and view (Outline, Preview, Overprint, or Pixel Preview). And if View > Proof Colors is on, the current proof profile is also listed.

⊗ Pool table.ai @ 66.67% (CMYK/Preview)

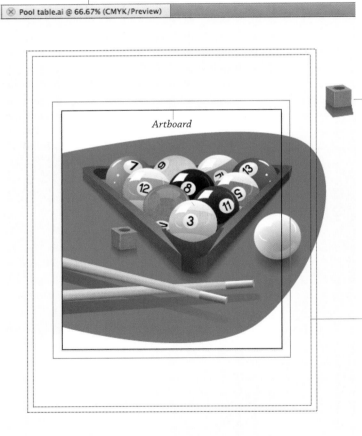

Artboard

The area outside the artboards is called the canvas.* Objects on the canvas save with the file but don't print unless they extend partially onto an artboard, within the current bleed region. You can create and stash objects in the canvas area and drag them into any artboard when needed.

The red rectangle defines the bleed region, which can be specified in the New Document dialog when you create your file, in the Document Setup dialog at any time, or in the Print dialog. To be part of a bleed, your artwork must extend into the canvas area.

The inner dotted rectangle represents the actual printable area. It takes into account the printer's nonprintable margins at the edge of the paper, and is controlled by the specifications of the currently chosen printer (see Chapter 31). The outer dotted rectangle represents the paper size.

*In Adobe Photoshop, the image is contained in what is known as the live canvas area, whereas in Illustrator, the artboard is called the "live" area and the "nonlive" area surrounding it is called the canvas area. Mighty confusing, when you consider that both programs are in the Adobe Creative Suite!

Adding artboards to a document

By default, every Illustrator document contains one artboard. The dimensions for a document's first artboard are chosen in the New Document dialog. Using the Artboard tool, you can add more artboards, as well as scale them individually, change their orientation, and reposition them within the canvas area. Only one artboard can be active at a time. Artboards can be printed and exported individually or sequentially.

If you were to create a corporate identity package for a client, for example, you could create a business card, stationery, and a brochure on separate artboards within the same document. Or you could create a series of separate but related graphics for the same website or animation project, a multipage PDF file, or components of a package design — all within the same document. Any colors or graphic, paragraph, or character style definitions that you create will be available for all the artboards in the document.

Illustrator CS5 features a new Artboards panel. **A** ★ Using the panel, you can create, select, duplicate, and delete artboards; change their order or arrangement; and open the Artboard Options dialog.

To add an artboard with the Artboard tool:

1. With a document open, press Cmd--/Ctrl-- to zoom out, if necessary, then hold down the Spacebar and drag to display the current artboard and some of the canvas area to the right of it.

2. Do either of the following:
   Choose the **Artboard** tool ⬚ (Shift-O).
   Deselect by clicking a blank area of the artboard. On the Control panel, click **Document Setup**, then click **Edit Artboards**.

3. Drag to create a new artboard next to (or above or below) the existing one. **B** Artboards are assigned numbers automatically based on the sequence in which they are created.

4. To scale an artboard, see page 10.

5. To exit artboard editing mode, either press Esc (the last tool that was selected will reselect) or click a different tool.

A *The Artboards panel*

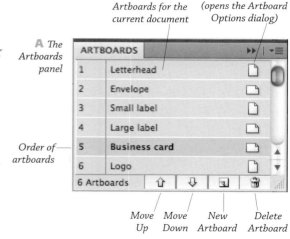

Artboards for the current document

Orientation icon (opens the Artboard Options dialog)

Order of artboards

Move Up   Move Down   New Artboard   Delete Artboard

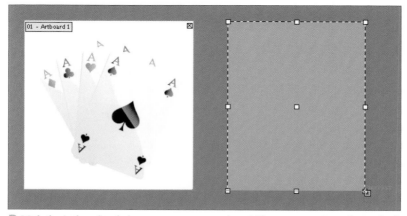

B *With the Artboard tool, drag to create a new artboard. Here, we are using a Smart Guide to align a new artboard with an existing one (see pages 100–101).*

To duplicate an artboard and its contents:

Do either of the following:

On the Artboards panel, drag an artboard listing to the **New Artboard** button. ★ In the document, the duplicate artboard will appear to the right of the existing ones.

Choose the **Artboard** tool (Shift-O), activate the **Move/Copy Artwork with Artboard** button on the Control panel, then Option-drag/Alt-drag an artboard. **A–B** Press Esc.

➤ To rename an artboard, choose the Artboard tool, click the artboard, then change the name in the Name field on the Control panel. Another method is to double-click the orientation icon next to an artboard listing on the Artboards panel, then change the name in the Artboard Options dialog that opens. ★

USING THE STATUS BAR

Depending on which category is selected on the Show submenu on the status bar menu in the lower left corner of the document window, the bar displays the current Artboard Name, ★ Current Tool, Date and Time, Number of [available] Undos, or Document Color Profile. (For fun, Option-click/Alt-click the status bar menu to find out the number of shopping days 'til Christmas, and other vital statistics!)

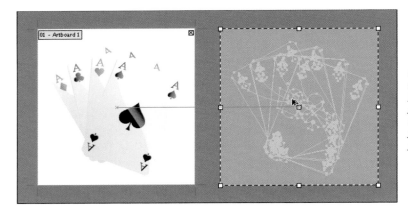

A *To copy an artboard and its contents, activate the Move/Copy Artwork with Artboard button on the Control panel, then with the Artboard tool, Option-drag/Alt-drag the artboard.*

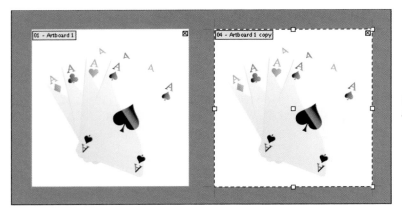

B *The duplicate artboard and its contents appear.*

To duplicate an artboard but not its contents:

Do one of the following:

On the Artboards panel, click the artboard to be duplicated, then click the **New Artboard** button. ★ A The duplicate artboard will appear to the right of all the existing ones.

Choose the **Artboard** tool (Shift-O), deactivate the **Move/Copy Artwork with Artboard** button on the Control panel, then Option-drag/Alt-drag an artboard (add Shift if you want to constrain the movement). Press Esc to exit artboard editing mode.

Choose the **Artboard** tool, click in an existing artboard, click the **New Artboard** button on the Control panel, position the artboard preview rectangle in the document window, then click to make the artboard appear. (You can also hold down Option/Alt and click to create additional copies of it.) Press Esc to exit artboard editing mode.

➤ To create an artboard based on a rectangular path, select the path, then choose Convert to Artboards from the Artboards panel menu.

Deleting artboards

To delete an artboard but not its contents:

Do either of the following:

Choose the **Artboard** tool (Shift-O), then in the upper right corner of the artboard to be deleted, click the Delete icon. You could also click the artboard to be deleted, then press Delete/Backspace or click the Delete Artboard button on the Control panel. Press Esc.

On the Artboards panel, click the listing for the artboard to be deleted (or Cmd-click/Ctrl-click multiple listings), then click the **Delete Artboard** button. ★

➤ To delete all the artboards in a document that don't contain any artwork (except the original artboard, which must remain), from the Artboards panel menu, choose Delete Empty Artboards. ★

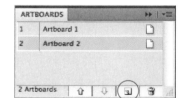

A *We selected an artboard, then clicked the New Artboard button on the Artboards panel. A new blank artboard appeared, the same size as the original.*

FITTING AN ARTBOARD TO ARTWORK ★

➤ If your document contains just one artboard and you want to fit it exactly to all the artwork in the document, choose Object > Artboards > Fit to Artwork Bounds.

➤ To fit an artboard around specific artwork, choose the Selection tool (V), then drag a marquee around that artwork. Activate the artboard by clicking its listing on the Artboards panel, then choose Object > Artboards > Fit to Selected Art.

The two commands mentioned above are also available on the Presets menu on the Control panel when the Artboard tool is selected.

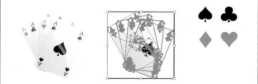

With a group of objects selected, we chose Object > Fit to Selected Art.

Modifying artboards

To change the location, scale, or orientation of an artboard:

1. To display all the artboards in the document window, choose View > **Fit All in Window** or press Cmd-Option-0/Ctrl-Alt-0.

2. Choose the **Artboard** tool ⬚ (Shift-O), then click an artboard to select it.

3. To reposition the artboard and its contents, activate the **Move/Copy Artwork with Artboard** button ⬚ on the Control panel, then drag the artboard. Or to reposition the artboard relative to the artwork, deactivate the Move/Copy Artwork with Artboard button before dragging (reactivate the button when you're done).**A**

   ➤ You can use Smart Guides (Cmd-U/Ctrl-U) to align the top, center, or side of the artboard to other artboards (see pages 100–101).

4. To scale the artboard, do any of the following:

   From the **Preset** menu on the Control panel, choose a predefined size.

To scale the artboard manually, drag a side or corner handle. You can use the on-object readouts for exact dimensions.* **B** To scale the artboard proportionally, Shift-drag a handle.

Enter new values in the **W** and/or **H** fields on the Control panel. Note: If Constrain Proportions is checked in the Artboard Options dialog, the same option will be activated on the Control panel; see page 12. (To learn which unit abbreviations you can use in Illustrator, see page 382.)

5. To change the orientation of the artboard, click the **Portrait** ⬚ or **Landscape** ⬚ button on the Control panel.

6. Press Esc.

➤ You can also change the size and orientation of an artboard in the Artboard Options dialog (see page 12).

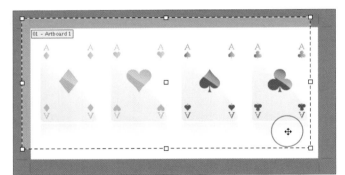

A To move an artboard while keeping its contents stationary, deactivate the Move/Copy Artwork with Artboard button on the Control panel, then with the Artboard tool, drag the artboard.

B To scale an artboard manually, drag one of its handles with the Artboard tool.

*If the readouts aren't displaying, go to Illustrator/Edit > Preferences > Smart Guides, and check Measurement Labels.

Aligning and rearranging artboards

If you prefer not to align your artboards manually, you can use the new Rearrange Artboards dialog to quickly arrange them in neat rows or columns. If you change the order of the artboard listings on the Artboards panel before opening the dialog, the artboards will be rearranged automatically based on that sequence.

To rearrange or realign the artboards in your document: ★

1. *Optional:* To control the order in which the dialog will arrange the artboards, change the order of any artboard listing on the Artboards panel by dragging it upward or downward (or by clicking a listing, then clicking the Move Up ⇧ or Move Down ⇩ button on the panel).

2. From the Artboards panel menu, choose **Rearrange Artboards**.

3. In the dialog, **A–B** click a **Layout** option: Grid by Row, Grid by Column, Arrange by Row, or Arrange by Column.

   If desired (and if these options are available), change the number of **Rows** or **Columns**, or change the **Spacing** value for the distance between the rows and columns.

   Check **Move Artwork with Artboard** to have your artwork stick with the artboards as they're moved (unless for some reason you want the artboards to move and the art to remain stationary).

4. Click OK.**C** All the artboards will display in the document window, in their new configuration (and also in a new order, if you followed step 1).

➤ To cycle among multiple artboards when the Artboard tool is selected, hold down Option/Alt and press an arrow key on your keyboard. To fit an artboard in the document window, see page 28.

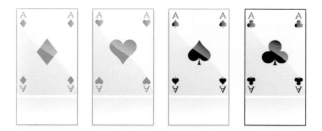

A *The original artwork contains four artboards in a row.*

B *You can use the Rearrange Artboards dialog to realign the artboards in your document, or to rearrange them based on the current order of listings on the Artboards panel. We clicked the second Layout button and chose a Rows value of 2.*

C *Now the artboards are arranged in two columns and two rows.*

Choosing artboard options

Note: The options that you see in the Artboard Options dialog are also available on the Control panel when the Artboard tool is selected.

To choose artboard options:

1. To open the Artboard Options dialog, A do either of the following:

   On the Artboards panel, double-click the orientation icon □ □ for an artboard listing. ★

   Choose the **Artboard** tool, □ click an artboard in the document, then click the **Artboard Options** button ▦ on the Control panel.

2. For the currently selected artboard, you can change the artboard Name, choose a Preset size or enter new Width and/or Height values (check Constrain Proportions if you want to preserve the current aspect ratio), change the artboard Orientation, or change its *x,y* Position.

3. For video output, check which guides you want to Display: **Show Center Mark** displays crosshairs in the center of the artboard; **Show Cross Hairs** displays a line at each of the four midpoints of the artboard; and **Show Video Safe Areas** displays guides that mark the viewable area of the artboard (see Illustrator Help).

4. Check **Fade Region Outside Artboard** to have the area outside all the artboards display as dark gray (not white) when the Artboard tool is selected. Also check Update While Dragging to have the artboard area display as a medium gray while an artboard is being dragged.

5. Click OK. If the Artboard tool is selected, press Esc.

➤ *Beware!* The Delete button in the Artboard Options dialog deletes the currently selected artboard, not the current values in the dialog.

A *Use the Artboard Options dialog to scale, and choose display options for, the current artboard.*

CHOOSING A DISPLAY OPTION FOR ARTBOARDS VIA THE CONTROL PANEL

When the Artboard tool is selected, you can turn the guide marks on or off via the Display Options menu on the Control panel. The option that currently has a check mark can be turned on or off quickly by clicking the button next to the menu.

Saving a document in the Adobe Illustrator (ai) format

When saving an Illustrator file, you can choose one of these seven formats: Adobe Illustrator (ai), Illustrator EPS (eps), Illustrator Template (ait), Adobe PDF (pdf), Adobe FXG (fxg), SVG Compressed (svgz), or SVG (svg). Files in these formats can be reopened and edited in Illustrator.

You should keep your file in the Adobe Illustrator (ai) format if you're going to print it directly from Illustrator or if you're going to import it into a program that reads this format, such as InDesign. If you're going to display the file online or export it to an application that doesn't read Illustrator (ai) files, you will need to save a copy of it in a different format such as Adobe PDF (see Chapter 32).

To save a file in the Adobe Illustrator (ai) format:

1. If the file has never been saved, choose File > Save (Cmd-S/Ctrl-S). If the file has already been saved, choose File > Save As. In either case, the Save As dialog opens.

2. Enter a name in the Save As/File Name field.

3. Navigate to the desired drive and folder.

4. From the Format/Save as Type menu, choose **Adobe Illustrator (ai)**.

5. Click Save. The Illustrator Options dialog opens. Leave Illustrator CS5 as the choice on the Version menu. (For the legacy formats of Illustrator, see the sidebar at right.)

6. Under Fonts, enter a percentage in the **Subset Fonts When Percent of Characters Used Is Less Than** field to save the fonts being used in the artwork as part of the document. If not all the characters in a particular font are being used, you can opt to have Illustrator embed just a subset of its characters, as opposed to the whole font, to help reduce the file size. For example, at a setting of 50%, the entire font will be embedded only if more than 50% of its characters are used in the file, and the Subset option will apply if fewer than 50% of the font characters are used in the file. Characters in embedded fonts will display and print on any system, even those in which they aren't installed. However, bear in mind that the higher the Subset Fonts percentage, the more characters will be embedded, and the larger the file size. At a setting of 100%, all the characters in a font are embedded.

7. Under **Options**, check any of the following:

   Create PDF Compatible File to enable the file to be read by other applications that support the PDF format, such as Photoshop. We recommend checking this option, despite the fact that it increases the file size.

   Include Linked Files to save a copy of any linked files with the document (see Chapter 22).

   If you chose a profile in the Edit > Assign Profile dialog, check **Embed ICC Profiles** to embed those profiles in the file so it will be color-managed properly.

   Use Compression to compress vector data (and PDF data, if included) to help reduce the file size. With this option checked, the Save command may process more slowly.

   Save Each Artboard to a Separate File, then click All or enter a Range. ★ With this option off, multiple artboards will be saved in one file.

8. Click OK. The file with the new name remains open onscreen; the file with the original name closes but is preserved on disk.

➤ The Save a Copy command keeps the original file open onscreen and saves the copy with the new name to disk. See "To save a copy of a file" on the next page.

SAVING FILES IN EARLIER CS VERSIONS

To save a CS5 file in an earlier Illustrator CS format, in the Illustrator Options dialog, choose the desired format from the Version menu (see step 5 on this page). Saving to an earlier CS version can cause unexpected text reflows. Avoid saving a file in a pre-CS version of Illustrator, as those versions can't save such document features as multiple artboards, live effects, Live Paint groups, and transparency. The Transparency options are available only for very early legacy formats.

If you save a document that contains multiple artboards to an earlier version of Illustrator (such as CS3) and check Save Each Artboard as a Separate File in the Illustrator Options dialog, ★ the result will be a separate file for each artboard, along with a master file in which each artboard has been converted to a guide.

The prior version of your document is overwritten each time you use the Save command. Do yourself a favor and save often — don't be shy about it! And be sure to create backups of your work frequently, too.

To resave a file:

Choose File > **Save** (Cmd-S/Ctrl-S).

When you use the Save a Copy command, the original version of the file stays open onscreen and a copy of it is saved to disk.

To save a copy of a file:

1. Choose File > **Save a Copy** (Cmd-Option-S/ Ctrl-Alt-S). The Save a Copy dialog opens.
2. To save the file in the Illustrator (ai) format, follow steps 2–8 on the preceding page. Or for other formats, see Chapter 32.

To revert to the last saved version of a file:

1. Choose File > **Revert**.
2. When the alert dialog opens, click Revert.

Ending a work session

To close a document:

1. To close a tabbed document, click the ✖ on the window tab.

   To close a floating document in the Mac OS, click the close (red) button in the upper left corner of the document window or press Cmd-W. To close a floating document in Windows, click the close box in the upper right corner of the document window or press Ctrl-W.
2. If the file contains unsaved changes, an alert dialog will appear.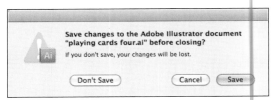 Click Don't Save to close the file without saving your edits, or click Save to resave the file before closing it, or click Cancel to back out of the deal.

To quit/exit Illustrator:

1. In the Mac OS, choose Illustrator > **Quit Illustrator** (Cmd-Q).

   In Windows, choose File > **Exit** (Ctrl-Q) or click the close box for the application window.
2. All open Illustrator files will close. If any of the open files contain unsaved changes, an alert dialog will appear. To resave the file(s), click Save, or to quit/exit Illustrator without saving your edits, click Don't Save.

A *If you try to close a file that contains unsaved changes, this prompt will appear.*

SHORTCUTS FOR THE SAVE DIALOGS

	Mac OS	Windows
Save the edits in a previously saved file (no dialog opens), or open the Save As dialog if the file hasn't yet been saved	Cmd-S	Ctrl-S
Open the Save As dialog	Cmd-Shift-S	Ctrl-Shift-S
Open the Save a Copy dialog	Cmd-Option-S	Ctrl-Alt-S

CLOSING OPEN FILES QUICKLY

Close all tabbed windows	Right-click a window tab and choose Close All from the context menu
Close all floating windows (Mac OS only)	Option-click the close button on one of the document windows
Close all tabbed and floating windows	Press Cmd-Option-W/ Ctrl-Alt-W

Choosing the proper color settings for Illustrator is a crucial step before creating artwork. In this chapter, you'll learn how to use color settings to manage and maintain color consistency among documents and output devices, synchronize the color settings of all the programs in your Adobe Creative Suite, change document color profiles, and finally, soft-proof your artwork onscreen for the chosen output device.

Introduction to color management

Problems with color can creep up on you when the various hardware devices and software packages you use treat color differently. If you were to open an Illustrator graphic in several different imaging programs or Web browsers, the colors might look completely different in each case, and may not look the same as they did onscreen in Illustrator. Print the graphic, and the results could be different yet again. In some cases, you might find such discrepancies to be slight and unobjectionable, but in other cases, they can wreak havoc with your design and turn your project into a disaster.

A color management system can solve most of these problems by acting as a color interpreter. Such a system knows how each device and program understands color, and by using color profiles (mathematical descriptions of the color space of each device), makes the proper adjustments so the colors in your files look the same as you move them from one program or device to another. Illustrator, Photoshop, and other programs in the Adobe Creative Suite use the standardized ICC (International Color Consortium) profiles to tell your color management system how specific devices use color. Whether you're planning a traditional print run or will be using the same artwork for multiple purposes (such as for Web and print), your work stands to benefit from color management.

In Illustrator, you'll find most of the color management controls in the Edit > Color Settings dialog. It gives you access to preset management settings for various publishing situations, including press and Web output, and also lets you choose custom settings. There are two main areas in the basic dialog:

► The **Working Spaces** options govern how RGB and CMYK colors are displayed in your document and serve as the default color profiles for new Illustrator documents.

Continued on the following page

MANAGE COLOR

2

➤ The **Color Management Policies** options for RGB and CMYK color files govern how Illustrator manages color when you open a document that doesn't have an attached color profile, or if the document's profile doesn't match the current color settings in Illustrator.

Choosing the correct color settings will help keep your document colors consistent from the onscreen version to final output. The abundance of options in the Color Settings dialog may appear complex at first, but you and your documents will benefit if you take the time to learn about them.

Note: For high-end print output, ask your print shop to recommend specific color management settings to ensure a smooth color management workflow.

The display types

There are two basic types of computer displays: CRT (cathode ray tube, as in a traditional TV set) and LCD (liquid crystal display, or flat panel). The display performance of a CRT fluctuates due to its analog technology and the fact that its display phosphors (which produce the glowing dots that you view onscreen) tend to fade over time. CRT displays can be calibrated reliably for only around three years.

An LCD display uses a grid of fixed-sized liquid crystals that filter color coming from a backlight source. Although you can adjust only the brightness on an LCD (not the contrast), the LCD digital technology offers more reliable color consistency than a CRT, without the flickering that is characteristic of a CRT. The newest LCD models provide good viewing angles, display accurate color, use the desirable daylight temperature of 6500K for the white point (an industry-standard color temperature), and are produced under tighter manufacturing standards than CRTs. Moreover, in most cases the color profile that is provided with an LCD display (and that is installed in your system automatically) describes the display characteristics accurately.

➤ Both types of displays lose calibration gradually, so you may not notice a change until the colors are way off. To maintain good color consistency for your display, try to stick to a regular monthly calibration schedule. Our calibration software reminds us to recalibrate our display via a monthly onscreen alert.

Calibrating your display

The first step toward achieving color consistency is to calibrate your display by adjusting the contrast and brightness, gamma, color balance, and white point.

In the Mac OS, Illustrator relies on the Calibrate utility, which is found in the Displays panel (Color tab) in System Preferences. The utility generates an ICC profile that the operating system refers to in order to display colors accurately onscreen.

If you're using a Windows machine, or to generate a more complete profile in the Mac OS (which we recommend doing), you'll need to purchase and use a hardware calibrator. Calibrate your display with it, and save the settings as an ICC profile. Thereafter, that profile will be available to the Adobe color management system and will be used by all the color-managed applications in your Adobe Creative Suite.

WHAT ARE COLOR SPACES AND PROFILES?

➤ Each device, such as a camera or computer display, is able to capture and reproduce a particular range (or gamut) of color, which is known as its color space.

➤ The mathematical description of the color space of each device is called the color profile. The color management system uses the color profile to define the colors in a document.

➤ Illustrator uses the document profile to display and edit artwork colors, or if the document doesn't have a profile, Illustrator uses the current working space profile (the profile you will choose in the Color Settings dialog) instead.

Choosing color settings for Illustrator

To choose color settings for Illustrator:

1. Choose Edit > **Color Settings** (Cmd-Shift-K/ Ctrl-Shift-K). The Color Settings dialog opens (**A**, page 19).

2. Choose a preset from the **Settings** menu. The four basic presets are summarized as follows:

   Monitor Color sets the RGB working space to your display profile. This is a good choice for video output, but not for print output.

   North America General Purpose 2 meets the requirements for screen and print output in the United States and Canada. All profile warnings are off.

   North America Newspaper manages color for output on newsprint paper stock.

   North America Prepress 2 manages color to conform with common press conditions in the United States and Canada. This is the recommended preset for commercial print output. The default RGB color space that is assigned to this setting is Adobe RGB. When CMYK documents are opened, their color values are preserved.

   North America Web/Internet is designed for online output. All RGB images are converted to the sRGB color space.

3. At this point you can click OK to accept the predefined settings or you can proceed with the remaining steps to choose custom settings.

4. The **Working Spaces** menus govern how RGB and CMYK colors will be treated in documents that lack an embedded profile. You can either leave these settings as they are or choose custom options. The RGB options that we recommend using are discussed below (see also the third tip on the following page). For the CMYK setting, you should ask your output service provider which working space to choose.

   Adobe RGB (1998) encompasses a wide range of colors and is useful when converting RGB images to CMYK images. This working space is recommended for inkjet and commercial printing, but not for online output.

   ColorMatch RGB contains a smaller range of colors than Adobe RGB (1998) but, because it matches the color space of Radius Pressview displays, is suitable for print work.

   ProPhoto RGB contains a very wide range of colors and is suitable for output to high-end dye sublimation and inkjet printers.

   sRGB IEC61966-2.1 is a good choice for Web output, as it reflects the settings for an average computer display. Many hardware and software manufacturers use it as the default space for scanners, low-end printers, and software.

5. From the RGB and CMYK menus in the Color Management Policies area, choose a color management policy for Illustrator to use when the profile in a document doesn't match the current color settings you have chosen for Illustrator:

   Off to prevent files from being color-managed when imported or opened.

   Preserve Embedded Profiles if you will be working with both color-managed and non-color-managed documents and you want each document to keep its own profile.

   Convert to Working Space if you want all your documents to be converted to the current color working space. This is usually the best choice for Web output.

   Choose **Preserve Numbers (Ignore Linked Profiles)** to have Illustrator preserve embedded profiles (and the numeric values of colors used in the file) for CMYK documents but ignore profiles for linked CMYK imagery.

   For **Profile Mismatches,** check **Ask When Opening** to have an alert appear if the color profile in a file you're opening doesn't match the working space for Illustrator. If you choose this option, you can override the current color management policy via an alert dialog upon opening a document.

   Check **Ask When Pasting** to have Illustrator display an alert when a color profile mismatch crops up as you paste or drag and drop a color image into your document. If you choose this option, you can override the current color management policy via an alert dialog when pasting.

Continued on the following page

For files that have **Missing Profiles**, check **Ask When Opening** to have Illustrator display an alert offering you the opportunity to assign the current working spaces profile or a custom profile to files as you open them.

6. *Optional:* If you've chosen custom color settings that you want to save for later use, click Save. To have your custom file appear on the Settings menu, save it in the default location. In the Mac OS, that location is Users/[user name]/Library/Application Support/Adobe/Color/Settings. In Windows XP, the location is C:\Documents and Settings\[user name]\Application Data\Adobe\Color\Settings. And in Windows 7, the location is C:\Users\[user name]\AppData\Roaming\Adobe\Color\Settings.

7. Click OK.

➤ To learn about the various alert dialogs that may appear onscreen as you open a file, see page 63.

➤ To reuse your saved settings, choose the file name from the Settings menu in the Color Settings dialog. To load a settings file that wasn't saved in the Settings folder (and therefore isn't listed on the Settings menu), click Load, locate the desired file, then click Open.

➤ We discourage use of the Monitor RGB and ColorSync RGB color spaces because they rely on a profile that is specific to each computer system. The result is that a document that was created on your computer could look different on someone else's computer, which defeats the whole point of using color management.

DESIGNING FOR THE COLOR-BLIND

At some point in your career, you may be hired to design graphics, such as signage, that are fully accessible to color-blind viewers. In fact, some countries require signage in public spaces to comply with the Color Universal Design (CUD) guidelines. The View > Proof Setup > Color Blindness – Protanopia-Type and Color Blindness – Deuteranopia-Type commands in Illustrator simulate how your document will look to viewers that have common forms of color blindness.

In case you're not familiar with those two terms, for a protanope, the brightness of red, orange, and yellow is dimmed, making it hard for such a person to distinguish red from black or dark gray. Protanopes also have trouble distinguishing violet, lavender, and purple from blue because the reddish components of those colors look dimmed. Deuteranopes are unable to distinguish between colors in the green-yellow-red part of the spectrum and experience color blindness similar to that of protanopes, without the problem of dimming.

For color and design suggestions, enter "color blindness" in the search field in Illustrator Help.

Color Settings

Synchronized: Your Creative Suite applications are synchronized using the same color settings for consistent color management.

OK

Cancel

Settings: North America Prepress 2

Load...

☐ Advanced Mode

Save...

Working Spaces

RGB: Adobe RGB (1998)

CMYK: U.S. Web Coated (SWOP) v2

The Working Spaces options govern the display of RGB and CMYK colors and serve as the default color profiles for new documents.

Color Management Policies

RGB: Preserve Embedded Profiles

🔒 CMYK: Preserve Numbers (Ignore Linked Profiles)

Profile Mismatches: ☑ Ask When Opening

☑ Ask When Pasting

Missing Profiles: ☑ Ask When Opening

The Color Management Policies govern how colors are treated when you open a file that lacks a color profile or when a file's profile conflicts with the currently chosen color settings

Description:

Preparation of content for common printing conditions in North America. CMYK values are preserved. Profile warnings are enabled.

Rest the pointer over a menu or option, and read information about it here in the Description area.

A *When you choose a preset from the Settings menu in the Color Settings dialog, the other options are chosen for you automatically. You can customize any preset by choosing settings.*

Synchronizing the color settings

When the color settings in another Adobe Creative Suite program, such as Photoshop, don't match the current settings in Illustrator, an alert displays at the top of the Edit > Color Settings dialog in Illustrator.**A** If you don't have a complete Adobe Creative Suite installed in your system, you'll have to start up each of your Adobe applications and fix their color settings by hand. If a whole suite is installed, you can use the Suite Color Settings dialog in Bridge to synchronize the color settings of all the programs.

Note: Before synchronizing the color settings via Bridge, make sure you've chosen the proper settings in Illustrator (see pages 17–19).

To synchronize the color settings among Creative Suite applications via Bridge:

1. On the Application bar in Illustrator, click the **Go to Bridge** button. **Br**

2. In Bridge, choose Edit > **Creative Suite Color Settings** (Cmd-Shift-K/Ctrl-Shift-K). The Suite Color Settings dialog opens, **B** showing the same list of settings as found in the Color Settings dialog when Advanced Mode is unchecked.

3. Click the settings preset you chose in Illustrator, then click Apply. Bridge will change (synchronize) the color settings of the other Adobe Creative Suite applications to match the selected preset.

A *This alert in the Color Settings dialog informs us that the color settings in our Creative Suite applications aren't synchronized with one another.*

B *Use the Suite Color Settings dialog to synchronize the color settings of all the Adobe Creative Suite applications that are installed in your system.*

Changing the document profile

When a file's profile doesn't match the current working space or is missing a color profile altogether, you can use the Assign Profile command to assign the correct one. You may notice visible color shifts if the color data of your file is reinterpreted to match the new profile, but rest assured, the color data in the actual document is preserved.

To change or delete a document's color profile:

1. With a file open in Illustrator, choose Edit > **Assign Profile**. The Assign Profile dialog opens.**A**

2. Do one of the following:

   To remove the color profile from the document, click **Don't Color Manage This Document**. The current working space will now control the appearance of colors in the artwork.

   If your document doesn't have an assigned profile or if its profile is different from the current working space, click **Working** [document color mode and the name of the current working space] to assign that profile.

   To assign a different profile to your document, click **Profile**, then choose the desired profile from the menu. This won't change or convert any color data in your artwork.

3. Click OK.

EMBEDDING A COLOR PROFILE WHEN SAVING A FILE

When you use the File > Save As command to save a file in a format that supports embedded profiles, such as Adobe Illustrator (ai), the Illustrator Options dialog opens. In that dialog, you can check the Embed ICC Profiles option to embed a profile into the document, if one has been assigned.

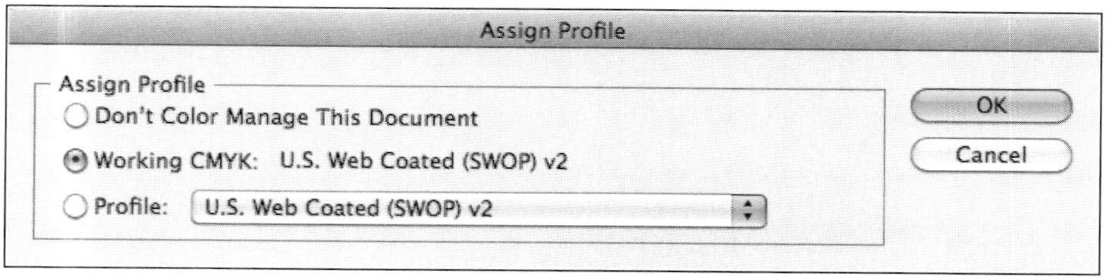

Assign Profile
Assign Profile
○ Don't Color Manage This Document
⦿ Working CMYK: U.S. Web Coated (SWOP) v2
○ Profile: U.S. Web Coated (SWOP) v2

OK
Cancel

A *Use the Assign Profile dialog to either delete a file's color profile or assign a new one. The profile chosen here will also be listed as the Document Profile in the Color Management panel of the File > Print dialog.*

Proofing a document onscreen

Specifying a color management setup is all well and good, but once you start creating some Illustrator artwork, you will need to get an idea of how it's going to look in print or online. You can do this by viewing a soft proof of your document onscreen. Although this method is less accurate than viewing a press proof or viewing the file in a browser, it can give you a general idea of how your artwork would look if it were printed using CMYK inks or displayed online on a Windows or Macintosh display.

To proof colors onscreen for commercial printing or online output:

1. From the View > **Proof Setup** submenu, choose a type of output display to be simulated:

   Working CMYK to simulate colors for the commercial press that is currently chosen on the CMYK menu under Working Spaces in the Edit > Color Settings dialog in Illustrator.

   For an RGB document, choose **Legacy Macintosh RGB (Gamma 1.8)** or **Internet Standard RGB (sRGB)** ★ to simulate colors for online output using the legacy Mac gamma (1.8) or Windows gamma (2.2) as the proofing space.

   For an RGB document, choose **Monitor RGB** to simulate colors using the custom display profile for your monitor.

   To create a proofing model for a specific output device, choose **Customize**. The Proof Setup dialog opens.A From the **Device to Simulate** menu, choose the color profile for your target output device, then check or uncheck **Preserve CMYK (or RGB) Numbers**. This option is available only when the document color mode of the current file matches the mode of the output device

profile that is currently chosen on the Device to Simulate menu (e.g., if the document color mode is CMYK and the proofing profile is a CMYK profile). With this option checked, colors will look as if they're not converted to the proofing space. With this option unchecked, Illustrator colors will appear as though converted, and you'll need to choose a **Rendering Intent** (see the sidebar). Click OK.

2. *Optional:* The Display Options (On-Screen) are available for some profiles. Simulate Paper Color simulates the soft white of actual paper, based on the current proof profile, and Simulate Black Ink simulates the dark gray that many printers produce when printing black.

3. Click OK.

4. The View > Proof Colors command will be checked automatically, so you can see the soft proof onscreen. The name of the device being simulated will be listed in the document tab. Uncheck the command when you're done.

Proof Setup

Device to Simulate:	U.S. Sheetfed Coated v2
	☐ Preserve CMYK Numbers
Rendering Intent:	Perceptual

Display Options (On–Screen)
☐ Simulate Paper Color
☑ Simulate Black Ink

A *Use the Proof Setup dialog to choose custom options for soft-proofing your Illustrator files.*

THE RENDERING INTENTS

➤ Perceptual changes colors in a way that seems natural to the human eye, while attempting to preserve the appearance of the overall document. This is a good choice for documents that contain continuous-tone images.

➤ Saturation changes colors with the intent of preserving vivid colors but in doing so compromises color fidelity. Nevertheless, it's a good choice for charts and business graphics, which normally contain fewer colors than continuous-tone images.

➤ Absolute Colorimetric maintains the color accuracy only of colors that fall within the destination color gamut (i.e., the color range of your printer), but in doing so sacrifices the accuracy of colors that are outside that gamut.

➤ Relative Colorimetric is the default intent for all the Adobe presets in the Color Settings dialog. It compares the white, or highlight, of your document's color space to the white of the destination color space (the white of the paper, in the case of print output), and shifts colors where needed. This is the best Rendering Intent option for documents in which most of the colors fall within the color range of the destination gamut, because it preserves most of the original colors.

In this chapter, you will become acquainted with basic features of the Illustrator interface, such as the Application bar, document tabs, and panels. You will learn how to arrange document windows, change the document zoom level, fit an artboard in the document window, bring a different part of a document into view, change the screen display mode and document view, save and choose custom view settings, reconfigure the panel groups and docks, and save and manage your custom workspaces. By the end of the chapter, you will know how to configure your workspace to suit your usual workflow — and even better, you will have the skills to create custom workspaces for various kinds of tasks.

Features of the Illustrator workspace

In Windows — and when displayed in the Mac OS — an Application frame houses the Application bar, tabbed document windows, the Control panel, and all the other panels. Mac OS users, we recommend keeping the frame visible (see the next page). Note: We also refer to the application window in Windows as the "Application frame." The Application frame cannot be hidden in Windows.

Although you have the option to float individual document windows onscreen or dock them as multiple tabs within a floating window, we recommend docking them as tabs within the Application frame instead, for several reasons. First, the Application frame conveniently blocks out any Desktop clutter; without the frame, you would have to spend time enlarging your document windows to hide the clutter. Second, the frame displays your document against a neutral light gray background, which is helpful when you need to judge the colors in your artwork. And third, when your document is displayed in Normal Screen mode, the viewing area expands or contracts dynamically as you hide or show the panels or collapse or expand any of the panel docks (see page 32).

Continued on the following page

WORKSPACES

3

To show (or hide) the Application frame in the Mac OS:

To show the Application frame, check Window > **Application Frame** 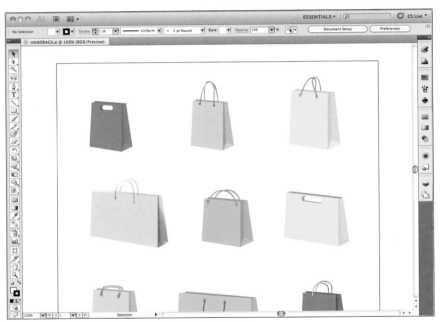 (or to hide it, uncheck the command).

➤ You can resize the Application frame by dragging an edge or a corner.

➤ To minimize the Application frame in Windows, click the Minimize button; or to do this in the Mac OS, double-click the Application bar.

A *In the Mac OS, we prefer to work with the Application frame showing.*

To use the Application bar:

Use the button and menus on the Application bar to manage your workspace. **B** If the bar is hidden in the Mac OS, choose Window > **Application Bar**. In Windows, the main Illustrator menus also display on the Application bar.

To search for info at Adobe.com and other websites, enter a keyword or phrase in the Search for Help field, then press Return/Enter.

Go to Adobe Bridge   *Arrange Documents menu for arranging multiple documents onscreen*   *The current workspace*   *Menu for accessing, saving, and deleting workspaces*

B *These controls are available on the Application bar in the Mac OS.*

Using tabbed document windows

You can dock multiple open document windows into the Application frame as a series of tabs, and then display any document easily by clicking its tab.

To dock document windows into the Application frame as tabs:

Do any of the following:

To dock a floating document window manually, drag its title bar to the tab area (just below the Control panel) of the Application frame, and release the mouse when the blue drop zone bar appears.**A**

If one or more documents are already docked as tabs and you want to dock all floating document windows into the Application frame, right-click a tab and choose **Consolidate All to Here** from the context menu.**B** Or on the Arrange Documents menu ▦ on the Application bar, click the **Consolidate All** (first) icon ▣; this icon is available even when all documents are floating.

To set a preference so that all documents you subsequently open will dock as tabs automatically, go to Illustrator/Edit > Preferences > User Interface and check **Open Documents as Tabs**.

➤ To cycle among the currently open documents, press Cmd- ~ (tilde)/Ctrl- Tab.

➤ To fit an artboard in the document window, see page 28.

➤ To turn a tabbed document window into a floating one, either right-click the tab and choose Move to New Window, or drag the tab downward out of the tab area. To dock one floating document window into another one, drag its title bar to just below the title bar of the other window.

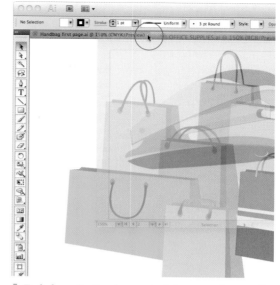

A *To dock one floating document window as a tab manually, drag its title bar to the tab area of the Application frame, and release the mouse when the blue drop zone bar appears.*

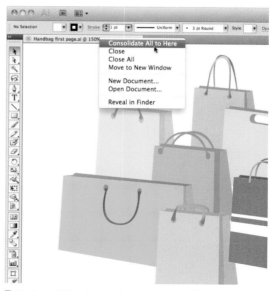

B *To dock all floating windows into the Application frame, right-click a document tab and choose Consolidate All to Here.*

Arranging document windows

By using icons on the Arrange Documents menu on the Application bar, you can quickly display multiple documents in various layouts, such as two documents arranged side by side or vertically, or four or six documents in a grid.

To display multiple tabbed document windows:

On the Application bar, click the **Arrange Documents** menu icon to open the menu, then click one of the available icons (the availability of icons depends on the number of open documents).**A**

➤ If any open documents are floating when you click an option on the Arrange Documents menu, they will be docked as tabbed windows automatically.

Just as effortlessly, you can go back to displaying one document at a time.

To redisplay one tabbed document window:

Do either of the following:

Right-click a document tab and choose **Consolidate All to Here** from the context menu.

On the Arrange Documents menu on the Application bar, click the **Consolidate All** (first) icon.

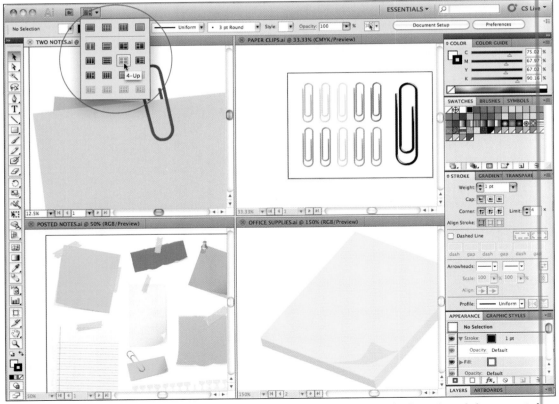

A *We chose the 4-Up view from the Arrange Documents menu. A different zoom level can be chosen for each document window.*

Changing the zoom level

By changing the zoom level for your document, you can display multiple artboards, one artboard, or a magnified detail of your artwork. The current zoom level is listed as a percentage between 3.13% and 6400% on the document tab or title bar and in the lower left corner of the document window. The zoom level has no bearing on the output size.

There are many ways to change the zoom level in a document. The fastest method is via the keyboard, because you can do it with any tool selected. Pick a few methods that you like, memorize them, and ignore the rest.

To change the zoom level:

Do any of the following:

Use any of the shortcuts that are listed in the sidebar at right.

Choose a preset percentage from the zoom menu in the lower left corner of the document window. A Or choose Fit on Screen from the same menu to fit the entire artboard within the current document window size.

Make sure no objects are selected, then right-click in the document and choose Zoom In or Zoom Out.

Double-click the zoom field in the lower left corner of the document window, type the desired zoom level, then press Return/Enter. Or if you want to try out a zoom value without exiting the zoom field, press Shift-Return/Shift-Enter.

Display the Navigator panel.✳ Click the Zoom Out or Zoom In button, or move the Zoom slider, or Cmd-drag/Ctrl-drag across a section of the preview to magnify the area of the document that it corresponds to.

➤ To move a different part of your magnified artwork into view, see the next page.

➤ You can change the zoom level while the screen is redrawing.

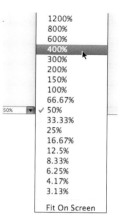

A *You can choose a preset percentage from the zoom menu in the lower left corner of the document window.*

SHORTCUTS FOR ZOOMING IN AND OUT

	Mac OS	Windows
Fit current artboard in the window	Cmd-0 (zero)	Ctrl-0 (zero)
Fit all artboards in the window	Cmd-Option-0 (zero)	Ctrl-Alt-0 (zero)
Actual size	Cmd-1	Ctrl-1
Zoom in	Cmd- + (plus) or Cmd-Spacebar click or drag	Ctrl- + (plus) or Ctrl-Spacebar click or drag
Zoom out	Cmd- – (minus) or Cmd-Option-Spacebar click	Ctrl- – (minus) or Ctrl-Alt-Spacebar click

USING THE ZOOM TOOL

We think the other methods described on this page are more convenient to use than the Zoom tool 🔍 (Z), but if you decide to use it, select it, then do any of the following:

➤ In the document window, click in the center of, or drag a marquee across, the area to be magnified. The smaller the marquee, the higher the zoom level.

➤ Option-click/Alt-click in the document window to reduce the zoom level.

➤ Drag a marquee and then, without releasing the mouse, press and hold down the Spacebar, move the marquee over the area to be magnified, and release the mouse.

Fitting an artboard in the document window

To fit an artboard to the bounds of the document window, use either one of these methods.

To fit an artboard within the document window: ★

Do either of the following:

On the Artboards panel, double-click an artboard name. **A** Or if the chosen artboard is already displaying, just click the name once.

Using the artboard navigation controls at the bottom of the document window, do either of the following: From the **Artboard Navigation** menu, choose an artboard number, **B** or click the First, Previous, Next, or Last arrow.

The chosen artboard will zoom to fit within the document window.

➤ To merely activate an artboard without fitting it to the document window, click in it with the Selection tool (in the document) or click an artboard number in the leftmost column of the Artboards panel.

➤ To learn more about artboards, see pages 7–12.

Moving an area of a document into view

To move a different area of a document into view:

Do either of the following:

Choose the **Hand** tool (H) or hold down the Spacebar to turn the current tool into a temporary Hand tool, and drag the artwork to the desired position.

Display the Navigator panel, then drag the Proxy Preview area (red outlined box) on the panel.

➤ If your cursor is inserted in a type object, pressing the Spacebar will add spaces to the text. If you're using a type tool and you want to move the document in the window without switching tools, see the sidebar on page 247.

➤ You can also move a different part of a document into view by clicking any of the scroll arrows at the edge of the document window.

A *To fit an artboard within the document window, double-click its listing on the Artboards panel.*

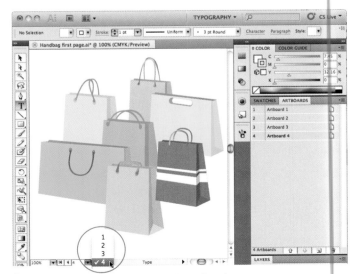

B *Choose an artboard number from the Artboard Navigation menu.*

Changing the screen mode

The three screen modes control the display of various features of the Illustrator interface.

To change the screen mode for Illustrator:

Press (and keep pressing) F to cycle through the three screen modes, or from the **Screen Mode** menu at the bottom of the Tools panel, A choose one of the following:

Normal Screen Mode B (the default mode) to display the Application frame (if that option is on), menu bar, Application bar, document tabs, and panels, with the Desktop visible behind everything. This is the only mode in which a tabbed document window resizes dynamically as you hide or show the panels or resize a panel

dock (in the Mac OS, you must display the Application frame to see how this works).

Full Screen Mode with Menu Bar C to display the document in a maximized window with the menu bar, Application bar, scroll bars, and panels visible, but not the document tabs or document title bar.

Full Screen Mode to display the illustration in a maximized window with the scroll bars visible but all the Illustrator features (and the Dock/Taskbar) hidden.

✓ Normal Screen Mode
Full Screen Mode with Menu Bar
Full Screen Mode

A *Choose from the Screen Mode menu at the bottom of the Tools panel.*

B *With our document in Normal screen mode, we pressed Tab to hide all the panels and the Control panel; the document window enlarged to fill the area left by the panels. If we were to redisplay the panels (by pressing Tab again), the document window would shrink to its former size.*

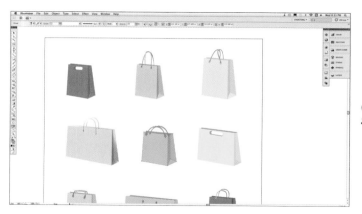

C *Here we have chosen the Full Screen Mode with Menu Bar option.*

Switching document views

A document can be displayed and edited in four different views: Preview, Outline, Pixel Preview, and Overprint Preview. In all the views, the other View menu commands — Hide/Show Edges, Artboard, Print Tiling, Slices, Guides, and Grid — are accessible. (For Overprint Preview view, see page 403.)

To switch document views:

Do any of the following:

Press Cmd-Y/Ctrl-Y to toggle between **Preview** view **A** and **Outline** view **B** (View > Preview and View > Outline). In Preview view, all fill and stroke colors and all placed images are visible; in Outline view, objects display as wireframes with no fill or stroke colors. Another option is to deselect (click a blank area of the document), then right-click in the document and choose Outline or Preview from the context menu. The screen redraws more quickly in Outline view.

To activate a 72-ppi view so you can see what your vector graphics would look like if you were to rasterize them and view them in a Web browser, choose View > **Pixel Preview** **C** (or

press Cmd-Option-Y/Ctrl-Alt-Y), and also choose View > Actual Size (Cmd-1/Ctrl-1). See also the sidebar below.

➤ Cmd-click/Ctrl-click the visibility (eye) icon for a layer (not an individual object) on the Layers panel ⬤ to toggle Preview and Outline views for just that layer. See also the sidebar on page 185.

SNAPPING ARTWORK TO THE PIXEL GRID

➤ When you choose the Pixel Preview view command, View > Snap to Pixel is also enabled (Snap to Grid becomes Snap to Pixel). Edges of objects will snap to the nearest pixel grid line as you move or reshape them, and horizontal and vertical edges will look crisper onscreen. This reduces the need for anti-aliasing, which makes objects look smoother but also less crisp.

➤ To view a representation of the pixel grid in Pixel Preview view, check Show Pixel Grid (Above 600% Zoom) in Illustrator/Edit > Preferences > Guides & Grid, and choose a document zoom level of 600% or higher. ★

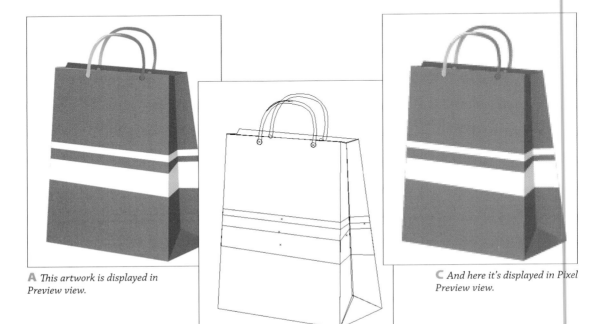

A *This artwork is displayed in Preview view.*

C *And here it's displayed in Pixel Preview view.*

B *Here it's displayed in Outline view.*

Creating custom views

You can save up to 25 custom views in the current document, and you can switch among them by using either the View menu or their assigned shortcuts. Each custom view can include a zoom level, the display of a specific artboard, and a choice of Preview or Outline view.

To save a custom view:

1. Do all of the following:

   Choose a **zoom** level for your document.

   If the document contains multiple artboards, display the one you want to choose a view for (see page 28).

   Choose **Preview, Outline** (Cmd-Y/Ctrl-Y), or **Pixel Preview** (Cmd-Option-Y/Ctrl-Alt-Y) view.

2. Choose View > **New View**. The New View dialog opens.**A**

3. In the Name field, type a descriptive name for the new view, for easy identification (as in "160% view, Preview, Artboard 4").

4. Click OK. The view is now listed on, and can be chosen from, the bottom of the View menu.

   ➤ Unfortunately, custom views can be created only for a specific document — not for the application. However, custom views can be saved as part of a document template (see page 5).

To rename or delete a custom view:

1. Choose View > **Edit Views**.

2. In the Edit Views dialog, click the view to be renamed or deleted.**B**

3. Do either of the following:

   Change the name in the **Name** field.

   Click **Delete** to delete the view.

4. Click OK. The View menu will update to reflect your edits.

   ➤ If you want to rename more than one view, you have to click OK and then reopen the dialog for each one. It's a simple little system.

A *Type a Name for a custom view in the New View dialog.*

B *In the Edit Views dialog, click a view name, then change the Name or click Delete.*

Configuring the panel groups and docks

In Illustrator, the panels are as indispensable as the tools. You can easily minimize, collapse, or hide them so they don't intrude on your document space when you're not using them, and expand or display them when you need to access them.

In the predefined workspaces (see page 34), the panels are arranged in docks on the right side of your screen — except for the Tools panel, which is docked on the left side. The panels are stored in groups within the docks (**A**, next page). In this section, we'll show you how to open and close the panels, and reconfigure the panel groups and docks to suit your workflow. For a description and illustration of the individual panels, see the next chapter.

To show or hide the panels:

To show a panel: Choose the panel name from the Window menu. The panel will display either in its default group and dock or in its last open location (floating or in a dock). To bring a panel to the front of its group, click its tab (the panel name). Some panels can also be opened temporarily via a link on the Control panel or Appearance panel; see the sidebar on page 42.

Close a panel or group: To close (but not collapse) a panel, right-click the panel tab and choose Close from the context menu. To close a whole panel group, choose Close Tab Group from the context menu. To close a group that's collapsed to icons, expand the dock first by clicking the Expand Panels button.

Hide or show all the panels: Press Tab to hide or show all the open panels, including the Tools panel, or press Shift-Tab to hide or show all the panels except the Tools panel.

Make hidden, docked panels reappear: After you have hidden the panels via the Tab or Shift-Tab shortcut, move the pointer over the dark gray vertical bar inside the right edge of the Application frame. The panel docks (but not freestanding panels) will redisplay temporarily. Move the pointer away from the panels, and they'll disappear again. Note: If this isn't working, redisplay the panels, then right-click any panel icon or tab and choose Auto-Show Hidden Panels from the context menu.

➤ Every panel has a menu ▀≡ in the upper right corner, from which you can choose options for that panel.

To reconfigure the panels:

Expand a panel that's collapsed to an icon: Click the icon or panel label. If Auto-Collapse Icon Panels is checked in Illustrator/Edit > Preferences > User Interface and you open a panel from an icon, it will collapse back to the icon when you click elsewhere. With this preference unchecked, the panel will remain expanded; to collapse it back to an icon, click the Collapse to Icons button ▮▮ on the panel bar, or click the panel icon or label in the dock.

➤ To quickly access the Auto-Collapse Iconic Panels option from a context menu, right-click any panel tab, bar, or icon.

Maximize or minimize an expanded panel or group (vertically): Double-click the panel name or the gray bar. For some panels, such as Character, Color, or Color Guide, you can cycle through its three states (display more or fewer options) by clicking the expand/collapse arrow icon ↕ on the tab.

Collapse a whole dock to icons or to icons with labels: Click the Collapse to Icons button ▮▮ at the top of the dock (**B**, next page), or double-click the dark horizontal gray bar. Repeat to expand it.

Change the width of an expanded dock; or expand icons to icons with labels, or vice versa: Position the mouse over the vertical left edge of the dock (↔ cursor), then drag horizontally (**C**, next page).

Move a panel to a different slot in the same group: Drag the panel tab to the left or right.

Move a panel into a different group: Drag the panel tab over the title bar of the desired group, and release the mouse when the blue drop zone border appears (**D**, next page).

Change the location of a panel group in a dock: Drag the gray title bar upward or downward, and release the mouse when the horizontal blue drop zone bar is in the desired location (**E**, next page).

Create a new dock: Drag a panel tab or gray title bar sideways over the vertical left edge of the dock (**F**, next page), and release the mouse when the blue vertical drop zone bar appears.

Reconfigure a dock that's collapsed to icons: The methods are similar to those for an expanded group. Drag the group "title" bar (double dotted line) ∷∷∷∷ to the edge of a dock to create a new dock;

Instructions continue on page 34

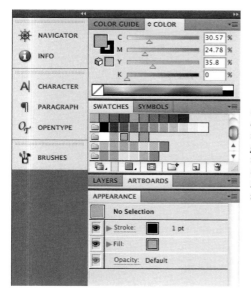

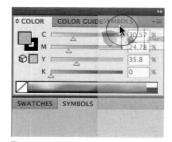

A *The panels in the left dock are collapsed to icons with labels (in three groups), whereas ones in the right dock are expanded (in four groups). The Layers/Artboards group is minimized vertically.*

D *A blue drop zone border appears as we drag the Symbols panel to the title bar of the Color/Color Guide group.*

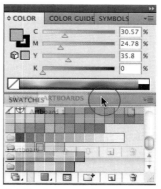

B *We clicked the Collapse to Icons button to collapse the whole right dock to icons. The panel groups were preserved.*

E *A blue horizontal drop zone bar appears as we move a panel group upward to a new slot in the same dock.*

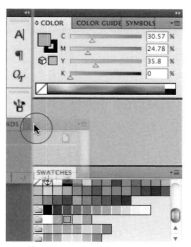

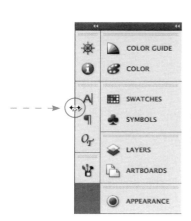

C *We dragged the edge of the left dock to the right to shrink it to just icons (no labels).*

F *A blue vertical drop zone bar appears as we drag a panel out of a dock, to create a new dock for it.*

or drag the title bar upward or downward between groups to restack it (look for a horizontal drop zone line); or drag the title bar into another group to add it to that group (look for a blue drop zone border).**A–B**

Float a docked panel or group: Drag the panel tab, icon, or gray title bar out of the dock. To stack floating panels or groups, drag the top bar of one so it meets the bottom of another, and release the mouse when a blue drop zone bar appears.

➤ To reset the panels to their default visibility states and locations, choose Essentials from the Workspace menu on the Application bar.

➤ To prevent a floating panel from docking as you move it around onscreen, hold down Cmd/Ctrl.

➤ If you inadvertently take the panel docks out of the Application frame, drag the dark gray bar (at the top) to the right edge of the Application frame, and release the mouse when a vertical blue drop zone line appears.

Choosing and saving workspaces

When you choose a predefined Illustrator workspace, the panels and panel groups that are most suited to a particular sphere of work appear onscreen. Among the specialty workspaces are Automation, Painting, Printing and Proofing, Typography, and Web. On the following page, you'll learn how to create and save custom workspaces for different purposes.

To choose a predefined workspace:

From the **Workspace** menu on the Application bar, choose a predefined workspace.**C**

➤ The arrangement of panels on a computer with dual displays is saved as a single workspace. You could put all the panels in one display, or put the ones you use most often in one display and those you use less often in the other.

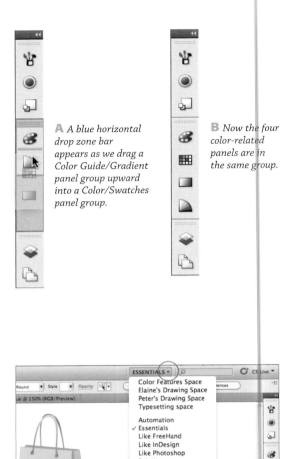

A *A blue horizontal drop zone bar appears as we drag a Color Guide/Gradient panel group upward into a Color/Swatches panel group.*

B *Now the four color-related panels are in the same group.*

C *On the Workspace menu on the Application bar, user-defined workspaces are listed first, followed by the preset workspaces.*

If the predefined workspaces don't suit your needs, you can hide, show, collapse, or expand any of the panels or docks. Even better, instead of tediously repeating those steps each time you start a work session, why not save your custom settings as a workspace? Saved workspaces are available on the Workspace menu (on the Application bar) for all documents. You can save multiple workspaces for different kinds of tasks.

To save a custom workspace:

1. If you like, you can use any of the preset workspaces on the Workspace menu as a starting point. Configure the Illustrator workspace by doing any or all of the following:

   Position the panels that you normally use where you want them, including the Tools panel and any library panels (such as any of the PANTONE color books). Put them in the desired groups and in the desired locations in one or more docks.

   Expand any of the panel docks, or collapse them to icons or icons with labels. For instance, you could expand the panels that you use frequently in one dock, and collapse the ones you use less frequently to icons in another dock.

   Resize any of the pickers, including any of those that open from the Control panel, such as the Swatches panel or the Brush Definition picker. For the Swatches panel, you can choose an option from the Show Swatch Kinds menu.

   Choose a View (e.g., a thumbnail or swatch size) for any panel from its menu.

   Open any tearoff toolbars for tool groups that you use frequently (such as for the type tools or for the Rectangle and its related tools).

2. From the Workspace menu on the Application bar, choose **Save Workspace**.

3. In the Save Workspace dialog, A enter a descriptive Name for the workspace.

4. Click OK. Your workspace (and any other user-saved workspaces) will be listed on, and can be chosen from, the Workspace menu on the Application bar.

➤ You can't save an artboard number, zoom level, or custom view as part of a workspace.

A *Type a Name for your new custom workspace in the Save Workspace dialog.*

To rename, delete, or duplicate a saved workspace:

1. From the Workspace menu on the Application bar, choose **Manage Workspaces**.

2. In the Manage Workspaces dialog, 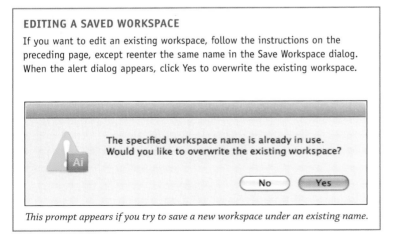A do any of the following:

   To **rename** a workspace, click the workspace name, then type the desired name in the field.

   To **duplicate** a workspace, click an existing workspace, then click the New Workspace button. Rename the duplicate workspace, if desired (a good idea).

   To **delete** a workspace, click the workspace name, then click the Delete Workspace button.

3. Click OK.

➤ If no workspaces are selected in the Manage Workspaces dialog when you click the New Workspace button, the new workspace will be based on the current state of the panels and other features of the Illustrator interface.

A *Use the Manage Workspaces dialog to rename or delete any of the custom workspaces that you have saved.*

EDITING A SAVED WORKSPACE

If you want to edit an existing workspace, follow the instructions on the preceding page, except reenter the same name in the Save Workspace dialog. When the alert dialog appears, click Yes to overwrite the existing workspace.

This prompt appears if you try to save a new workspace under an existing name.

This chapter will help you become more intimately acquainted with the Illustrator interface features that you will be using continually as you work: the panels. In the preceding chapter, you learned how to arrange them onscreen. Here you will see what the individual panels look like and be introduced to their specific functions — from choosing color swatches (Swatches panel) to switching among artboards (Artboards panel) to editing layers (Layers panel). Note: In-depth instructions for using specific panels are amply provided throughout this book.

You can read through this chapter with or without glancing at or fiddling with the panels onscreen, and also use it as a reference guide as you work. The panel icons are shown on the next page to help you identify them quickly. After that, you'll find instructions for using the Tools panel, a brief description of each tool, an introduction to the Control panel, then finally a description and illustration of the other Illustrator panels and their features (in alphabetical order). The panels open from the Window menu.

PANELS

4

CHOOSING VALUES IN A PANEL OR DIALOG

➤ To change a value incrementally, click in a field in a panel or dialog, then press the up or down arrow key on the keyboard.

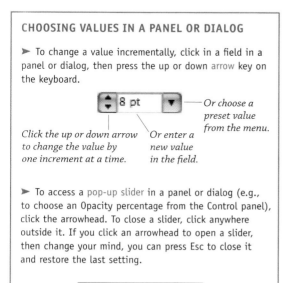

Click the up or down arrow to change the value by one increment at a time.   *Or enter a new value in the field.*   *Or choose a preset value from the menu.*

➤ To access a pop-up slider in a panel or dialog (e.g., to choose an Opacity percentage from the Control panel), click the arrowhead. To close a slider, click anywhere outside it. If you click an arrowhead to open a slider, then change your mind, you can press Esc to close it and restore the last setting.

The Illustrator panel icons

Identifying the panel icons

Each panel in Illustrator has a unique icon.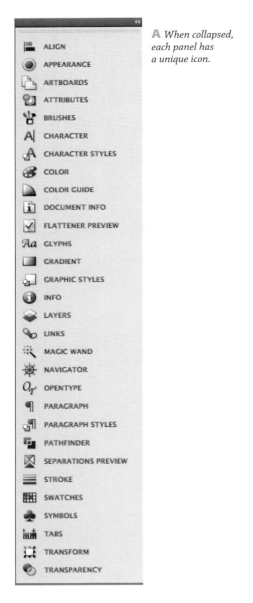
If you keep the panels collapsed to conserve
screen space, you can identify them by their
icons. To identify a panel icon, use the tool tip.

A *When collapsed, each panel has a unique icon.*

ALIGN
APPEARANCE
ARTBOARDS
ATTRIBUTES
BRUSHES
CHARACTER
CHARACTER STYLES
COLOR
COLOR GUIDE
DOCUMENT INFO
FLATTENER PREVIEW
GLYPHS
GRADIENT
GRAPHIC STYLES
INFO
LAYERS
LINKS
MAGIC WAND
NAVIGATOR
OPENTYPE
PARAGRAPH
PARAGRAPH STYLES
PATHFINDER
SEPARATIONS PREVIEW
STROKE
SWATCHES
SYMBOLS
TABS
TRANSFORM
TRANSPARENCY

USING THE CONTEXT MENUS

When you right-click* in the document window,
depending on where you click and which tool happens to be selected, a menu of context-sensitive
commands pops up onscreen. Many panel thumbnails,
names, and features also have related context menus.
If a command is available on a context menu (or can
be executed quickly via a keyboard shortcut), we let
you know in our instructions, to spare you a trip to
the main menu bar.

Undo
Redo Move
Perspective ▸
Isolate Selected Path
Group
Join
Average...
Make Clipping Mask
Make Compound Path
Make Guides
Transform ▸
Arrange ▸
Select ▸

This is the context menu for a selected object.

ENTERING VALUES IN THE ILLUSTRATOR PANELS

Apply a value and highlight the next field	Tab
Apply a value and highlight the previous field	Shift-Tab
Apply a value and exit the panel	Return/Enter

Mac OS users: If your mouse doesn't have a right-click button, hold down Control and click to open the context menu.

The Tools panel

Using the Tools panel

The Tools panel contains 81 tools that are used for creating and editing objects, as well as color controls, a menu or icons for choosing a drawing mode, and a menu for choosing a screen mode. If the panel is hidden, choose Window > Tools to display it. To convert its layout from single-column to double-column, or vice versa, double-click the dark gray bar at the top or click the arrowheads icon. To move the panel, drag the gripper bar or the dark gray bar.

Click once on a visible tool to select it, or click and hold on a tool that has a tiny arrowhead to choose a related tool from a fly-out menu. You can cycle through tools on the same menu by Option/Alt clicking the visible tool.

To create a standalone tearoff toolbar,**A–B** press and hold on the arrowhead for the current tool, then release the mouse when it's over the vertical tearoff bar on the far right side of the tool menu. To move a tearoff toolbar, drag the top bar. To restore a tearoff toolbar to the Tools panel, click its close button.

To access a tool quickly, use the letter shortcut that is assigned to it. The shortcuts are listed in parentheses on the next two pages, and also in tool tips onscreen.* **C**

Some tools can also be accessed temporarily via a toggle key. For example, pressing Cmd/Ctrl turns the current tool into a temporary selection tool. You'll learn other tool toggles as you proceed through this book.

To turn the tool pointer into a crosshairs icon for more precise positioning, go to Illustrator/Edit > Preferences > General and check Use Precise Cursors. Or if you prefer to keep that preference off, you can turn the pointer into a crosshairs icon temporarily by pressing the Caps Lock key.

You can choose options for the current tool from the Control panel (see page 42). Some tools, such as the Paintbrush and Pencil tools, have a related options dialog, which opens when you double-click the tool or when you click the tool and then press Return/Enter.

A *Open a tearoff toolbar by choosing a tearoff bar.*

B *A tearoff toolbar is created.*

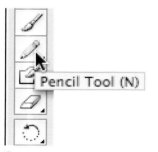

C *Use tool tips to learn the tool shortcuts.*

HIDING AND SHOWING PANELS AND TOOLBARS	
Hide or show all the currently open panels and tearoff toolbars, including the Tools panel.	Tab
Hide or show all the currently open panels and tearoff toolbars except the Tools panel.	Shift-Tab

*If the tool tips aren't displaying, go to Illustrator/Edit > Preferences > General and check Show Tool Tips.

The Tools panel illustrated

Gripper bar, for moving the panel

Selection (V) *Selects, moves, and transforms entire objects*

Direct Selection (A) *Selects and reshapes objects by their anchor points and segments*

Magic Wand (Y) *Selects objects based on their color and opacity attributes*

Lasso (Q) *Selects individual points and segments on a path via a free-form marquee*

Pen (P) *Draws paths that are composed of curved and/or straight segments*

Type (T) *Creates and edits horizontal type*

Line Segment (\) *Draws separate straight lines at any angle*

Rectangle (M) *Draws rectangles and squares*

Paintbrush (B) *Creates Calligraphic, Scatter, Art, Bristle, ★ or Pattern brush strokes*

Pencil (N) *Draws paths in a freehand style*

Blob Brush (Shift-B) *Creates closed shapes, or reshapes them, in a freehand style*

Eraser (Shift-E) *Erases sections of objects*

Rotate (R) *Rotates objects*

Scale (S) *Enlarges and shrinks objects*

Width (Shift-W) ★ *Reshapes an object's stroke*

Free Transform (E) *Rotates, scales, reflects, shears, distorts, or applies perspective to objects*

Shape Builder (Shift-M) ★ *Combines objects*

Perspective Grid (Shift-P) ★ *Puts objects into one-, two-, or three-point perspective*

Mesh (U) *Creates and edits multicolored mesh objects*

Gradient (G) *Changes the position, length, radius, or angle of existing gradients*

Eyedropper (I) *Samples and applies paint or type attributes*

Blend (W) *Creates shape and color blends between objects*

Symbol Sprayer (Shift-S) *Sprays symbol instances into a set*

Column Graph (J) *Creates column graphs*

Artboard (Shift-O) *Creates and reconfigures artboards in a document*

Slice (Shift-K) *Defines slice areas of a document*

Hand (H) *Moves the document in its window*

Zoom (Z) *Changes the zoom level of a document*

Fill *(press **X** to toggle or click to activate) The color, gradient, or pattern that fills the inside of a path*

Swap Fill and Stroke (Shift-X) *Swaps the current fill and stroke colors*

Stroke *(press **X** to toggle or click to activate) The color or pattern that's applied to a path*

Default Fill and Stroke (D) *Applies a fill color of white and 1-pt. stroke of black*

None (/) *Removes the current stroke or fill color*

Gradient (>) *Reapplies the last gradient fill*

Drawing modes: *Draw Normal, Draw Behind, or Draw Inside ★*

Color (<) *Reapplies the last solid stroke or fill color*

Screen modes (F) *Change the size of the document window and control the display of Illustrator features*

The tearoff toolbars*

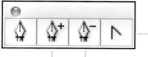

Convert Anchor Point (Shift-C) *Converts corner points to smooth points, and vice versa*

Add Anchor Point (+) **Delete Anchor Point (–)**

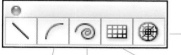

Polar Grid *Creates circular grids*

Arc *Creates curved segments* **Spiral** *Creates spiral lines* **Rectangular Grid** *Creates rectangular grids*

Reflect (O) *Creates a mirror reflection of an object*

LIQUIFY TOOLS *(apply distortion)*

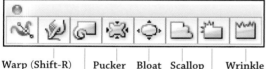

Warp (Shift-R) *Distorts objects* **Pucker** **Bloat** **Scallop** **Wrinkle**

Twirl **Crystallize**

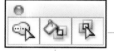

Live Paint Selection (Shift-L) *Selects sections of a Live Paint group*

Live Paint Bucket (K) *Recolors faces and edges in a Live Paint group*

Measure *Measures the distance between two points*

SYMBOLISM TOOLS *(edit symbol instances)*

Symbol Styler

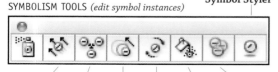

Symbol Shifter **Symbol Scruncher** **Symbol Sizer** **Symbol Spinner** **Symbol Stainer** **Symbol Screener**

Print Tiling *Positions the printable page*

Group Selection *Selects whole groups (and nested groups)*

Area Type *Creates and edits type horizontally inside an object* **Vertical Type** *Creates and edits vertical type*

Type on a Path *Creates and edits type horizontally along a path* **Vertical Area Type** *Creates and edits type vertically inside an object* **Vertical Path Type** *Creates and edits type vertically along a path*

Rounded Rectangle **Ellipse (L)** **Polygon** **Star** **Flare** *Creates drawings of lens flares*

Path Eraser *Erases sections of paths*

Smooth *Smooths path segments*

Knife *Carves up paths*

Scissors (C) *Splits paths*

Reshape *Reshapes sections of paths*

Shear *Skews objects*

Slice Select *Selects slices, for Web output*

*The tearoff toolbars for the Perspective Grid and Graph tools aren't illustrated here.

The Control panel

The Control panel houses many frequently used controls conveniently under one roof, and changes contextually depending on what tool and kind of object are selected. Two of the many variations are shown below. For example, you can use this panel to apply fill and stroke colors; change an object's variable width profile, brush stroke definition, or opacity; apply basic type attributes, such as the font and point size; align and distribute multiple objects; access controls for editing symbols, Live Trace, and Live Paint objects; and embed or edit linked images.

When no objects are selected, you can use this panel to choose default fill, stroke, brush, style, and opacity settings for the current document and quickly access the Document Setup or Preferences dialog by clicking the button of the same name.

To move the Control panel to the top or bottom, respectively, of the Application frame or your screen, choose Dock to Top or Dock to Bottom from the menu at the right end of the panel. Or if you prefer to make the panel free-floating, drag the gripper bar on the far left side. To control which options display on the panel, uncheck or check any of the items on the main part of the panel menu.

OPENING A TEMPORARY PANEL

► Click a link (word or letter that has a blue underline) on the Control panel to open a related panel. For example, you could click Stroke to open a temporary Stroke panel, or click Opacity to open a temporary Transparency panel (see the first figure below).

► Click the Stroke or Fill color square on the Control panel to open a temporary Swatches panel, or Shift-click either square to open a temporary Color panel.

► You can open other temporary panels by clicking a thumbnail or arrowhead. For example, you could click the Style thumbnail or arrowhead to open a temporary Graphic Styles panel.

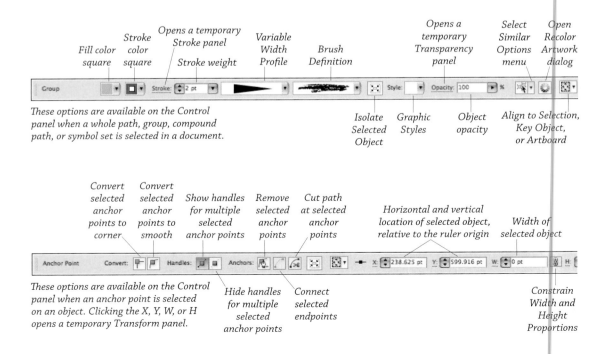

Fill color square | Stroke color square | Opens a temporary Stroke panel | Stroke weight | Variable Width Profile | Brush Definition | Opens a temporary Transparency panel | Select Similar Options menu | Open Recolor Artwork dialog

These options are available on the Control panel when a whole path, group, compound path, or symbol set is selected in a document.

Isolate Selected Object | Graphic Styles | Object opacity | Align to Selection, Key Object, or Artboard

Convert selected anchor points to corner | Convert selected anchor points to smooth | Show handles for multiple selected anchor points | Remove selected anchor points | Cut path at selected anchor points | Horizontal and vertical location of selected object, relative to the ruler origin | Width of selected object

These options are available on the Control panel when an anchor point is selected on an object. Clicking the X, Y, W, or H opens a temporary Transform panel.

Hide handles for multiple selected anchor points | Connect selected endpoints | Constrain Width and Height Proportions

The other essential panels illustrated*

Align panel

The buttons on the top two rows of the Align panel align and/or distribute two or more objects along their centers or along their top, left, right, or bottom edges. Objects can be aligned to a selection, an artboard, or a key object (one of the selected objects). Buttons at the bottom of the panel redistribute (equalize) the spacing among three or more objects. See pages 105–106. This panel can also be used to align anchor points (see page 164). Align buttons also appear on the Control panel when multiple objects are selected.

SHOWING OR HIDING PANEL OPTIONS

Some of the panels in Illustrator have extra options, which you may or may not see at first. To display or show a panel's full options, click the double arrow on its tab.

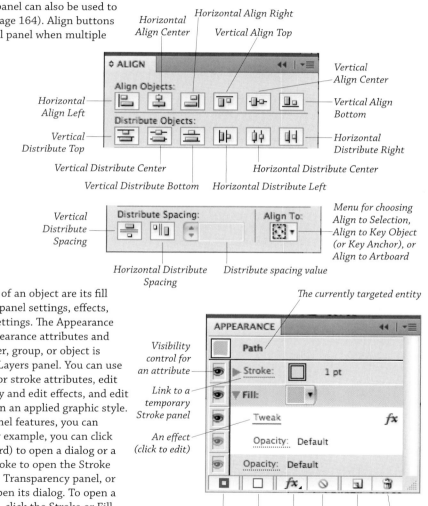

Horizontal Align Center
Horizontal Align Right
Vertical Align Top
Horizontal Align Left
Vertical Align Center
Vertical Align Bottom
Vertical Distribute Top
Horizontal Distribute Right
Vertical Distribute Center
Horizontal Distribute Center
Vertical Distribute Bottom
Horizontal Distribute Left
Vertical Distribute Spacing
Horizontal Distribute Spacing
Distribute spacing value
Menu for choosing Align to Selection, Align to Key Object (or Key Anchor), or Align to Artboard

Appearance panel

The appearance attributes of an object are its fill color, stroke color, Stroke panel settings, effects, and Transparency panel settings. The Appearance panel lists the specific appearance attributes and settings for whichever layer, group, or object is currently targeted on the Layers panel. You can use the panel to add extra fill or stroke attributes, edit or remove attributes, apply and edit effects, and edit individual attributes within an applied graphic style.

Using convenient in-panel features, you can edit attributes quickly. For example, you can click a link (blue underlined word) to open a dialog or a temporary panel: Click Stroke to open the Stroke panel, Opacity to open the Transparency panel, or the name of an effect to open its dialog. To open a temporary Swatches panel, click the Stroke or Fill color square, then click the thumbnail or arrowhead (or Shift-click the latter to open a temporary Color panel). See Chapter 14.

The currently targeted entity
Visibility control for an attribute
Link to a temporary Stroke panel
An effect (click to edit)
Add New Stroke
Add New Fill
Add New Effect
Duplicate Selected Item
Delete Selected Item
Clear Appearance

For the Kuler panel, see page 131. The Actions, Flash Text, SVG Interactivity, and Variables panels aren't covered in this book.

Artboards panel ★ 🗋

In addition to displaying a list of all the artboards
in the current document, the Artboards panel lets
you display, create, rename, and duplicate artboards;
change their order; rearrange them in the document;
choose options for them; change their orientation;
and delete them. The Artboard Options dialog opens
when you double-click the artboard orientation icon,
which is located to the right of the artboard name.
See pages 7–12 and 28.

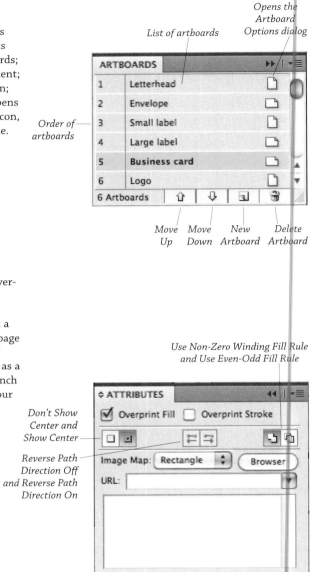

List of artboards

*Opens the
Artboard
Options dialog*

*Order of
artboards*

*Move
Up* *Move
Down* *New
Artboard* *Delete
Artboard*

Attributes panel 🔲

The "catchall" Attributes panel lets you choose overprint options for an object (see page 403), show
or hide an object's center point (see page 101),
switch the fill between color and transparency in a
compound path, change an object's fill rule (see page
338), choose a shape for an image map area, and
enter a Web address for an object to designate it as a
hot point on an image map. Click Browser to launch
the Web browser that is currently installed on your
system.

*Use Non-Zero Winding Fill Rule
and Use Even-Odd Fill Rule*

*Don't Show
Center and
Show Center*

*Reverse Path
Direction Off
and Reverse Path
Direction On*

Brushes panel

There are five varieties of decorative brushes that you can apply to paths: Calligraphic, Scatter, Art, Bristle, and Pattern. This can be done either by choosing the Paintbrush tool and a brush and then drawing a shape, or by applying a brush to an existing path.

To personalize your brush strokes, you can create and edit custom brushes. If you modify a brush that's being used in a document, you'll be given the option via an alert dialog to update the paths with the revised brush. Brushes on the Brushes panel save with the current document. See Chapter 23.

To open a temporary Brushes panel, click the Brush Definition thumbnail or arrowhead on the Control or Appearance panel.

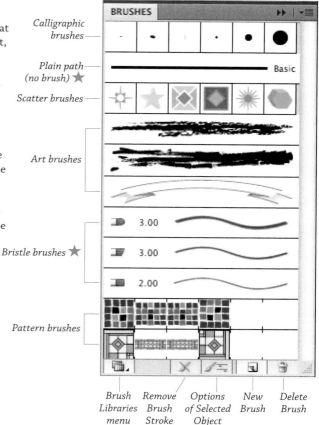

Calligraphic brushes

Plain path (no brush)

Scatter brushes

Art brushes

Bristle brushes

Pattern brushes

Brush Libraries menu — Remove Brush Stroke — Options of Selected Object — New Brush — Delete Brush

Character panel

You will use the Character panel to apply type attributes: font (family), font style, font size, leading, kerning, tracking, horizontal scale, vertical scale, baseline shift, character rotation, underline, strikethrough, an anti-aliasing method, and a language to be used for hyphenation. See pages 255–258 and 272.

When a type tool or a type object is selected, the Control panel also provides some basic type controls. To open a temporary Character panel, click Character on the Control panel.

Font — Tekton Pro
Font Style — Bold
Font Size — 12 pt   *Leading* — 15 pt
Kerning — Auto   *Tracking* — 0
Horizontal Scale — 100%   *Vertical Scale* — 100%
Baseline Shift — 0 pt   *Character Rotation* — 0°
Underline
Strikethrough   Sharp — *Anti-aliasing method*
Language: English: USA

Hyphenation Language for the current document

Character Styles panel

A character style is a collection of settings for type characters, including a font (family), font style, font size, leading, tracking, and kerning. Unlike paragraph styles, which apply to whole paragraphs, character styles are used to quickly format small bits of type (such as bullets, boldfaced words, italicized words, or large initial caps) to distinguish them from the main text. When you edit a character style, any text in which it is being used updates accordingly. Using the Character Styles panel, you can create, apply, edit, store, duplicate, and delete styles. See pages 266–269. (Compare this panel with the Paragraph Styles panel, which is shown on page 52.)

Color panel

Use the Color panel to mix a global process color or set a tint percentage for a spot color, and apply that color to an object's fill or stroke. Choose a color model for the panel, such as RGB or CMYK, from the panel menu. Quick-select a solid color or black, white, or None from the color ramp at the bottom of the panel. See page 117.

To open a temporary Color panel, Shift-click the Fill or Stroke color square or arrowhead on the Control panel or the Appearance panel.

Color Guide panel

Use the Color Guide panel to generate color schemes from a base color by choosing a harmony rule and/or a variation type (Tints/Shades, Warm/Cool, or Vivid/Muted). You can click any variation swatch to apply it as a fill or stroke color to one or more selected objects. You can also save variations from the Color Guide panel as a group to the Swatches panel, or edit the current color group via the Edit Colors dialog. See pages 115 and 128–130.

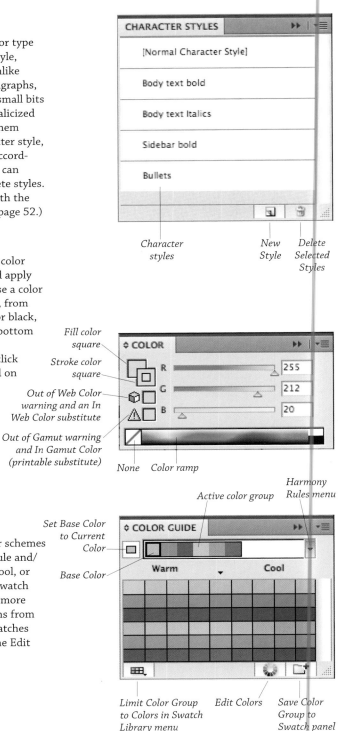

Character styles

New Style

Delete Selected Styles

Fill color square

Stroke color square

Out of Web Color warning and an In Web Color substitute

Out of Gamut warning and In Gamut Color (printable substitute)

None   Color ramp

Harmony Rules menu

Active color group

Set Base Color to Current Color

Base Color

Warm   Cool

Limit Color Group to Colors in Swatch Library menu

Edit Colors

Save Color Group to Swatch panel

Document Info panel

The Document Info panel only provides information. It lists data about artwork in your document, based on which category is chosen on the panel menu: Document (all data), or all Objects, Graphic Styles, Brushes, Spot Color Objects, Pattern Objects, Gradient Objects, Fonts, Linked Images, Embedded Images, or Font Details. If Selection Only is selected on the menu, the panel lists only data pertaining to the currently selected object(s). See page 410.

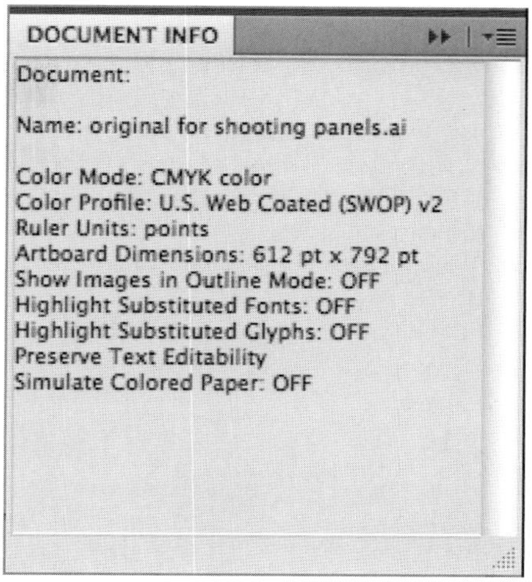

Flattener Preview panel

Artwork that contains semitransparent objects must be flattened before it is printed. Using the Highlight menu options in the Flattener Preview panel, you can preview which objects in your document will be affected by flattening, adjust the flattening settings, then click Refresh to preview the effect of the new settings in your artwork. See page 406.

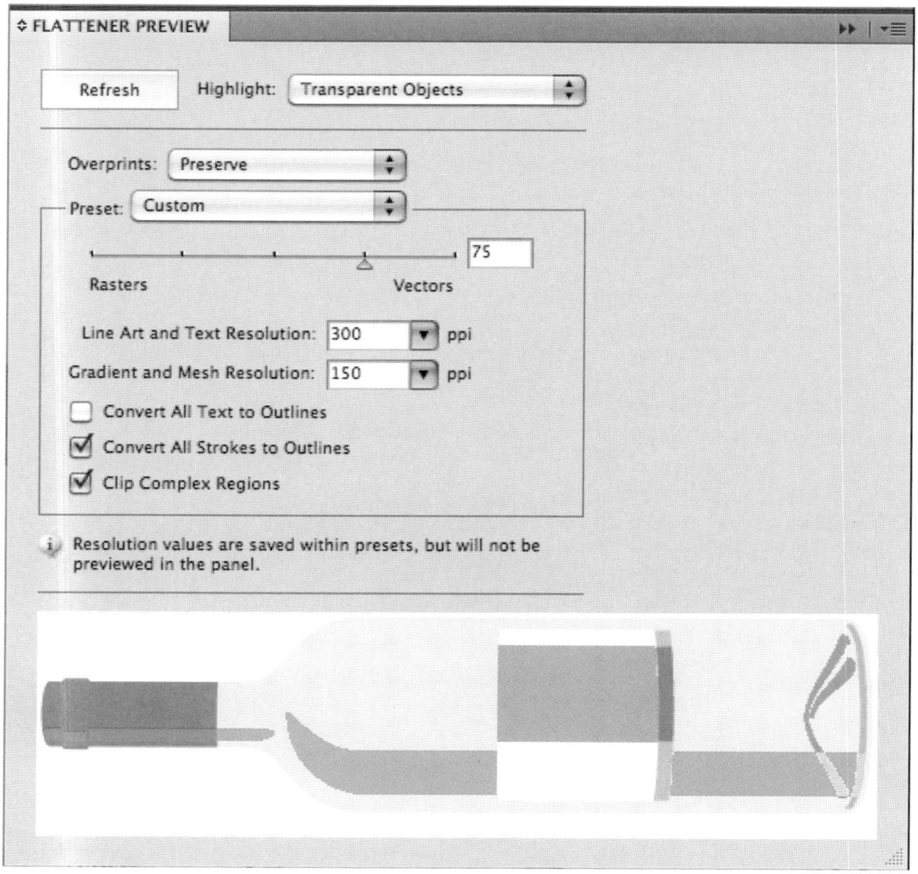

DOCUMENT INFO

Document:

Name: original for shooting panels.ai

Color Mode: CMYK color
Color Profile: U.S. Web Coated (SWOP) v2
Ruler Units: points
Artboard Dimensions: 612 pt x 792 pt
Show Images in Outline Mode: OFF
Highlight Substituted Fonts: OFF
Highlight Substituted Glyphs: OFF
Preserve Text Editability
Simulate Colored Paper: OFF

FLATTENER PREVIEW

Refresh   Highlight: Transparent Objects

Overprints: Preserve

Preset: Custom

75

Rasters   Vectors

Line Art and Text Resolution: 300 ppi
Gradient and Mesh Resolution: 150 ppi

☐ Convert All Text to Outlines
☑ Convert All Strokes to Outlines
☑ Clip Complex Regions

ℹ Resolution values are saved within presets, but will not be previewed in the panel.

Glyphs panel 𝕬𝖆

Using the Glyphs panel, you can find out which character variations (alternate glyphs) are available for any given character in a specific OpenType font, and insert glyphs from that font into your document (including glyphs that can't be entered via the keyboard). See page 261.

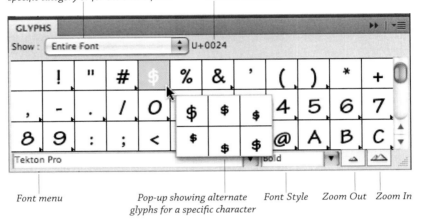

Via the Show menu, you can control whether the panel displays glyphs in a specific category or for the entire font.

Unicode for the currently selected character

Font menu

Pop-up showing alternate glyphs for a specific character

Font Style *Zoom Out* *Zoom In*

Gradient panel ▥

The Gradient panel lets you create, apply, and edit gradients, which are soft, gradual blends between two or more colors. You can adjust the amount of a color by dragging its stop, choose a different color or opacity value for a selected stop, click below the gradient slider to add new colors, move a midpoint diamond to change the location where two adjacent colors are mixed equally, reverse the gradient colors, or change the overall gradient type or angle. For a radial gradient, you can also change the aspect ratio to make the gradient more oval or more round. See Chapter 24.

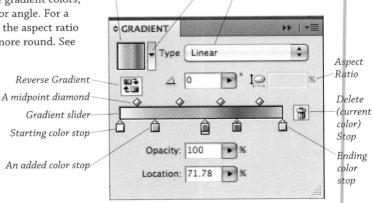

Gradient Fill square

Gradient menu (of swatches)

Gradient Type: Radial or Linear

Aspect Ratio

Reverse Gradient

A midpoint diamond

Gradient slider

Starting color stop

An added color stop

Delete (current color) Stop

Ending color stop

Graphic Styles panel 🔲

The Graphic Styles panel enables you to store and apply collections of appearance attributes, such as multiple solid-color fills or strokes, transparency and overprint settings, blending modes, brush strokes, and effects. Using graphic styles, you can apply attributes quickly and create a cohesive look among multiple objects or documents (you can think of them as paragraph styles for type). See Chapter 16. To open a temporary Graphic Styles panel, click the Style thumbnail or arrowhead on the Control panel.

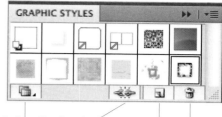

Graphic Styles Libraries menu — Break Link to Graphic Style — New Graphic Style — Delete Graphic Style

Info panel ⓘ

If no objects are selected in the current document, depending on the current tool, the Info panel lists the *x,y* (horizontal and vertical) location of the pointer in the document window. If an object is selected, the panel lists the location of the object relative to the ruler origin, its width and height, and data about its fill and stroke colors (the color components; or the name of a pattern or gradient; or a color name or number, such as a PANTONE number). While an object is being transformed, the panel lists pertinent information, such as a percentage value for a scale transformation or an angle of rotation. When a type tool and type object are selected, the panel displays type specifications. When the Measure tool is used, the Info panel opens automatically and lists the distance and angle the tool has just calculated.

Layers panel 🔷

The indispensable Layers panel lets you add and delete layers and sublayers in a document. You can also use this panel to select, target, restack, duplicate, delete, hide, show, lock, unlock, merge, change the view for, or create a clipping set for a layer, sublayer, group, or individual object. When your artwork is finished, you can use a command on the panel menu to flatten the document into one layer or release all the objects to separate layers for export as a Flash animation. See Chapter 13.

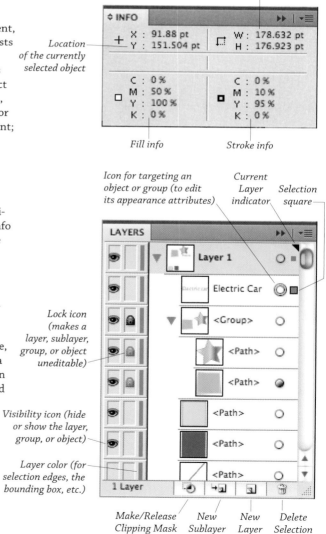

Width and height of the currently selected object

Location of the currently selected object

Fill info — Stroke info

Icon for targeting an object or group (to edit its appearance attributes) — Current Layer indicator — Selection square

Lock icon (makes a layer, sublayer, group, or object uneditable)

Visibility icon (hide or show the layer, group, or object)

Layer color (for selection edges, the bounding box, etc.)

Make/Release Clipping Mask — New Sublayer — New Layer — Delete Selection

Links panel

When you place an image from another application, such as Photoshop, into an Illustrator document, you can opt to have Illustrator embed a copy of the image into the file (and thereby increase the file size but allow the program to color-manage it) or merely link the image to your document (and keep the file size to a minimum but require the original file to be available for print output). Using the Links panel, you can monitor the status of linked images, convert a linked image to an embedded one, open a linked image in its original application for editing, and restore the link to an image that is missing or modified. See pages 292–295.

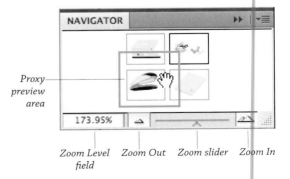

Modified Linked Image indicator   *Missing Image indicator*

Relink   *Go to Link*   *Update Link*   *Edit Original*

Magic Wand panel

The Magic Wand tool selects objects that have the same or a similar fill color, stroke color, stroke weight, opacity, or blending mode as the currently selected object. Using the Magic Wand panel, you choose attributes for the tool to select, and a tolerance value for each attribute. For example, if you were to check Opacity, choose an opacity Tolerance of 10%, then click an object that has an Opacity of 50%, the tool would find and select objects in the document that have an Opacity between 40% and 60%. See page 97.

Navigator panel

The Navigator panel has two main functions. To move the current document in its window, drag or click in the proxy preview area (red outlined box). To change the document zoom level, use the zoom controls at the bottom of the panel. To both zoom to and bring a specific area of a document into view, Cmd-drag/Ctrl-drag in the proxy preview area.

Proxy preview area

Zoom Level field   *Zoom Out*   *Zoom slider*   *Zoom In*

OpenType panel O_T

Among the Roman OpenType font families that ship with Illustrator, the fonts that contain an expanded character set and a large assortment of alternate glyphs are labeled with the word "Pro." By clicking a button on the OpenType panel, you can specify which alternate characters (glyphs) will appear in your text when you type the requisite key or keys. The special characters for a given font may include ligatures, swashes, titling characters, stylistic alternates, ordinals, and fractions. You can also use the panel to specify options for numerals, such as a style (e.g., tabular lining or oldstyle) and a position (e.g., numerator, denominator, superscript, or subscript). See page 262.

OPENING THE PANELS FOR EDITING TYPE

Illustrator has eight panels that are used for editing type: Character, Character Styles, Flash Text, Glyphs, OpenType, Paragraph, Paragraph Styles, and Tabs. All of them can be opened via the Window > Type submenu; the Glyphs panel can also be opened via the Type menu. Four of them have default shortcuts, as listed below.

	Mac OS	Windows
Character	Cmd-T	Ctrl-T
OpenType	Cmd-Option-Shift-T	Ctrl-Alt-Shift-T
Paragraph	Cmd-Option-T	Ctrl-Alt-T
Tabs	Cmd-Shift-T	Ctrl-Shift-T

Paragraph panel ¶

Use the Paragraph panel to apply settings that affect entire paragraphs, such as horizontal alignment, indentation, spacing before or after, and automatic hyphenation. Via the panel menu, you can choose hanging punctuation and composer options and open a dialog for choosing justification or hyphenation options. See pages 259, 263–265, and 270.

The Align Left, Align Center, and Align Right buttons are also available on the Control panel when a type object is selected. To open a temporary Paragraph panel, click Paragraph on the Control panel.

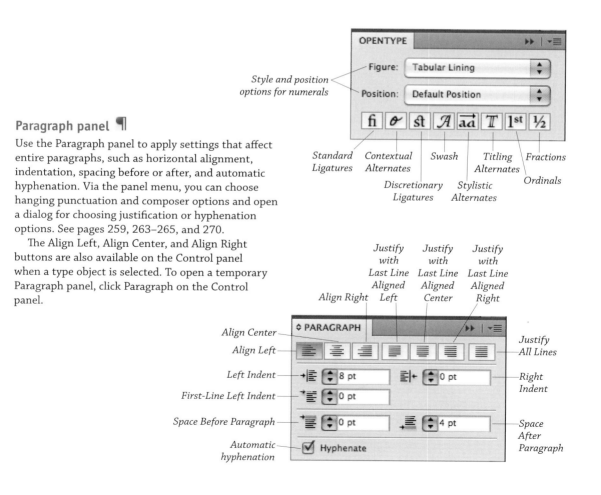

Paragraph Styles panel

A paragraph style is a collection of paragraph specifications (including horizontal alignment, indentation, spacing before or after, word spacing, letter spacing, hyphenation, and hanging punctuation) and character attributes, such as the font family, font style, and font size. When you apply a paragraph style to one or more selected paragraphs, the type is reformatted with the specifications in that style. When you edit a paragraph style, the type it's assigned to updates accordingly. Using paragraph (and character) styles, you can typeset text more quickly and with less effort. Styles also enable you to keep the formatting consistent among multiple type objects in the same document or among multiple documents. This panel lets you create, apply, edit, store, duplicate, and delete paragraph styles for the current document. See pages 266–269.

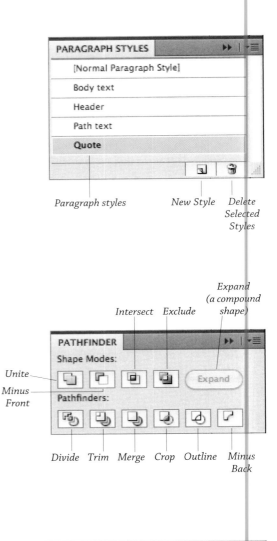

Paragraph styles   New Style   Delete Selected Styles

Pathfinder panel

Depending on how they are applied, the Shape Mode commands on the top row of the Pathfinder panel combine selected, overlapping objects into one or more standard paths or into a compound shape. The Expand button converts a compound shape into either a path or a compound path (the latter if the command originally produced a cutout shape). The Pathfinder buttons on the bottom row of the panel produce flattened, cut-up shapes from multiple selected objects. See pages 334–336. Be sure to also learn about the new Shape Builder tool, which we give instructions for on pages 327–331.

Intersect   Exclude   Expand (a compound shape)

Unite
Minus Front

Divide   Trim   Merge   Crop   Outline   Minus Back

Separations Preview panel

The Separations Preview panel gives you an idea of how the individual C, M, Y, and K color components in a CMYK document will separate to individual printing plates during the commercial printing process. You can use the panel to check that a color is properly set to knock out colors beneath it in your artwork, or to check whether a color is properly set to overprint on top of the other colors. Other uses for the panel are to monitor the use of spot colors in the artwork, to verify that any spot color is set to knock out colors beneath it, and to determine whether a specific black is a rich black (a mixture of C, M, Y, and K inks) or a simple black that contains only the K component. See pages 402–403.

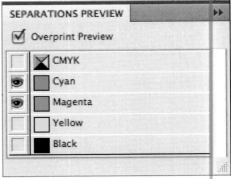

Stroke panel ≣

The stroke attributes affect the appearance of an object's path (edge). By using the Stroke panel, you can choose a stroke weight (thickness), a cap (end) style, and a corner (join) style, and control how the stroke aligns to the path. You can also use the panel to create a dashed (or dotted) line or border; apply an arrowhead and/or tail style; and change the stroke width profile. See pages 120–122, page 156, and page 158. To open a temporary Stroke panel, click Stroke on the Control or Appearance panel.

Swatches panel ▦

Use the Swatches panel to choose, store, and apply solid colors, patterns, gradients, and color groups. If you click a swatch, it becomes the current fill or stroke color (depending on whether the Fill or Stroke square is active on the Tools panel and Color panel), and it is applied to all currently selected objects.

Double-clicking a swatch opens the Swatch Options dialog, in which you can change the swatch name or change its type to global process, nonglobal process, or spot. Via commands on the panel menu, you can merge swatches and perform other tasks. See pages 114, 116, 118, 124–127, and 132. To open a temporary Swatches panel, click the Fill or Stroke square or arrowhead on the Control or Appearance panel.

Symbols panel ♣

Symbols are Illustrator objects that are stored on the Symbols panel and save with the current document. Using symbols, you can quickly and easily create a complex collection of objects, such as a bank of trees or clouds. To create one instance of a symbol, you simply drag from the Symbols panel onto the artboard; to assemble multiple instances quickly into what is known as a symbol set, you use the Symbol Sprayer tool.

The other symbolism tools let you change the position, stacking order, proximity, size, rotation angle, or transparency of multiple instances in a set, or gradually apply a color tint or graphic style — while maintaining the link to the original symbol on the panel. If you edit the original symbol, all instances of that symbol in the document update automatically. See Chapter 28.

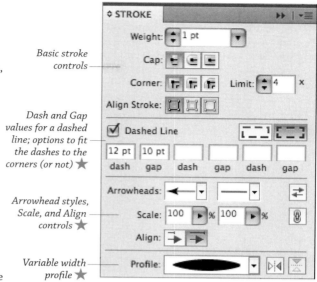

Basic stroke controls

Dash and Gap values for a dashed line; options to fit the dashes to the corners (or not) ★

Arrowhead styles, Scale, and Align controls ★

Variable width profile ★

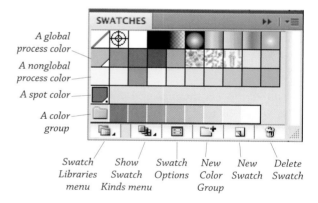

A global process color

A nonglobal process color

A spot color

A color group

Swatch Libraries menu — Show Swatch Kinds menu — Swatch Options — New Color Group — New Swatch — Delete Swatch

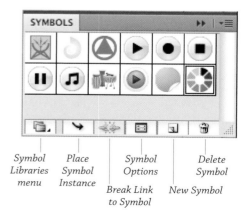

Symbol Libraries menu — Place Symbol Instance — Symbol Options — Break Link to Symbol — New Symbol — Delete Symbol

Tabs panel

The only way to accurately align columns of text is by using tabs and the Tabs panel. Using the panel, you can insert, move, and change the alignment of custom tab markers (tab stops), specify a leader (such as a period character, to produce a dotted line), and specify a character for your text to align to (such as a decimal point). See pages 270–271.

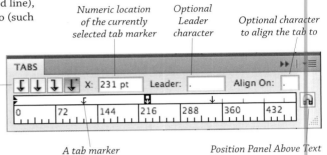

Numeric location of the currently selected tab marker

Optional Leader character

Optional character to align the tab to

Left-, Center-, Right-, and Decimal-Justified alignment buttons for horizontal type (or Top-, Center-, and Bottom-Justified buttons for vertical type)

A tab marker

Position Panel Above Text

Transform panel

The Transform panel lists the location, width, height, rotation angle, and shear angle of the currently selected object, and can be used to change those values. By clicking a point on the Reference Point locator, you can control what part of the object the transformations are calculated from. The panel can also be used to align selected objects to the pixel grid. Via commands on the panel menu, you can control whether just the object, the object and a fill pattern, or just the fill pattern is transformed. See pages 142–143.

To open a temporary Transform panel, click the X, Y, W, or H link on the Control panel (or click the word "Transform," if those fields aren't showing). A reference point icon and X, Y, W, and H fields also appear on the Control panel when one or more paths are selected.

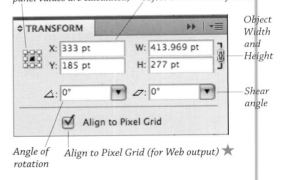

Reference Point (the part of the object from which panel values are calculated)

Location of the selected object on the x and y axes

Object Width and Height

Shear angle

Angle of rotation

Align to Pixel Grid (for Web output) ★

Transparency panel

You can use the Transparency panel to change the blending mode or opacity of a layer, group, or individual object. See Chapter 27. The Make Opacity Mask command on the panel menu generates an editable opacity mask, which hides parts of a layer or group (that technique isn't covered in this book).

To open a temporary Transparency panel, click the Opacity link on the Control or Appearance panel. You can also change the opacity of an object via the Control panel.

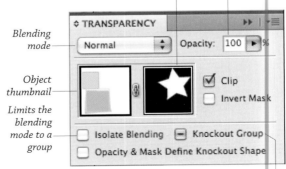

Opacity mask thumbnail

Object Opacity

Blending mode

Object thumbnail

Limits the blending mode to a group

Prevents objects in a group from showing through one another

In this chapter, you will open files via the Open command and via Bridge, a separate application that serves as a conduit among Adobe Creative Suite programs. You will also learn how to customize the Bridge window and use it to preview, open, label, rate, group, find, rename, delete, move, copy, and assign keywords to files. (Bridge is included with Illustrator.)

Opening files from Illustrator

Follow the instructions below if you want to open Illustrator files using the Open command in Illustrator. Or if you prefer to use Bridge to open files — as we do and recommend — turn the page and start reading from there. (To learn how to import files from other programs into Illustrator, see Chapter 22.)

To open a file from Illustrator:

1. Do either of the following:

   Choose File > **Open** (Cmd-O/Ctrl-O).

   If you've just launched Illustrator and the Adobe Illustrator CS5 welcome screen is displaying, click **Open**.

2. In the Mac OS, to list files only in the formats that Illustrator can read, choose Enable: All Readable Documents. In Windows, to list all files, readable and not, either choose Files of Type: All Formats or choose a specific format.

3. Locate and click a file name, then click Open. If an alert dialog about a color profile or missing font appears, see page 63; if an alert dialog pertaining to imported images appears, see page 289.

➤ To reopen a recently opened file, choose the file name from the File > Open Recent Files submenu.

➤ If you open an Illustrator CS3 document that contains crop areas into Illustrator CS5, those areas will convert to artboards. You may be prompted to specify how you want the crop areas to be converted.

To open an Illustrator file from the Macintosh Desktop or Windows Explorer:

Double-click the icon for an Illustrator file. The file name may include one of the following extensions: .ai, .eps, .ait, .fxg, .svgz, or .svg.

In the Mac OS, you can also open a file by dragging its icon over the Adobe Illustrator CS5 application icon on the Dock.

Illustrator will launch if it isn't already running.

BRIDGE

5

IN THIS CHAPTER

Launching Adobe Bridge

The excellent navigation controls and large thumbnail previews in Bridge make locating and opening files a snap. There are many useful features in Bridge to explore, such as the ability to organize file thumbnails into collections and collapsible stacks, assign keywords to files, and filter the display of thumbnails by various criteria.

To launch Adobe Bridge:

Do one of the following:

In the Mac OS or in Windows, on the Application bar in Illustrator, click the **Go to Bridge** button ▣ (Cmd-Option-O/Ctrl-Alt-O).

In the Mac OS, double-click the **Adobe Bridge CS5** application icon ▣ or click the **Bridge** icon ▣ on the Dock.

In Windows, click the Start button, choose All Programs, then click **Adobe Bridge CS5.**

Features of the Bridge window

First, we'll identify the main sections of the Bridge window (**A**, next page). The two rows of buttons and menus running across the top of the window are referred to jointly as the toolbar. The second row of the toolbar is also called the Path bar.

In the default workspace, Essentials, the main window is divided into three panes: a large pane in the center and a vertical pane on either side. Each pane contains one or more panels, which are accessed via tabs: Favorites, Folders, Filter, Collections, Export, Content, Preview, Metadata, and Keywords. Using panels in the side panes, you can manage files, filter the display of thumbnails, and display file data; the Content panel displays document thumbnails. You can hide, show, or resize any of the panels or move any panel into a different pane. At the bottom of the Bridge window are controls for changing the thumbnail size and format. To customize the Bridge workspace, see pages 58–59 and 64–65.

We'll explore the toolbar features and most of the panels in depth in this chapter. To help you get oriented, here is a brief description of the panels:

The **Favorites** panel displays a list of folders that you've designated as favorites, for quick and easy access (see page 61).

The **Folders** panel contains a scrolling window with a hierarchical listing of all the top-level and nested folders on your hard disk. See page 60.

By clicking various criteria in the **Filter** panel on or off, you can filter which file thumbnails in the current folder display in the Content panel. See page 72.

The **Collections** panel displays the names (and folder icons) for collections, which are user-created groups of file thumbnails. Using collections, you can organize and access your file thumbnails without having to relocate the actual files. See pages 69–70.

The **Content** panel displays thumbnails for files (and, optionally, for nested folders) within the current folder. In the lower right corner of the Bridge window, you can click a View Content As button to control whether, and in what format, metadata displays in the Content panel (see page 65). The Content panel is used and illustrated throughout this chapter.

The **Preview** panel displays a large preview of one or more document (or folder) thumbnails that are selected in the Content panel. If a document you are previewing contains multiple artboards, controls are provided for navigating through them. If the thumbnail for a video file is selected in the Content panel, a controller for playing the video displays in this panel. Or if a multipage PDF file is selected, you can click the left or right arrow to preview pages in the file. See pages 60–61.

In the **Metadata** panel, you can find detailed information about the currently selected file, within expandable categories. The File Properties category, for example, lists such data as the file name, format, date created, and date modified. For a closeup of this panel, see the sidebar on page 61 (see also Bridge Help).

Use the **Keywords** panel to assign descriptive keywords to files, such as the client or project name or the subject matter of the artwork. You can search for file thumbnails based on the keywords that are assigned to them, and display thumbnails based on keywords by using the Filter panel (see page 73).

Note: The Export and Inspector panels aren't covered in this book.

Browse Quickly by Preferring Embedded Images

Options for thumbnail quality and preview generation

Filter Items by Rating menu

Sort menu

Rotate selected thumbnails

Create New Folder

Delete Item

Display thumbnails in descending order or ascending order

Open Recent File menu

Get Photos from Camera

Return to last Adobe Creative Suite application

Refine menu (Review Mode, Batch Rename, File Info)

Open in Camera Raw

Output menu (Web or PDF)

Name of currently displayed folder

Workspace switcher

Workspace menu

For the navigation controls on the toolbar, see page 60.

Path bar

A Features of the Bridge window are identified above. You'll learn about their functions throughout this chapter.

Thumbnail Size slider

Lock Thumbnail Grid (displays grid lines between full thumbnails)

View Content as Thumbnails

View Content as List

View Content as Details

Choosing a workspace for Bridge

To reconfigure the Bridge window quickly, choose one of the predefined workspaces. (To create and save custom workspaces, see pages 64–66.)

To choose a workspace for Bridge:

Do one of the following:

In the workspace switcher on the upper toolbar, click **Essentials**, **Filmstrip**, **Metadata** (List View for the thumbnails), **Output**, **Keywords**, **Preview**, **Light Table**, **Folders**, or a user-saved workspace. A If you want to display more workspace names, pull the gripper bar to the left. B

From the **Workspace** menu on the workspace switcher, choose a workspace C (and A–C, next page).

Press the shortcut for one of the first six workspaces on the switcher (as listed on the Workspace menu): Cmd-F1/Ctrl-F1 through Cmd-F6/Ctrl-F6. The shortcuts are assigned automatically to the first six workspaces on the switcher, based on their current order from left to right.

➤ The Output workspace has a different purpose from the other workspaces, and is not covered in this book.*

➤ To resize the thumbnails for any workspace, see page 64.

To change the order of workspaces on the switcher:

Do either of the following:

Drag a workspace name to the left or right.

Right-click a workspace name and choose a different name from the context menu.

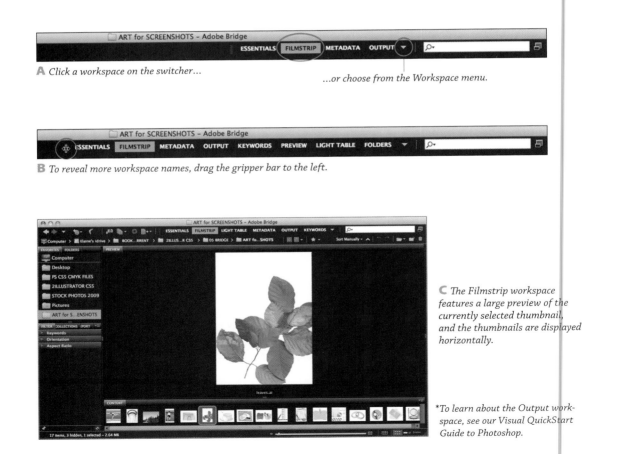

A *Click a workspace on the switcher...*

...or choose from the Workspace menu.

B *To reveal more workspace names, drag the gripper bar to the left.*

C *The Filmstrip workspace features a large preview of the currently selected thumbnail, and the thumbnails are displayed horizontally.*

To learn about the Output workspace, see our Visual QuickStart Guide to Photoshop.

A *In the Essentials workspace, all the panels are showing.*

B *In the Preview workspace, the Metadata and Keywords panels are hidden to make room for a large preview, and the thumbnails are displayed vertically.*

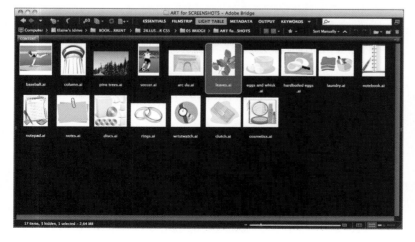

C *The Light Table workspace allows you to display the largest number of thumbnails in a folder, because the Content panel takes up the whole Bridge window.*

Previewing graphics in Bridge

For navigating to and opening folders, Bridge provides controls on the toolbar and in the Folders and Favorites panels.

To select and preview graphics in Bridge:

1. Do any of the following:

   In the **Folders** panel, navigate to the folder to be opened. You can use the scroll arrows, and you can expand or collapse any folder by clicking its arrowhead.

   Display the contents of a folder by clicking its icon in the **Folders** panel or by double-clicking its thumbnail in the **Content** panel. Note: For folder thumbnails to display in the Content panel, View > Show Folders must be checked.

   Click the **Go Back** button ◀ on the toolbar **A** to step back through the last folders viewed, or the **Go Forward** button ▶ to reverse those steps.

   Click a folder name in the **Favorites** panel.

   From the **Go to Parent or Favorites** menu ▾ on the toolbar, choose a parent or favorites folder.

   Click a folder name on the **Path** bar (choose Window > Path Bar to display the bar).

   From one of the menus ▸ on the Path bar, choose a folder. If another submenu displays,
   click yet another folder; repeat until the desired folder is reached.

   ➤ To display thumbnails for files in all the nested subfolders inside the current folder, choose Show Items from Subfolders from its menu.▸ To restore the normal view, click the Cancel button ◯ on the Path bar.

2. In the **Content** panel, do either of the following:

   Click a thumbnail. A colored border will appear around it, and data about the file will be listed in the Metadata panel. An enlarged preview of the graphic will also display in the Preview panel, if that panel is showing.

   To select multiple files, Cmd-click/Ctrl-click nonconsecutive thumbnails; or click the first thumbnail in a series of consecutive thumbnails, then Shift-click the last one.**B**

Go Back and Go Forward   Go to Parent or Favorites   Reveal Recent File or Go to Recent Folder menu

Path bar

A *These are the navigation controls in Bridge.*

The Preview panel displays an enlargement of one or more selected thumbnails, so you can shop and compare.

B *Cmd-click/Ctrl-click multiple thumbnails in the Content panel to compare them in the Preview panel.*

3. If the file for the currently selected thumbnail contains multiple artboards, you can cycle through them by clicking the left or right arrow below the preview or by entering the desired artboard number in the field and then pressing Return/Enter.**A**

➤ A number in the upper left corner of a document thumbnail indicates that it belongs to a group, called a stack. To display all the document thumbnails in a stack, click the number; to collapse the stack, click the number again. To learn more about stacks, see page 67.

➤ When a document thumbnail is selected, you can cycle through other thumbnails in the same folder by pressing an arrow key. To quickly locate and select a particular thumbnail, start typing the file name (you don't need to click anywhere first).

To add a folder to the Favorites panel:

Do either of the following:

Drag a folder icon from the Content panel or from the Desktop into the Favorites panel.

Right-click a folder in the Folders or Content panel and choose **Add to Favorites**.

➤ Via check boxes in the Favorite Items area of Adobe Bridge CS5/Edit > Preferences > General, you can control which system folders appear in the top part of the Favorites panel.

➤ To remove a folder from the list of Favorites, right-click it and choose Remove from Favorites.

VIEWING A FILE'S METADATA

When you click the thumbnail for an Illustrator document, information about the file displays in expandable categories in the Metadata panel. You can use the IPTC Core category in this panel to attach creator, description, copyright, and other information to the currently selected file: Click the field next to a listing, enter or modify the file description information, press Tab to cycle through and edit other data, then click the Apply button ■ in the lower right corner.

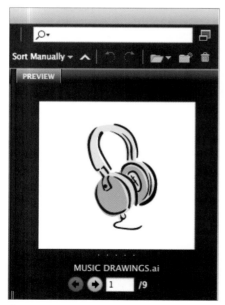

A *In the Preview panel, you can cycle through multiple artboards in an Illustrator document by clicking the left or right arrow or by entering the desired artboard number in the field.*

Opening files from Bridge

You can open as many files in Illustrator as the currently available RAM and scratch disk space on your computer can accommodate. (To learn how to import files from other programs into Illustrator, see Chapter 22.)

To open files from Bridge into Illustrator:

1. In the Content panel, display the thumbnails for the documents you want to open.

2. Do either of the following:

   Double-click a thumbnail.

   Click a thumbnail or select multiple thumbnails, then double-click one of them or press Cmd-O/ Ctrl-O.

   Illustrator will launch, if it isn't already running, and the chosen documents will appear onscreen.

3. If the Font Problems dialog or an alert about a color profile appears, see the next page. If an alert about a linked image file appears, see the sidebar on page 289.

➤ To locate a file in Finder/Explorer, right-click its thumbnail in Bridge and choose Reveal in Finder/Reveal in Explorer from the context menu. The folder that the file resides in will open in a window in Finder/Explorer and the file icon will be selected.

➤ By default, the Bridge window stays open after you use it to open a file. To have the Bridge window close/minimize as you open a file, hold down Option/Alt while double-clicking the file thumbnail.

To reopen a recently opened file:

To reopen a file that was recently opened and then closed, do one of the following:

Choose from the **Open Recent File** menu on the right side of the Path bar.

Choose from the File > **Open Recent** submenu.

From the **Reveal Recent File or Go to Recent Folder** menu on the toolbar, choose Adobe Illustrator > **Recent Adobe Illustrator Files**, then in the Content panel, click the thumbnail for a file to open it. To redisplay an "actual" folder when you return to Bridge, click the Go Back arrow or a Favorites folder.

GETTING TO ILLUSTRATOR QUICKLY

If Illustrator was the last Creative Suite application you were working in, you can get back to it quickly from Bridge by clicking the Return to Adobe Illustrator button on the toolbar. Illustrator will launch, if it isn't already running.

RESPONDING TO ALERT DIALOGS UPON OPENING A FILE

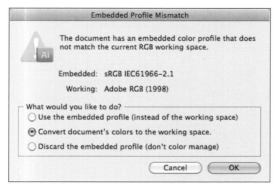

If you open a file in Illustrator that is using a missing font (the font isn't available or isn't installed), the Font Problems dialog will appear. You can click Open to let the document open with a substitute font. If a missing font subsequently becomes available in the system, it will also become available on the font menus in Illustrator and the type will redisplay correctly without any action required on your part.

The Font Problems alert dialog will appear if any of the fonts that are being used in the file you are opening are missing.

If the file's color profile doesn't match the current working space for Illustrator, the Embedded Profile Mismatch alert dialog will appear. Click Use the Embedded Profile (Instead of the Working Space) if you must keep the document's current profile, or for better consistency with your color management workflow, we recommend clicking Convert Document's Colors to the Working Space to convert the profile to the current working space. Click OK. (See also pages 17–18 and 21.)

If this Embedded Profile Mismatch alert dialog appears, indicate whether you want to continue to use the embedded profile or convert the file to the current working space.

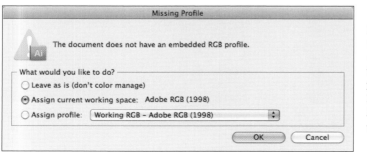

If the Missing Profile alert dialog appears, click Assign Current Working Space. Listed next to this option will be the profile that is used in the Color Settings preset you chose for Illustrator on pages 17–18. In an RGB workflow, that profile will be Adobe RGB (1998); in a CMYK workflow, it will be U.S. Web Coated (SWOP) v2.

If this Missing Profile alert dialog appears, click Assign Current Working Space to convert the file to the current working space for Illustrator.

Customizing the Bridge workspace

To display or hide the panels:

On the **Window** menu, check which panels you want to show or hide.

► To quickly hide (and then show) the side panes, press Tab or double-click the dark vertical bar between a side pane and the middle pane.

► To display just the Content panel in a compact window, click the Switch to Compact Mode button ⬛ in the upper right corner of the Bridge window. Click it again to restore the full window.

To configure the panes and panels manually:

Do any of the following:

To make a panel or panel group taller or shorter, drag its horizontal gripper bar upward or downward.**A**

To make a whole pane wider or narrower, drag its vertical gripper bar to the left or right;**B** the adjacent pane will resize accordingly.

You can minimize/maximize some panels by double-clicking the panel tab.

To move a panel into a different group, drag the panel tab, and release the mouse when the blue drop zone border appears around the desired group.

To display a panel as a separate group, drag its tab between two panels, and release the mouse when the horizontal blue drop zone line appears.

► To save a Bridge layout as a user-created workspace for easy access in the future, see page 66.

To resize the document thumbnails:

At the bottom of the Bridge window, drag the **Thumbnail Size** slider **C** or click the **Smaller Thumbnail Size** button ⬜ or **Larger Thumbnail Size** button.⬜

► To display only full thumbnails, with grid lines between them, click the Lock Thumbnail Grid button ▦ at the bottom of the Bridge window. With this option on, the thumbnails won't reshuffle if you resize the Content panel.

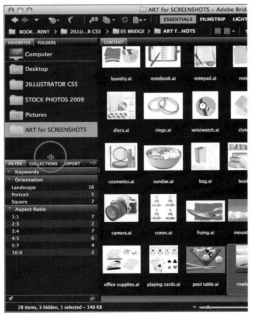

A We are moving the gripper bar upward to shorten the Favorites panel group and lengthen the Filter panel group.

B We are moving the gripper bar for the right pane to the left to widen the Preview and Metadata panels.

C Use the Thumbnail Size slider to resize the thumbnails in the Content panel.

To control the format in which metadata displays in the Content panel:

1. In the lower right corner of the Bridge window, click one of these buttons: **A View Content as Thumbnails** (minimal file data), **View Content as Details** (more file data),**B** or **View Content as List** (small thumbnails with columns of data).

   ➤ If the View Content as List button is activated, you can change the column order by dragging any column header to the left or right.

2. To control which categories of metadata display below or next to the file thumbnails when the View Content as Thumbnails button is activated, go to Adobe Bridge CS5/Edit > Preferences > Thumbnails, then select from any or all of the **Details: Show** menus. For example, to display the file size, choose Size.

➤ When the View Content as Thumbnails button is activated, you can toggle the display of data on and off by pressing Cmd-T/Ctrl-T.

METADATA IN THE TOOL TIPS

If Show Tooltips is checked in Adobe Bridge CS5/Edit Preferences > Thumbnails and you rest the pointer on a document thumbnail, the tool tip will list the metadata for that file. Uncheck the option if the tool tips become annoying.

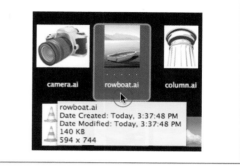

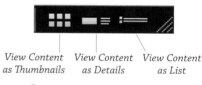

View Content as Thumbnails   View Content as Details   View Content as List

A *These buttons control the display of metadata in the Content panel.*

B *When the View Content as Details button is activated, metadata displays next to the file thumbnails.*

Saving custom workspaces

If you save your customized workspaces, you'll be able to access them again quickly at any time and will avoid having to reconfigure your workspace each time you launch Bridge.

To save a custom workspace for Bridge:

1. Do all of the following:

   Choose a size and location for the overall Bridge window.

   Arrange the panel sizes and groups as desired.

   Choose a thumbnail size for the Content panel.

   Choose a sorting order from the Sort menu at the top of the Bridge window (see page 72).

   Click a View Content button.

2. From the **Workspace** menu on the workspace switcher, choose **New Workspace**.

3. In the New Workspace dialog, **A** enter a Name for the workspace, check Save Window Location as Part of Workspace and/or Save Sort Order as Part of Workspace (both are optional), then click Save.

   Note: Your new workspace will be listed first on the workspace switcher, and will be assigned the first shortcut (Cmd-F1/Ctrl-F1). To change the order of the workspaces on the bar, drag any workspace name horizontally to a different slot. When you do this, the shortcuts will be reassigned based on the new order.

➤ To delete a user-saved workspace, from the Workspace menu, choose Delete Workspace. From the menu in the dialog, choose the workspace to be deleted, then click Delete.

Resetting the Bridge workspace

When you make a manual change to a saved workspace, the change sticks with the workspace even if you switch to a different one. For instance, if you were to change the thumbnail size for the default Filmstrip workspace, click the Essentials workspace, then click back on the Filmstrip workspace, the new thumbnail size would still display. Via the commands for resetting workspaces, you can restore the default settings to any individual predefined (standard Adobe) or user-saved workspace or to all the predefined workspaces.

To reset the Bridge workspace:

Do either of the following:

To restore the default settings to one workspace, right-click the workspace name and choose **Reset**.

To restore the default settings to all the Adobe predefined workspaces, choose **Reset Standard Workspaces** from the Workspace menu.

A *In the New Workspace dialog, enter a Name for your custom workspace and choose options for it.*

CHOOSING COLORS FOR THE BRIDGE INTERFACE

In Adobe Bridge CS5/Edit > Preferences > General (Cmd-K/Ctrl-K), you can choose a User Interface Brightness (gray) value for the side panes; a different Image Backdrop value for the Content and Preview panels and for the background behind files when displayed in Full Preview View, Slideshow, or Review Mode; and an Accent Color for the border around selected folders, thumbnails, and stacks.

Using thumbnail stacks

Before learning about stacks, you need to know how to rearrange file thumbnails in the Content panel.

To rearrange thumbnails manually:

Drag any thumbnail (or select, then drag multiple thumbnails) to a new location. Okay, that was a no-brainer. The header on the Sort menu switches to "Sort Manually."

➤ Thumbnails remain where you place them unless you change the sorting order or perform a stacking operation.

One method for controlling how many thumbnails display at a given time is to group them into stacks. You can select the thumbnails for a stack based on any characteristic, such as the client, the project, or the subject matter of the artwork.

To group thumbnails into a stack:

1. Shift-click or Cmd-click/Ctrl-click to select multiple thumbnails.**A** The thumbnail in the selection that appears first in the Content panel is going to become the "stack thumbnail" (will display on top of the stack).

2. Press Cmd-G/Ctrl-G or right-click one of the selected thumbnails and choose Stack > **Group as Stack**.**B** A stack looks like a couple of playing cards in a pile, with the stack thumbnail on top. The number in the upper left corner (called the "stack number") tells you how many thumbnails the stack contains.

To select the thumbnails in a stack:

To expand, display, and select all the thumbnails in a stack, click the stack number (click it again to collapse the stack).

To select all the thumbnails in a stack while keeping the stack collapsed, click the stack border (the bottom "card") or Option-click/Alt-click the stack thumbnail (the top one in the stack). Note that although the stack is collapsed, because it is selected, all the thumbnails it contains are displaying in the Preview panel, if that panel is showing.

To rearrange thumbnails within a stack:

To move a thumbnail to a different position in an expanded stack, click it to deselect the other selected thumbnails, then drag it to a new spot (as shown by the vertical drop zone line).

To move a whole stack:

1. Collapse the stack, then Option-click/Alt-click the stack thumbnail. The borders of both "cards" in the stack should now be highlighted.

2. Drag the document thumbnail (not the border).

➤ If you drag the top thumbnail of an unselected stack, you'll move just that thumbnail, not the whole stack.

To add a thumbnail to a stack:

Drag a thumbnail over a stack thumbnail or into an open stack.

To remove a thumbnail from a stack:

1. Click the stack number to expand the stack.

2. Click a thumbnail to be removed (to deselect the other thumbnails), then drag it out of the stack.

To ungroup a stack:

1. Click the stack number to expand and select all the thumbnails in the stack.

2. Press Cmd-Shift-G/Ctrl-Shift-G (Stacks > Ungroup from Stack) or right-click the stack and choose Stack > **Ungroup from Stack**. The stack number and border will disappear.

A We selected six thumbnails to be grouped into a stack...

B ...then chose the Group as Stack command.

Searching for files

To find files via Bridge:

1. In Bridge, choose Edit > **Find** (Cmd-F/Ctrl-F). The Find dialog opens. A

2. From the **Look In** menu in the Source area, choose the folder to be searched (by default, the current folder is listed). To select a folder that's not on the list, choose Look In: Browse, locate the desired folder, then click Choose/OK.

3. From the menus in the **Criteria** area, choose search criteria (e.g., Filename, Date Created, Keywords, or Rating), choose a parameter from the adjoining menu, and enter data in the field. To add another criterion to the search, click the ⊕ button, or to remove a row of fields, click ⊖.

4. From the **Match** menu, choose "If any criteria are met" to find files based on one or more of the criteria you have specified, or choose "If all criteria are met" to narrow the selection to files that meet all of the criteria.

5. Check **Include All Subfolders** to also search through any of the subfolders that are contained within the folder you chose in step 2.

6. *Optional:* Check Include Non-indexed Files to search through files that Bridge hasn't yet indexed (any folder Bridge has yet to display). This could slow down the search.

7. Click Find. The search results will be placed in a temporary folder called Search Results: [name of source folder] and will display in the Content panel. B The folder will be listed on the Path bar and on the Reveal Recent File or Go to Recent Folder menu 🔳 on the Bridge toolbar.

8. To create a collection from the search results, see the following page.

➤ To discard the current search results and initiate a new search, click New Search, or to cancel the results, click the Cancel button. ✖

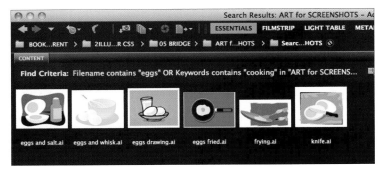

A *Use the Find dialog to search for and locate files based on various criteria.*

QUICK SEARCH FOR A FILE

In the Favorites panel, click Computer, then double-click the thumbnail for your hard disk; or navigate to a particular folder. In the search field 🔍▾ on the Bridge toolbar, type the name of the file you're looking for, then press Return/Enter.

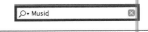

B *The search results from the Find command display in the Content panel. The parameters that we used for the search and the name of the folder that was searched are listed as the Find Criteria.*

Creating and using collections

The collection features in Bridge provide a useful way to catalog and access files without your actually having to relocate them. There are two kinds of collections: a Smart Collection that is created from the results of a Find search, and what we call a "nonsmart" collection, which is created by dragging thumbnails manually to a collection icon.

To create a Smart Collection:

1. Click the tab for the Collections panel. (If it's hidden, choose Window > Collections Panel.)

2. Perform a search via the Edit > Find command (see the preceding page). When the search is complete, click the **Save as Smart Collection** button at the top of the Content panel. **A**

3. A new Smart Collection icon appears in the Collections panel. Type a name in the highlighted field, then press Return/Enter. **B**

➤ To add a collection to the Favorites panel, right-click the icon and choose Add to Favorites.

➤ To delete a collection, click it, click the Delete Collection button, then click Yes in the alert. Not to worry: This won't delete the actual files.

To display the contents of a collection:

Click its icon in the Collections panel.

If you edit an existing Smart Collection based on altered criteria in a new search, the collection contents will update automatically.

To edit a Smart Collection:

1. In the Collections panel, click the icon for an existing Smart Collection.

2. At the top of the Content panel or in the lower left corner of the Collections panel, click the **Edit Smart Collection** button. **C**

3. The Edit Smart Collection dialog opens. It looks like the Find dialog, which is shown on the preceding page. To add another criterion, click the next ⊕ button, choose and enter the criterion, and choose "If any criteria are met" from the Match menu. You can also change the source folder and/or change the original criteria.

4. Click Save. The results of the new search will display in the Content panel.

   Note: If you move a thumbnail from a Smart Collection into a folder that wasn't used in the search (or move the actual file), it will be removed from the collection, but not from your hard disk. Don't delete a thumbnail from a Smart Collection, however, unless you want Bridge to delete it from your hard disk!

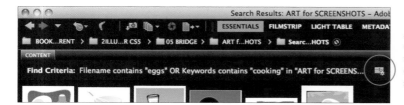

A To create a Smart Collection, click the Save as Smart Collection button in the Content panel.

B A new Smart Collection appears on the Collections panel. Type a name for it in the field.

C To edit a Smart Collection, click a Smart Collection icon on the Collections panel, then click the Edit Smart Collection button at the bottom of the panel.

You can also create a collection without running a search first. We call this a "nonsmart" collection. You can add to a nonsmart collection by dragging thumbnails into it (you cannot do this for a Smart Collection).

To create a nonsmart collection:

1. On the Content panel, select the document thumbnails to be placed into a collection. On the **Collections** panel, click the **New Collection** button, then click Yes in the alert dialog.

2. On the Collections panel, rename the collection,**A** then press Return/Enter. The number of thumbnails the collection contains is listed next to the name. ★

To add thumbnails to a nonsmart collection:

1. Display the Collections panel.

2. Drag one or more thumbnails from the Content panel over a nonsmart collection icon. **B**

➤ You can copy and paste thumbnails from a Smart Collection into a nonsmart one, or from one nonsmart collection into another.

To remove thumbnails from a nonsmart collection:

1. On the Collections panel, click the icon for a nonsmart collection to display its contents.

2. Select the thumbnails to be removed, then click **Remove from Collection** at the top of the Content panel.**C**

If you rename a file or move it from its original location on disk, Bridge will try to update the link to any nonsmart collections the file is part of. If Bridge is unsuccessful at this, follow these steps.

To relink a missing file to a nonsmart collection:

1. On the Collections panel, click the collection to which you need to relink one or more files.

2. Next to the Missing File Detected alert at the top of the Content panel, click **Fix**.**D**

3. In the Find Missing Files dialog, click Browse, locate and select the missing file, then click Open. Click OK to exit the dialog.

A To create a new collection, click the New Collection button, then type a name for it in the highlighted field.

C To take selected thumbnails out of the currently selected collection, click Remove from Collection.

B Drag thumbnails to a nonsmart collection listing to add them to that collection.

D To relink a file that's missing from a collection, click Fix.

Rating and labeling thumbnails

If you assign thumbnails a star rating and/or color label, you'll be able to filter their display based on the presence or absence of that rating or label and find them easily via the Filter panel (see the following page) and via the Find command. You can also apply a Reject rating to thumbnails that you want to hide from the Content panel (if you're not quite ready to delete the actual files from your hard disk).

To rate and label thumbnails:

1. Select one or more thumbnails in the Content panel.

2. Do any of the following:

   From the Label menu, choose a Rating (number of stars) and/or a Label (color-coded strip, to appear below the thumbnail).

   Right-click a thumbnail in the Content panel, and from the Label submenu on the context menu, choose a category.

   Right-click in the Preview panel and choose a star rating and/or a label.

   Click a thumbnail, then click any one of the five dots below it; stars will appear.**B** To remove a star, click the star to its left. To remove all the stars from a thumbnail, click to the left of the first star.**C** (If you don't see the dots or stars, enlarge the thumbnails and they should appear.)

   Press one of the keyboard shortcuts that is listed on the Label menu.

   To label the losers with a red "Reject" label, choose Label > Reject (Option-Delete/Alt-Del).**D** If Show Reject Files is unchecked on the View menu, all rejected thumbnails will be hidden.

➤ If tool tips get in the way of your adding or removing stars, go to Adobe Bridge CS5/Edit > Preferences > Thumbnails and uncheck Show Tooltips.

➤ You can rename the Label categories in the Labels panel of the Preferences dialog for Bridge.

To remove ratings or labels from thumbnails:

1. Select one or more document thumbnails in the Content panel.

2. Do either or both of the following:

   Choose Label > **No Rating** or press Cmd-0/Ctrl-0 (zero).

   Choose Label > **No Label**.

A *This thumbnail has an Approved (green) rating.*

B *We clicked the third dot on this thumbnail to assign a 3-star rating…*

C *…but then we changed our minds, so we clicked to the left of the stars to remove them.*

D *This poor thumbnail has a Reject rating.*

Choosing a sorting order

The order in which thumbnails display in the Content panel is determined by the criterion that is checked on the Sort menu. This order applies to all folders and thumbnails in Bridge, not just to the currently selected one. By applying ratings and/or labels, choosing a sorting order, and checking categories in the Filter panel (see below), you'll be able to locate the files you need more quickly and efficiently. The sorting order also affects the batch and automate commands in Bridge, because the commands process files based on the current sequence of thumbnails.

To choose a sorting order for thumbnails:

From the **Sort** menu on the Path bar, choose a sorting order (such as By Date Created). **A** All thumbnails (except those that are in stacks) will be rearranged in the Content panel. To restore the last manual sort (rearrangement of the thumbnails by dragging), choose Manually.

➤ To reverse the current order, click the Ascending Order ▲ or Descending Order ▼ arrowhead.

Filtering the display of thumbnails

The Filter panel lists data that is specific to files in the current folder, such as their label, star rating, date created, or keywords. When you check specific criteria in the panel, only thumbnails meeting those criteria display in the Content panel. Thumbnails in stacks are ignored by this panel.

To filter the display of thumbnails:

Do either of the following:

On the **Filter Items by Rating** menu ▲▼ on the Bridge toolbar, **B** check the desired criteria.

On the **Filter** panel, click the arrowhead to expand any category, such as Labels or Ratings, then check a criterion. **C** To require that additional criteria be met, check more listings, either in the same category or in other categories. For example, to display only files that have a 3-star rating, check the 3-star listing under Ratings. (To remove a criterion, click the listing again.)

➤ To prevent the current filters (check marks) from clearing when you display other folders, click the Keep Filter When Browsing 📌 button on the panel. The button will display a highlight color.

➤ To remove all check marks from the Filter panel, click the Clear Filter ⊘ button at the bottom of the panel or press Cmd-Option-A/Ctrl-Alt-A.

A From the Sort menu on the Path bar, choose a sorting order for your selected thumbnails.

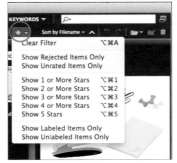

B Control which thumbnails display via the Filter Items by Rating menu.

C Because we checked the 3-star ranking in the Filter panel (under the Ratings category), only thumbnails matching that criterion (that have three stars) are displaying in the Content panel.

THE FILTER PANEL IS DYNAMIC

The categories that are listed on the Filter panel (e.g., Ratings, Keywords, Date Modified) change dynamically depending on what data is available for files in the currently selected folder and what categories are checked on the Filter panel menu. For instance, if you haven't applied ratings to any files in the current folder, there won't be a Ratings category; if you apply a rating to one of the thumbnails, a Ratings category will appear.

Assigning keywords to files

Keywords (words that are assigned to files) are used by search utilities to locate files and by file management programs to organize them. In Bridge, you can create parent keyword categories (for events, people, places, etc.), and nested subkeywords within those categories, and then assign them to your files. You can locate files by entering keywords as search criteria in the Find dialog, build a Smart Collection based on a search for keywords, or display files by checking listings under Keywords in the Filter panel.

To create keywords and subkeywords:

1. Display the Keywords panel. To create a new parent keyword category, click the **New Keyword** button, ⊞ then type a keyword.

2. To create a nested subkeyword, click a parent keyword, click the **New Sub Keyword** button, ⊞ type a word, then press Return/Enter.  To add more subkeywords, click the parent keyword first. You can also create nested sub-subkeywords.

➤ You can move (drag) any subkeyword from one parent keyword category into another.

➤ For more about keywords, see Adobe Bridge Help.

To assign keywords to files:

1. Select one or more document thumbnails in the Content panel. If keywords are already assigned to any of those files, they will be listed at the top of the Keywords panel; you can assign more.

2. Check the box for one or more subkeywords. **B** (Although you can assign a parent keyword to a file, we can't think of a reason for doing so.) To remove a keyword from a file, uncheck the box.

➤ The keywords that are assigned to the files in the current folder are also listed in the Keywords category in the Filter panel.

➤ To assign keywords via the File Info dialog, select one or more thumbnails, then from the Refine menu ▦ on the Bridge toolbar, choose File Info (Cmd-I/Ctrl-I). In the Keywords field of the Description tab, enter keywords, separated by semicolons or commas. Be on the alert for typing errors!

➤ If you import a file into Bridge that contains keywords that you want to add as permanent subkeywords, right-click each italicized subkeyword under Other Keywords in the Keywords panel and choose Make Persistent from the menu.

A We created a new parent keyword called "Office supplies," kept that category selected, then via the New Sub Keyword button, added subkeywords to it.

B We selected multiple file thumbnails, then assigned a subkeyword to them by checking the box.

USING THE KEYWORDS PANEL

Rename a parent keyword or a subkeyword	Right-click the word, choose Rename from the context menu, then type a name (this won't alter any already embedded data).
Delete a parent keyword or a subkeyword	Click the word, then click the Delete Keyword button. 🗑 (You can't undo this.) If that keyword is assigned to any files, it will now be listed in italics.
Find a keyword or subkeyword on the list	Type the word in the search field at the bottom of the panel. Choose a search parameter from the menu. 𝒫▾

Exporting the Bridge cache

When the contents of a folder are displayed in the Content panel in Bridge for the first time, the program creates a cache file containing information about those files, such as the data it uses to display ratings, labels, and high-quality thumbnails. Having the cache helps speed up the display of thumbnails when you choose that folder again. If you want this data to be included with files that you copy to a removable disc or to a shared folder on a network, you have to build the cache files and export them to the current folder first.

To export the Bridge cache to the current folder:

1. Choose Adobe Bridge CS5/Edit > Preferences > Cache. In the Cache area, check **Automatically Export Cache to Folders When Possible**, then click OK.

2. Display a folder in Bridge.

3. Choose Tools > Cache > **Build and Export Cache**. In the dialog, check **Export Cache to Folders**, (keep the Build 100% Previews option off), and click OK.

4. Two hidden cache files will be placed in the current folder, one named .BridgeCache (the metadata cache) and the other named .BridgeCacheT (the thumbnail cache).

   Now if you use the File > Move To (or Copy To) command in Bridge to move (or copy) selected thumbnails, the folder cache you just created will also move or copy, thanks to the export prefer- ence that you checked.

➤ To display the cache file icons in the Content panel, choose View > Show Hidden Files.

Thumbnail cache files sometimes cause display problems. Purging the cache for the current folder may solve the problem, because it prompts Bridge to rebuild the cache.

To purge the cache files from Bridge:

Do either of the following:

To purge the cache files from the current folder, choose Tools > Cache > **Purge Cache for Folder** "[current folder name]." Two new (hidden) cache files will be generated.

To purge the cache files for multiple selected thumbnails, right-click one of them and choose **Purge Cache for Selection**.

Managing files using Bridge

To create a new folder:

1. Via the Folders panel or the Path bar, navigate to the folder in which you want the new folder to appear.

2. Click the **New Folder** button 📑 at the right end of the Bridge toolbar, type a name in the high- lighted field below the new folder, then press Return/Enter.

To delete a file or folder:

1. Click a file or folder thumbnail (or Cmd-click/ Ctrl-click multiple thumbnails).

2. Press Cmd-Delete/Ctrl-Backspace, then click OK in the alert dialog.

➤ Change your mind? To retrieve a deleted file or folder, double-click the Trash icon/Recycle Bin for the operating system, then drag the item into the Content panel in Bridge.

To rename a file or folder:

1. Click a thumbnail, then click the file or folder name. The name will become highlighted.

2. Type a new name (for a document, don't try to delete the extension), then press Return/Enter or click outside the name field.

To move or copy files between folders:

Method 1 (by dragging)

1. Click the Folders panel tab. Navigate to (but don't click) the folder or subfolder that you want to move files into.

2. Select one or more thumbnails in the Content panel, then drag them over the folder name in the Folders panel to move them, or hold down Option/Ctrl and drag them over a folder name to copy them.

Method 2 (via the context menu)

1. Select one or more thumbnails in the **Content** panel.

2. Right-click one of the selected thumbnails, then from the **Move To** or **Copy To** submenu on the context menu, do either of the following:

   Select a folder name under **Recent Folders** or **Favorites**.

   Select **Choose Folder**. Locate a folder in the Choose a Folder dialog, then click Choose/OK.

In Illustrator, all paths consist of straight and/or curved line segments that are connected by anchor points. Paths can be closed, such as polygons and ovals, or open, such as lines and spirals. In the instructions below, we show you how to select and delete unwanted objects. Following that are instructions for using the Rectangle, Rounded Rectangle, Ellipse, Polygon, Star, Line Segment, and Spiral tools, with which you can produce geometric objects quickly and easily.

In the next chapter, you will learn to draw in a loose, freehand manner. Once you master these basics, you will learn how to select paths for editing (Chapter 8), copy and align them (Chapter 9), apply colors to them (Chapter 10), and change their shape (Chapters 11 and 12). Other methods for creating objects, such as by using the Pen tool, type tools, and tracing commands, are discussed in later chapters.

Selecting and deleting objects

You'll be creating many different shapes in this chapter, and your artboard may soon become crowded with junk. To remove an object you've just created, choose Edit > Undo (Cmd-Z/Ctrl-Z). To remove an object that's been lying around, do the following.

To select and delete objects:

1. Choose the **Selection** tool (V), then click the object to be deleted, or drag a marquee around multiple objects to be deleted.

2. Press Delete/Backspace.

➤ If you used the Direct Selection tool to select points on an object, you can press Delete/Backspace twice to delete the whole object.

THINGS TO DO BEFORE CREATING OBJECTS!

➤ From the Tools panel, choose the drawing mode of Draw Normal. ★ On the occasion that you want a new object to appear behind an existing selected one, choose Draw Behind mode instead. For Draw Inside mode, see pages 343 and 347. To cycle through the modes, press Shift-D.

➤ If your document contains multiple artboards, via the Artboard Navigation menu at the bottom of the document window or the Artboards panel, ★ display the artboard you want to add the objects to.

➤ Once your document contains multiple layers, click a layer to contain the new object (see Chapter 13).

GEOMETRIC OBJECTS

IN THIS CHAPTER

CHOOSING COLORS QUICKLY

Methods for choosing and applying fill and stroke colors are explained fully in Chapter 10. In the meantime, if you want to choose a fill and stroke color for the tools you will be using in this chapter, see "A quick color primer" on page 83.

Creating rectangles and ellipses

To create a rectangle or an ellipse by dragging:

1. Choose the **Rectangle** tool ▢ (M) or the **Ellipse** tool ⬭ (L).

2. Drag diagonally.**A** As you drag, a wireframe representation of the rectangle or oval will display. When you release the mouse, the rectangle or oval will be selected, and the current fill and stroke settings will be applied to it.**B–C**

   You can also use these modifiers while dragging:

   To draw the object from its center, Option-drag/Alt-drag.

   To move the rectangle or ellipse as you draw it, before releasing the mouse, Spacebar-drag.

   To draw a square with the Rectangle tool or a circle with the Ellipse tool, Shift-drag.

To create a rectangle or an ellipse by specifying dimensions:

1. Choose the **Rectangle** tool (M) or the **Ellipse** tool (L).

2. Click on an artboard. The Rectangle or Ellipse dialog opens.**D**

3. Enter **Width** and **Height** values. To create a circle or a square, enter a value in the Width field, then click the word Height (or vice versa) — the value in one field will be copied to the other one.

4. Click OK.**E**

➤ To learn how to choose measurement units for Illustrator, see page 382.

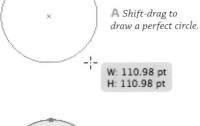

A *Shift-drag to draw a perfect circle.*

W: 110.98 pt
H: 110.98 pt

B *The current fill and stroke settings are applied automatically.*

C *To create type on a circle, see page 251.*

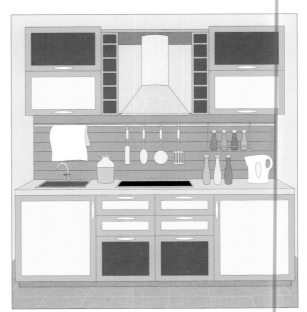

D *Enter values in the Ellipse (or Rectangle) dialog.*

E *The cabinetry in this art was created using rectangles. To duplicate objects, see page 102.*

To create a rounded rectangle:

1. Choose the **Rounded Rectangle** tool.

2. Drag diagonally. As you drag, a wireframe representation of the rounded rectangle will display.**A** When you release the mouse, the rounded rectangle will be selected and the current fill and stroke settings will be applied to it.**B–C**

➤ As you create an object with the Rounded Rectangle tool, keep the mouse button down and keep pressing the up arrow to make the corners more round, or the down arrow to make them more square. Or press (don't hold) the left or right arrow to toggle between square and round corners.

➤ To draw a rounded rectangle of a specific size, choose the Rounded Rectangle tool, click on an artboard, then enter Width, Height, and Corner Radius values. The Corner Radius value, which controls the degree of curvature in the corners of rounded rectangles, can also be specified in Illustrator/Edit > Preferences > General. When changed in one location, the value updates in the other location automatically.

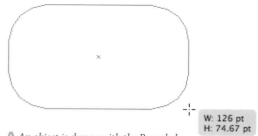

A *An object is drawn with the Rounded Rectangle tool.*

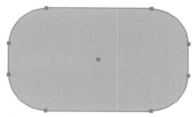

B *The rounded rectangle remains selected after it's drawn.*

C *This retro pattern contains rounded rectangles of various sizes and colors. (To create fill patterns, see pages 135–136.)*

DISPLAYING ON-OBJECT READOUTS

Turn on the View > Smart Guides feature (it should have a check mark), and in Illustrator/Edit > Preferences > Smart Guides, check Measurement Labels. With these settings in place, the following will occur:

➤ As you create an object, its exact Width and Height dimensions will display in a readout.

➤ When the Selection or Direct Selection tool is above an anchor point or the center point of an object, a readout indicating its exact X (horizontal) and Y (vertical) locations will display.

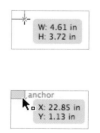

Here's a quick introduction to one of the many commands on the Effect menu: Round Corners. Effects produce appearances, which are nonpermanent, editable changes. To learn more about effects, see Chapter 15.

To round the corners of an existing object:

1. Select one or more objects.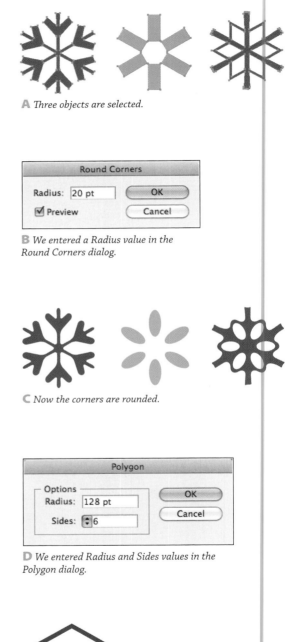

2. On the Effect menu, under Illustrator Effects, choose Stylize > **Round Corners**.

3. In the dialog, check Preview. Enter a **Radius** value (for the radius of the curve, in points), B then press Tab to preview the new setting.

4. Click OK. C If you want to edit the Round Corners setting for the object at any time, display the Appearance panel, ⦿ then click Round Corners.

5. Make sure the New Art Has Basic Appearance option is checked on the Appearance panel menu, so any new objects you create won't have the Appearance panel settings that you have chosen.

Creating polygons

With the Polygon, Star, and Spiral tools, as with the other tools discussed in this chapter, all you have to do is drag in an artboard or enter values in the tool dialog.

To create a polygon by clicking:

1. Choose the **Polygon** tool. ◯

2. Click where you want the center of the polygon to be located. The Polygon dialog opens. D

3. Enter a **Radius** value for the distance from the center of the object to the corner points.

4. Choose a number of **Sides** for the polygon by clicking the up or down arrow or by entering a number — 3 for a triangle, 4 for a rectangle, etc. The sides will be of equal length.

5. Click OK. E A polygon will appear where you clicked, and the current fill and stroke settings will be applied to it automatically (see Chapter 10).

A *Three objects are selected.*

Round Corners

Radius: 20 pt   OK

☑ Preview   Cancel

B *We entered a Radius value in the Round Corners dialog.*

C *Now the corners are rounded.*

Polygon

Options
Radius: 128 pt   OK

Sides: 6   Cancel

D *We entered Radius and Sides values in the Polygon dialog.*

E *A polygon is created. This object has a dark brown stroke and a fill color of None.*

To create a polygon by dragging:

1. Choose the **Polygon** tool.

2. Drag in an artboard, starting from where you want the center of the polygon to be located.

   While dragging, do any of the following:

   To scale the polygon, drag away from or toward the center.

   To rotate the polygon, drag in a circular direction.

   To constrain the bottom edge of the polygon to the horizontal axis, hold down Shift.

   To add sides to or delete sides from the polygon, press the up or down arrow key.

   To move the polygon without scaling it, hold down the Spacebar.

3. When you release the mouse, the polygon will be selected, and the current fill and stroke settings will be applied to it.

➤ To align a new object with an existing object while drawing it, use Smart Guides (see pages 100–101).

Creating stars

To create a star by clicking:

1. Choose the **Star** tool.

2. Click where you want the center of the star to be located. The Star dialog opens. **A**

3. Enter **Radius 1** and **Radius 2** values, in points. The higher value is the distance from the center of the star to its outermost points; the lower value is the distance from the center of the star to the innermost points. The greater the difference between the two values, the narrower the arms of the star.

4. Choose a number of **Points** for the star by clicking the up or down arrow, by clicking in the field and then pressing the up or down arrow key, or by entering a number.

   ➤ To create a star that looks similar to the one shown in **B**, make the Radius 1 value twice the value of Radius 2, and choose 5 as the Points value.

5. Click OK.

➤ You can rotate the completed star (or any other object) via its bounding box. See page 137.

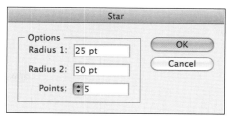

A *We entered Radius and Points values in the Star dialog.*

B *A star is born.*

CREATING ART FROM BASIC BUILDING BLOCKS

You can create illustrations like this one by using basic geometric objects as building blocks, such as ellipses, rectangles, and rounded rectangles.

To create a star by dragging:

1. Choose the **Star** tool. ☆

2. Drag in an artboard, starting from where you want the center of the star to be located.

   While dragging, do any of the following:

   To scale the star, drag away from or toward its center.

   To rotate the star, drag in a circular direction.

   To constrain two points of the star to the horizontal axis, drag with Shift held down.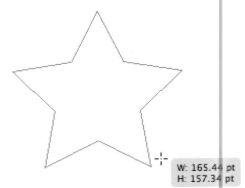

   To add points to or delete points from the star, press the up or down arrow key. **B**

   To move the star, drag with the Spacebar held down.

   To make each pair of shoulders (opposing segments) parallel to each other, drag with Option/Alt held down.

   To increase or decrease the length of the arms of the star while keeping the inner radius points constant, drag away from or toward the center of the star with Cmd/Ctrl held down. **C**

3. When you release the mouse, the star will be selected and the current fill and stroke settings will be applied to it. **D**

➤ Hold down ~ (tilde) while dragging quickly with the Star or Polygon tool to create progressively larger (separate) copies of the object. The more rapidly you drag, the farther apart the copies will be from one another. You can apply new stroke colors and settings to the copies afterward.

A *While dragging with the Star tool, we are holding down Shift to constrain two points of the star to the horizontal axis.*

W: 165.44 pt
H: 157.34 pt

W: 167.52 pt
H: 167.52 pt

B *We pressed the up arrow key to add points to the star.*

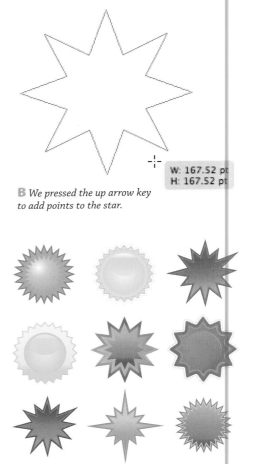

D *To apply gradients to objects, see Chapter 24. To move (extend) the points on a star, see page 148.*

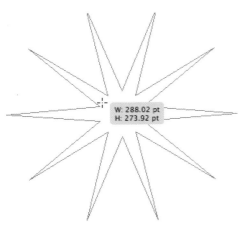

W: 288.02 pt
H: 273.92 pt

C *We dragged with Cmd/Ctrl held down to elongate the arms of the star.*

Next, we'll show you how to use the Line Segment and Spiral tools (on the Line Segment tool pop-out menu), which create independent objects or groups of objects.

Creating line segments

The Line Segment tool creates straight lines. Each time you release the mouse and drag again with this tool, a new, separate path is created.

To draw a line segment by dragging:

1. Choose the **Line Segment** tool ＼ (\).

2. Drag to draw a line. **A–B** As you do so, you can do any of the following:

    To have the line extend outward from the point of origin, drag with Option/Alt held down.

    To constrain the line to the nearest 45° increment, drag with Shift held down.

    To move the line, drag with the Spacebar held down.

  ➤ To create multiple separate lines of varied lengths from the same center point but at different angles, drag in a circular direction with ~ (tilde) held down. Move the mouse rapidly as you create the copies to spread them apart.

To create a line segment by entering values:

1. Choose the **Line Segment** tool ＼ (\).

2. Click where you want the segment to begin. The Line Segment Tool Options dialog opens.

3. Enter the desired line **Length**, then press Tab.

4. Enter an **Angle** or move the dial.

5. *Optional:* Check Fill Line to assign the current fill color to the line, in addition to the current stroke color, which is assigned automatically (see Chapter 10). The fill color won't be revealed unless you reshape the line into a curve or an angle. With Fill Line unchecked, the line will have a fill of None, but you can apply a fill color (and also change the stroke color) after exiting the dialog.

6. Click OK.

  ➤ To restore the factory-default settings to the Line Segment Tool Options dialog, Option-click/ Alt-click the Reset button (Cancel becomes Reset).

DÉJA VU

When you open the options dialog for the Rectangle, Ellipse, Rounded Rectangle, Polygon, Star, Line Segment, or Spiral tool (by clicking an artboard with the tool), the last-used settings display — whether the last object was created by dragging or by using the dialog. To quickly create additional objects using the current options settings, click an artboard with the tool, then press Return/Enter to exit the dialog.

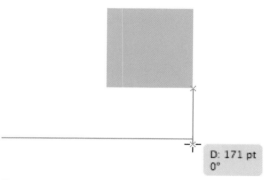

A *Shift is held down as a line is drawn, to constrain it to the horizontal axis. A Smart Guide (in green) is also being used to align the line to another object (see pages 100–101).*

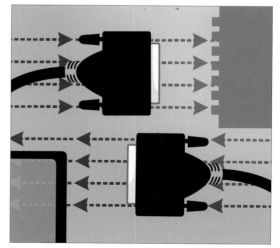

B *To create a dashed line, see page 122. To add an arrowhead to a line, see page 121.*

Creating spirals

To create a spiral by dragging:

1. Choose the **Spiral** tool.

2. Drag in the document window, starting from where you want the center of the spiral to be.

3. While dragging, do any of the following: **A**

   To scale the spiral, drag away from or toward the center.

   To control how tightly the spirals wind toward the center (the Decay value), Cmd-drag/Ctrl-drag slowly away from or toward the center.

   To add segments to or delete segments from the center of the spiral, press the up or down arrow key.

   To rotate the spiral, drag in a circular direction.

   To move the spiral, drag with the Spacebar down.

4. When you release the mouse, the spiral will be selected, and the current fill and stroke settings will be applied to it. **B–C**

Creating pixel-perfect artwork for the Web ★

▶ To make your artwork look as crisp as possible onscreen, particularly any straight horizontal or vertical edges, check **Align New Objects to Pixel Grid** in the Advanced area of the New Document dialog when you create your document. If you forgot that step, you can align objects that you subsequently create to the pixel grid by choosing the same option on the Transform panel menu.

▶ To align existing objects (except type objects) to the pixel grid, select them, then check **Align to Pixel Grid** on the Transform panel. As you move or transform the objects or change their stroke weight, they will snap to the grid. To quickly select all the objects in your document that aren't aligned to the pixel grid, choose Select > Object > **Not Aligned to Pixel Grid**. Note: If you move pixel-aligned and non-pixel-aligned objects simultaneously, their relative positions will be preserved.

▶ To see a representation of the pixel grid onscreen, choose a zoom level of 600% or higher. In Illustrator/Edit > Preferences > Guides & Grid, check **Show Pixel Grid (Above 600% Zoom)**, and also turn on View > **Pixel Preview**. See also page 30.

A We drew this spiral with the Spiral tool.

B We applied the Streamer brush from the Borders_Novelty brush library to the spiral. To learn about brushes, see Chapter 23.

C Spirals can be altered in several ways, such as by applying brush strokes, a shear transformation, or effects. You will learn those techniques later in this book.

If you enjoy sketching in a loose, free-hand manner, the Pencil, Paintbrush, and Blob Brush tools will be right up your alley. Each tool has its own special attributes, which we explore in this chapter. Paths drawn with these tools can be reshaped by using any of the techniques described in Chapters 11 and 12. In fact, in addition to being used to create objects, the Pencil and Blob Brush tools also have a reshaping function.

A quick color primer

Before exploring the freehand drawing tools, learn how to quickly set the fill color, stroke color, and stroke weight. Do this via either the Control panel or the in-panel editing feature of the Appearance panel.

To choose a fill or stroke color:

1. Choose the **Selection** tool ▸ (V), then click an object or drag a marquee around multiple objects.

2. Do either of the following:

    On the Control panel, click the Fill or Stroke square or arrowhead,**A** then on the temporary Swatches panel, click a swatch.

    On the Appearance panel,● click the square for the Fill or Stroke listing, click the color square or arrowhead, then on the temporary Swatches panel, click a swatch.**B**

    Note: To choose a fill or stroke color of None, click the **None** button ☑ on the Swatches panel.

To choose a stroke weight:

Do either of the following:

On the Control panel, click the up or down Stroke Weight arrow.

On the Appearance ● panel, click the Stroke link, then click the up or down Stroke Weight arrow on the temporary Stroke panel that opens.

Fill square   Stroke square   Stroke Weight

A *To open a temporary Swatches panel, click the Fill or Stroke square on the Control panel...*

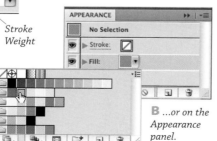

B *...or on the Appearance panel.*

FILL AND STROKE DEFINED

► The fill, which is applied to the inside of a closed or open object or to a face within a Live Paint group, can be a solid color, a pattern, a gradient, or None (of the above).

► The stroke, which is applied to the path of a closed or open object, can be a solid color (or None), and can be dashed or continuous. To a stroke, you can apply a Scatter, Calligraphic, Art, Bristle, or Pattern brush, but not a gradient.

Note: To learn more about choosing and applying fill and stroke colors, see Chapter 10.

Note: For optimal results when using the Pencil, Paintbrush, or Blob Brush tool, draw with a pressure-sensitive tablet and a stylus. (Not to worry, though —although it's recommended, it's not mandatory.)

Drawing with the Pencil tool

The Pencil tool has three distinct functions: You can drag in a blank area of the artboard to create a new, open path (as described in the instructions below); drag along the edge of an existing, selected path to reshape it (see page 155); or drag from an endpoint of an existing open path to add segments to it (see page 153).

Note: To choose default settings for the Pencil tool, see page 86.

To draw with the Pencil tool:

1. Choose the **Pencil** tool ✎ (N).

2. Choose a stroke color and weight, and a fill color of None.

3. Draw lines (a dotted line will appear while you draw). You can release the mouse between strokes. That's all there is to it. (Well, except for the artistic part!)

4. Press Cmd-Y/Ctrl-Y to toggle the display of the artwork with its current color settings (Preview view) **A** and a wireframe representation (Outline view).

5. *Optional:* To apply a brush to a selected path, keep the artwork selected, show the Brushes panel ✿ or click the Brush Definition menu ⎯⎯ Basic ▾ on the Control panel, ★ then click a brush. (You can also choose a brush for the tool before drawing the artwork.) To learn about brushes, see Chapter 23.

   To change the contour of a selected path, choose from the Variable Width Profile menu on the Control panel.**B–C** ★

➤ To create a closed path with the Pencil tool, start drawing the path, then finish drawing it with Option/Alt held down.

➤ To close an existing Pencil path with a straight segment, choose the Selection tool (V), click the line, then press Cmd-J/Ctrl-J.

➤ If you want to draw perfectly straight lines or nice, smooth curves, you could go mad trying to do it with the Pencil tool! Use the Line Segment or Pen tool instead.

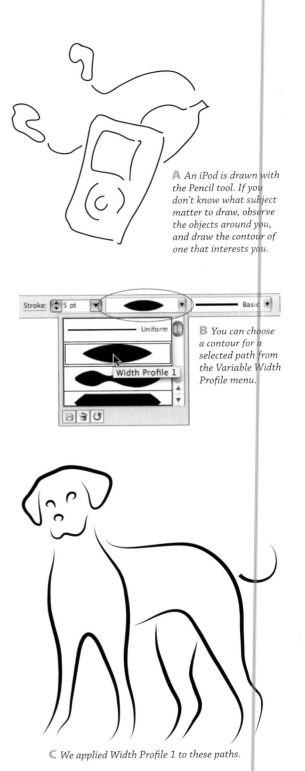

A An iPod is drawn with the Pencil tool. If you don't know what subject matter to draw, observe the objects around you, and draw the contour of one that interests you.

B You can choose a contour for a selected path from the Variable Width Profile menu.

C We applied Width Profile 1 to these paths.

Drawing with the Paintbrush tool

If you use a stylus and a pressure-sensitive tablet, the Paintbrush tool will respond to pressure. The harder you press on the tablet, the wider the stroke.

Note: To choose options for the Paintbrush tool, see the following page.

To draw with the Paintbrush tool:

1. Choose the **Paintbrush** tool ✒ (B).

2. Choose a stroke color and weight, and a fill color of None.

3. Show the Brushes panel 🖌 or click the Brush Definition menu ⬛ on the Control panel, ★ then click a brush. We recommend choosing a Bristle or Art brush (see Chapter 23).

4. Do either of the following:

   To draw open paths, draw separate lines. **A–B**

   To draw a closed path, drag to draw the path, then Option-drag/Alt-drag to close it (release Option/Alt last).

5. *Optional:* To change the contour of a selected path, choose from the Variable Width Profile menu on the Control panel. ★

➤ To change the width of a Bristle brush between strokes, press [or]. To change the opacity of the brush, press a number key (e.g., 5 for 50% opacity, 9 for 90% opacity, and 0 for 100% opacity). ★

When you remove a brush stroke from a path, it is given a plain, basic shape. Similarly, if you remove a width profile from a path, it is given a uniform width.

To remove a brush stroke or width profile from a path: ★

1. Select the path.

2. On the Control panel, do either or both of the following:

   To restore the default width profile, from the **Variable Width Profile** menu, choose **Uniform**.

   To remove a brush, from the **Brush Definition** menu, choose the **Basic** brush.

➤ When an object that contains a brush stroke is selected, you can click the Stroke listing on the Appearance panel to make a Brush Definition menu appear. And if you click the Stroke link on that panel, a Variable Width Profile menu displays on a temporary Stroke panel.

A *These objects were drawn with an Art brush chosen for the Paintbrush tool.*

B *We applied assorted fill colors to the objects.*

A CHECKLIST OF THINGS TO DO BEFORE YOU BEGIN DRAWING (A FRIENDLY REMINDER)

➤ Display an artboard.

➤ Choose a drawing mode (usually Draw Normal 🔲) from the bottom of the Tools panel. ★

➤ If your document contains multiple layers, click a layer.

Choosing options for the Pencil and Paintbrush tools

The Pencil or Paintbrush tool can be customized in two ways: by choosing settings on the Control panel or via the tool's options dialog. Changes to the tool options affect only lines you subsequently draw, not existing ones.

To choose options for the Pencil or Paintbrush tool:

1. Do either of the following:

   Double-click the **Pencil** tool ✐ (or press N to choose the tool, then press Return/Enter).

   Double-click the **Paintbrush** tool ✐ (or press B to choose the tool, then press Return/Enter).

2. In the Tolerances area of the options dialog: **A**

   Choose a **Fidelity** value. **B–C** A low Fidelity setting produces many anchor points and paths that accurately follow the movement of your mouse, whereas a high setting produces fewer anchor points and smoother but less accurate paths.

   Choose a **Smoothness** percentage. The higher the Smoothness, the fewer the irregularities and anchor points in the path.

3. Check any of the following options:

   Fill New Pencil Strokes or **Fill New Brush Strokes** to have new paths (whether they are open or closed) fill automatically with the current fill color. The default setting for this option is off.

   Keep Selected to have the paths stay selected after they're created. This saves you a step if you are likely to add to a path right after drawing it.

   Edit Selected Paths to activate the reshaping function of the tool (see page 155). The Within: [ ] Pixels value is the minimum distance the pointer must be from a path for the tool to reshape it. Uncheck this option if you want to be able to draw multiple lines or brush strokes near one another without reshaping any existing selected paths.

4. Click OK. **D**

   ➤ Click Reset in the Pencil or Paintbrush Tool Options dialog to restore the default settings for the tool.

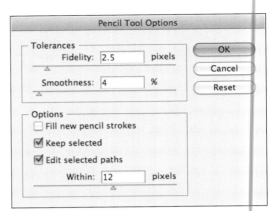

A *The Pencil tool has its own options dialog.*

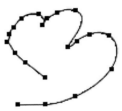

B *This line was drawn with the Pencil tool at a low Fidelity setting.*

C *This line was drawn with the Pencil tool at a high Fidelity setting.*

D *Each stroke in this drawing is a separate path.*

Drawing with the Blob Brush tool

The Blob Brush is a versatile, dual-purpose tool. It lets you draw closed paths in a loose, freehand style, and also lets you reshape existing closed paths, regardless of which tool they were created with. The tool is similar to a traditional felt-tip marker, with two advantages: It enables you to reshape your strokes after they're drawn and it's odor-free! If you like to draw artwork "by hand," you'll probably take an instant liking to it. "Blob Brush tool" is a cumbersome name to say aloud, but it's a fun tool to use.

On this page, you'll learn how to create objects with the Blob Brush tool; on the next page, you'll choose options for the tool; and on page 160, you'll master its reshaping function.

To draw with the Blob Brush tool:

1. Choose the **Blob Brush** tool 🖋 (Shift-B).

2. On the Control or Appearance panel, click the **Stroke** thumbnail or arrowhead 🔲▾ to open a temporary Swatches panel, then click a solid-color swatch on the panel.

3. Position the brush cursor over an artboard. Press [to decrease the brush tip size or] to increase it.

4. Draw lines, as you might with a traditional marking pen.**A–B** Let the lines crisscross or touch one another. When you release the mouse, a new closed path or compound path is created (unlike the stroked paths that are produced by the Paintbrush and other freehand tools).

5. *Optional:* Without changing the stroke color, draw a connecting line from one end of a Blob Brush shape to the other end, to connect them.

6. Choose the Selection 🔺 or Direct Selection 🔺 tool, then click the new shape. The original stroke color on the object has been converted to a fill color, and the stroke color has been removed (changed to the setting of None).

7. *Optional:* For the selected Blob Brush path, via the Appearance or Control panel, change the Opacity percentage.

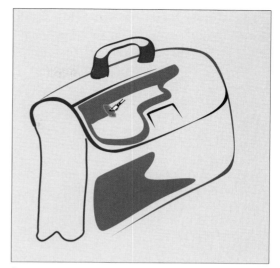

A *A briefcase is drawn with the Blob Brush tool.*

B *Other areas of "shading" were drawn with the Blob Brush.*

Choosing options for the Blob Brush tool

To choose options for the Blob Brush tool:

1. Double-click the **Blob Brush** tool. The Blob Brush Tool Options dialog opens. **A**

2. Check **Keep Selected** to have the Blob Brush objects remain selected after they are created. We check this option so we can see more easily when our Blob Brush objects are being merged.

3. Check **Merge Only With Selection** to permit new Blob Brush strokes to merge only with selected unstroked objects, or uncheck this option to allow new strokes to merge with any unstroked objects that have the same fill color as the brush, whether they are selected or not. (To merge shapes with this tool, see page 160.)

4. Under Tolerances, choose a low **Fidelity** setting to produce many anchor points and paths that follow your mouse movements more accurately, or a high setting to produce fewer anchor points and smoother but less accurate paths. Also choose a **Smoothness** value to preserve or smooth out irregularities in the path.

5. For the brush **Size**, **Angle**, and **Roundness** options, **B–C** see steps 4–7 in the instructions for editing a Calligraphic brush on pages 302–303 (the Diameter option discussed there is equivalent to the Size option here).

6. Click OK.

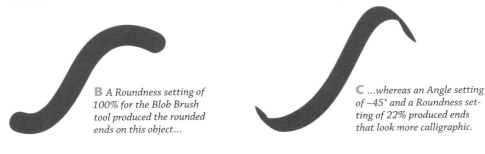

A *You can customize the behavior of the Blob Brush tool via its options dialog.*

B *A Roundness setting of 100% for the Blob Brush tool produced the rounded ends on this object…*

C *…whereas an Angle setting of −45° and a Roundness setting of 22% produced ends that look more calligraphic.*

As a prerequisite to learning the many editing techniques in Illustrator, you need to master the methods for selecting and deselecting objects. The simple fact is that an object must be selected before it can be edited. The many selection controls in Illustrator include five tools, an assortment of Select menu commands, and a selection area on the Layers panel. In this chapter, in addition to learning all the selection methods, you will learn how to group objects, isolate groups and objects for editing, and save your selections for future access. Once you master these fundamental skills, you'll be ready to learn how to copy and align objects (in the next chapter) and then plunge into the fun stuff, such as recoloring, transforming, reshaping, and applying effects.

The five selection tools

The basic functions of the selection tools are introduced here. Step-by-step instructions for using these tools are given elsewhere in this chapter.

Use the **Selection** tool ▸ (V) to select or move a whole object or group, **A** and to select all of an object's points (see page 91). This tool can also be used to scale, reflect, or rotate an object via its bounding box (see page 137).

Continued on the following page

A *The Selection tool selects whole objects.*

SELECT

8

Use the **Direct Selection** tool ↖ (A) to select one or more individual anchor points or segments on a path. **A** If you click a curve segment with this tool, the direction handles and anchor points for that segment become visible (see page 92). (The anchor points for straight segments don't have direction handles — they just have anchor points.)

Although the **Group Selection** tool ↖ can be used to select all the anchor points on an individual path, the main purpose of this tool is for selecting groups (of objects) that are nested inside larger groups. Click once with this tool to select an object in a group, click a second time to select the entire group that object belongs to, click a third time to select the parent group it's nested within, and so on. The Group Selection tool can be selected from the Direct Selection tool pop-out menu, or accessed temporarily when the Direct Selection tool is selected by holding down Option/Alt.

➤ Instead of using the Group Selection tool, we prefer to put our groups into isolation mode. An advantage of this method is that it makes other objects temporarily uneditable. See page 94.

Use the **Lasso** tool 🔾 (Q) to select anchor points and segments by dragging a freeform marquee around them. **B** (See page 96.)

The **Magic Wand** tool ✨ (Y) selects objects that contain the same or a similar fill color, stroke color, stroke weight, opacity, or blending mode as the object you click, depending on the current tool settings on the Magic Wand panel. **C** (See page 97.)

Note: In the illustrations on these pages, we hid the bounding box for the selected object(s) (Cmd-Shift-B/Ctrl-Shift-B).

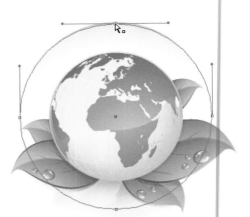

A *The Direct Selection tool selects individual anchor points and segments on a path.*

B *The Lasso tool selects anchor points and segments via a freeform marquee.*

C *The Magic Wand tool selects objects that have the same or a similar fill color, stroke color, stroke weight, opacity, or blending mode as an object you click.*

Using the Selection tool

To select one or more objects:

1. Make sure the View > **Smart Guides** option has a check mark (Cmd-U/Ctrl-U). Also go to Illustrator/Edit > Preferences > Smart Guides, and make sure the **Object Highlighting** option is checked.

2. Choose the **Selection** tool ▸ (V).

3. Do one of the following:

   Because Smart Guides are on (with the Object Highlighting preference enabled), the edge of the path will be highlighted as you move the pointer over it. Click the path. **A**

   If the object has a color fill, your document is in Preview view, and the Object Selection by Path Only option is off (see the sidebar at right), you can click the object's fill.

   Position the pointer outside one or more objects to be selected, then drag a marquee across all or part of them. The whole path will become selected, even if you marquee just a portion of it. **B–C**

With the Selection tool, you can add objects to or subtract objects from a selection.

To add objects to or subtract objects from a selection:

Choose the **Selection** tool ▸ (V), then Shift-click on or Shift-drag a marquee around any unselected objects to add them to the selection, or do the same for any selected objects to deselect them.

SELECTING OBJECTS BY PATH ONLY

If Object Selection by Path Only is checked in Illustrator/Edit > Preferences > Selection & Anchor Display, in order to select an object, you must click a segment or anchor point on the path. When this option is unchecked, you don't have to be as precise about where you click: If the object contains a fill (not None) and the document is in Preview view, you can click the fill or the path.

SELECTING UNDERLYING OBJECTS ★

If Command/Control Click to Select Objects Behind is checked in Preferences > Selection & Anchor Display and you want to select objects that are hidden behind other objects at the current pointer location, Cmd-click/Ctrl-click (and keep clicking).

A We selected a path with the Selection tool (in the figures on this page, the bounding box is hidden).

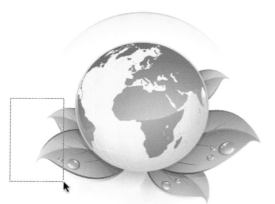

B We marqueed a few paths with the Selection tool.

C The paths within the marquee became selected.

Using the Direct Selection tool

As a prerequisite to reshaping objects (which you will do in Chapter 12), you need to learn how to select individual points and segments. It's important to be precise about which components you select.

To select or deselect anchor points or segments with the Direct Selection tool:

1. Open the Illustrator/Edit > Preferences dialog. In the Selection & Anchor Display panel, check Highlight Anchors on Mouse Over (to choose other Anchor Point and Handle Display preferences, see page 380). And in the Smart Guides panel of the same dialog, check Object Highlighting and Anchor/Path Labels. Click OK.

2. Turn on View > **Smart Guides** (Cmd-U/Ctrl-U). (The command should have a check mark.)

3. Choose the **Direct Selection** tool ⸢ (A).

4. Do one of the following:

   To select a segment, click the path.**A**

   To select an anchor point, pass the pointer over an anchor point (the point enlarges temporarily), then click.**B–C**

   Position the pointer outside one or more objects, then drag a marquee across the anchor points or segments you want to select.**D** Only the points or segments you marquee will become selected.**E**

5. *Optional:* To select additional anchor points or segments, or to deselect individual selected anchor points or segments, Shift-click them or Shift-drag a marquee around them.

➤ To access the Selection or Direct Selection tool temporarily (whichever one was used last) when using a non-selection tool, hold down Cmd/Ctrl.

Selecting objects via a command

The Select commands select objects whose characteristics are similar to those of the last selected object or the currently selected one.

To select objects via a command:

Do any of the following:

Select an object to base the search on, or deselect all objects to base the search on the last object that was selected. From the Select > **Same** submenu, choose one of the available commands, such as Fill & Stroke, Fill Color, Opacity, Stroke

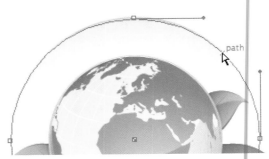

A *A curve segment is clicked with the Direct Selection tool.*

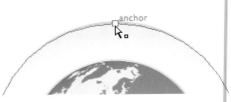

B *As you move the pointer over an anchor point, it becomes enlarged temporarily. Click the point to select it.*

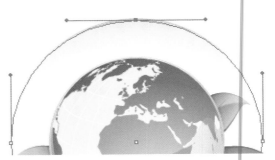

C *Selected anchor points are solid, unselected ones are hollow.*

D *A marquee is made with the Direct Selection tool.*

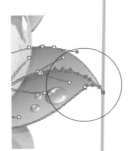

E *Only anchor points within the marquee became selected.*

Color, or Stroke Weight.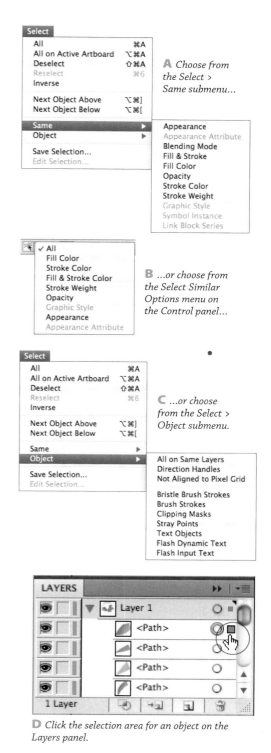 Most of these commands are also found on the **Select Similar Options** menu on the Control panel B (the menu isn't available for some kinds of objects). Read about the Select Same Tint % preference on page 378.

Select one or more objects, then from the Select > **Object** submenu, C choose **All on Same Layers** to select all the objects on the layer the object resides in (or if the currently selected objects are on more than one layer, from those layers), or choose **Direction Handles** to select all the direction handles on the currently selected object or objects (see pages 147 and 148).

With or without selecting an object first, from the Select > **Object** submenu, choose one of the following: **Bristle Brush Strokes** or **Brush Strokes** to select all objects that have those types of brush strokes; **Clipping Masks** to select masking objects (to display their edges); **Stray Points** to select lone points that don't belong to any paths (for deletion); or **Text Objects** to select all type objects.

The last command you chose from the Select Similar Options menu on the Control panel displays as an icon in the menu button, for quick access.

To reapply the last used Select Similar Objects command:

Select an object, then click the **Select Similar Objects** button (next to the menu).

Selecting objects via the Layers panel

To select objects via the Layers panel:

1. Display the Layers panel.

2. Do either of the following:

   If the listing for the object to be selected isn't visible on the Layers panel, reveal it by clicking the expand/collapse triangle for its top-level layer, sublayer, or group. Next, at the far right side of the panel, click the selection area for the object. A colored square appears (each top-level layer is automatically assigned a different color). D

   To select all the objects on a layer or sublayer, click in the selection area for the whole layer.

➤ To learn more about selecting objects via the Layers panel, see pages 178–180.

A Choose from the Select > Same submenu...

B ...or choose from the Select Similar Options menu on the Control panel...

C ...or choose from the Select > Object submenu.

D Click the selection area for an object on the Layers panel.

Working with groups

When objects are in a group, you can select, isolate, copy, paste, or edit them as a unit. You can group different kinds of objects (e.g., type objects with placed images), and you can edit individual objects in a group without having to ungroup them first.

To put objects into a group:

1. Do either of the following:

   Choose the **Selection** tool ▶ (V). In the document, Shift-click or drag a marquee around all the objects to be grouped.

   Shift-click the selection area at the far right side of the Layers panel to make a selection square appear for each object to be put in a group (click the expand/collapse arrow, if necessary, to reveal the object listings). Or if you want to select all the objects on a layer, click the selection square for the layer.

2. Right-click in the document window and choose **Group** from the context menu (Cmd-G/Ctrl-G).**A** All the objects in the group will be put on the layer of the topmost selected object.

The easiest and quickest way to edit individual objects in a group is to put the group into isolation mode.

To edit grouped objects in isolation mode:

1. In Illustrator/Edit > Preferences > General, make sure **Double Click to Isolate** is checked.

2. Choose the **Selection** tool ▶ (V), then double-click a group in your artwork.**B**

3. Objects within the group are shown in full color and are editable; objects outside the group are temporarily dimmed and uneditable. A dark gray isolation mode bar appears at the top of the document window, which lists the name of the selected layer and group. An Isolation Mode listing also appears on the Layers panel.

4. You can click and edit objects in an isolated group with the Selection tool, or click and edit individual points or segments with the Direct Selection tool.**C** With the Selection tool, you can also double-click any nested group within the current parent group to isolate it. To navigate through nested groups, click <Group> or the arrowhead on the isolation mode bar.

5. To exit isolation mode, click the isolation mode bar or press Esc.

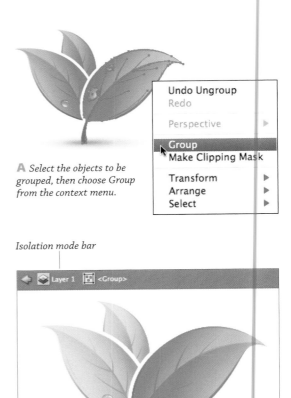

A *Select the objects to be grouped, then choose Group from the context menu.*

Isolation mode bar

B *We double-clicked the leaf group on the right to put it into isolation mode; the other objects are temporarily dimmed.*

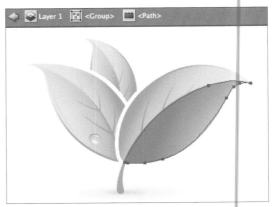

C *We double-clicked an object in the group to further isolate it. The name of the object appears on the isolation mode bar.*

Before creating an object or placing an image into an Illustrator document, you can specify which group you want it to belong to.

To add a new object to a group:

1. Choose the **Selection** tool ➤ (V), then double-click a group to isolate it.

2. Draw a new object or objects.**B** A listing for each new object you create will appear within the group listing on the Layers panel.

3. *Optional:* On the Layers panel, expand the listing for the group that you added an object to, then drag the new object listing to a different stacking position within the group.

4. To exit isolation mode, click the gray isolation mode bar at the top of the window or press Esc.

A *We double-clicked the leaf group on the right to isolate it. The other objects are temporarily dimmed.*

To add an existing object to a group:

1. With the **Selection** tool ➤ (V), click the object to be added to a group.

2. Choose Edit > **Cut** (Cmd-X/Ctrl-X).

3. Double-click the group to isolate it.

4. Choose Edit > **Paste** (Cmd-V/Ctrl-V). Drag the object to position it, then click the gray isolation mode bar at the top of the document window to exit isolation mode.

➤ To add an existing object to a group via the Layers panel, see page 181.

Sometimes a group has to be disbanded — er, ungrouped.

To ungroup a group:

1. To select the group, choose the **Selection** tool ➤ (V), then either click the group in the document window or click the selection area for the group listing on the Layers panel.

2. Do either of the following:

   Right-click the artboard and choose **Ungroup** from the context menu.

   Choose Object > **Ungroup** (Cmd-Shift-G/Ctrl-Shift-G).

   The group listing disappears from the Layers panel, but the objects remain selected.

➤ Keep choosing the same command to ungroup nested groups (groups within parent groups).

➤ To learn how to select groups and grouped objects via the Layers panel, see page 180.

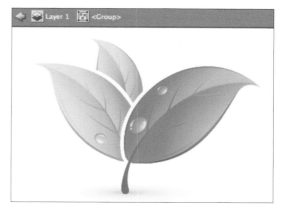

B *We added two new objects (the water droplets) to the isolated group.*

Isolating individual objects

Not only can you put a whole group into isolation mode, but you can also edit individual objects in this mode, whether they're in a group or not. This option is useful for isolating objects in complex artwork.

Note: Throughout this book, when we instruct you to select an object for editing, remember that in most cases you can simply isolate the object instead.

To isolate an individual object:

1. Do either of the following:

   In Illustrator/Edit > Preferences > General, make sure **Double Click to Isolate** is checked. Choose the Selection tool ▶ (V) then double-click an object.

   To isolate an object in a group, choose Direct Selection tool ▶ (A), then click the object. Next, click the **Isolate Selected Object** button ⊞ on the Control panel or right-click the object and choose **Isolate Selected Path**.

2. A dark gray **isolation mode** bar appears at the top of the document window, bearing the name of the selected object.**A**

3. Edit the object.

4. To exit isolation mode, click the gray isolation mode bar at the top of the window or press Esc.

Using the Lasso tool

Say you need to select a few points on one path and a few points on a nearby path. With the Direct Selection tool, you could click the points individually (tedious), or if the points in question happen to fall conveniently within a rectangular area, you could marquee them. To select points in complex artwork, our preferred method is to drag around them with the Lasso tool. Don't use this tool to select whole paths.

To select or deselect points or segments with the Lasso tool:

1. Deselect (click a blank area of the artboard).

2. Choose the **Lasso** tool ⬚ (Q), then drag to encircle segments or points.**B–C** You can drag right across any path. You don't need to close the selection; just release the mouse when the desired points have been lassoed.

3. *Optional:* Shift-drag around any unselected points or segments to add them to the selection, or Option-drag/Alt-drag around any selected points or segments to deselect them.

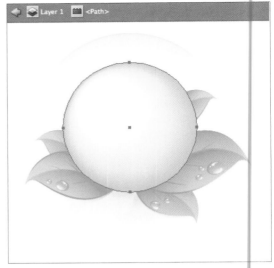

A *We double-clicked a circle object to isolate it.*

B *We are wending our way around parts of objects with the Lasso tool.*

C *Only the points and segments we marqueed became selected.*

Using the Magic Wand tool

The Magic Wand tool selects all the objects in a document that have the same or a similar fill color, stroke color, stroke weight, opacity, or blending mode as the object you click, depending on which options are checked on the Magic Wand panel.

To choose options for the Magic Wand tool:

1. To show the Magic Wand panel, double-click the **Magic Wand** tool ✹ (Y) or choose Window > **Magic Wand**.

   If all three sections of the panel aren't showing, click the up/down arrowhead on the panel tab to make them appear.

2. On the left side of the panel,**A** check which attributes you want the tool to select: **Fill Color**, **Stroke Color**, **Stroke Weight**, **Opacity**, or **Blending Mode**.

3. For each option you checked in the preceding step (except Blending Mode), choose a **Tolerance** value. Choose a low value to select only objects whose colors, weights, or opacities match (or are very similar to) the one you will click with the tool, or choose a high value to allow the tool to select a broader range of those attributes. For Fill Color or Stroke Color, choose a Tolerance (0–255 for an RGB document or 0–100 for a CMYK document); for the Stroke Weight, choose a weight Tolerance (0–1000 pt); for the Opacity, choose a percentage (0–100).

4. To permit the Magic Wand tool to select objects on all layers, check **Use All Layers** on the panel menu (the default setting), or uncheck this option to permit the tool to select objects only on the current top-level layer.

➤ The Reset command on the Magic Wand panel menu resets all fields on the panel to their default values and unchecks all the options except Fill Color.

IN THE CROSSHAIRS

If Use Precise Cursors is checked in Illustrator/ Edit > Preferences > General, the Lasso and Magic Wand tool pointers will be a crosshairs icon ⁃¦⁃ instead of the tool icon. Use the crosshairs when a task requires precise positioning of the pointer.

To use the Magic Wand tool:

1. Choose the **Magic Wand** tool ✹ (Y).

2. To create a new selection, click an object in the document window. Depending on the current settings on the Magic Wand panel, other objects containing the same or a similar fill color, stroke color, stroke weight, opacity, or blending mode may become selected.**B–C**

3. Do either of the following:

   To add to the selection, Shift-click another object.

   To subtract from the selection, Option-click/ Alt-click one of the selected objects.

A *Choose default settings for the Magic Wand tool on its panel.*

B *The first two water droplets have an opacity of 100%; the third one has an opacity of 50%. We checked Fill Color and Opacity for the Magic Wand tool, then clicked the fill of the leftmost object. Only the middle droplet, which has the same fill color and opacity as the first one, became selected.*

C *This time we used the Magic Wand tool with the Opacity option off. All three objects became selected, because their opacity settings were ignored as a factor.*

Saving selections

Via the Save Selection command, you can save any selection under a custom name. To reselect the same objects quickly, simply choose the name of your saved selection on the Select menu.

To save a selection:

1. Select one or more objects.

2. Choose Select > **Save Selection**.

3. In the Save Selection dialog, 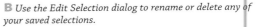A enter a descriptive name, then click OK. To reselect those objects at any time, simply choose the selection name from the bottom of the **Select** menu.

▶ To rename or delete a saved selection, choose Select > Edit Selection. Click a selection name, then change it or click Delete. B Click OK.

Selecting and deselecting all objects

To select all the objects in a document:

Choose Select > **All** (Cmd-A/Ctrl-A). All unlocked objects in your document will become selected, regardless of whether they're on an artboard or in the scratch area. This command won't select locked objects or objects on hidden layers (for which the visibility icon on the Layers panel is off).

▶ If a text cursor is flashing in a text block when you choose the Select > All command, all the text in the block will become selected (instead of all the objects in your document).

To prevent objects from being modified, you must make sure they're deselected.

To deselect all the objects in a document:

Do either of the following:

Choose Select > **Deselect** (Cmd-Shift-A/Ctrl-Shift-A).

Choose any selection tool (or hold down Cmd/Ctrl), then click a blank area of the document.

▶ To deselect an individual object in a selection of multiple objects, Shift-click it with the Selection tool. To deselect an object in a group, see page 180.

The Inverse command deselects all selected objects and selects all the unselected ones.

To invert a selection:

Choose Select > **Inverse**.

A *By saving your selections, they will be easy to reselect.*

B *Use the Edit Selection dialog to rename or delete any of your saved selections.*

Once you have created multiple objects in a document, you'll undoubtedly find a need to reposition, copy, or realign them. In this chapter, you'll learn how to move objects with the assistance of Smart Guides; duplicate, align, and distribute objects; and create and use ruler guides, guide objects, and the grid to position objects manually.

Moving objects

In these instructions, you will learn the simplest and most straightforward method for moving objects: by dragging. In conjunction with a great feature called Smart Guides (see the next page), dragging will take care of most of your moving needs.

To move an object or group by dragging:

1. Choose the **Selection** tool ▶ (V).

2. Do either of the following:

   Drag the object's path (this can be done in Outline or Preview view).

   If the document is in Preview view, the object has a fill, and the Object Selection by Path Only feature is off in Illustrator/Edit > Preferences > Selection & Anchor Display, you can drag the object's fill.**A** This can also be done with the Direct Selection tool.

➤ Hold down Shift while dragging an object to constrain the movement to a multiple of 45°.

➤ To learn other techniques for moving objects, such as the Transform panel, Control panel, and Transform Each command, see pages 142–145.

9

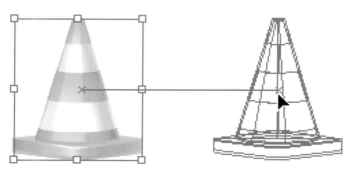

A *With the aid of a Smart Guide, a group is dragged along the horizontal axis.*

Aligning objects with the help of Smart Guides

Smart Guides are various kinds of nonprinting labels or lines that appear onscreen temporarily when you create, move, duplicate, or transform an object. For example, "magnetic" alignment guides appear onscreen when you move an object. You can use them, say, to align an object along the horizontal or vertical axis, or to align the edge of an object to the edge of an artboard or to the edge of another object. You can also use Smart Guides when repositioning artboards. This feature is easier done than said, so give it a try.

To align objects with the help of Smart Guides:

1. Confirm that the View > **Smart Guides** (Cmd-U/ Ctrl-U) feature is on (has a check mark), and that the View > Snap to Grid and Pixel Preview features are off.

2. To establish the necessary preferences for Smart Guides, go to Illustrator/Edit > Preferences (Cmd-K/Ctrl-K) > Smart Guides, and check all six option boxes.* **A** Switch to the Selection & Anchor Display panel, check Snap to Point, then click OK.

3. Choose the **Selection** tool ▶ (V).

4. Drag an object, releasing the mouse when the object snaps to any of the following:

   An **alignment guide** that denotes the edge of another object.**B**

   The **center point** of another object.**C**

   An **anchor point** on the edge of another object (**A**, next page).

   The edge of an **artboard**.

   ➤ The measurement label (in the gray rectangle) lists the current horizontal distance (dX) and vertical distance (dY) the selection has been moved from its original location.

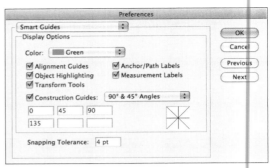

A *Check all six of the Display Options check boxes in the Smart Guides panel of the Preferences dialog.*

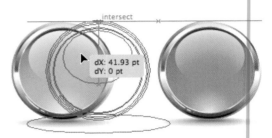

B *A horizontal alignment guide appears at the moment when the edge of the group we're moving aligns with the top edge of another group.*

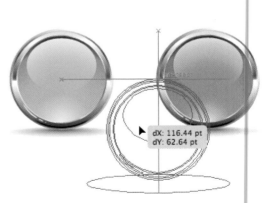

C *We're aligning the center point of a group with the intersection of two alignment guides — in this case, to the center point of another object. The measurement label (in the gray box) lists the distance the group has been dragged.*

Although you won't be using all of the different types of Smart Guides in this task, you may find it convenient to activate all of them so they will be available for other tasks.

➤ Smart Guides vanish as quickly as they appear. To create guides that remain onscreen, see page 107.

➤ The Smart Guides preferences are described in detail on page 384. For example, you can establish specific angles for Smart Guides or change their color to make them contrast better with colors in your artwork. To use the Transform Tools option for Smart Guides, see page 139.

➤ Smart Guides provide useful information even when the mouse is merely hovering over an object.**B**

HIDING OR SHOWING AN OBJECT'S CENTER POINT

To hide (or show) the center point on one or more selected objects, display the Attributes panel, 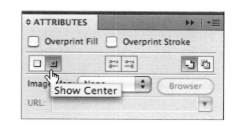 then click the Don't Show Center button (or the Show Center button) on the panel. To hide or show the center point for all objects in the current document, choose Select > All (Cmd-A/Ctrl-A) before clicking the button. Note: If the Show Center buttons aren't visible on the panel, click the up/down arrowhead in the panel tab.

The center point is visible on this object (upon rollover)... ...and disappears when the pointer is moved away.

A *Because the Snap to Point option is on (in the Selection & Anchor Display panel of the Preferences dialog), when the pointer of an object we drag is over an anchor point on another object, it becomes a white arrowhead.*

B *Object highlighting (the blue border) and anchor/path labels (the green text labels) display when the pointer is over the edge or an anchor point of an object, with the mouse button up. The measurement label on the right lists the x,y location of that anchor point.*

Duplicating objects

To duplicate an object or group, you can use any of the following techniques:

➤ Dragging (instructions on this page)

➤ Arrow keys (sidebar on this page)

➤ The Clipboard (facing page)

➤ The Offset Path command (page 104)

➤ The Rotate, Reflect, Scale, or Shear tool (pages 140–141)

➤ The Transform panel (pages 142–143)

➤ The Transform Each command (page 144)

➤ The Transform effect (page 145)

➤ The Layers panel (page 182)

To duplicate an object or group in the same document:

1. Choose the **Selection** tool ▸ (V).

2. Option-drag/Alt-drag an object's path or fill (not its bounding box).**A–B** Release the mouse before you release Option/Alt. To constrain the copy to an increment of 45°, include Shift in the shortcut (learn about the Constrain Angle on pages 378–379). To use Smart Guides for alignment while creating the duplicate, see the two previous pages.

➤ To repeat the last transformation (such as the creation of a duplicate), press Cmd-D/Ctrl-D.

➤ To duplicate an object in a group and make the copy a member of the group, Option-drag/Alt-drag it with the Direct Selection tool. Or if you want the duplicate to appear outside the group, select it with the Direct Selection tool, choose Edit > Copy, then choose Edit > Paste.

When you drag an object between documents, a copy of the object appears in the target document automatically.

To drag and drop an object or group between documents:

1. Open two documents as docked tabbed windows.

2. Choose the **Selection** tool ▸ (V).

3. Drag an object or group to the tab of the target document, pause until the target document window displays, then release the mouse where you want the duplicate object to appear.

➤ To drag and drop an object from a group, use the Direct Selection tool.

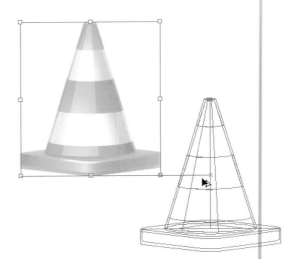

A *The quickest way to copy a group or an object is simply to Option-drag/Alt-drag it. Note the double-arrowhead pointer.*

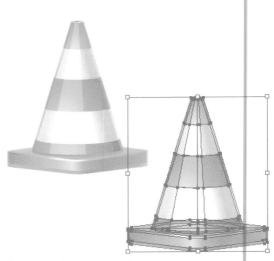

B *A copy of the group is made.*

COPYING OBJECTS BY USING AN ARROW KEY

Choose the Selection tool, select an object, then press Option-Shift-arrow/Alt-Shift-arrow to copy the object and move the copy in the direction of the arrow by 10 times the current Keyboard Increment value in Illustrator/Edit > Preferences > General (or press Option-arrow/Alt-arrow to move the copy by the current increment). The default increment is 1 pt.

If you select an object or a group and choose the Cut or Copy command, the object or group is placed onto the Clipboard, which is a temporary storage area in your computer's system memory. The contents of the Clipboard are replaced each time you choose Cut or Copy. The Paste command places the current Clipboard contents on the currently selected layer in the center of the currently active document window. The current Clipboard contents can be pasted an unlimited number of times.

Objects are copied to the Clipboard in the PDF and/or AICB format, depending on the current settings in Illustrator/Edit > Preferences > File Handling & Clipboard (see page 389).

To duplicate or move objects between documents using the Clipboard:

1. Open two documents.

2. With the Selection tool ✛ (V) or via the Layers panel, select the object(s) or group to be copied or moved.

3. Do either of the following:

    To put a copy of the object(s) or group onto the Clipboard while leaving the original(s) in place, choose Edit > **Copy** (Cmd-C/Ctrl-C).

    To put the object(s) or group onto the Clipboard and delete it from the current document, choose Edit > **Cut** (Cmd-X/Ctrl-X).

4. Click the tab for the target document.

5. Choose Edit > **Paste** (Cmd-V/Ctrl-V). The Clipboard contents will appear in the center of the document window. If the document is in Draw Normal mode, the contents will appear within the current layer. For the other paste commands, see the sidebar at right.

    Note: If an object is selected and Draw Inside mode is activated, the Clipboard contents will paste inside that object. ★ Or if the document is in Draw Behind mode, the Clipboard contents will be stacked behind the currently selected object.

➤ To restack an object in front of or behind another object, use the Layers panel (see page 181).

➤ On page 137, you will learn how to transform an object or group via its bounding box. In the meantime, if you want to hide (or show) the bounding box, which displays on all selected objects, choose View > Hide Bounding Box (or Show Bounding Box) or press Cmd-Shift-B/Ctrl-Shift-B. **A–B**

PASTING TO THE ORIGINAL LAYER

To have the Clipboard contents always paste to the top of the layer or sublayer from which they were copied or cut, turn the Paste Remembers Layers option on via the Layers panel menu. To allow the Clipboard contents to paste onto whichever layer happens to be selected at the time, leave this option off. Note: If this option is on and you copy or cut an object, delete the object's layer, then use the Paste command, the object will paste onto a brand new layer.

OTHER PASTE COMMANDS ON THE EDIT MENU

➤ Paste in Front (Cmd-F/Ctrl-F) and Paste in Back (Cmd-B/Ctrl-B) paste the Clipboard contents in the current artboard, at the same horizontal and vertical (x/y) location from which they were copied or cut, stacked in front of or behind the current selection, respectively.

➤ Paste in Place (Cmd-Shift-V/Ctrl-Shift-V) pastes the Clipboard contents in the current artboard, at the same x/y coordinates as they were copied from (instead of in the center of the document window). ★

➤ Paste in all Artboards (Cmd-Option-Shift-V/Ctrl-Alt-Shift-V) pastes the Clipboard contents at the same x/y coordinates in every artboard in the current document. We recommend using the Cut command first (instead of Copy) because Paste in All Artboards will paste a copy of the object on top of the original. ★ Note: The contents may land outside any artboards that are smaller.

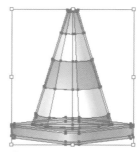

A *The Bounding Box feature is on for Illustrator, so the bounding box displays around this selected group.*

B *Here the Bounding Box feature is turned off.*

The Offset Path command duplicates a path and offsets the duplicate path around or inside the original object by a specified distance. The duplicate is given the same fill and stroke attributes as the original object. The command also reshapes the duplicate automatically so it fits nicely around the original path. You might not use this command on a regular basis, but it can come in handy if you happen to need a precisely scaled copy of an object.

To offset a duplicate of a path:

1. Select an object.

2. Choose Object > Path > **Offset Path**. The Offset Path dialog opens.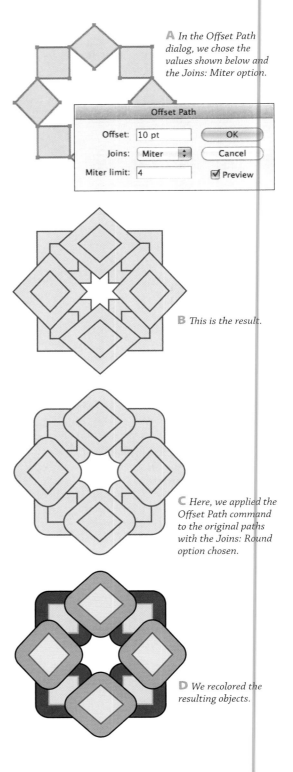A Check Preview.

3. In the Offset field, enter the distance the duplicate path is to be offset from the original. Make sure this value is larger or smaller than the stroke weight of the original path so the duplicates will be visible.

   For a closed path, a positive offset value will create a new path that is larger than the original one, and a negative value will create a path that is smaller than the original one. For an open path, both positive and negative values create a wider closed path, in the same shape as the original stroke.

4. Choose a **Joins** (bend) style for the shape of the joints in the duplicate: **Miter** (pointed),B **Round** (rounded),C or **Bevel** (beveled).

5. *Optional:* Change the Miter Limit value for the point at which a mitered (pointed) corner becomes a beveled one. A high Miter Limit (13 or greater) creates long, pointy corners; a low Miter Limit (4 or less) creates beveled corners.

6. Click OK. The offset path will be a separate path from, and will be stacked behind or in front of, the original path.D Regardless of whether the original object was open or closed, the resulting offset path will be closed.

➤ The Offset Path command can also be applied as an editable effect via Effect > Path > Offset Path. To learn about effects, see Chapter 15.

A *In the Offset Path dialog, we chose the values shown below and the Joins: Miter option.*

B *This is the result.*

C *Here, we applied the Offset Path command to the original paths with the Joins: Round option chosen.*

D *We recolored the resulting objects.*

Aligning and distributing objects via buttons

To line up objects neatly in a row or column (such as buttons for a Web page or blocks of point type), rather than trying to position them by eye, use the convenient controls on the Align or Control panel.

To align or distribute objects:

1. For alignment, select two or more objects or groups; or for distribution, select three or more objects. (If all the objects are in the same group, you can isolate the group before selecting the objects.)

2. Do either of the following:

   Display the Align panel. ■ A To display the full panel, click the arrows on the panel tab.

   Display the Control panel. B The align buttons also may not display if the Application frame is too narrow; enlarge the frame and the buttons should appear. If you still don't see the buttons, confirm that Align is checked on the panel menu.

3. On the Align panel menu or in Illustrator/ Edit > Preferences > General, check **Use Preview Bounds** to have Illustrator factor in an object's stroke weight and any applied effects when calculating an alignment or distribution command, or turn this option off to have Illustrator ignore the stroke weight and any effects. (By default, the stroke thickness extends halfway outside the path.)

4. Do either of the following:

   From the **Align To** menu, ⊞▾ choose **Align to Selection** (the default setting) to reposition some or all of the selected objects within the bounding box of the overall selection, depending on which Align Objects button you click in the next step.

   To specify which object in the selection remains stationary (becomes the "key" object), click that object now; it will now have a thicker border.

Continued on the following page

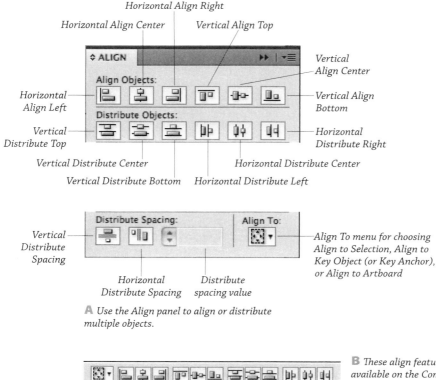

Horizontal Align Right
Horizontal Align Center
Vertical Align Top
Vertical Align Center
Horizontal Align Left
Vertical Align Bottom
Vertical Distribute Top
Horizontal Distribute Right
Vertical Distribute Center
Horizontal Distribute Center
Vertical Distribute Bottom
Horizontal Distribute Left
Vertical Distribute Spacing
Align To menu for choosing Align to Selection, Align to Key Object (or Key Anchor), or Align to Artboard
Horizontal Distribute Spacing
Distribute spacing value

A Use the Align panel to align or distribute multiple objects.

B These align features are also available on the Control panel when multiple objects are selected.

Or alternatively, choose **Align to Key Object** from the Align To menu to have the topmost of the selected objects in the stacking order on the Layers panel become the key object.

➤ To cancel the key object, choose Align to Selection from the Align To menu, or choose Cancel Key Object from the panel menu, or click the object again.

5. Do either of the following:

On the Align or Control panel, click one or more of the **Align Objects** buttons **A–B** and/or **Distribute Objects** buttons.**C**

On the Align panel, specify the desired distance to be placed between the objects by using the **Distribute Spacing** menu or field, then click either or both of the two Distribute Spacing buttons.

➤ Change your mind? To apply a different Align panel option, first nix the last one by using the Undo command (Cmd-Z/Ctrl-Z).

➤ If you choose Align to Artboard from the Align To menu ⊞▾ on the Align or Control panel, depending on which Align Objects or Distribute Objects button you click, at least two of the selected objects will align with the top, right, bottom, or left edge of the current artboard. If you were to click, say, the Vertical Distribute Top button, the top of the topmost object would align to the top of the artboard, the bottom of the bottommost object would align to the bottom of the artboard, and the remaining objects would be distributed evenly between them.

➤ To align objects to the pixel grid, see "Creating pixel-perfect artwork for the Web" on page 82.

➤ If the objects don't align perfectly, make sure they all have the same Align Stroke setting on the Stroke panel (see page 120).

➤ To align multiple anchor points on one or more objects, see page 164.

A *These are the original objects.*

B *We clicked the Vertical Align Bottom button first.*

C *Then we clicked the Horizontal Distribute Center button.*

Creating ruler guides

For most purposes, Smart Guides work quite well for arranging objects, but they're fleeting. If you need guides that stay onscreen (unless they're hidden intentionally), and that also have magnetism, create ruler guides by following these instructions. Ruler guides don't print.

To create ruler guides:

1. Choose View > Guides > **Show Guides** (Cmd-;/ Ctrl-;), or if the command is listed as Hide Guides, leave it be.

2. *Optional:* To create a new top-level layer to contain the guides you're about to create, Option-Shift-click/Alt-Shift-click the New Layer button ◰ on the Layers panel. In the Layer Options dialog, name the layer "Guides," then click OK. Keep the new Guides layer selected.

3. If the rulers aren't showing at the top and left sides of the document window, choose View > Rulers > **Show Rulers** (Cmd-R/Ctrl-R).

4. Drag one or more guides from the horizontal or vertical ruler onto your artboard, **A–B** noting its location by the dotted line on the opposite ruler as you do so. (The higher the zoom level, the finer the ruler increments.) Each guide is listed individually on the Layers panel as a <Guide>.

   Note: If you want to limit a guide to a particular artboard rather than have it extend across the whole canvas, choose the Artboard tool, click the artboard, then drag to create the guide. ★

➤ To control whether the zero point (where the horizontal and vertical rulers meet) and the ruler increments apply to just the current artboard or stretch across all the artboards in your document (are global), right-click a ruler and choose Change to Artboard Rulers or Change to Global Rulers from the context menu. To switch between the two options quickly, press Cmd-Option-R/ Ctrl-Alt-R. ★

➤ To learn about locking, unlocking, and clearing guides, see page 109.

➤ Option-drag/Alt-drag from the horizontal ruler to create a vertical guide, or from the vertical ruler to create a horizontal guide.

➤ You can choose a different color for guides in Illustrator/Edit > Preferences > Guides & Grid (see page 383).

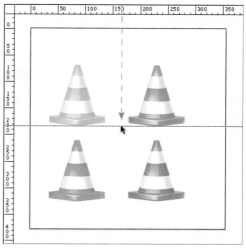

A *A guide is dragged from the horizontal ruler.*

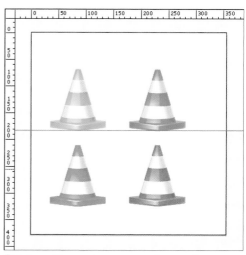

B *Ruler guides remain onscreen unless you choose to hide or delete them.*

MAKE IT SNAPPY

Turn on View > Snap to Point. Next, drag the edge, an anchor point, or the center point of an object near a guide (or near an anchor point on another object). The pointer turns white when it's over a point and the object snaps to the guide (or point). In Preferences > Selection & Anchor Display, you can change the Snap to Point value (the maximum distance between the pointer and the target within which the snap occurs); the default value is 2 px.

Creating guides from objects

Thus far we have shown you how to work with two kinds of guides: Smart Guides and ruler guides. Here you will learn how to convert a standard path into a guide. The process is reversible, meaning the guide can be converted back to a standard object at any time. Like ruler guides, guides that are made from objects don't print.

To create a guide from an object:

1. Click the selection square on the Layers panel for an object, **A** a group of objects, or an object in a group. It can't be a symbol, type, an object in a blend or distortion envelope, or a Live Paint group. You can copy the object and work with the copy, if you like. Note: If the object you convert to a guide is part of a group, the guide will be listed in that group.

2. Do either of the following:

   Choose View > Guides > **Make Guides** (Cmd-5/Ctrl-5).**B**

   Right-click the artboard and choose **Make Guides** from the context menu.

➤ You can transform or reshape an object guide, provided the guides in your document aren't locked (see "To lock or unlock all guides" on the next page). The guide can be selected (and hidden) via the Layers panel (see pages 179 and 184); look for the <Guide> listing. Remember to relock the guide after editing it.

When you release an object guide, the object regains its former fill and stroke attributes.

To release a guide that was made from an object:

1. On the Layers panel, make sure none of the guides to be released have a lock icon.

2. Do either of the following:

   To release one guide, in the document window, Cmd-Shift-double-click/Ctrl-Shift-double-click the edge of the guide.

   To release one or more guides, make sure the guides aren't locked (see the first task on the next page). Select the guide to be released, either manually or by clicking its selection square on the Layers panel (or Shift-click multiple selection squares), then right-click in the document and choose **Release Guides** from the context menu (Cmd-Option-5/Ctrl-Alt-5).

A We selected a three-sided polygon (a triangle).

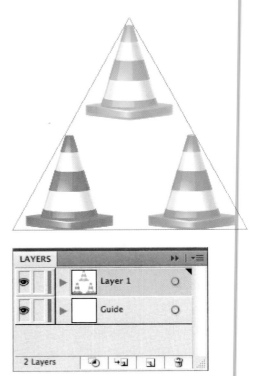

B We used the Make Guides command to convert the polygon to a guide, then aligned the cone object groups within the guide. (We put our guide on a separate layer.)

Locking and unlocking guides

To select or move ruler or object guides, you must make sure they're unlocked first.

To lock or unlock all guides:

Deselect all objects, then right-click in the document and choose **Lock Guides** from the context menu (Cmd-Option-;/Ctrl-Alt-;).

➤ To hide (or show) guides, choose Hide Guides (or Show Guides) from the context menu.

You can easily lock or unlock (as well as hide or show) ruler and object guides individually, because each one has its own <Guide> listing on the Layers panel.

To lock or unlock guides individually:

1. Make sure the Lock Guides command is off (see the instructions above).

2. On the Layers panel, click in the edit (lock) column for any guide to lock or unlock it. The padlock icon appears or disappears.

Clearing guides

To clear one guide:

1. Make sure either all guides are unlocked or at least the guide you want to remove is unlocked.

2. Choose the **Selection** tool (V), then click the ruler guide or guide object to be removed.

3. In the Mac OS, press Delete; in Windows, press Backspace or Del.

4. To relock all the remaining guides, deselect all objects, then right-click in the document window and choose Lock Guides.

The Clear Guides command removes all ruler and object guides from your document.

To clear all guides:

Choose View > Guides > **Clear Guides**.

TIPS FOR WORKING WITH GUIDES

➤ If you drag all your guides into one guides-only layer, you will be able to lock or unlock all of them at once by clicking the edit icon for that layer, or lock or unlock any guide individually via its own edit icon.

➤ If the current color assigned to the guides is similar to the selection color for the layer that contains the <Guide> listings, it may be hard to tell when the guides are selected. To change the layer selection color, double-click the layer name, then in the Layer Options dialog, choose a Color from the menu. Or change the color that is assigned to the guides instead, in Illustrator/Edit > Preferences > Guides & Grid (Guides: Color).

Using the grid

The grid is like nonprinting graph paper. You can use it as a framework to arrange objects on, either by eye or by using the Snap to Grid feature. The first step, logically, is to display the grid.

To show the grid:

Do either of the following:

Choose View > **Show Grid** (Cmd-"/Ctrl-").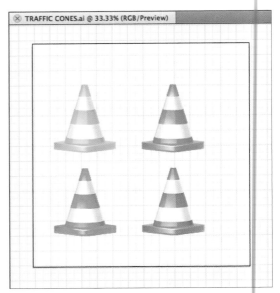

Deselect all, then right-click and choose **Show Grid** from the context menu.

To hide the grid, either choose View > Hide Grid or choose Hide Grid from the context menu.

➤ You can change the grid style (lines or dots), color, or spacing in Illustrator/Edit > Preferences > Guides & Grid. With the Grids in Back preference checked (the default setting), the grid displays behind all objects rather than in front of them.

To snap objects to the grid:

1. Choose View > **Snap to Grid** (Cmd-Shift-"/Ctrl-Shift-") to make the check mark appear.

2. With the Selection tool ▸ (V), drag an object near a gridline; the edge of the object will snap to the gridline. This feature works whether the grid is showing or not.

   Note: When the Snap to Grid command is on, Smart Guides won't display (even if the Smart Guides option is on). If you like to use Smart Guides to align objects, as we do, when you're done using the grid, be sure to hide it, and also remember to turn off the Snap to Grid feature.

➤ If the View > Pixel Preview feature is on, View > Snap to Grid becomes View > Snap to Pixel, which is turned on automatically. See the sidebar on page 30. Note that Smart Guides don't display when the Pixel Preview option is on.

A *The grid is showing in this document.*

In the preceding four chapters you mastered creating, selecting, and positioning objects. In this comprehensive chapter, you will apply colors and patterns to them. You will learn what kinds of colors are suitable for print or Web output and master the basic color controls in Illustrator. You will also fill the inside or edge of an object with a solid color or pattern using various panels and tools, save and organize swatches in the Swatches panel, copy swatches between files, choose stroke attributes, use the Color Guide and Kuler panels, replace colors in your artwork, invert colors, colorize grayscale images, blend fill colors between objects, and create and edit fill patterns.

Using color in Illustrator

The fill, which is applied to the inside of an object or an area in a Live Paint group, can be a solid color, a pattern, or a gradient (or None). The stroke, which is applied to an object's path, can be a solid color, a pattern (or None) but not a gradient, and it can be dashed or continuous. You can apply a brush to an object's stroke, make it into an arrow, or as we describe on page 156, change the stroke profile. The path that you apply a fill and/or stroke to can be open or closed.

The fill and stroke colors in the current or last selected object — or new colors that you choose when no objects are selected — display on the Tools, Color, Control, and Appearance panels. **A** The two current colors are applied to new objects automatically.

Continued on the following page

Fill square   Stroke square

A *The current stroke and fill colors display on the Tools, Control, Color, and Appearance panels.*

10

IN THIS CHAPTER

In this chapter, you will use the Color, Swatches, Color Guide, Kuler, and Appearance panels; the Color Picker; swatch library panels; and the Eyedropper tool to create and apply colors and patterns. And you will use the Control, Stroke, and Appearance panels to change the stroke weight, style (dashed or solid), alignment (position on the path), and endcaps, and apply arrowheads.

Beyond this chapter, there are many fill and stroke features to explore. In Chapter 12, you will create nonuniform stroke widths using variable width profiles and the Width tool. In Chapter 14, you will apply multiple fill and stroke attributes; in Chapter 18, you will apply colors with the Live Paint Bucket tool; in Chapter 24, you will create and save gradients; and in Chapter 29, you will use the Recolor Artwork dialog to assign new colors or color groups to your artwork.

Colors for your output medium

Before getting into the specific coloring features of Illustrator, you need to know what types of colors are suitable for your artwork and target output medium.

Colors for print output

A **spot** color is a predefined mixture of specific inks that is printed via an individual printing plate. Your print shop would create PANTONE 7489C (a medium green), for instance, by mixing ink percentages of 60 cyan, 0 magenta, 80 yellow, and 7 black. To choose a spot color, you need to flip through a fan guide for a matching system (such as PANTONE); pick a named, numbered spot color; then locate that color in Illustrator. You can use just spot colors if your document doesn't contain any photos, gradients, or other continuous-tone elements. Because each spot color adds to the printing cost, the budget for a project will determine how many can be used.

In commercial **process** printing, minute dots of the four process colors — cyan (C), magenta (M), yellow (Y), and black (K) — are printed from four separate plates. On the final print, your eyes (and mind) blur the dots together and read them as solid colors. If you examine a photograph in a magazine or catalog with a magnifying lens or loupe, you will see the actual dots. You can choose premixed process colors from a matching system, such as TRUMATCH or PANTONE Process, or enter specific process color percentages in the Color panel **A** or Color Picker.**B** The four-color process printing method must be used if your artwork contains continuous tones. (See also **A**, next page.)

QUICK ACCESS TO COLORING PANELS

To quickly open a color-related panel, either click its icon or use one of these methods:

Appearance panel ◉	Press Shift-F6
Color panel 🎨	Shift-click the Fill or Stroke square or arrowhead on the Control panel;* or click, then Shift-click the Fill or Stroke square on the Appearance panel; or press F6
Swatches panel ▦	Click the Fill or Stroke square or arrowhead on the Control panel, or click the Fill or Stroke square on the Appearance panel twice*

*When opened from the Control or Appearance panel, these panels stay open only temporarily.

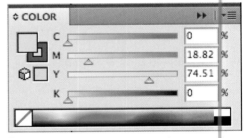

A For print output, choose colors in the CMYK color model. CMYK colors can be mixed on the Color panel...

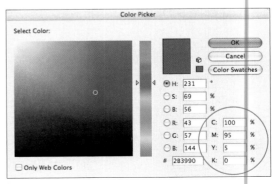

B ...or in the Color Picker.

In Illustrator, you can create and apply nonglobal process colors, which can only be edited individually in selected objects, or global process colors, which can be changed either individually in selected objects or globally in all objects in which they are being used, by editing the color swatch. To learn how this works, see page 132.

If the budget for your project allows, you can print a file using process colors, and add a spot color or two, say, for a key graphic, such as a logo.

Colors for Web output

For Web and video output, you should choose **RGB** colors (the acronym stands for red-green-blue).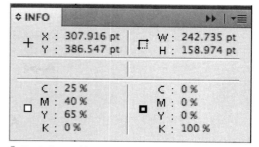 Modern computer video systems display millions of colors, so you don't need to restrict yourself to Web-safe colors for Web graphics. In other words, ignore the non-Web-safe icon 🔲 if it displays in the Color Picker, and keep the Only Web Colors option unchecked.

Note: For good color matching between the document that you see onscreen and the medium in which it will be published, make sure you have chosen the proper color management settings (see Chapter 2).

In the New Document dialog, as you create a document, you can choose CMYK or RGB as the document color mode. Any colors you mix or choose in that document will conform automatically to the chosen mode. If you change the document color mode, all the colors in the artwork will be converted to the new mode. Note that the gamut of RGB colors is larger than the gamut of CMYK colors.

Note: If the final output for your file will be an inkjet print (the inkjet print won't merely be used as a mockup or proof before commercial proofing and printing), choose RGB Color as the document mode.

To change the document color mode:

1. To be on the safe side, copy your file by using the File > Save As command (Cmd-Shift-S/ Ctrl-Shift-S).

2. Choose File > Document Color Mode > **CMYK Color** (for commercial print output) or **RGB Color** (for Web output or inkjet printing). The current document color mode is listed in the document tab.

▶ If you need to reverse a document color mode change, don't choose the former mode. Instead, choose Edit > Undo immediately.

A *The Info panel lists the components (or swatch name) of the fill and stroke in the currently selected object(s). If the colors in those objects are different, the color readout areas on the panel will be blank.*

B *For Web output, choose colors in the RGB color model.*

STAYING IN THE MODE

▶ You can create either process CMYK colors or RGB colors in a document, but not both. Any process colors that you create in a document will conform automatically to the current document color mode, regardless of which mode is chosen on the Color panel menu (see page 117). The same holds true for the Color Mode menu in the Swatch Options dialog when you edit a swatch (see page 132).

▶ Embedded placed and pasted images are converted to the current document color mode automatically.

▶ The Object > Rasterize dialog displays a color option for just the current document color mode (see page 206).

Using the basic color controls

Note: To choose new default colors for future objects, deselect all before choosing fill and stroke colors.

To apply a fill or stroke color, gradient, or pattern via a temporary Swatches panel:

1. Select one or more objects, or isolate an object.

2. Do any of the following:

   On the Control panel, click the Fill square or arrowhead,**A** then on the temporary Swatches panel that opens, click a solid-color, gradient, or pattern swatch.**B–C**

   On the Control panel, click the Stroke square or arrowhead, then on the temporary Swatches panel, click a solid-color or pattern swatch. You can change the stroke weight by using the adjacent arrows, menu, or field (see also page 120).

   On the Appearance panel,◉ click the Fill or Stroke listing,**D** click the color square or arrowhead,**E** then on the temporary Swatches panel, click a swatch.

To apply a fill or stroke color of None:

1. Select one or more objects, or isolate an object.

2. Do one of the following:

   On the Tools panel or the Color panel,⊞ click the Fill or Stroke square, then either click the **None** button ☐ or press /.

   On the Control panel, click the Fill or Stroke square or arrowhead, then click the **None** button ☐ on the temporary Swatches panel.

   On the Appearance panel,◉ click the Fill or Stroke listing, then press /.

Fill color Stroke color

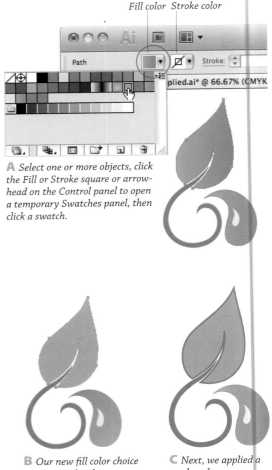

A *Select one or more objects, click the Fill or Stroke square or arrowhead on the Control panel to open a temporary Swatches panel, then click a swatch.*

B *Our new fill color choice appears in the object.*

C *Next, we applied a stroke color.*

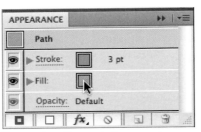

D *Click the Fill or Stroke listing on the Appearance panel.*

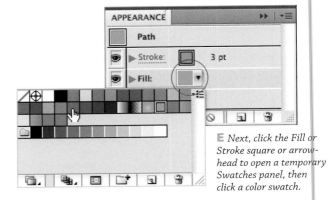

E *Next, click the Fill or Stroke square or arrowhead to open a temporary Swatches panel, then click a color swatch.*

You can also apply a solid color to objects by using the Color Picker dialog or the Color Guide panel.

To apply a solid fill or stroke color using the Color Picker:

1. Select one or more objects, or isolate an object.

2. On the Tools or Color panel, double-click the Fill or Stroke square. The Color Picker opens.

3   Click a hue on the vertical bar in the middle of the dialog (or move the slider), then click a brightness and saturation value of that hue in the large square.**A** You could also define a color by entering HSB, RGB, or CMYK values.

    If your document is going to be printed and the Out of Gamut icon ⚠ appears in the dialog, click the swatch below the icon to replace the chosen color with the closest printable one.

4. Click OK.

➤ If the fill or stroke colors differ among selected objects, a question mark **?** appears in the Fill and/or Stroke square on the Tools, Color, and Control panels. The new fill or stroke color you choose will apply to all the selected objects.

➤ A gradient can't be applied as a stroke color. For a workaround to this limitation, see page 336.

To apply a variation of a current color via the Color Guide panel:

1. Select one or more objects, or isolate an object.

2. On the Tools or Color panel, click the Fill or Stroke square.

3. Display the Color Guide panel.

4. Click the **Set Base Color to Current Color** button ▣ in the upper left corner of the panel, then click a color variation swatch in the panel.**B** For more about this panel, see pages 128–130.

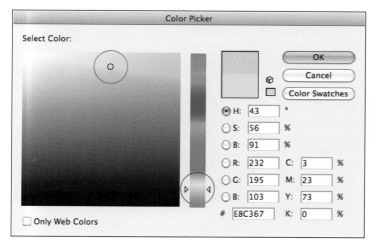

A *In the Color Picker, click a hue on the vertical bar, then click a variation of that color in the large square.*

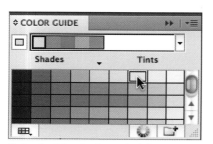

B *On the Color Guide panel, click a variation of the current color.*

SEEING THINGS IN BLACK AND WHITE

➤ To apply a white fill and a black stroke of 1 pt., click the Default Fill and Stroke button ⌐ on the Tools panel or press D.

➤ To apply a white or black fill or stroke separately, select an object, click the Fill or Stroke square on the Color panel, then click the White or Black selector in the bottom right corner of the Color panel (shown below) or click the White or Black swatch on the Swatches panel.

Saving colors as swatches

The Swatches panel is used for storing and applying solid process and spot colors, patterns, gradients, and color groups. Swatches that you add to the panel save only with the current file. To learn more about this panel, see pages 124–127.

To save the current fill or stroke color as a swatch:

1. Do either of the following:

   Select or isolate an object that contains the color you want to save as a swatch.

   With no objects selected, choose a color via the Color Picker or the Color Guide panel (see the preceding page) or specify values via the Color panel (see the facing page).

2. Display the Swatches panel so it stays open, either expanded in a dock or as a floating panel.

3. Do one of the following:

   Drag the Fill or Stroke square from the Color panel to the Swatches panel.A

   Drag a color from the Color Guide panel to the Swatches panel.

   Click the Fill or Stroke square on the Color or Tools panel, then Option-click/Alt-click the **New Swatch** button at the bottom of the Swatches panel.

To save the colors being used in a document as swatches:

Do either of the following:

Deselect all objects, then from the Swatches panel menu, choose **Add Used Colors**.

Select one or more objects, then from the Swatches panel menu, choose **Add Selected Colors**.

Note: Both of the above-mentioned commands convert nonglobal process colors to global process colors (see page 132).

➤ To rename a swatch, double-click it, then type a new Swatch Name in the Swatch Options dialog.

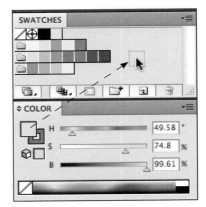

A *To save a color as a swatch, drag from the color square on the Color panel to the Swatches panel.*

SHORTCUTS FOR COLORING

Toggle the Fill and Stroke squares on the Tools and Color panels	Press X
Make the fill color the same as the stroke color, or vice versa	Drag one square over the other on the Tools panel or Color panel
Swap the current fill and stroke colors	Press Shift-X or click the Swap Fill and Stroke button on the Tools panel
Apply a fill of None	Click the None button on the Color or Tools panel, or press /
Reapply the last solid color	Click the Last Color button on the Color panel or the Color button on the Tools panel, or press <
Reapply the last gradient after applying a solid color or None	Click the Gradient button on the Tools panel, or press >

Default Fill and Stroke (D) — Swap Fill and Stroke (Shift-X)

Fill square — Stroke square

Color (<) — None (/)
Gradient (>)

These color controls are located at the bottom of the Tools panel.

Choosing colors via the Color panel

In these steps, you will define a CMYK color for print output by specifying numeric values on the Color panel or mix an RGB color for Web output by moving the sliders.

To choose a color via the Color panel:

1. Select one or more objects, or isolate an object (or to choose colors for an object to be created, deselect all).

2. Do one of the following:

   On the Color panel, ☞ click the Fill or Stroke square.

   On the Control panel, Shift-click the Fill or Stroke square or arrowhead to open a temporary Color panel.

   On the Appearance panel, ● Shift-click the Fill or Stroke square or arrowhead to open a temporary Color panel (or if the square isn't active, click and then Shift-click it).

3. Choose a color model from the Color panel menu:

   Grayscale to choose a gray shade.

   RGB to define a color for video or Web output. For Web output, we recommend using this color model instead of the Web Safe RGB model.

   HSB to define a color according to its hue (location on the color wheel), saturation (purity), and brightness values.

   CMYK to define a process color for print output.

4. For print output, get the exact percentages for a color from a printed fan guide for a matching system (such as PANTONE Process Coated), then enter C, M, Y, and K values.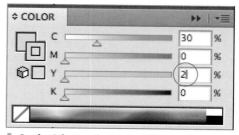

   For Web output, click a color in the color ramp at the bottom of the panel, then move the R, G, and B sliders to mix the desired color.

5. *Optional (but recommended):* To save the new color as a nonglobal process color swatch, Option-click/Alt-click the New Swatch button 🔲 on the Swatches panel.

▶ To quickly cycle through the available color models for the Color panel, Shift-click the color ramp at the bottom of the panel.

▶ Colors can also be defined numerically via the Color Picker (see page 115).

A *On the Color panel, click the Fill or Stroke square, choose a color model from the panel menu, then either enter percentages from a swatch book (for print output) or move the sliders.*

SELECTING TYPE FOR RECOLORING

▶ To recolor all the type in a block, select it with the Selection tool first.

▶ To recolor just a portion of the type in a block, select that passage with a type tool first.

▶ To recolor the object the type is on or inside (not the type), select the path with the Direct Selection tool first.

KEEPING COLORS WITHIN THE GAMUT

If the current RGB or HSB color has no CMYK equivalent (and therefore can't be printed on a commercial press), an Out of Gamut warning ⚠ appears below the Fill and Stroke squares on the Color panel. If you click the icon or swatch, Illustrator will replace it with the closest equivalent printable color.

Applying colors from a library

In these instructions, we'll show you how to access and apply spot or process colors from a matching system (such as PANTONE) or swatches from one of the predefined Adobe color libraries.

To access swatches from a library:

1. *Optional:* Select one or more objects or isolate an object that you want to apply a color to, and click the Fill or Stroke square on the Tools or Color panel.

2. From the **Swatch Libraries** menu 🗀 in the lower left corner of the Swatches panel (or from a submenu on that menu), choose a library name. If you want to open a library from a matching system (for print output), choose that system from the Color Books submenu (see the sidebar at right); or to reload the default swatches, choose from the Default Swatches submenu.

   The chosen library will open in a floating panel. You can scroll in or enlarge the panel, if necessary, to reveal more colors.

3. If you click a swatch in a Color Books library or click a color group icon 🗀 in any library, that color or color group will appear on the Swatches panel immediately. For other colors, do either of the following:

   On the library panel, click a swatch or hold down Cmd/Ctrl or Shift and click multiple swatches, then choose **Add to Swatches** from the library panel menu.**A**

   Drag a swatch or a selection of multiple swatches from the library panel to the Swatches panel.

➤ Once you have opened one library, you can cycle through other libraries by clicking the Load Next Swatch Library ▶ or Load Previous Swatch Library ◀ button on the library panel.

➤ To control whether a library panel reappears when you relaunch Illustrator, check or uncheck Persistent on the library panel menu.

➤ To close a whole library panel, click its close box. To close just one library on a panel, right-click its tab and choose Close from the context menu.

➤ You can't modify swatches on a library panel (note the non-edit icon 🖉 in the lower right corner). However, you can edit any swatch once you have added it to the Swatches panel.

➤ To locate a particular color, choose Show Find Field from the library panel menu, then start typing the desired name or number in the field.

USING THE COLOR BOOK BRANDS

ANPA colors are used in the newspaper industry.

DIC Color Guide and TOYO Color Finder colors are used in Japan.

FOCOLTONE process colors are designed to help prevent registration problems and lessen the need for trapping.

HKS process colors and HKS spot colors (without the word "Process" in the name) are used in Europe.

PANTONE process colors and PANTONE spot colors (without the word "Process" in the name) are widely used in the commercial print industry in North America.

TRUMATCH process colors include 40 tints and shades of each hue, organized differently from PANTONE colors.

AVOIDING NASTY COLOR SURPRISES

As you learned in Chapter 2, the Color Settings command in Illustrator uses monitor and printer device profiles and output intents in conjunction with the system's color management utility to ensure accurate color matching between the onscreen display of artwork and the final output. Unfortunately, even with the best color management system in place, you can't proof process and spot colors for commercial printing onscreen — however tempted you may be to trust what you see. Instead, always pick spot colors and look up process color formulas in a printed fan guide for a color matching system that is used in your locale. And before you authorize a print run, be sure to tell your print shop that you will need to view at least one color proof.

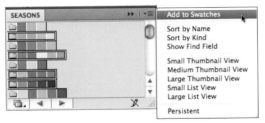

A *Select one or more swatches or color groups on a library panel, then choose Add to Swatches from the panel menu to make them appear on the Swatches panel.*

Changing the tint percentage

You can achieve a pleasing range of tints (and help to keep your project within budget) with just one black and one spot color printing plate by applying an assortment of tint percentages of the spot color to different objects. You can also change the percentage of any global process color (see also page 132).

To change the tint percentage of a spot or global process color:

1. Select one or more objects that contain the same spot or global process color. On the Swatches panel, a spot color swatch will have a dot in the lower right corner, a global process color swatch will have a white triangle in the corner.

2. Do either of the following:

   On the Color panel, click the Fill or Stroke square, then move the **T** (Tint) slider. **A**

   To open a temporary Color panel, Shift-click the Fill or Stroke square on the Control panel; or on the Appearance panel, click, then Shift-click the Fill or Stroke square. Move the **T** (Tint) slider. **B**

➤ If Select Same Tint % is checked in Illustrator/ Edit > Preferences > General, the Fill Color, Stroke Color, and Fill & Stroke Color commands on the Select Similar Options menu on the Control panel will select only objects that contain the same color and tint percentage as the currently selected object. With this preference unchecked, the above-mentioned commands will select all tint percentages of the same color.

➤ If the objects you select contain the same spot or global process color in different tint percentages, a question mark will display in the Fill or Stroke square. The tint percentage you choose will apply to all the selected objects.

QUICK RECOLORING BY DRAGGING

You can quickly apply a fill color, gradient, or pattern or a stroke color or pattern without having to select an object first. Click the Fill or Stroke square on the Tools or Color panel, then drag a swatch from the Swatches panel or Color Guide panel, or from the Fill square on the Color panel, onto any object (it doesn't matter which tool is selected).

A *On the Color panel, move the Tint slider.*

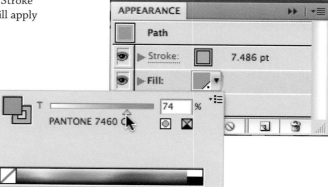

B *You can also change the Tint percentage on a temporary Color panel, which you can access from the Appearance panel, as shown here, or from the Control panel.*

Changing the stroke weight, alignment, caps, and joins

In addition to changing the color of a stroke, you can also change the stroke weight, its position on the path, and its style (dashed or solid, rounded or sharp corners, flat or rounded ends). You can also choose settings to make it look like an arrow. First, learn how to change the weight. (To use the Profile options on the Stroke panel, see page 156.)

To change the weight of a stroke:

1. Select one or more objects, isolate an object, or select some type.

2. In any of these locations, change the stroke weight by clicking the up or down arrow, by entering a value, or by choosing a value from the menu:

   In the **Weight** area of the Stroke panel.≣ A

   In the **Stroke Weight** area of the Control panel.

   On the Appearance panel ● (click the Stroke square to display the Stroke Weight controls).B

➤ Shift-click the up or down Stroke Weight arrow to change the value by a larger interval.

➤ For a list of the units and abbreviations that can be used in Illustrator fields, see page 382.

➤ A stroke that is narrower than .25 pt. may not print. Check with your print shop.

To change the alignment of a stroke on a path:

1. Select one or more closed paths, or isolate a closed path. To see the effect of the align options, either make the stroke fairly wide or zoom in on your artwork.

2. Display the full Stroke panel ≣ (see the sidebar on this page).

3. Click one of these buttons: **Align Stroke to Center** ◘ (the default setting), **Align Stroke to Inside,**◘ or **Align Stroke to Outside.**◘ C–E

➤ When aligning paths (see pages 105–106), make sure they have the same Align Stroke setting.

To change the stroke cap or corner style:

1. Select one or more objects or isolate an object, and apply a fairly wide stroke to it.

2. Display the full Stroke panel.≣

3. To modify the endpoints of a solid line or all the dashes in a dashed line, click one of the **Cap** buttons: (**A–B**, next page).

DISPLAYING THE STROKE PANEL

➤ Click the Stroke panel icon ≣ in a panel dock. To display its full set of options, click the double arrowheads on the panel tab.

➤ To open a full but temporary Stroke panel, click the underlined Stroke link on the Control panel (objects with mixed stroke attributes can be selected).

➤ To open a full but temporary Stroke panel when one object is selected or when multiple objects that have the same stroke attributes are selected, click the underlined Stroke link on the Appearance panel.

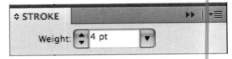
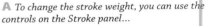

A *To change the stroke weight, you can use the controls on the Stroke panel...*

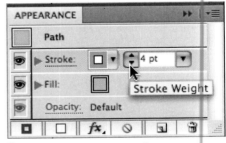

B *... or on the Appearance panel.*

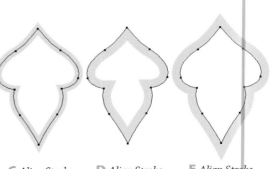

C *Align Stroke to Center* D *Align Stroke to Inside* E *Align Stroke to Outside*

Butt Cap ⊏ to create squared ends in which the stroke stops at the endpoints, or to create short, rectangular dashes. Use this option when you need to align your paths very precisely.

Round Cap ⊏ to create semicircular ends or elliptical dashes.

Projecting Cap ⊏ to create squared ends in which the stroke extends beyond the endpoints (by half current stroke weight), or to create rectangular dashes.

4. To modify the joins on corner points (not the curve points) of the path, click a **Corner** button:

Miter Join ⊦ to produce pointed bends.

Round Join ⊦ to produce semicircular bends.

Bevel Join ⊦ to produce beveled bends. The sharper the angle in a path, the wider the bevel.

5. *Optional:* Change the Miter Limit value for the minimum length a mitered (pointed) corner must have to become a beveled corner. Don't fret over how this works; just use a high Miter Limit value (12 or higher) to create sharp, pointy corners or a low Miter Limit value (4 or lower) to create beveled corners.

➤ To learn the difference between corner and curve points, see page 279.

Creating arrows

To add an arrowhead and/or tail to a path: ★

1. Select one or more objects or isolate an object — preferably an open path. Apply a stroke color to it and choose a weight.

2. Display the full Stroke panel.≣

3. From the **Arrowheads** pickers, choose an arrowhead style for the starting point of the path and a tail style for the endpoint of the path.

➤ To swap the two styles on the path, click the Swap Start and End Arrowheads button.⇄

4. *Optional:* To scale the arrowhead or tail on the object, use the respective Scale slider. Or to scale both ends at once, click the link icon first.**C**

5. *Optional:* To change the alignment of the arrowhead and tail on the path, click the Extend Arrow Tip Beyond End of Path button ⇥ or the Place Arrow Tip at End of Path button.⇥

➤ To remove an arrowhead or tail from a selected path, choose None from the menu.

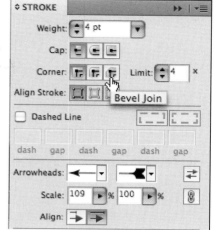

A To identify the Cap and Corner buttons on the Stroke panel, use the tool tips.

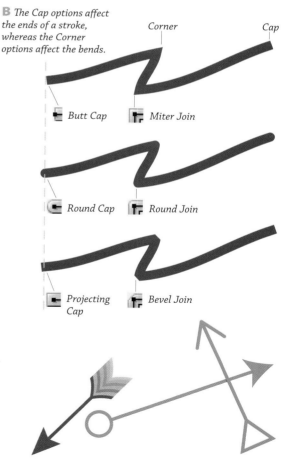

B The Cap options affect the ends of a stroke, whereas the Corner options affect the bends.

Corner   Cap

⊏ *Butt Cap*   ⊦ *Miter Join*

⊏ *Round Cap*   ⊦ *Round Join*

⊏ *Projecting Cap*   ⊦ *Bevel Join*

C Arrowheads and tails are applied to these paths.

Creating a dashed stroke

Using the Dashed Line controls, you can easily create a dashed stroke that has either uniform or varied dash lengths and spacing.

To create a dashed (or dotted) stroke:

1. Select one or more objects, or isolate an object. Make sure the stroke has a color and that its weight is 1 pt. or more.

2. Display the full Stroke panel.≡

3. Click a **Cap** button for the shape of the ends of the dashes (see the preceding page).

4. Check **Dashed Line**.

5. Enter a value in the first **Dash** field for the length of the first dash, then press Tab.**A**

6. *Optional:* Enter a value in the first Gap field (for the length of the first gap following the first dash), then press Tab to proceed to the next field or press Return/Enter to exit the panel. If you don't enter a gap value, the dash value will also serve as the gap value. You can enter values in a nondefault measurement unit (see page 382).

7. *Optional:* To create dashes of varying lengths, enter values in the other dash fields. If you don't do this, the first dash value will be used for all the dashes, and all the dashes will have a uniform length. Ditto for the gaps.

8. To control how the dashes fit around the corners of the object, click the **Preserves Exact Dash and Gap Lengths** button ⌐ ⌐ for no adjustment at the corners, or click the **Aligns Dashes to Corners and Path Ends, Adjusting Lengths to Fit** button [⌐] (that's a mouthful!) to have the dashes adjust to fit symmetrically at the corners. ★ We chose the first option for the top two figures in **B** and the second option for the bottom two figures.

➤ To create a dotted line, click the second Cap button (Round Cap), enter a dash value of 0, and enter a gap value that is equal to or greater than the stroke weight. For example, for a stroke weight of 15 pt., you would enter a dash value of 0 and a gap value between 20 and 30 pt.

➤ To save a dashed stroke as a graphic style, drag a path to which that stroke is applied to the Graphic Styles panel (see page 215).

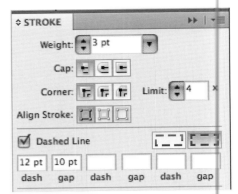

A *These Dashed Line settings will produce dashes that are 12 pt. long and are separated by 10-pt. gaps.*

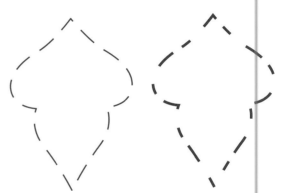

Weight 1 pt., Dash 14, Gap 9, Butt Cap

Weight 2 pt., Dash 8, Gap 15, Dash 15, Gap 8, Butt Cap

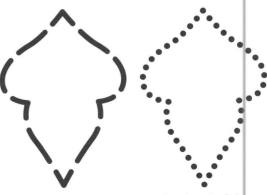

Weight 4 pt., Dash 24, Gap 8, Round Cap

Weight 4.6 pt., Dash 0, Gap 7.8, Round Cap and Join

B *These dashed strokes were created using various settings.*

Using the Eyedropper tool

When you click an object with the Eyedropper tool, it samples the object's color and stroke attributes, displays them on the Color, Stroke, and Appearance panels, and applies them to selected objects — in one quick, easy step.

To sample and apply colors with the Eyedropper tool:

1. *Optional:* To specify default settings for which attributes the Eyedropper tool picks up and applies, double-click the tool ✐ (or click the tool, then press Return/Enter). In the Eyedropper Options dialog, check which attributes are to be picked up and applied (all are checked by default), uncheck the attributes to be ignored, then click OK.

2. *Optional:* Select one or more objects. They will be recolored instantly with the attributes you are going to sample with the Eyedropper in step 4.

3. Choose the **Eyedropper** tool ✐ (I).

4. Click an object in your artwork that contains the desired attributes.**A** It can be any kind of object (even a color in a placed image), and it can contain a solid color, pattern, or gradient. The object doesn't have to be selected. Depending on the current Eyedropper Options settings, the sampled colors may appear in the Fill and/or Stroke squares on the Tools, Color, Appearance, and Transparency panels, and the sampled stroke settings may appear on the Stroke panel.

   If you selected any objects before using the Eyedropper tool, the sampled attributes will be applied to those objects.**B**

➤ Option-click/Alt-click an object to do the opposite of the above — that is, apply color attributes from the currently selected object to the object you click.**C–D**

➤ To have the Eyedropper tool sample only the color you click it on (no other attributes), click the Fill or Stroke square on the Tools or Color panel, then Shift-click the color to be sampled.

➤ To preserve a sampled color for future use, drag it from the Fill or Stroke square on the Color panel to the Swatches panel.

A *Select one or more objects, then with the Eyedropper tool, click an object that contains the desired attributes.*

B *The attributes you sample will be applied instantly to the selected object(s).*

C *Another method is to Option-click/ Alt-click with the Eyedropper tool to apply attributes from the currently selected object to the one you click.*

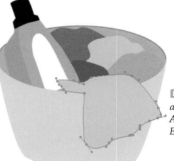

D *This is the result after we Option/ Alt clicked with the Eyedropper tool.*

Using the Swatches panel

Via the Swatches panel menu, you can control which categories and size of swatches the panel displays.

To choose display options for the Swatches panel:

1. Display the Swatches panel. ⊞

2. To control which categories of swatches display on the panel, from the **Show Swatch Kinds** menu, 🔳 choose Show All Swatches for all types (colors, gradients, patterns, and groups), **A** Show Color Swatches for just solid colors and color groups, Show Gradient Swatches for just gradients, Show Pattern Swatches for just patterns, or Show Color Groups for just color groups.

3. From the panel menu, choose one of these views for the currently chosen category of swatches: Small Thumbnail View, Medium Thumbnail View, Large Thumbnail View, Small List View, or Large List View. The medium and large thumbnail views are useful for identifying gradients and patterns. In the two list views, icons representing the color type and mode for each solid color also display. **B**

4. *Optional:* From the panel menu, choose Sort by Name to sort the nongrouped swatches alphabetically by name or numerically by their color contents; or choose Sort by Kind (when all swatch categories are displayed) to sort swatches in the following order: solid colors, gradients, patterns, color groups.

▶ To locate a particular swatch, choose Show Find Field from the panel menu, click in the field, then start typing the swatch name. Choose the command again to hide the field.

▶ You can drag a swatch, or multiple selected swatches, to another location on the panel. Color groups are always listed last.

▶ To learn the difference between global and nonglobal colors, see page 132.

Global process colors have a white corner but no dot. *Nonglobal process colors are plain.* *Spot colors have a dot.*

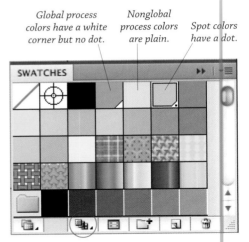

A *All four kinds of swatches (color, gradient, pattern, and color groups) are displayed on this Swatches panel because Show All Swatches is chosen on the Show Swatch Kinds menu. This panel is in Large Thumbnail view.*

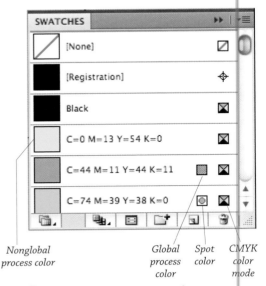

Nonglobal process color   *Global process color*   *Spot color*   *CMYK color mode*

B *When the Swatches panel is in a list view, icons representing the color type and document color mode display on the right side.*

A convenient way to organize swatches on the Swatches panel is to put them into color groups. If you're coordinating a group of solid colors for a client, for a specific design, or by theme, putting them in a group will allow you to locate and display them more easily.

When the panel is in a thumbnail view, the colors in each group are lined up in a row, beginning with the folder icon, and each group name can be identified via its tool tip. When the panel is in a list view, the name of the color group is listed next to the folder icon, followed by a nested listing of the colors in the group.

To create a color group from swatches:

1. Deselect.

2. On the Swatches panel, ▦ Shift-click to select contiguous solid-color swatches or Cmd-click/ Ctrl-click to select multiple swatches (sorry, no gradients, patterns, or the color None).**A**

3. Click the **New Color Group** button ◻⁺ at the bottom of the panel.

4. In the New Color Group dialog, enter a Name, then click OK. The new group appears on the Swatches panel.**B**

   Note: To add a swatch to an existing color group, drag the swatch from the Swatches or Color Guide panel into the group or onto the group icon.

➤ You can also create a color group using the Color Guide panel (see pages 128–130), the Kuler panel (see page 131), or the Recolor Artwork or Edit Colors dialog (see Chapter 29). To edit a color group via one of those dialogs, double-click the group icon on the Swatches panel.

➤ To rename a color group, click its folder icon, then choose Color Group Options from the panel menu. Change the name, then click OK.

➤ To restack a color group among other color groups, drag its icon upward or downward.

To create a color group from artwork:

1. With the Selection tool or via the Layers panel, select the artwork that contains the colors to be put in a new color group.**C**

2. Click the **New Color Group** button ◻⁺ on the Swatches panel.

3. In the New Color Group dialog, enter a name for the group, click **Selected Artwork** (check the desired options), then click OK.**D**

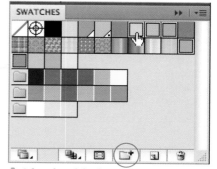

A *Select the solid-color swatches to be put into a group, then click the New Color Group button.*

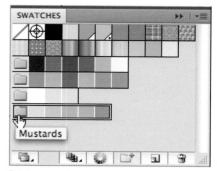

B *The new color group appears on the panel.*

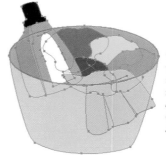

C *Select the artwork that contains the colors to be put into a group, then click the New Color Group button on the Swatches panel.*

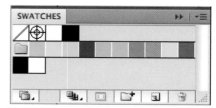

D *The new color group appears on the panel.*

To copy swatches between Illustrator files:

1. Open the file into which you want to load swatches.

2. From the **Swatch Libraries** menu ▦. at the bottom of the Swatches panel, choose **Other Library**. The Select a Library to Open dialog opens.

3. Locate and click the Illustrator file you want to copy swatches from, then click Open. A library of swatches opens, bearing the name of the source file.

4. Do one of the following:

   Click a swatch in the source library panel.

   Click a color group icon on the source library panel.**A–B**

   Cmd-click/Ctrl-click or Shift-click multiple swatches, then choose Add to Swatches from the library panel menu.

5. If the Swatch Conflict dialog appears, see the sidebar at right.

► To quickly append spot or global process colors from one file to another, do either of the following: Copy and paste an object or group that contains those colors from one document to another, or drag the object or group from one Illustrator document window onto the tab, and then into the window, of the other document. To append nonglobal process colors, do the same, then drag from the Fill and/or Stroke square on the Color panel to the Swatches panel.

RESOLVING A SWATCH CONFLICT

► The Swatch Conflict dialog will appear as you copy swatches or objects between files if a global process color has the same name, but different color percentages, as an existing swatch in the current document. Click Merge Swatches to have the offending swatch adopt the color values of the existing one, or click Add Swatches to add the offending swatch to the document (a number is appended to its name). Note: To apply the current Options setting to any other name conflicts that crop up and to prevent the alert dialog from opening repeatedly, check Apply to All.

► If a conflict arises between spot colors, Illustrator will merge the new swatch into the existing one.

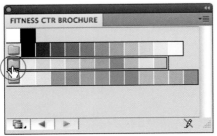

A We opened a library of swatches from another file, then clicked a color group.

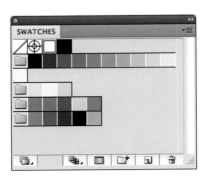

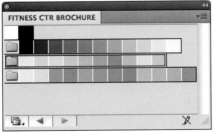

B The color group appeared on the Swatches panel for the current document.

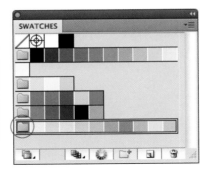

To duplicate a swatch:

1. On the Swatches panel, click the swatch you want to duplicate, then click the **New Swatch** button 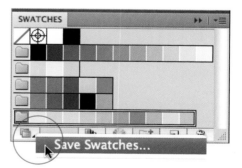 on the panel. The New Swatch dialog opens.

2. Change the swatch name, if desired, check Global or not (see page 132), then click OK.

➤ To bypass the dialog as you duplicate a swatch, click the swatch, then Option-click/Alt-click the New Swatch button (or drag the swatch over the button).

To delete swatches from the panel:

1. On the Swatches panel, do one of the following:

   Click a swatch.

   Click the icon for a color group.

   Cmd-click/Ctrl-click (or Shift, then Shift-click) multiple swatches or color groups.

   To select only the swatches that aren't being used in your artwork, choose **Show All Swatches** from the **Show Swatch Kinds** menu, then choose **Select All Unused** from the panel menu.

2. Click the **Delete Swatch** button at the bottom of the Swatches panel, then click Yes in the alert dialog; or to bypass the prompt, Option-click/Alt-click the Delete Swatch button.

➤ If you delete the swatch for a spot or global process color (or for a pattern or gradient that contains a spot or global process color) that is currently in use in your document, a nonglobal process color equivalent of the deleted color is applied to those objects automatically (see page 132).

➤ To restore a deleted swatch or swatches, choose Undo immediately. If you unintentionally delete a nonglobal solid color (not a global process or spot color), gradient, or pattern that's being used in the current file and it's too late to use the Undo command, you can retrieve the swatch by selecting an object in which it is being used, then dragging the Fill and/or Stroke square from the Color panel to the Swatches panel.

➤ If you want to restore swatches from a default library or any other library, see page 118.

By saving your favorite swatches and color groups as custom libraries, you'll be able to load them onto the Swatches panel for use in any document.

To save a library of swatches:

1. Make sure the Swatches panel contains only the swatches or color groups to be saved in a library.

   ➤ To delete all the swatches that aren't being used in your artwork, choose Show All Swatches from the Show Swatch Kinds menu, choose Select All Unused from the Swatches panel menu, then click the Delete Swatch button.

2. From the **Swatch Libraries** menu at the bottom of the Swatches panel, choose **Save Swatches.** A The Save Swatches as Library dialog opens.

3. Type a name for the library in the Save As field, keep the default location, and click Save.

4. User-saved libraries are listed on, and can be opened from, the User Defined submenu on the Swatches Libraries menu.

A *To save the swatches currently on the panel as a library, choose Save Swatches from the Swatch Libraries menu.*

Using the Color Guide panel

Use the Color Guide panel to generate color schemes from a base color by choosing a harmony rule and/or a variation type (Tints/Shades, Warm/Cool, or Vivid/Muted). You can apply any resulting swatch as a fill or stroke color, save variations from the panel as a group to the Swatches panel, or edit the current color group via the Edit Colors dialog.

This panel might prove useful if you want to apply a set of coordinated colors quickly, if your projects require you to work with an approved group of colors, or if you simply want to see how a different range of hues, tints, or saturation values might look in your artwork. To get acquainted with the panel, start by choosing options for it.

To choose variation options for the Color Guide panel:

1. Show the Color Guide panel, 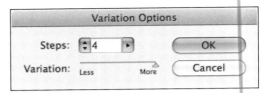 then choose **Color Guide Options** from the panel menu. The Variation Options dialog opens.**A**

2. Click the up/down arrow to set the number of variation **Steps** (columns of colors) to be displayed on either side of the colors in the central column, and move the **Variation** slider to control how much the colors can vary from those in the central column.

3. Click OK.**B**

➤ To make the swatches wider, enlarge the Color Guide panel by dragging its left or right edge.

To apply color variations via the Color Guide panel:

1. From the **Limit Color Group to Colors in Swatch Library** menu at the bottom of the Color Guide panel, choose None.

2. To make a color appear on the panel, do either of the following:

   Select an object,**C** click the Fill or Stroke square on the Tools or Color panel, then in the upper left corner of the Color Guide panel, click the **Set Base Color to Current Color** button.

   With no objects selected, click the Fill or Stroke square on the Tools or Color panel, click a swatch on the Swatches panel, or mix a color on the Color panel.

3. The active color group displays at the top of the Color Guide panel. To control what types of variations are derived from the active color

A *In the Variation Options dialog box, specify the number of Steps (variations) to be displayed on the Color Guide panel, and a degree of Variation for those colors.*

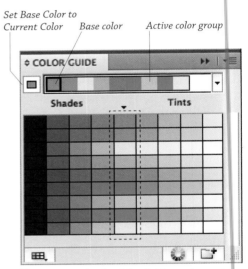

B *The options for this Color Guide panel are set to 4 Steps (four colors on either side of the central column) and the maximum amount of Variation (More). The original colors from the active color group display in the central column.*

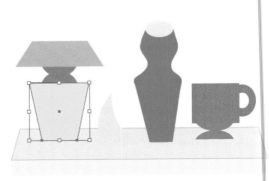

C *An object is selected.*

group, choose a variation type from the panel menu:

Show Tints/Shades adds progressively more black to the variations on the left side of the central column and progressively more white to the variations on the right.

Show Warm/Cool adds progressively more red to the variations on the left and progressively more blue to the variations on the right.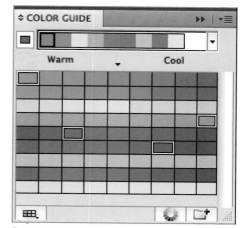

Show Vivid/Muted progressively reduces the saturation of colors on the left and progressively increases the saturation of colors on the right.

4. To apply a color variation, do either of the following:

   To recolor the currently selected object, click a color in the active group at the top of the panel or click a variation in the main part of the panel.

   Drag a variation swatch over any selected or unselected object.**B**

➤ When you click a variation on the Color Guide panel, that color becomes the current color. If you then click the Set Base Color to Current Color button, the active color group changes and new variations are generated.

➤ To limit the harmony and variation colors on the Color Guide panel to the colors in a specific library, from the Limit Color Group to Colors in Swatch Library menu, ▦ choose a library name (e.g., Earthtone or Color Books > PANTONE Solid Coated). The library name will be listed at the bottom of the panel, and only colors from that library will display as variations on the panel and on the Harmony Rules menu (see the next page). To remove the current restriction, choose None from the same menu.

➤ Tints/Shades is the only variation that doesn't convert spot colors to process colors. To replace a spot color in a selected object with a different spot color, click one of the variations that has a dot in the lower right corner.

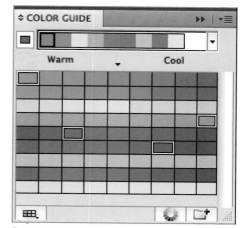

A *We chose the Warm/Cool variation type for this Color Guide panel.*

B *We dragged variation swatches from the Color Guide panel over some of the objects in the artwork. The colors we used are shown selected in the panel above.*

Another easy way to change the variations on the Color Guide panel is by choosing a harmony rule, such as Complementary, Analogous, or High Contrast. A new color group and variations are generated from the same base color, in accordance with the chosen rule.

To create a color group and variations based on a harmony rule:

1. To establish a base color on the Color Guide panel, 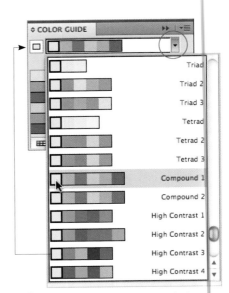 follow step 2 in "To apply color variations via the Color Guide panel" on page 128.

2. On the Color Guide panel, click to open the **Harmony Rules** menu (to the right of the active color group),**A** then click a rule. A new color group displays at the top of the panel. Below that, you'll see the variations that Illustrator has generated from the new color group.**B**

3. *Optional:* To produce a new color group and variations based on the chosen harmony rule, click a variation or a color in the active color group, then click the Set Base Color to Current Color button. You can also choose a different rule.

4. To recolor an object, select it, click the Fill or Stroke square on the Color panel, then click a color variation swatch, or drag a swatch over any selected or unselected object.**C**

The color group and variations on the Color Guide panel are transitory. They change as soon as you reset the base color, choose a different harmony rule, or click a swatch on the Swatches panel. Thankfully, you can save either the active color group or selected variations as a color group to the Swatches panel.

To add colors from the Color Guide panel to the Swatches panel:

1. On the Color Guide panel, do either of the following:

   To save the active color group, deselect any selected variations by clicking the blank area.

   Cmd-click/Ctrl-click the desired color variations.

2. Click the **Save Color Group to Swatch Panel** button. The new group appears on the Swatches panel.

   ➤ To save just a single variation instead of a whole color group, drag that variation from the Color Guide panel to the Swatches panel.

A *When you choose a harmony rule from the menu on the Color Guide panel, the base color stays the same, but the color group changes to abide by the new rule.*

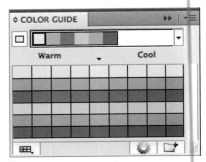

B *A new color group and variations appear on the panel, based on the new harmony rule.*

C *We dragged some new color variations onto objects in this artwork.*

Using the Kuler panel

Kuler (pronounced "cooler") is a free, Web-hosted Adobe application that lets users create and upload color groups, called color themes. By using the Kuler panel in Illustrator, you can access and browse through those themes. And with a click of a button, you can add a selected theme to the Swatches panel for the current document. An Internet connection is required.

To access color themes via the Kuler panel:

1. Open a document in Illustrator.

2. Display the Kuler panel by choosing Window > Extensions > **Kuler**.

3. Do either of the following:

   In the search field at the top of the panel, enter a theme name (or an exact keyword tag or creator name, if you happen to know it), then press Return/Enter to run the search.**A**

   ➤ You can sort of free-associate when entering a theme (e.g., "sunset," "Paris," "Monet," "wine," "grapes"). If you get few or no results, the criterion you've entered is probably too narrow. For example, "Navajo rug" yielded only one color theme for us, but "Navajo" yielded many.

   Choose a theme category from the first menu and a time criterion from the second menu.

4. To view more results based on the same search criterion, click the **View Next Set of Themes** button ⬇ at the bottom of the panel, if available.

5. To add a Kuler color group to your Swatches panel in Illustrator, click the group on the Kuler panel, then click the **Add Selected Theme to Swatches** button ⊞ at the bottom of the panel.

➤ To save your search criteria for quick future access, choose Custom from the first menu on the Kuler panel. In the dialog, enter the criteria to be saved, then click Save. To run a search based on your saved criteria, choose the search name from the same menu.

➤ To view more information about a selected color theme on the Kuler website, click the arrowhead for that theme ▶ and choose View Online in Kuler. If an alert about the Flash Player appears, follow the instructions to install the player.

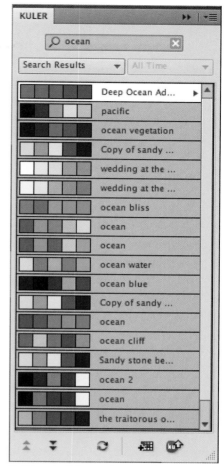

A *Using the Kuler panel, you can browse through color themes online and add select themes to the Swatches panel in Illustrator.*

➤ To learn more about Kuler, visit http://kuler. adobe.com. You can generate themes from photographs, upload your favorite themes to make them available to other users, etc.

➤ To refresh the panel with the latest Kuler themes, click the Refresh the Themes from the Kuler Community button ↻ at the bottom of the panel.

Replacing colors in your artwork

Via the Select Similar Options menu on the Control panel, you can quickly select multiple objects that have an attribute in common, such as the same fill color, then apply a replacement color to all the selected objects.

To replace a color, stroke attribute, or opacity setting throughout a document:

1. Select an object that contains a spot color(s), nonglobal process color(s), stroke weight, or other attribute that you want to change, and which is also in use in other objects.

2. From the **Select Similar Options** menu 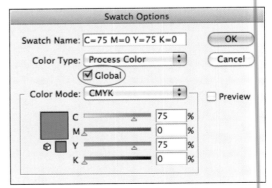 on the Control panel, choose an option, such as Fill Color, Stroke Color, or Fill & Stroke Color.

3. To change any attributes, such as those chosen in the prior step, do any of the following:

   Click the Fill or Stroke square on the Tools or Color panel, then click a different swatch on the Swatches or Color Guide panel or in an open swatch library panel, or mix a new color on the Color panel. Tint percentages for spot colors will remain the same.

   Choose a new stroke weight or other stroke attributes on the Stroke or Appearance panel.

   Change the Opacity percentage on the Control or Appearance panel.

4. Deselect (Cmd-Shift-A/Ctrl-Shift-A).

A global process color swatch is one for which Global is checked in the Swatch Options dialog. When you edit the values of a global process color swatch, the color updates automatically in all the objects that contain it — whether those objects are selected or not.

To change a process color from nonglobal to global:

1. Double-click a nonglobal process color swatch on the Swatches panel. Global process color swatches have a white corner and no dot; nonglobal process colors are plain (no corner, no dot).

2. The Swatch Options dialog opens. A Check **Global**, then click OK.

   ➤ To make a global swatch nonglobal, uncheck Glogal in the Swatch Options dialog.

To edit the values of a global process color:

1. Double-click a global process color swatch on the Swatches panel.

2. In the Swatch Options dialog, check Preview, edit the color by moving the sliders, then click OK. Existing tint percentages are preserved.

To replace a global process color that's being used in multiple objects, instead of recoloring one object at a time, you simply replace the current color swatch with a new one, and the replacement color appears in all the objects (even if they're not selected). Existing tint percentages are preserved.

To replace a global process color swatch:

1. Deselect all objects.

2. Do one of the following:

   From the Swatch Libraries menu 🗔. on the Swatches panel, choose a library name. Click a color on the library panel, then Option-drag/Alt-drag it over the global process color swatch on the Swatches panel that you want to replace.

   Click the Fill or Stroke square on the Color panel, then mix a new color using the Color panel (or double-click either square and mix a color via the Color Picker); or click a color on the Color Guide panel. Option-drag/Alt-drag the Fill or Stroke square over the global process color swatch on the Swatches panel that you want to replace.

   On the Swatches panel, Option-drag/Alt-drag one global color swatch over another.

   ➤ If you Option-drag/Alt-drag a nonglobal process color swatch over a global process swatch, the resulting swatch will be a global process color.

A *Double-click a swatch to open the Swatch Options dialog, then check or uncheck the Global option.*

Inverting colors

The Invert Colors command on the Edit menu converts multiple nonglobal process colors in selected objects to their opposite values on the color scale. The command doesn't convert spot colors, global process colors, gradients, or patterns.

To invert multiple nonglobal process colors:

1. Select one or more objects (or an imported image).**A**

2. Choose Edit > Edit Colors > **Invert Colors**.**B**

A *This is the original placed image.*

B *We applied the Invert Colors command.*

Colorizing grayscale images

To colorize a grayscale image:

1. Open or place a grayscale EPS, JPEG, PCX, PDF, PSD, or TIFF image into an Illustrator document.**C** To learn about the File > Open and File > Place commands, see Chapter 22.

   Note: You can't colorize a linked EPS image, but you can colorize an embedded EPS image. (To embed an image, uncheck the Link option in the Place dialog.)

2. Click the grayscale image that you have imported into Illustrator.

3. Click the Fill square on the Color panel, then apply a color via the Color, Swatches, or Color Guide panel, or via the Color Picker.**D** Gray areas will be recolored; white background areas will remain opaque white.

➤ Another option is to convert an imported, embedded image to grayscale via Edit > Edit Colors > Convert to Grayscale, then colorize it by following steps 2–3, above.

C *We placed this grayscale Photoshop image into an Illustrator document.*

D *We colorized the image by clicking a solid brown color on the Swatches panel.*

Blending fill colors

To blend fill colors between objects:

1. Select three or more objects that contain fill colors, or isolate a group.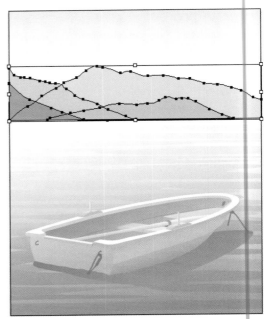 None of the objects should have a fill of None. The more objects you use, the more gradual the blend will be.

   Note: The two objects that are either farthest apart or frontmost and backmost can contain different nonglobal colors or different tints of the same global process or spot color. The objects may not contain patterns, gradients, different global process colors, or different spot colors. And they can't be type objects.

2. From the Edit > **Edit Colors** submenu, choose one of the following commands:

   Blend Front to Back to use the fill colors of the frontmost and backmost objects as the starting and ending colors in the blend. This works irrespective of the *x/y* location of the objects in the artwork.**B**

   Blend Horizontally to use the fill colors of the leftmost and rightmost objects as the starting and ending colors in the blend.

   Blend Vertically to use the fill colors of the topmost and bottommost objects as the starting and ending colors in the blend.

   Selected objects that are stacked between the frontmost and backmost objects or between the two outermost objects will be assigned intermediate blend colors. The original stroke colors and weights will remain the same, and the objects will remain on their respective layers.

A *A group is put in isolation mode.*

B *The Blend Front to Back command is applied.*

Creating and editing fill patterns

When creating a pattern, as an optional step you can use a rectangle to control the amount of white space around the pattern or to crop away parts of objects that you want to exclude from the pattern.

To define a pattern:

1. *Optional:* To define an area for the pattern, choose the Rectangle tool ▭ (M), then drag a rectangle. To help prevent a printing error, make it no larger than an inch (6 picas) square. Apply a fill and stroke of None to the rectangle if you don't want it to be an element in the pattern, or apply a fill color to it if you do. On the Layers panel, click in the edit (second) column for the rectangle object to lock it; the padlock icon 🔒 appears.

2. Draw an object or objects of any kind to be used for the pattern. For example, you could create geometric objects with the Rectangle, Ellipse, Polygon, Spiral, or Star tool. The objects can contain brush strokes. To copy an object along an axis, Option-Shift-drag/Alt-Shift-drag it with the Selection tool. To position the objects precisely, you can use Smart Guides (see pages 100–101) or the Align buttons (see pages 105–106). Note: Complex attributes in a pattern, such as gradients, could cause a printing error.

3. Deselect. If you drew a rectangle (step 1, above), unlock it by clicking its edit icon on the Layers panel.

4. With the Selection tool ▶ (V), marquee all the objects for the pattern. **A**

5. Do either of the following:

   Choose Edit > **Define Pattern**.

   Drag the selection onto the Swatches panel, deselect the objects, then double-click the new swatch.

6. The New Swatch or Swatch Options dialog opens. Type a Swatch Name, then click OK. The new pattern appears on the Swatches panel. **B**

7. The new pattern can be applied as a fill or stroke to any object. **C**

➤ To transform (e.g., scale) a pattern fill without transforming the object, see page 139.

➤ Creating a symmetrical pattern takes patience and skill. To learn more, enter "create seamless geometric patterns" in the search field in Adobe Help.

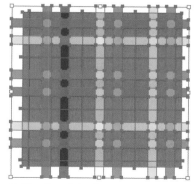

A *We selected the objects for a pattern, then chose the Define Pattern command.*

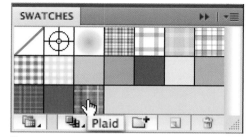

B *The pattern swatch appeared on the Swatches panel.*

C *We used the pattern to fill a type object.*

You can edit any pattern, including any predefined Illustrator pattern.

To edit a pattern:

1. Drag a pattern swatch from the Swatches panel or from a pattern swatch library panel onto a blank area of the artboard.

2. With the Selection tool ▶ (V), double-click the group to isolate it, then modify the pattern objects.**A** To select individual anchor points or segments, use the Direct Selection tool ▶ (A). Click the isolation mode bar to exit that mode.

3. With the Selection tool ▶ (V), Option-drag/ Alt-drag the group onto the original pattern swatch.**B** The pattern will update in any objects in which it's being used.**C**

➤ To save an edited pattern as a new swatch, drag the selection onto the Swatches panel without holding down Option/Alt. Double-click the new swatch to rename it.

➤ To reposition a pattern fill or stroke in an object without moving the object, hold down ~ (tilde) and drag inside it with the Selection tool.

➤ To expand a pattern fill into separate objects, select an object that contains the pattern, choose Object > Expand, check Fill, then click OK. The former fill pattern will be divided into the original shapes that the pattern tile was created from, nested as groups below a clipping mask (labeled as <Clipping Path> on the Layers panel). Each nested group may also contain its own clipping path. You can reshape the mask, delete it, or release it (select it via the Layers panel, then choose Object > Clipping Mask > Release).

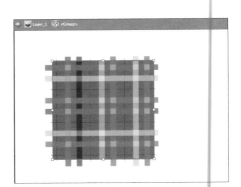

A We dragged the pattern to be edited from the Swatches panel to the artboard, double-clicked the group to isolate it, then changed the color of the background rectangle to gray.

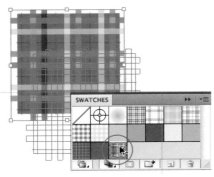

B We exited isolation mode, selected all the objects, then with Option/Alt held down, dragged them over the original swatch.

C The edited pattern updated in the type object in which it was being used.

Illustrator provides several ways to rotate, scale, reflect, distort, shear, or apply perspective to an object. These methods include manipulating the object's bounding box and using the multipurpose Free Transform tool, the individual transformation tools, the Transform panel, the Control panel, the Transform Each command, and the Transform effect.

Transforming an object via its bounding box

One of the simplest ways to transform an object is via its bounding box. Note that this method doesn't allow you to move the reference point or make copies.

To transform an object via its bounding box:

1. With the Selection tool, select one or more objects, or double-click an object or group to isolate it. If the bounding box feature is off, press Cmd-Shift-B/ Ctrl-Shift-B (View > Show Bounding Box).

2. Do either or both of the following:

   Drag a corner handle to **scale** the object along two axes, or drag a midpoint handle to scale it along one axis, or Shift-drag to scale it proportionally, or Option-drag/Alt-drag to scale it from its center, **A–B** or Option-Shift-drag/Alt-Shift-drag to scale it proportionally from its center. Note: If you isolate a group, click an object in the group to display its bounding box.

   To **rotate** the object, move the pointer slightly outside a corner handle (the pointer will be a curved double arrow), then drag in a circular direction.

A *Option-drag/Alt-drag an object or group to scale it from its center.*

B *The group is enlarged.*

TRANSFORM

11

Using the Free Transform tool

The multipurpose Free Transform tool lets you rotate, scale, reflect, distort, shear, or apply perspective to an object. However, unlike the other transformation tools, this tool doesn't let you move the reference point or make copies.

To use the Free Transform tool:

1. With the Selection tool, select one or more objects, or double-click a nongrouped object to isolate it. A

2. *Optional:* Copy the object, if you want to transform a copy of it instead of the original.

3. Choose the **Free Transform tool** (E).

4. Do any of the following:

   To **scale** the object(s), do one of the following: Drag a corner handle to scale the object along two axes, drag a midpoint handle to scale it along one axis; Shift-drag to scale it proportionally; Option-drag/Alt-drag to scale it from its center; or Option-Shift-drag/Alt-Shift-drag a corner handle to scale it proportionally from its center.

   To **rotate** the object, position the pointer outside it, then drag in a circular direction; Shift-drag to rotate the object in increments of 45°.

   To **shear** the object, start dragging a midpoint handle, then hold down Cmd/Ctrl and continue to drag. B To constrain the shearing to the horizontal or vertical axis, drag a midpoint handle, then hold down Cmd-Shift/Ctrl-Shift and continue to drag. To shear the object from its center, start dragging a midpoint handle, then hold down Cmd-Option/Ctrl-Alt and continue to drag.

   To **reflect** the object, drag a midpoint handle all the way across it. To reflect the object from its center, Option-drag/Alt-drag a midpoint handle.

   To **distort** any kind of object except editable type, start dragging a corner handle, then hold down Cmd/Ctrl and continue to drag. C

   To apply **perspective** to any kind of object except editable type, start dragging a corner handle, then hold down Cmd-Option-Shift/Ctrl-Alt-Shift and continue to drag. D

A *This is the original object.*

B *We sheared the object.*

C *Then we distorted the object.*

D *Finally, we applied a perspective transformation.*

As we showed you on pages 100–101, Smart Guides can be helpful when aligning objects or points to one another. In these instructions, Smart Guides are used while an object is transformed.

To transform objects with the help of Smart Guides:

1. Go to Preferences (Cmd-K/Ctrl-K) > Smart Guides, make sure Transform Tools and Measurement Labels are checked, then click OK.

2. Make sure View > **Smart Guides** is on (Cmd-U/Ctrl-U).

3. Select the object(s) or group to be transformed, or isolate an object.

4. Choose the **Free Transform** tool ▦ (E).

5. As you drag to transform the object, Smart Guides will appear onscreen temporarily.**A–C** Move the pointer along a Smart Guide to apply the transformation on that axis. The angle of rotation or other transformation data will display in the measurement label.

➤ You can also use Smart Guides with the Rotate ↻ (R), Reflect ⊠ (O), Scale ▨ (S), or Shear tool.⤵ Those tools are discussed on the next two pages.

➤ In Preferences > Smart Guides, you can choose a different set of Construction Guides angles for Smart Guides or enter custom angles.

CHOOSING PREFERENCES FOR TRANSFORMATIONS

When performing transformations, there are three options in Illustrator/Edit > Preferences (Cmd-K/Ctrl-K) > General you should know about:

➤ When transforming objects, the default horizontal angle is 0° and the default vertical angle is 90°. The default starting point for measuring the degree of an angle is the horizontal *(x)* axis (the three o'clock position). To create a new default setting, enter a custom Constrain Angle.

➤ If Transform Pattern Tiles is checked when you transform an object that contains a pattern fill or stroke, the pattern will also transform.* Note: If you subsequently fill the object with a different pattern, the current transform values will apply to the replacement pattern. If you want to restore the default values to a pattern, apply a solid color, then reapply the pattern.

➤ Via the Scale Strokes & Effects check box, you can control whether an object's stroke and effects also scale when an object is scaled.*

This option can also be turned on or off via the Transform panel menu.

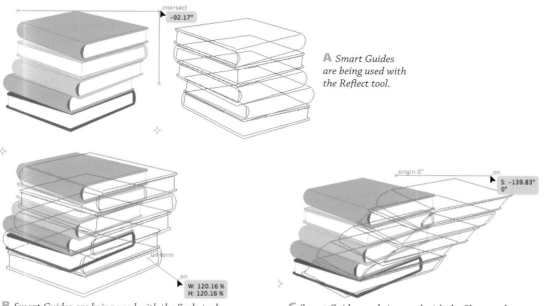

A *Smart Guides are being used with the Reflect tool.*

B *Smart Guides are being used with the Scale tool.*

C *Smart Guides are being used with the Shear tool.*

Using the Scale, Rotate, Shear, and Reflect tools

To transform an object by using the Scale, Rotate, Shear, or Reflect tool:

1. With the Selection tool, select one or more objects, or double-click an object or group to isolate it. If you isolate a group, click an object in the group to display its bounding box.

2. When using one of the transform tools that you will choose next, you can either let the object transform from its center (the default behavior) or set a custom reference point for Ilustrator to transform the object from by clicking near the object (the pointer will turn into an arrowhead). In either case, before dragging, position the mouse (button up) far away from the center or reference point, for better control.**A–B** (And don't forget to use those handy Smart Guides!)

Do any of the following:

Choose the **Scale** tool 🔲 (S), then drag away from or toward the object.

Choose the **Rotate** tool ⟲ (R), then drag around the object.

Choose the **Shear** tool, 🔲 then drag away from the object.**C–D**

Choose the **Reflect** tool 🔲 (O), click to establish a reference point, then click or drag to define the axis of reflection (or to reflect the

A *We clicked to establish a reference point with the Rotate tool, repositioned the mouse, and are dragging in a circular direction.*

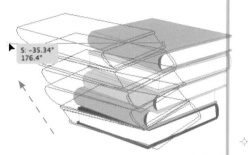

B *We clicked to establish a reference point with the Shear tool, repositioned the mouse, and are dragging diagonally to the left.*

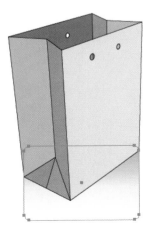

C *We selected the shadow object...*

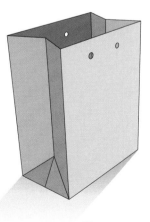

D *...then sheared it along the horizontal axis.*

object along the nearest 45° angle, Shift-click or Shift-drag).**A–B**

Some additional options:

To transform a copy of the object, start dragging, then hold down Option/Alt and continue to drag (release Option/Alt last).

To transform the object at an increment of 45° or to scale it proportionally, or to constrain a shear to the horizontal or vertical axis, start dragging, then hold down Shift and continue to drag (release Shift last).**C**

To transform a copy of the object along an increment of 45° or to copy and scale it proportionally, start dragging, then hold down Option-Shift/Alt-Shift and continue to drag.

To flip and scale the object simultaneously, drag completely across it with the Scale tool.

➤ To transform a pattern but not the object when using the Rotate, Reflect, Scale, or Shear tool, drag with ~ (tilde) held down.

➤ To reset an object's reference point to the default location, choose the Selection tool, deselect, then reselect the object.

> **APPLYING TRANSFORMATIONS VIA A DIALOG**
>
> ➤ To apply a transformation via a dialog, select one or more objects or a group, then right-click the selection and choose Transform > Rotate, Reflect, Scale, or Shear from the context menu. In the dialog that opens, check Preview. If you want to transform a copy of the selected object(s), after choosing values, click Copy instead of OK to exit the dialog.
>
> ➤ To transform an object from a user-defined reference point instead of the center, with the Rotate ○ (R), Reflect 🖽 (O), Scale 🖾 (S), or Shear tool 🖎, Option-click/Alt-click on or near the object. The dialog opens.
>
> ➤ If an object's fill or stroke contains a pattern and you want the pattern to transform along with the object, check both Objects and Patterns in the transform dialog; or to scale the pattern but not the object, uncheck Objects. These options are also available on the Transform panel menu.

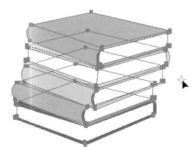

A *We clicked to establish a reference point with the Reflect tool...*

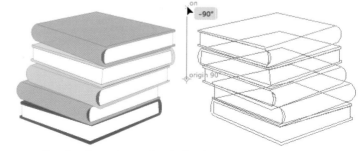

B *...then dragged upward with Shift held down.*

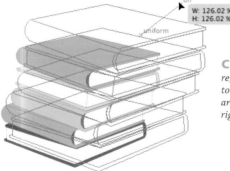

C *We clicked to establish a reference point with the Scale tool, repositioned the mouse, and are dragging toward the upper right with Shift held down.*

Using the Transform and Control panels

Use the Transform panel to move, scale, rotate, or shear an object by an exact amount or percentage.

To move, scale, rotate, or shear an object using the Transform panel:

1. With the Selection tool, select one or more objects, or double-click an object or group to isolate it. If you isolate a group, click an object in the group to display its bounding box.

2. Do either of the following:

   Show the Transform panel.

   To open a temporary Transform panel, click the blue X, Y, W, or H link on the Control panel. Or if your application frame or window is too narrow for those letters to display, click Transform.

3. To control which part of the object the X and Y values are calculated from, click a handle on the reference point locator on the left side of the panel.**A** (The other values will be calculated relative to the object's bounding box.)

4. If the object contains a pattern, from the Transform panel menu, choose **Transform Object Only**, **Transform Pattern Only**, or **Transform Both**.

5. If you're going to scale the object, check or uncheck **Scale Strokes & Effects** on the panel menu to control whether the object's stroke and any applied effects will also scale (this option can also be turned on or off in Illustrator/Edit > Preferences > General).

6. As you enter or choose values, use one of the shortcuts in the sidebar (at right) to apply them:

   To move the object horizontally, change the **X** value. Increase the value to move the object to the right, or lower it to move the object to the left.

   To move the object vertically, change the **Y** value. Increase the value to move the object downward, or lower it to move the object upward. ★

   To scale the object, enter percentage or absolute **W** (width) and/or **H** (height) values. To scale the object proportionally, either click the Constrain Width and Height Proportions button 🔗 first (a bracket displays next to it) or if the button is off, press Cmd-Return/Ctrl-Enter after entering the value.

SHORTCUTS FOR APPLYING TRANSFORM PANEL VALUES

Apply the value and exit the panel	Return/Enter
Apply the value and select the next field	Tab
Apply the value and reselect the same field	Shift-Return/ Shift-Enter
Apply the value, exit the panel, and clone the object	Option-Return/ Alt-Enter
Highlight the next field and clone the object (Mac OS only)	Option-Tab

A *Reference point locator*

Width and height of selected object

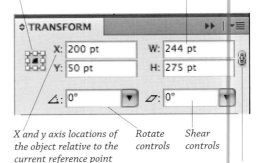

X and y axis locations of the object relative to the current reference point

Rotate controls

Shear controls

Constrain Width and Height Proportions (here the button is in its off state)

Enter or choose a positive **Rotate** value to rotate the object counterclockwise, or a negative value to rotate it clockwise.

To shear (slant) the object to the right, enter or choose a positive **Shear** value; or to shear to the left, enter or choose a negative Shear value.

7. From the panel menu, you can choose the **Flip Horizontal** or **Flip Vertical** command.

➤ To apply a transformation as an editable and removable effect, see page 145.

➤ With Use Preview Bounds checked in Illustrator/ Edit > Preferences > General (the default setting), the W and H values on the Transform, Control, and Info panels are calculated based on the full dimensions of an object, including the weight and width of its stroke and any applied effects. With this option off, the dimensions of the basic path are listed instead.

➤ To learn about the Align New Objects to Pixel Grid option on the Transform panel menu, see page 82.

Note: If your application frame is too narrow to display the X, Y, W, and H controls on the Control panel and it can't be widened, follow the steps on the preceding page instead of the ones below.

To move or scale an object using the Control panel:

1. Select an object or group, or isolate an object.

2. On the Control panel, **A** do either or both of the following:

   To move the object, choose or enter new **X** (horizontal) and/or **Y** (vertical) values.

   To scale the object, choose or enter **W** (width) and/or **H** (height) values. To scale the object proportionally, click the Constrain Width and Height Proportions button 🔗 first.

➤ You can click in a field on this (or any other) panel and press the up or down arrow on the keyboard to change the value incrementally.

LETTING ILLUSTRATOR DO THE MATH

In the W, H, X, or Y field on the Transform or Control panel, you can let Illustrator perform simple math (see below). When entering values, you can use any of these units of measure: p, pt, ", in, mm, cm, q, or px. To apply a new value, press Tab or Return/Enter.

➤ To perform addition, to the right of the current number and unit, enter a plus sign, then a number (as in "+2"). For example, to move an object horizontally to the right, you would enter a plus sign after the current X value and unit, followed by the amount you want it to move. To perform subtraction, enter a minus sign (as in "–2") instead of a plus sign.

➤ To multiply the current value, after the current value and unit, type an asterisk (*), then a number. For example, to reduce an object's scale by half, click to the right of the current value and unit, then type "*.5" (e.g., 4p would become 2p). For division, enter / instead of an asterisk.

➤ To multiply a value by a percentage, select the current value and unit, then enter a number and the percent symbol (%). To reduce the width or height to three-quarters of its current value, for example, enter "75%" (e.g., 4p would become 3p).

Here the Constrain Width and Height Proportions button is in its "on" state.

A *Reposition an object or group by changing the X and/or Y values on the Control panel, or scale it by changing the W and/or H values.*

Using the Transform Each command

The transformation tools transform multiple objects relative to a single, common reference point, whereas the Transform Each command transforms objects relative to their individual center points.**A** If you want your artwork to look less regular and more hand-drawn, apply this command to multiple objects with the Random option checked.

To perform multiple transformations via the Transform Each command:

1. Select one or more objects (preferably two or more). If you're going to check the Random option in step 4, make sure the objects aren't in a group.

2. Right-click one of the objects and choose Transform > **Transform Each** (Cmd-Option-Shift-D/Ctrl-Alt-Shift-D).

3. Check Preview, and move the dialog out of the way, if necessary.

4. Do any of the following **B**:

   Click a different **reference** point 🔳 (the point from which the transformations will be calculated).

   Move the **Scale: Horizontal** or **Vertical** slider (or enter a percentage, then press Tab) to scale the objects horizontally or vertically from their individual reference points.

   Increase the **Move: Horizontal** value to move the objects to the right, or decrease it to move them to the left; increase the **Vertical** value to move the objects downward, or decrease it to move the objects upward. ★

   Enter a **Rotate: Angle** value and then press Tab, or move the dial.

   Check **Reflect X** or **Reflect Y** to flip the objects.

   Check **Random** to let Illustrator apply random transformation values within the range that you have chosen for Scale, Move, or Rotate. For example, at a Rotate Angle of 35°, a different angle between 0° and 35° will be used for each selected object. Keep unchecking and rechecking Preview to get different random effects.

5. Click OK or click Copy.

This is the original arrangement of objects.

With the Rotate tool, we rotated all the objects 15°.

Here the objects were rotated 15° via the Transform Each command, with the Random option unchecked.

A *Our results from using the Rotate tool are compared with those from the Transform Each command.*

Transform Each		
Scale		OK
Horizontal:	126 %	Cancel
Vertical:	64 %	Copy
Move		
Horizontal:	30 pt	☐ Reflect X
Vertical:	0 pt	☐ Reflect Y
		🔳
Rotate		☐ Random
Angle:	0 °	☑ Preview

B *The Transform Each dialog lets you Scale, Move, Rotate, or Reflect an object according to random or fixed values.*

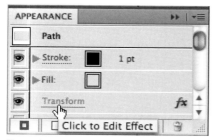

A *Use the Transform Effect dialog to apply editable transformations.*

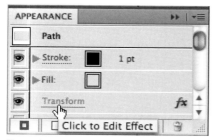

B *To edit a Transform effect, click the Transform listing on the Appearance panel.*

Using the Transform effect

When applied via the Transform Effect dialog, your transformation settings can be modified long after you close the dialog, and even after you close and reopen your document.

To use the Transform effect:

1. Select one or more objects.

2. From the Add New Effect menu *fx.* on the Appearance panel ● or from the Effect menu on the Illustrator menu bar, choose Distort & Transform > **Transform**.

3. The Transform Effect dialog looks and functions like the Transform Each dialog, with two exceptions: In the Transform Effect dialog, you can specify a number of **Copies**, and when the **Random** box is checked, the same random value for each option (Scale, Move, and Rotate) is applied to every selected object.**A** With these exceptions in mind, follow step 4 on the preceding page, then click OK to exit the dialog.

4. To edit the transformation at any time, select the object, then reopen the Transform Effect dialog by clicking Transform on the Appearance panel.**B** To learn more about appearances in Illustrator, see Chapter 14.

Repeating a transformation

By using the Transform Again command, you can quickly repeat the last transformation (using the last-used values) on any selected object. If the last object was cloned as it was transformed, Transform Again will produce another transformed copy.

To repeat a transformation:

1. Transform an object or group.**A**

2. Keep the object selected, or select another object or group.

3. Press Cmd-D/Ctrl-D or right-click the object or group and choose Transform > **Transform Again.B–C**

A *To create a sunburst, our first step was to rotate and copy a triangle at a 24° angle via the Rotate dialog.*

B *Next, we applied the Transform Again command 13 times, by pressing Cmd-D/Ctrl-D.*

C *Three curved objects are positioned in front of the sunburst.*

▶ *To clip the outer edges in this illustration, we drew a rectangle to encompass all the objects, selected all the objects, then pressed Cmd-7/Ctrl-7 to create a clipping mask (see Chapter 26).*

In Chapters 6 and 7 you learned how to draw paths without needing to think about their individual components. In this important chapter, you'll learn how to reshape a path's contour by manipulating the nuts and bolts that all paths are composed of: direction handles, anchor points, and segments. Once you learn how to change the position, number, or type (smooth or corner) of anchor points on a path, you'll be able to create just about any shape imaginable.

Other techniques covered in this chapter include learning how to quickly reshape all or part of a path with the Pencil, Paintbrush, Blob Brush, Path Eraser, Eraser, and Reshape tools; change the profile and width of a stroke; align anchor points; join endpoints; reshape objects via an Effect command; combine paths; and split and cut paths. This chapter also includes three practice exercises.

The building blocks of a path

In Illustrator, all paths are composed of straight and/or curved segments that are connected by anchor points. A path can be open, with two endpoints, or closed, with no endpoints. Smooth anchor points have a pair of direction handles that move in tandem, whereas corner anchor points have no direction handles, one direction handle, or a pair of direction handles that move independently.**A** By dragging the end of a direction handle, you can change the shape of the curve it's connected to. The angle of a direction handle controls the slope of the curve that leads into the anchor point; the length of a direction handle controls the height of the curve.

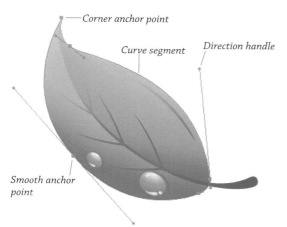

Corner anchor point

Curve segment *Direction handle*

Smooth anchor point

A *You can manipulate the basic components of a path manually by dragging, or by using a tool or command.*

RESHAPE

12

IN THIS CHAPTER

Moving points and segments

If you move an anchor point, the segments that are connected to it reshape, lengthen, or shorten accordingly. If you move a straight segment, the anchor points it's connected to move with it, whereas if you move a curve segment, the curve reshapes but the connecting anchor points remain stationary.

Note: For the instructions in this chapter, make sure Highlight Anchors on Mouse Over is checked in Illustrator/Edit > Preferences > Selection & Anchor Display. And while that dialog is open, you can also choose preferences for the display of anchor points and handles (see page 380).

To move an anchor point or a segment:

1. Choose the **Direct Selection** tool (A), and click a blank area of the document to deselect.

2. Move the pointer over the edge of an object, and do any of the following: Drag an anchor point (it will enlarge when the pointer is over it);**A** drag the middle of a segment;**B** or click an anchor point or segment, then press an arrow key. For the first two methods, you can use the Alignment Guides feature of Smart Guides for positioning.

➤ Shift-drag a point or segment to constrain the movement to a multiple of 45°.

➤ You can move more than one point at a time, even if they're on different paths. To select them first, Shift-click them individually or drag a marquee around them.

Reshaping curves

In the instructions above, you learned that you can drag an anchor point or a curve segment to reshape a curve. Another — and more precise — way to reshape a curve is to lengthen, shorten, or change the angle of the direction handles on a curve point.

To reshape a curve segment:

1. Choose the **Direct Selection** tool (A).

2. Click an anchor point or a curve segment.**C**

3. Do either of the following:

   Drag the end of a direction handle toward or away from the anchor point.**D**

   Rotate the end of a direction handle around the anchor point. You can use Shift to constrain the angle of the handle, or position the handle using the Alignment Guides feature of Smart Guides.

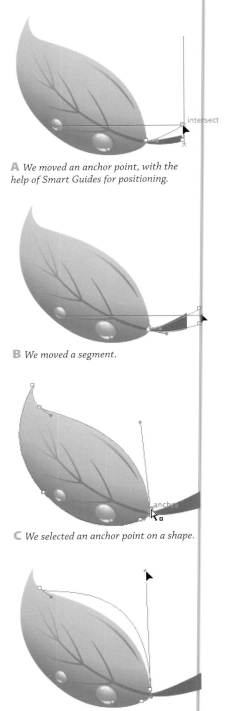

A *We moved an anchor point, with the help of Smart Guides for positioning.*

B *We moved a segment.*

C *We selected an anchor point on a shape.*

D *We dragged the end of a direction handle away from the anchor point, to reshape the curve.*

Converting points

Corner anchor points either have no direction handles, or they have direction handles that move independently of each other. The pair of direction handles on a smooth point always stays in a straight line and rotates in tandem (although they can be different lengths). With a click of a button, you can convert any corner point to a smooth point.

To convert a corner anchor point to a smooth anchor point:

1. In Illustrator/Edit > Preferences > Selection & Anchor Display, make sure **Highlight Anchors on Mouse Over** is checked. Click OK.

2. Choose the **Direct Selection** tool ▸ (A), and deselect.

3. Pass the pointer over a corner anchor point on a path, and when a point becomes highlighted (enlarged), click to select it.**A**

4. On the Control panel, click the **Convert Selected Anchor Points to Smooth** button.**▛ B–C** Direction handles will appear on the selected point, and the segments that are connected to it will become curved.

5. *Optional:* To reshape the curve, with the Direct Selection tool, drag either of the direction handles.**D**

➤ You can also convert a corner point to a smooth point by using the Convert Anchor Point tool (Shift-C). Move the pointer over a corner point, and when it becomes highlighted, drag away from it. Direction handles will appear as you drag.

➤ See also pages 283–284.

➤ To round the corners on a selected path by way of an editable and removable effect, use the Effect > (Illustrator Effects) Stylize > Round Corners command.**E–F** Once you have applied the effect, you can click the effect listing on the Appearance panel to reopen the Round Corners dialog at any time, and change the Radius value. See page 194. (To straighten out the rounded corners, delete the effect listing from the Appearance panel.)

See also pages 283–284. ... See page 194.

CREATING A TEAROFF TOOLBAR

To practice the techniques in this chapter, we recommend tearing off the toolbar for the Pen tool so the Pen and its cohorts are visible and easily accessible. (Later, once you memorize the shortcuts for accessing these tools, you won't need to display the toolbar.)

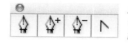

Display the tearoff toolbar for the Pen tools.

A *To convert a corner point to a smooth one, click it with the Direct Selection tool...*

B *...then click the Convert Selected Anchor Points to Smooth button on the Control panel.*

C *Direction handles appear for the selected anchor point.*

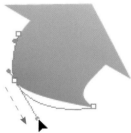

D *You can drag either direction handle to modify the curve.*

E *This original object has some sharp corners.*

F *The Effect > Stylize > Round Corners command rounded off the corners.*

To convert a smooth anchor point to a corner anchor point:

1. Choose the **Direct Selection** tool ⬚ (A), and deselect.

2. Pass the pointer over a smooth anchor point on a path, and when it becomes highlighted, click it. **A**

3. On the Control panel, click the **Convert Selected Anchor Points to Corner** button. **B** The direction handles will disappear from the anchor point.

➤ You can also convert a smooth point to a corner point by clicking it with the Convert Anchor Point tool ⬚ (Shift-C).

A *Click a smooth anchor point, then click the Convert Selected Anchor Points to Corner button on the Control panel.*

B *The smooth point is converted to a corner point.*

In these instructions, you will convert direction handles that stay in a straight line into handles that can be rotated independently of each other.

To rotate direction handles independently:

1. Choose the **Direct Selection** tool ⬚ (A).

2. Deselect, click the edge of an object to display its anchor points, then click a smooth point. **C**

3. Choose the **Convert Anchor Point** tool ⬚ (Shift-C).

4. Drag one of the direction handles on the point. The curve segment it is connected to will reshape as you drag. **D**

5. Choose the **Direct Selection** tool again (A), click the anchor point, then drag the other direction handle for the same anchor point. **E**

➤ To restore a corner point with direction handles that rotate independently to a smooth point, follow the instructions on the preceding page.

➤ When the Pen tool ⬚ (P) is selected, you can hold down Option/Alt to turn it into a temporary Convert Anchor Point tool.

➤ To select all the direction handles on one or more selected objects, from the Select > Object submenu, choose Direction Handles.

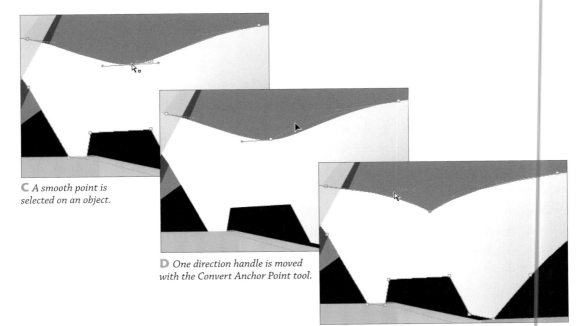

C *A smooth point is selected on an object.*

D *One direction handle is moved with the Convert Anchor Point tool.*

E *Then the second direction handle is moved.*

Adding points

Another way to reshape a path is by adding anchor points to it manually.

To add anchor points to a path manually:

1. Choose the **Selection** tool ▶ (V), then select or isolate an object.

2. Do either of the following:

   Choose the **Add Anchor Point** tool ⬙⁺ (+).

   Choose the **Pen** tool ⬙ (P), and make sure **Disable Auto Add/Delete** is unchecked in Illustrator/ Edit > Preferences > General (yes, it's a confusing double negative).

3. Click the edge of the object. A new, selected anchor point appears.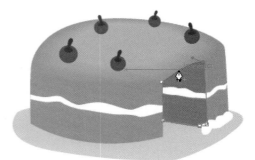 Repeat to add more points to the path, if desired.

   ➤ To locate the edge of a path, make sure Anchor/Path Labels is checked in Illustrator/ Edit > Preferences > Smart Guides, and turn on the Smart Guides feature (Cmd-U/Ctrl-U). As you move the pointer over the edge of an object, the word "path" or "anchor" will appear.

   Logically, an anchor point that you add to a curve segment will be a smooth point with direction handles, whereas an anchor point that you add to a straight segment will be a corner point with no direction handles.

4. *Optional:* With the Direct Selection tool (A), move the new anchor point.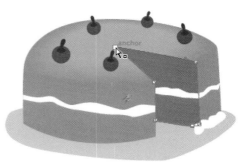 If it's a smooth point, you can also lengthen or rotate its direction handles.

   ➤ If you don't click precisely on a segment with the Add Anchor Point tool, an alert dialog may appear. Click OK, then try again.

   ➤ Hold down Option/Alt to turn the Add Anchor Point tool into a temporary Delete Anchor Point tool, or vice versa.

A *We clicked a segment to add a new point.*

B *We moved the new point.*

GETTING A GOOD CURVE

By paying attention to the placement of points, you can produce smoother curves. When reshaping paths (and while drawing them, as you will in Chapter 21), place points at the ends of a curve instead of at the middle.

It's hard to draw a symmetrical curve if you place a point at the high point.

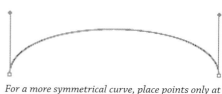

For a more symmetrical curve, place points only at the ends instead.

The Add Anchor Points command inserts one point between each pair of existing anchor points in a selected object.

To add anchor points to a path via a command:

1. Choose the Selection tool ➤ (V), then select the object(s) to which points are to be added.

2. Choose Object > Path > **Add Anchor Points.A–C** If desired, repeat to add yet more points.

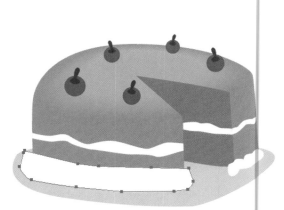

A *We added a simple long, round-ended object to this illustration.*

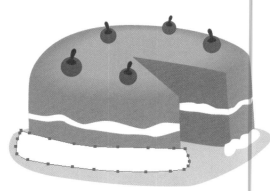

B *We applied the Add Anchor Points command to the object.*

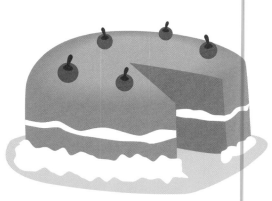

C *We applied Effect > Distort & Transform > Roughen to alter the shape. Because points were added to the path, we were able to keep the Roughen settings low, which produced less overall distortion.*

SELECTING TOOLS FOR RESHAPING PATHS

Pen tool	P
Add Anchor Point tool	+
Delete Anchor Point tool	–
Convert Anchor Point tool	Shift-C
Pencil tool	N
Paintbrush tool	B
Scissors tool	C
Lasso tool	Q
Disable the Auto Add/Delete function of the Pen tool	Shift
When the Pen tool is selected, access the last-used selection tool	Cmd/Ctrl
Convert the Add Anchor Point tool to the Delete Anchor Point tool, or vice versa	Option/Alt

You can add segments to a path with the Pencil tool, regardless of which tool the path was drawn with, and whether or not the path has an applied brush stroke. If a path does have a brush stroke, another way to add to it is by using the Paintbrush tool.

To add to an open path with the Pencil or Paintbrush tool:

1. Choose the Selection tool ▶ (V), then select or isolate an open path.

2. Double-click the **Pencil** tool ✎ (N) to open the options dialog for that tool. Or if the path has a brush stroke, you can double-click the **Paintbrush** tool ✎ instead.

3. In the tool preferences dialog, make sure **Edit Selected Paths** is checked, then click OK.

4. Position the pointer directly over the path, then draw an addition to the path. **A–B**

➤ If you end up with a new, separate path instead of an addition to an existing path, delete the new one. On your next try, make sure the pointer is directly over the path before you begin drawing. Or when using the Paintbrush tool, verify that the path you're adding a segment to has a brush stroke.

To add to an open path with the Pen tool:

1. Choose the **Pen** tool ✎ (P).

2. Position the pointer over the endpoint of an open path (the path doesn't have to be selected). A slash appears next to the Pen pointer when the tool is positioned correctly. **C**

3. Click the endpoint to make it a corner point, or drag from it to make it a smooth point. The point will become selected. **D**

4. Position the pointer where you want the next anchor point to appear, then click or drag.

5. If desired, continue to click to create more corner points or drag to create more smooth points. **E** Switch to another tool when you're done adding to the path.

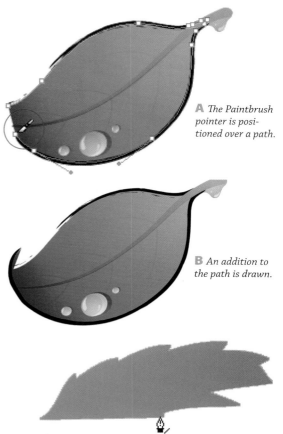

A *The Paintbrush pointer is positioned over a path.*

B *An addition to the path is drawn.*

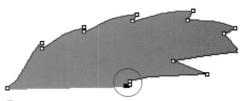

C *The pointer is positioned over an endpoint (note the slash next to the Pen icon).*

D *After the endpoint is clicked, it becomes solid.*

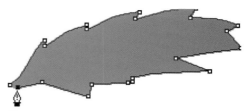

E *More points are then added to the same path.*

Deleting points

When you delete points from a closed path, it remains closed.

To delete anchor points from a path:

Method 1 (Pen tool)

1. Do either of the following:

   Choose the **Delete Anchor Point** tool ✒ (-).

   Choose the **Pen** tool ✒ (P), and make sure Disable Auto Add/Delete is unchecked in Illustrator/Edit > Preferences > General.

2. Cmd-click/Ctrl-click the edge of the object from which you want to delete anchor points.

3. Click an anchor point (don't press Delete!). **A** The point will be deleted. **B** Repeat to delete other anchor points, if desired.

➤ If you don't click precisely on an anchor point with the Delete Anchor Point tool, an alert dialog will appear. Click OK and try again.

Method 2 (Control panel)

1. Choose the **Direct Selection** tool ➤ (A).

2. Deselect, click the edge of an object to display its anchor points, then click a point (or Shift-click multiple points).

3. On the Control panel, click the **Anchors: Remove Selected Anchor Points** button. 🔧

A *We clicked an anchor point with the Delete Anchor Point tool (we could have used the Pen tool instead).*

B *We deleted the point.*

GETTING INTO ISOLATION MODE

The more we use isolation mode, the more we like it. You can switch to the Selection tool quickly by pressing V, then double-click an object or group to isolate it.

Reshaping objects with the Pencil or Paintbrush tool

With the Pencil and Paintbrush tools, you can reshape a path by dragging along its edge.

To reshape a path with the Pencil or Paintbrush tool:

1. Do either of the following:

    To reshape a path that doesn't have an applied brush stroke, choose the **Pencil** tool ✐ (N).

    To reshape a path that does have a brush stroke, choose the **Pencil** tool ✐ (N) or the **Paintbrush** tool ✐ (B).

2. Cmd-click/Ctrl-click a path to select it.

3. Position the pointer directly over the edge of the path, then drag along it. **A** The path will reshape instantly. **B**

    Note: Be sure to position the pointer precisely on the edge of the path when you begin and finish dragging. If you don't, you will create a new path instead of reshaping the existing one.

➤ Caps Lock reverses the current Use Precise Cursors setting in Illustrator/Edit > Preferences > General. That is, it turns a tool icon pointer into crosshairs, or vice versa.

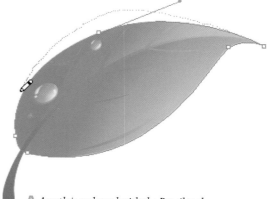

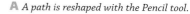

A *A path is reshaped with the Pencil tool.*

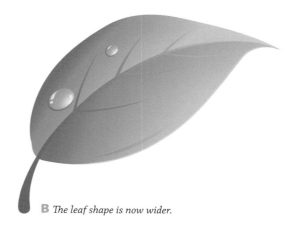

B *The leaf shape is now wider.*

Applying a variable width profile preset to an object's stroke

Using the new Profile options, you can quickly apply a preset nonuniform width to an object's stroke, to make it look more hand drawn.

To apply a variable width profile preset to an object's stroke: ★

1. Select or isolate a path. Apply a stroke color to it, and choose a Weight of at least 6 pt.**A**

2. Do either of the following:

   Display the Stroke panel.≡ If the full options aren't showing, click the arrowheads on the panel tab to make them appear. From the **Profile** menu at the bottom of the panel, choose a profile.**B–C**

   Choose a profile from the **Variable Width Profile** menu on the Control panel.

3. *Optional:* To flip the width profile along the path, on the Stroke panel, click the Flip Along button.◁ **D** (The change will be noticeable if you apply a profile in which the starting and ending widths are different, such as in Width Profile 2, Width Profile 4, or Width Profile 5.)

4. To restore the default stroke profile at any time, select or isolate the object, then choose **Uniform** from either of the menus listed in step 2 above.

➤ If an object that you have selected or targeted has a variable width profile, an asterisk will display next to the stroke weight value on the Appearance panel.

A *The stroke widths in the original artwork are uniform and boring.*

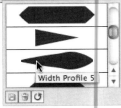

B *We are choosing Width Profile 5 from the Profile menu on the Stroke panel.*

C *The variable width profile gives the linework pizzazz. Vrrooom!*

D *We clicked the Flip Along button to flip the starting and ending thicknesses of the current stroke profile (Width Profile 5).*

Changing an object's stroke width using the Width tool

Using the new Width tool, you can change the width profile of an object's stroke manually.

To reshape an object's stroke using the Width tool: ★

1. Select or isolate a path, and apply a stroke color to it. (It can have an art or pattern brush applied to it, but not another type of brush.)

2. Choose the **Width** tool ✎ (Shift-W).

3. Move the pointer over a segment of a closed or open path, or over the endpoint of an open path. Click to make a width point (hollow diamond) appear and then, with the mouse button still down, drag outward from the path to lengthen the handles or inward to shorten them, **A–B** or Option-drag/Alt-drag one of the handles to change its length independently of its mate. **C**

4. *Optional:* You can drag any width point along the path to a new location (or Shift-drag a point to move the other width points along with it); duplicate a point by holding Option/Alt and dragging it; or delete a point by clicking it, then pressing Delete/Backspace.

➤ If any points on a stroke have handles of uneven lengths, you can click the Flip Across button ⧖ to flip the wider part of the stroke width to the other side of the stroke.

➤ To move specific multiple width points with the Width tool, Shift-click those points, release Shift, then drag. To deselect a selected width point, press Esc.

To adjust the stroke width by entering values:

1. Follow steps 1 and 2 above. Create width points or choose a width profile preset.

2. Double-click the path or an existing width point to open the Width Point Edit dialog. **D**

3. Click the Adjust Widths Proportionately icon,▣ if desired, to lengthen or shorten both handles simultaneously, then change the **Side 1** and/or **Side 2** values for the length of one or both handles; or enter a **Total Width** value for the combined length of both handles. For a more gradual change in width, allow handles on neighboring width points to adjust along with the selected one by checking **Adjust Adjoining Width Points**. Click OK.

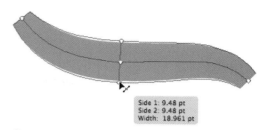

Side 1: 9.48 pt
Side 2: 9.48 pt
Width: 18.961 pt

A *To widen this path symmetrically, we dragged outward from it using the Width tool.*

Side 1: 13.537 pt
Side 2: 13.537 pt
Width: 27.073 pt

B *To flare the end of the stroke, we dragged from an endpoint outward using the Width tool.*

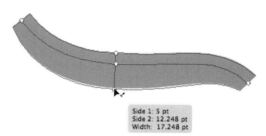

Side 1: 5 pt
Side 2: 12.248 pt
Width: 17.248 pt

C *Here we are holding down Option/Alt while dragging a handle to move it independently of its mate.*

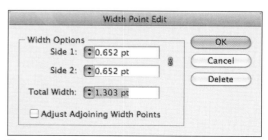

D *To move both handles outward, we are entering one Total Width value in the Width Point Edit dialog.*

On the preceding page you produced continuous width points using the Width tool. Here you will use discontinuous points to produce more abrupt changes in the width of the stroke.

To create a discontinuous width point:

1. Follow one of the tasks on the preceding two pages to make the stroke width on a path nonuniform, using three or more width points.

2. Select the **Width** tool, then click an existing width point on the path or create a new one. For the sake of this exercise, drag outward from the path to make the stroke fairly wide. **A**

3. Drag an adjacent width point **B** on top of the one that you just lengthened the handles of. **C** It is now a discontinuous width point. **D–E**

4. The discontinuous width point has two pairs of handles. To adjust the length of either pair, position the Width tool on the edge of the narrower or wider part of the stroke to locate a handle, then drag inward or outward from the path.

➤ You can double-click a discontinuous point with the Width tool to open the Width Point Edit dialog (**A**, next page), then enter specific values to adjust the length of each pair of handles. If you want to remove a pair of handles, check Single Width Only.

➤ To convert a discontinuous width point into a continuous one, drag it along the path, using the Width tool.

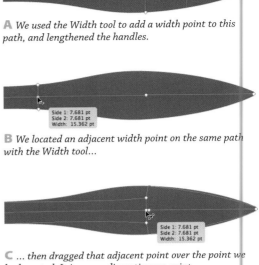

A *We used the Width tool to add a width point to this path, and lengthened the handles.*

B *We located an adjacent width point on the same path with the Width tool…*

C *… then dragged that adjacent point over the point we had created. It is now a discontinuous point.*

D *The result is an abrupt change in the stroke width.*

E *To add the stylized water objects below the boat, we made the width points on the royal blue stroke discontinuous, saved our custom width profile as a preset, then applied the new preset to two other paths. (We also clicked the Flip Along option for the profile on the middle path to change its orientation.)*

Width Point Edit		
Width Options		
Side 1: ▲▼ 8.248 pt	Side 1: ▲▼ 19.611 pt	OK
Side 2: ▲▼ 9.319 pt	Side 2: ▲▼ 41.943 pt	Cancel
Total Width: ▲▼ 17.568 pt	Total Width: ▲▼ 61.555 pt	Delete
☐ Single Width Only	☐ Single Width Only	

A *Double-click a discontinuous width point to open the Width Point Edit dialog, and edit the values for either or both pairs of handles.*

If you come up with a custom profile preset that you like, you can save it for future use.

To create a width profile preset: ★

1. Use the **Width** tool 🖌 to alter the stroke width of a path, and keep the path selected. **B**

2. At the bottom of the **Profile** preset picker (which you can access either from the Stroke panel or from the Variable Width Profile menu on the Control panel), click the **Add to Profiles** button. 🖫 **C** Enter a name for the profile in the dialog, then click OK.

3. The new profile will appear at the bottom of the picker and menu, and is available for all documents. **D**

➤ You can restore all the default profiles to the Profile preset picker by clicking the Reset Profiles button ↻ on the picker or menu, but be aware that when you click OK in the alert dialog, **E** any custom profiles on the picker and menu will be discarded. *Ouch!*

B *We created a custom stroke width on the blue path, and kept the path selected.*

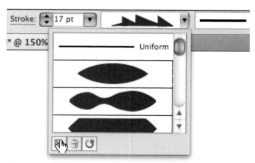

C *On the Variable Width Profile menu, we are clicking the Add to Profiles button.*

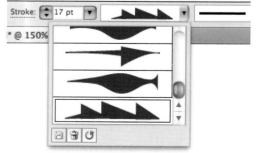

D *Our custom profile appears on the Variable Width Profile menu.*

Adobe Illustrator	
Replace current width profiles with default profiles?	
⚠ Ai	Replacing the current width profiles with default set of profiles will not preserve any custom profiles.
	Cancel　　OK

E *If you click the Reset Profiles button, this alert dialog will display.*

Reshaping objects with the Blob Brush tool

In addition to being a great tool for producing "magic marker" type drawings, as we showed you on page 87, you can drag with the Blob Brush tool to reshape or smooth the edges of existing closed paths. It can be used on any object that has a stroke of None: an ordinary path, a compound path, a masked object within a clipping mask, or on the start or end object of a live blend.

To reshape an object with the Blob Brush tool:

1. Select or isolate an object that was created with any tool except a type or symbol tool, **A** and make sure it has a stroke color of None. ☑ It can contain a solid fill color or a pattern, but not a gradient or a graphic style.

2. Choose the **Blob Brush** tool ☑ (Shift-B).

3. To add to the object, draw strokes around or across it. Your strokes will merge with the closed path. **B** Note: If your strokes produce a hole within the shape, the result will be a compound path (to learn about compound paths, see pages 337–339).

   To smooth the edge of the object by eliminating anchor points, hold down Option/Alt to access the Smooth tool temporarily, then drag along an edge of the object.

➤ Press [or] to decrease or increase the diameter of the Blob Brush tool. To choose other options for the tool, see page 88.

The versatile Blob Brush tool can also be used to merge multiple objects, but in a unique way—you draw strokes across them.

To combine objects using the Blob Brush tool:

1. Arrange two or more closed path objects near or overlapping each other (no type objects), and select them. They must have the same solid fill color or pattern and a stroke of None, and they must be listed consecutively on the same layer (see page 181). They may not contain a gradient or graphic style.

2. With the **Blob Brush** tool, ☑ draw strokes across the objects. Note: If your strokes produce a hole within the shape, the result will be a compound path.

A *To add shading to the cup, we created a basic polygon shape to use as a starting point, and kept it selected.*

B *We used the Blob Brush tool to reshape the object, to make it fit better on the side of the cup.*

EXERCISE: Draw and reshape objects in a freehand style

To master the art of drawing shapes by hand, you can use the Blob Brush tool to draw and reshape an object, **A–B** then erase any unwanted parts of it with the Eraser tool. **C** Finally, you can use the Smooth tool to smooth out any rough edges. **D** By using this great trio of tools, you can reshape a path without having to fiddle with those nasty anchor points or direction handles.

A *We double-clicked the Blob Brush tool, checked Merge Only with Selection, then clicked OK. To create foam on the top of a glass, we drew some shapes with the Blob Brush tool.*

B *We selected each new shape and used the Blob Brush tool to fill them in. We also enlarged the tan shape to create "drips."*

C *We used the Eraser tool to clean up the edges of the drip shapes.*

D *Finally, we used the Smooth tool to smooth some of the rough edges.*

Using the Reshape tool

The Reshape tool does a nice job of reshaping a path gently without distorting its shape. Give it a try and see if you like it. Note: Unfortunately, Smart Guides don't work with this tool.

To use the Reshape tool:

1. Choose the **Direct Selection** tool (A), deselect all, then click the edge of a path. Only one point or segment should be selected.

2. Choose the **Reshape** tool (it's on the same fly-out menu as the Scale tool).

3. Do one of the following:

   Drag any visible **anchor point** on the path. A tiny square border will display around the point when you release the mouse.

   Drag any **segment** of the path. A new square border point is created.

   Shift-click or marquee **multiple anchor points** on the path (a square will display around each one), then drag one of the square points. The selected portion of the path will maintain its overall contour as it elongates or contracts, and the rest of the path will stay put.

EXERCISE: Draw a brush with the Reshape tool

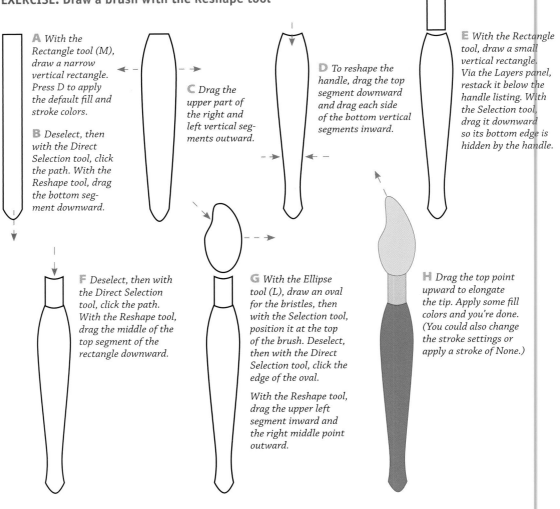

A *With the Rectangle tool (M), draw a narrow vertical rectangle. Press D to apply the default fill and stroke colors.*

B *Deselect, then with the Direct Selection tool, click the path. With the Reshape tool, drag the bottom segment downward.*

C *Drag the upper part of the right and left vertical segments outward.*

D *To reshape the handle, drag the top segment downward and drag each side of the bottom vertical segments inward.*

E *With the Rectangle tool, draw a small vertical rectangle. Via the Layers panel, restack it below the handle listing. With the Selection tool, drag it downward so its bottom edge is hidden by the handle.*

F *Deselect, then with the Direct Selection tool, click the path. With the Reshape tool, drag the middle of the top segment of the rectangle downward.*

G *With the Ellipse tool (L), draw an oval for the bristles, then with the Selection tool, position it at the top of the brush. Deselect, then with the Direct Selection tool, click the edge of the oval.*

With the Reshape tool, drag the upper left segment inward and the right middle point outward.

H *Drag the top point upward to elongate the tip. Apply some fill colors and you're done. (You could also change the stroke settings or apply a stroke of None.)*

Erasing sections of objects

The Eraser tool removes parts of objects that it passes over. The remaining parts of the objects are reconnected automatically to form closed paths.

To erase parts of objects:

1. If you want to limit the effect of the Eraser tool to specific objects (perhaps if there are many objects close together in your artwork, and you want to erase only some of them), select those objects first or put an object into isolation mode. Otherwise, deselect all.**A**

   Note: The object can be a Live Paint object or a compound path, it can be in a clipping mask, and it may contain gradients or patterns. The Eraser tool doesn't work on symbol instances, type objects, objects in a blend, or objects in a distortion envelope.

2. Choose the **Eraser** tool ✐ (Shift-E).

3. Do either of the following:

   Drag across parts of objects to be erased.**B–C** Hold down Shift while dragging to draw straight strokes at an increment of 45°.

   Option-drag/Alt-drag to create a marquee. Any parts of the artwork that fall within the rectangular marquee will be erased completely.

   ➤ Press [or] to decrease or increase the diameter of the Eraser tool. Double-click the tool icon to choose options for the tool shape.

   ➤ If you drag with the Eraser tool on the inside of an object — without crossing over the edge — a compound path will be produced.

A We drew this mountain range with the Pencil tool.

B With the Eraser tool, we erased sections of the object to create details in the mountains and lake.

USING THE PATH ERASER TOOL

To erase parts of a path without having to click points, choose the Path Eraser tool ✐ (the last tool on the Pencil tool fly-out menu). Select a path, then drag the eraser of the pencil pointer along the path.

C With a smaller diameter chosen for the Eraser tool, we made additional erasures. Finally, we placed two colored rectangles behind the mountain layer.

Aligning points

The Align buttons on the Control panel precisely realign selected endpoints or anchor points along the horizontal and/or vertical axis, and as a result, the paths those points belong to are reshaped.

To align points:

1. Choose the **Lasso** tool 🖑 (Q).

2. Drag to select two or more endpoints or anchor points **A** on the same path or on different paths.

3. On the Control panel, do any of the following:

   To align the points by moving them along the horizontal (*x*) axis, click one of the three **Horizontal Align** buttons.

   To align the points by moving them along the vertical (*y*) axis, click one of the three **Vertical Align** buttons.

   To overlap the points along both the horizontal and vertical axes, click a **Horizontal Align** button, then click a **Vertical Align** button. Use this method if you're planning to join the points into one point (see "To join two endpoints into one point" on the facing page).

   If you click a Left, Right, Top,**B** or Bottom **C** Align button, points will align to the leftmost, rightmost, topmost, or bottommost selected point, respectively. If you click a Center Align button,**D** points will align to a location that is equidistant between the points.

➤ If you Shift-select points with the Direct Selection tool (instead of dragging a selection marquee) before clicking an align button, points will align with and move toward the last selected point (the key anchor point), regardless of which Horizontal or Vertical Align button you click.

➤ To align selected points via a command, right-click and choose Average (Cmd-Option-J/Ctrl-Alt-J), then click Axis: Horizontal, Vertical, or Both in the dialog (fewer options are offered here than on the Control panel).

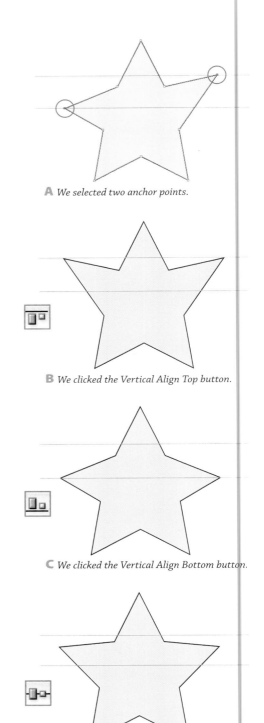

A *We selected two anchor points.*

B *We clicked the Vertical Align Top button.*

C *We clicked the Vertical Align Bottom button.*

D *We clicked the Vertical Align Center button.*

Joining endpoints

You can use the join controls in Illustrator to connect nonoverlapping endpoints with a new straight segment, or to join overlapping endpoints into one anchor point. Endpoints can be joined on the same open path (to close the path) or on separate open paths (to join them together). The method for joining endpoints into one point has been simplified. You don't have to average the endpoints first, and no dialog opens. Yippee!

To connect two endpoints with a segment: ★

1. Do either of the following:

   With the Direct Selection tool ▶ (A) or the Lasso tool 🔾 (Q), marquee two (or more) endpoints.**A**

   With the Selection tool ▶ (V) or the Layers panel, select one or more open paths. The objects can be in a group but they can't be compound paths, paths in a Live Paint group, or type objects.

2. Do one of the following: **B**

   Press Cmd-J/Ctrl-J (Object > Path > Join).

   Click the **Connect Selected End Points** button 🖉 on the Control panel.

   Right-click in the document and choose **Join**.

   Note: If you select multiple whole open paths with the Selection tool, the Join command will join the endpoints that are closest in proximity. The attributes from the topmost path will be applied to the newly combined object.

To join two endpoints into one point: ★

1. With the Direct Selection tool ▶ (A) or the Lasso tool 🔾 (Q), marquee two endpoints.

2. Do either of the following: **C**

   Press Cmd-Option-Shift-J/Ctrl-Alt-Shift-J.

   On the Control panel, click one of the three Horizontal Align buttons and one of the three Vertical Align buttons to position the two selected endpoints directly on top of each other, then do one of the following: Press Cmd-J/Ctrl-J, or click the **Connect Selected End Points** button 🖉 on the Control panel, or right-click in the document and choose **Join**.

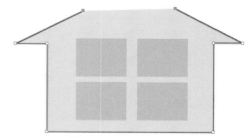

A *We selected two endpoints.*

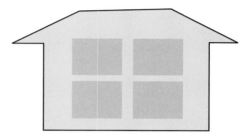

B *The Connect Selected End Points button created a straight segment between them.*

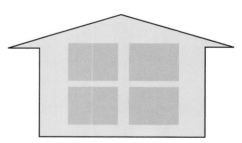

C *This is figure **A** after we clicked the Horizontal Align Center and Vertical Align Center buttons, then clicked the Connect Selected End Points button on the Control panel.*

Reshaping objects using commands

Some of the commands on the Effect menu can be used to explode simple shapes into more complex ones, with practically no effort on your part. For example, the Zig Zag effect, used in the steps below, adds anchor points to a path and then moves those points to produce waves or zigzags. Best of all, the Effect menu commands don't alter the actual path, so the results are both editable and removable. To explore effects more in depth, see Chapter 15.

To apply the Zig Zag effect:

1. Select an object. On the Appearance panel, click below the Opacity listing to make sure the Stroke and/or Fill listings are deselected.

2. From the **Add New Effect** menu *fx.* on the Appearance panel, choose Distort & Transform > **Zig Zag**.

3. The Zig Zag dialog opens.**A** Check Preview. Click Points: **Smooth** (at the bottom of the dialog) to create curvy waves, or **Corner** to create sharp-cornered zigzags.

4. Do either of the following:

   To move the added points by a percentage relative to the size of the object, click **Relative**, then move the Size slider.

   To move the added points by a specified distance, click **Absolute**, then choose or enter that distance via the **Size** slider or field.

5. Choose a number of **Ridges** per segment for the number of anchor points to be added between existing points. The greater the number of Ridges, the more complex the resulting object. If you enter a number, press Tab to preview its effect.

6. Click OK.**B–E**

➤ To edit the settings for the effect at any time, select the object, then click Zig Zag on the Appearance panel.

➤ To apply the Zig Zag effect to just an object's stroke, select the object, click the Stroke list-ing on the Appearance panel, then follow steps 2–6 above.**F–G** You could also try this with the Distort & Transform > Pucker & Bloat or Twist effect. To view the effect listing on the Appearance panel, click the expand arrowhead for the Stroke listing.

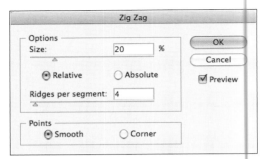

A *Choose settings for the Zig Zag effect.*

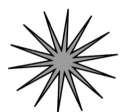

B *The original object is a star.*

C *The Zig Zag effect is applied (Size 20%, Relative, Ridges 4, Smooth).*

D *The original object is a circle.*

E *The Zig Zag effect is applied (Size 24%, Relative, Ridges 20, Corner).*

F *The original object is an ellipse.*

G *The Zig Zag effect is applied to just the object's stroke (Size 9%, Relative, Ridges 4, Smooth).*

If you use one of the "easy" tools to create objects, such as the Rectangle, Ellipse, Star, Blob Brush, Pencil, or Paintbrush, followed by any of the simpler reshaping techniques that are covered in this chapter, you will be able create artwork that looks complex without having to painstakingly draw it with the Pen tool. One of the easiest ways to create illustrations is to combine objects via a command on the Pathfinder panel. For example, to combine whole objects, rather than joining points one pair at a time, you can simply click the Unite button on the Pathfinder panel, as in the following steps.

To combine objects using a command:

1. Position two or more objects so they overlap one another at least partially. **A**

2. With any selection tool, marquee at least some portion of all the objects.

3. Display the Pathfinder panel. ▪

4. Click the **Unite** (first) button ▭ on the panel. Voilà! The individual objects are now combined into one closed object or compound path. It will automatically be given the attributes of the object that was originally on top. **B–F**

➤ To learn more about this panel, and also about the new Shape Builder tool, see Chapter 25.

➤ To learn about compound paths, see pages 337–339.

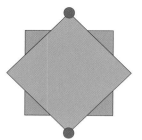

A *Arrange two or more objects so they overlap, then select them.*

B *We clicked the Unite button on the Pathfinder panel to combine the separate shapes into one compound shape.*

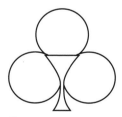

C *The original artwork consists of four objects.*

D *The Unite command is applied.*

E *The original artwork consists of four objects.*

F *The Unite command is applied (Macintosh to Granny Smith!).*

Slicing and dicing

The Scissors tool will open a closed path or split one open path into two. You can split a path either at an anchor point or in the middle of a segment.

To split a path with the Scissors tool:

1. Choose any selection tool, then click an object to display its points.

2. Choose the **Scissors** tool ✄ (C).

3. Click the object's path: If you click once on a closed path, it will turn into a single open path; if you click once on an open path, it will be split into two paths.

   If you click a segment, two new endpoints will appear, one on top of the other. If you click an anchor point, a new anchor point will appear on top of the existing one, and it will be selected.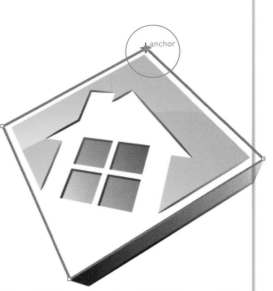**A**

4. To move the new endpoints apart, choose the **Direct Selection** tool ↘ (A), then either drag the selected endpoint away from its mate or press an arrow key.**B**

To split a path via the Control panel:

1. Choose the **Direct Selection** tool ↘ (A).

2. Click a path to display its anchor points, then click an anchor point to select it.

3. Click the **Cut Path at Selected Anchor Points** button ✁ on the Control panel. A new anchor point will appear on top of the existing one, and it will be selected.

4. To move the two new endpoints apart, drag the selected one.

A *We clicked an anchor point with the Scissors tool. You can click an anchor point or a segment.*

There is no segment, and therefore no stroke, between these two endpoints.

B *We moved the new endpoint on our newly opened path.*

The Divide Objects Below command uses an object like a cookie cutter to cut the objects below it, then deletes the cutting object.

To cut objects via the Divide Objects Below command:

1. Create or select an object that contains a solid-color fill and/or a stroke color, to be used as a cutting shape. It can't be a group or a Live Paint group.

   Optional: The Divide Objects Below command is going to delete the cutting object, so you may want to Option-drag/Alt-drag it to copy it first.

2. Place the cutting object on top of the object(s) to be cut.**A**

3. Make sure only the cutting object is selected.

4. Choose Object > Path > **Divide Objects Below**. The topmost shape (the cutting object) is deleted and the underlying objects are cut into separate paths where they met the edge of the cutting object.**B–C**

5. Deselect. You can use the Selection tool to select or isolate any of the objects, then recolor or move them. Any cut objects that were originally in a group will remain so.

➤ To prevent an object that is stacked below the cutting shape from being affected by the Divide Objects Below command, you can either lock it (see page 183) or hide it (see page 184).

A *The white leaf shape will be used as a cutting object (there are three objects below it).*

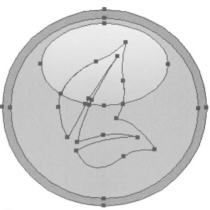

B *The Divide Objects Below command used the leaf shape to cut through the underlying objects.*

DIVIDE VERSUS DIVIDE OBJECTS BELOW

The Divide Objects Below command (this page) deletes the cutting object and leaves the resulting objects ungrouped, whereas the Divide button on the Pathfinder panel preserves the paint attributes of all the objects, including the topmost object, and puts the resulting paths in a group (see page 334). Divide usually produces smaller pieces than Divide Objects Below.

C *We applied different fill colors to the resulting divided paths.*

EXERCISE: Draw a glass of beer (or cream soda!)

1. With the Ellipse tool ◯ (L), draw a vertical oval that is approximately 3.5" wide by 5.5" high, and a smaller horizontal oval. With the Rectangle tool ▭ (M), draw a rectangle at the bottom of the vertical ellipse.

2. With the Selection tool, ▶ select all three shapes. Open the Art History > Impressionism library of swatches, then apply a pale blue-gray fill and a black stroke. **A** On the Pathfinder panel, click the Unite button. ▣

3. With the Delete Anchor Point tool ✎ (-), click to delete the points shown in **B**.

4. With the Direct Selection tool ▷ (A), drag a marquee to select the four bottom points of the stem. Click the Convert Selected Anchor Points to Smooth button ⌐ on the Control panel. To reshape the stem, move two points inward and two points outward individually: Click a point, then press an arrow key. **C** Adjust the bottom direction handles on the two lower points to reshape the bottom curve of the stem.

5. With the Ellipse tool, Option-drag/Alt-drag to create an oval the same width as the glass top, and fill it with a cream color. **D** With the Add Anchor Point tool ✎ (+), add five new points along the top of the oval. With the Direct Selection tool, select and drag each point separately, to make the oval look more like foam. **E**

6. Use the Selection tool (V) to select the glass shape. With the Scale tool ▨ (S), start dragging, then hold down Option/Alt and drag diagonally inward to create a slightly smaller copy. Apply a light tan fill color and a stroke of None. With the Delete Anchor Point tool (–), click the bottom two points on the scaled copy. With the Direct Selection tool, move the top two corner points on the scaled copy closer to the top corners of the original glass shape. **F**

7. Deselect. Double-click the Blob Brush tool. ✎ Set the Size to 40 pt, the Angle to 40°, and the Roundness to 22%; click OK. Click a darker tan fill color (and a Stroke of None), then drag vertically along the right edge of the glass to create shading. Double-click the tool again, change the Angle value to −40°, then click OK. Drag inside the left edge of the glass. **G**

8. With the Ellipse tool, draw an oval for the base of the glass, and apply the same colors as the glass. Via the Layers panel, restack it below the glass object.

9. Set the angle for the Blob Brush to 0. Create more areas of shading and highlights on the glass and stem. Cheers! **H**

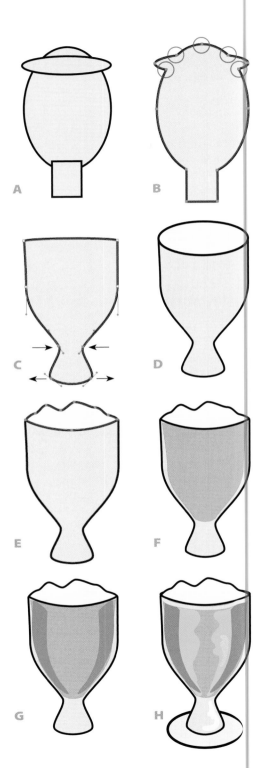

Until this point (unless you snuck ahead to this chapter!), you've been creating objects on a single, default layer that was created automatically when you created your document, and each new path was stacked above the last one automatically. In this chapter, you'll learn how to purposely change the stacking order of objects via the Layers panel.➭ A You will use the panel to create top-level layers and sublayers; delete layers and objects; select layer listings; select objects; restack, duplicate, lock, unlock, hide, and show layers; collect objects onto a new layer; release objects to layers; and finally, merge and flatten them.

Getting to know the Layers panel

With a document open, click the Layer 1 arrowhead on the Layers panel to expand the list of objects on that layer. Layer 1 is a top-level layer, meaning it isn't nested within another layer.

Continued on the following page

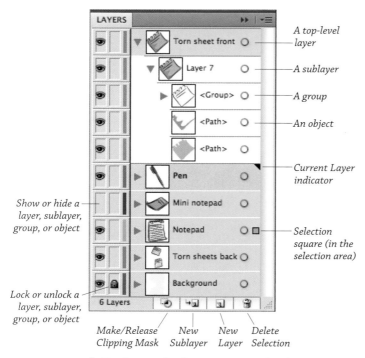

A top-level layer

A sublayer

A group

An object

Current Layer indicator

Show or hide a layer, sublayer, group, or object

Selection square (in the selection area)

Lock or unlock a layer, sublayer, group, or object

Make/Release Clipping Mask — New Sublayer — New Layer — Delete Selection

A *The objects in this document are nested within top-level layers and sublayers, at various stacking levels (the artwork is shown at the top of the page).*

You can add as many layers as you like to a document, depending on available system memory, and you can also create sublayers (nested layers) within any top-level layer. The actual objects that make up your artwork — paths, type, images, etc. — are nested within one or more top-level layers, or in groups or sublayers within top-level layers. The backmost layer in the document is listed last on the Layers panel.

When you create an object, it appears on the currently selected layer, but it can be moved to a different layer at any time, either individually or by restacking the whole layer or sublayer it resides in. The stacking order of objects in a document is unaffected by the number and the arrangement of artboards.

The Layers panel also has other important functions beyond enabling you to restack objects. You can use it to select, target (for appearance changes), show or hide, and lock or unlock any layer, sublayer, group, or individual object.

By default, each new vector object you create is listed as <Path> on the Layers panel, each placed raster image or rasterized object is listed as <Image> or by the name of the image file, each individual symbol instance is listed by the symbol name, each symbol set is listed as a generic <Symbol Set>, and each type object is listed by the first few characters in the object. Similarly, object groups are listed by such names as Live Paint Group, Compound Path, etc.

You may say "Whoa!" when you first see the number of listings on the Layers panel. Once you become accustomed to working with it, though, you may come to appreciate how much easier it makes even the simplest of tasks, such as selecting and locking objects.

Different Layers panel options can be chosen for each document.

To choose Layers panel options:

1. Choose **Panel Options** from the Layers panel menu. The Layers Panel Options dialog opens.**A**

2. Keep **Show Layers Only** unchecked; otherwise the panel will list only top-level layers and sublayers, not individual objects.

3. For the size of the layer and object thumbnails, click a **Row Size** of Small (12 pixels), Medium (20 pixels), or Large (32 pixels), or click Other and enter a custom size (12–100 pixels).**B**

> **ONE CATCHALL NAME**
>
> In this book, we often refer to the elements of an Illustrator document (paths, type, raster images, etc.) generically as objects, but when necessary, we identify specific kinds of objects (e.g., "symbol instances" or "clipping masks").

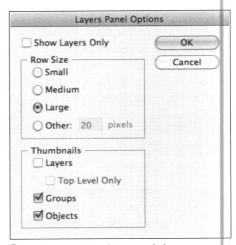

A *Via the Layers Panel Options dialog, you can customize the Layers panel for each file.*

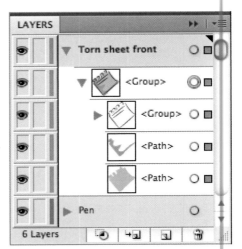
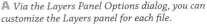

B *For this Layers panel, we chose the Large Row Size and turned Thumbnails off for Layers.*

4. Check which **Thumbnails** you want the panel to display: Layers, Groups, or Objects. If you check Top Level Only for layers, thumbnails will display for top-level layers but not for sublayers.

5. Click OK.

Creating layers

In these instructions, you'll learn how to create the granddaddy of layers — top-level layers.

To create a new top-level layer:

Method 1 (without choosing options)

1. On the Layers panel,● click the listing for a top-level layer. The new layer is going to appear above this layer.

2. Click the **New Layer** button ▨ at the bottom of the panel. To the new layer, Illustrator will assign the next available number in the sequence and the next available color, as listed on the Color menu in the Layer Options dialog.

Method 2 (choosing options)

1. On the Layers panel, click the listing for a top-level layer. The new layer is going to appear above the one you click.

2. Option-click/Alt-click the **New Layer** button.▨ **A** The Layer Options dialog opens.

3. Do any of the following:

   Change the layer **Name**.

   Via the **Color** menu, choose a highlight color for selections on the layer and for its listing on the Layers panel. Colors are assigned to new top-level layers based on their order on this menu.

   ➤ If the fill or stroke colors of objects on the layer are similar to the selection border color, consider choosing a different selection color, for contrast.

   Choose other layer options (see the sidebar on page 183).

4. Click OK.**B**

➤ Objects always reside in a top-level layer or sublayer (or in a group within either of the above) — they can't float around unassigned to any layer.

➤ To create a new top-level layer in the topmost position on the panel, regardless of which layer listing is currently selected, Cmd-click/Ctrl-click the New Layer button on the Layers panel. (Or if

Continued on the following page

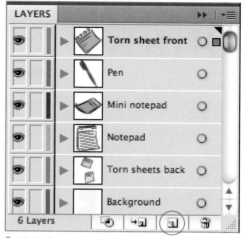

A *Click a layer, then Option-click/Alt-click the New Layer button. When the Layer Options dialog opens, choose options for, or rename, the new layer.*

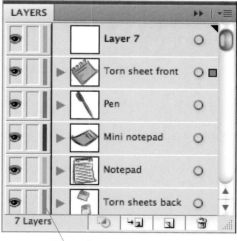

Layer color

B *The new layer (Layer 7) appears above the "Torn sheet front" layer, which was previously selected.*

ADDING LAYERS BELOW EXISTING ONES ★

If your document is in Draw Behind mode ▨ (Tools panel) when you create a new layer, the new layer will appear directly below the currently active one.

your document is in Draw Behind mode, 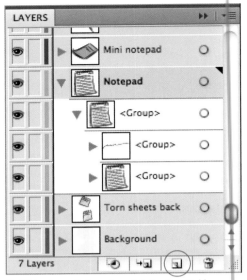 the same shortcut will create a new top-level layer at the bottom of the stack.)

➤ To rename any listing on the Layers panel, double-click it to open the options dialog, then enter a new name.

➤ Layers and sublayers are numbered in the order in which they're created, regardless of their position in the stacking order or their indent level.

Once you become accustomed to adding and using top-level layers, you'll be ready to add another tier to the hierarchy: sublayers. Every sublayer is nested within (indented within) either a top-level layer or another sublayer. If you create a new object or group of objects when a sublayer is selected, the new object or group will be nested within that sublayer. You don't necessarily have to create or use sublayers, but you may find they help you keep the panel organized, especially if your documents are complex.

By default, every sublayer has the same generic name: "Layer," but as with layers, you can rename them so they will be easier to identify (e.g., "green logo" or "inner petals" or "tyrannosaurus").

To create a sublayer:

1. On the Layers panel ◉ click the top-level layer (or sublayer) in which the new sublayer is to appear.

2. Do either of the following:

To create a new sublayer without choosing options for it, click the **New Sublayer** button. A–B

To choose options as you create a new sublayer, Option-click/Alt-click the **New Sublayer** button. In the Layer Options dialog, enter a Name, check or uncheck any of the options (see the sidebar on page 183), then click OK.

A *Click a layer listing, then click the New Sublayer button.*

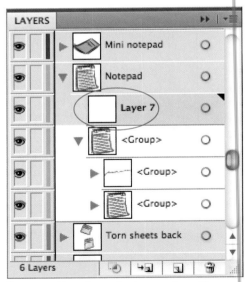

B *A new sublayer listing (in this case, Layer 7) appears within our "Notepad" layer.*

Deleting layers and objects

You know how to make 'em. Now you need to learn how to get rid of 'em.

Beware! When you delete a top-level layer or sublayer, all the objects that were on that layer are removed from the document.

To delete a layer, sublayer, group, or object:

1. On the Layers panel, click the layer, sublayer, group, or object to be deleted, or Cmd-click/Ctrl-click multiple listings. All the selected listings must be in the same sublayer, layer, or group. Also, you may click multiple listings at the same indent level (e.g., all top-level layers), but not listings from different indent levels (e.g., not ungrouped objects plus objects in a group).

2. Do either of the following:

   Click the **Delete Selection** button at the bottom of the Layers panel. **A–C** If you are deleting a layer or sublayer that contains objects, an alert dialog will appear; click Yes to proceed.

   To bypass the prompt, drag the highlighted layers or objects over the Delete Selection button.

   ➤ To retrieve a deleted layer and the objects it contained, use the Undo command immediately.

A *This is the original artwork.*

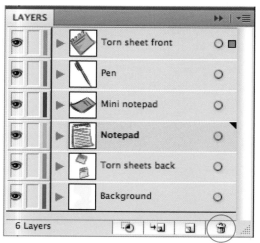

B *We highlighted the "Notepad" layer, then clicked the Delete Selection button.*

C *This is the artwork after we deleted the "Notepad" layer.*

Selecting listings on the Layers panel

If you want to control the stacking level at which a new object will appear in a document, before drawing the object, in addition to being aware of whether any objects are selected, you need to click a top-level layer, sublayer, group, or object listing on the Layers panel. The same holds true for objects that you paste, drag and drop, or place into a document.

If you select an object, the listing for its top-level layer or sublayer becomes selected automatically on the Layers panel, but the converse isn't true: Simply clicking a top-level layer or sublayer listing won't cause objects to become selected in the document window. Think of selecting layer listings (which is discussed on this page and the next) as a layer management technique, and of selecting the objects themselves (making their anchor points, and possibly their bounding box, appear) or targeting objects for appearance changes, as an essential first step in the process of editing.

Note: To learn how to select objects via the Layers panel, see pages 178–180. To learn how to target them for appearance changes, see the sidebar on page 178 and Chapter 14.

If your document is in Draw Normal mode 🖉 (Tools panel) and you create a new object (or place, paste, or drag and drop an object into your document), you will get different results depending on what you select first on the Layers panel: ★

➤ If you click a top-level layer or group listing first (but not a sublayer in that layer), the new object will be listed at the top of that top-level layer.

➤ If you click a sublayer listing first (and no objects are selected), the new object will appear within that sublayer.

➤ If you select an object first, the new object will appear at the top of the same layer or sublayer as the selected object, but outside any group on that layer or sublayer.

To select a layer, sublayer, group, or object listing on the Layers panel:

Click the name of a top-level layer, sublayer, group, or object, or click the area just to the right of the name — not the circle or the selection area at the far right side of the panel. The Current Layer indicator (black triangle) **A** moves to the layer that the item you clicked resides in.

> **USING DRAW BEHIND MODE ★**
>
> If your document is in Draw Behind mode 🖉 (Tools panel), the following will occur:
>
> ➤ If an object is selected when you create a new object, the new object will appear behind (and be listed below) the selected object on the current layer.
>
> ➤ If no objects are selected when you create a new object, the new object will appear behind (and be listed below) all the artwork on the current layer.
>
> Press Shift-D to cycle through the available drawing modes. To learn about Draw Inside mode, see page 343.

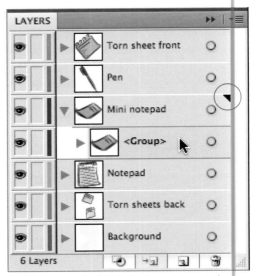

A When a group is clicked, the Current Layer indicator moves to the top-level layer that the group resides in.

If multiple layer listings (layers, sublayers, groups, or objects) are selected, you can restack them on the panel simultaneously or apply the same layer options to them. There are some rules to remember for this as well:

➤ You can select multiple sublayer listings within the same top-level layer, provided they're at the same nesting level, but you can't select multiple sublayer listings from different top-level layers.

➤ You can select multiple listings of the same category (e.g., multiple top-level layers) and nesting level, but you can't select multiple listings from different nesting levels (e.g., not both top-level layers and objects on another layer).

➤ You can select multiple object listings (such as a path and type) in the same top-level layer, but not from different top-level layers.

To select multiple layer listings:

1. On the Layers panel, click the listing for a top-level layer, sublayer, or object.

2. Do either of the following:

   Shift-click the name of another layer, sublayer, or object. The listings you click, plus any items of a similar kind that are stacked between them, will become selected.

   Cmd-click/Ctrl-click the names of other noncontiguous top-level layers, sublayers, or objects.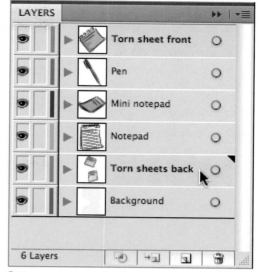

➤ Cmd-click/Ctrl-click to deselect any individual listings when multiple listings are selected.

➤ Although you can select multiple layer or sublayer listings, the Current Layer indicator displays for only one top-level layer or sublayer at a time.

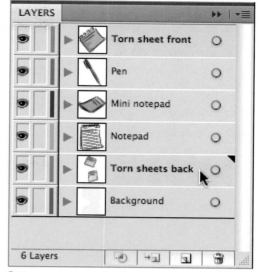

A *Two noncontiguous top-level layer listings are selected.*

Selecting objects via the Layers panel

In Chapter 8, you learned how to select objects using a variety of tools and commands. Here, you will learn how to select paths or groups via the Layers panel. The result is the same — the object's anchor points (and its bounding box, if that feature is on) become visible in the document window, and the object is ready for editing.

To select all the objects in a layer:

At the far right side of the Layers panel, click the **selection area** A for a top-level layer or sublayer. A colored selection square appears for every sublayer, group, and object on that layer (if the layer list is expanded), and every object on the layer, regardless of its indent level, becomes selected in the document window. The bounding box for the objects will also display, if that feature is on (View menu). B And unless the items are in a group, the target circle for each path and group will also become selected.

➤ To deselect an individual object, expand the list for its top-level layer or sublayer, then Shift-click the object's selection square.

To deselect all the objects in a layer:

Shift-click the selection square for the layer containing the objects you want to deselect. All the objects in the layer will be deselected, including the objects in any nested sublayers or groups.

THE CIRCLE OR THE SQUARE?

The difference between selecting and targeting should become clearer to you by the end of the next chapter.

➤ If you click either the target circle ◯ on the right side of the Layers panel for an object or group or the selection area next to the circle, that object or group becomes selected and targeted and its generic name (e.g., "Path," "Type," or "Group") is listed at the top of the Appearance panel.

➤ If you click the selection area for a top-level layer, all the objects or groups on the layer become selected and targeted for appearance changes, and its generic name (e.g., "Path" or "Mixed Objects") is listed on the Appearance panel. If you click the target circle for a top-level layer, all the objects on the layer become selected, but only the top-level layer is targeted, and "Layer" is listed at the top of the Appearance panel.

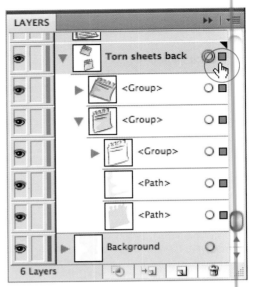

A *Click the selection area for a layer to select all the paths and groups within it. The selection squares appear, in the color that is currently assigned to that layer.*

B *All the paths and path groups on the "Torn sheets back" layer became selected in this artwork.*

To select an object via the Layers panel:

1. On the Layers panel, expand the top-level layer, sublayer, or group for the object to be selected.

2. At the far right side of the panel, click the selection area or target circle for the entity you want to select.

Via the Layers panel, you can select multiple groups or objects on different top-level layers or sublayers.

To select multiple objects on different layers:

1. On the Layers panel, make sure the listings for all the nested objects to be selected are visible (expand any layer or group lists, if necessary).

2. Click the selection area or target circle for any object, then Shift-click any other individual groups or objects to add them to the selection. The items don't have to be listed consecutively. **A–B**

➤ To deselect any selected object individually, Shift-click its selection square or target circle.

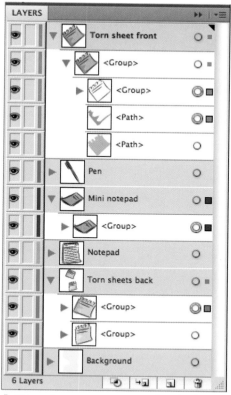

A *Objects from nonconsecutive stacking levels are selected (note the colored selection squares on the far right).*

B *Objects that we selected from different stacking levels are shown selected in the artwork.*

LOCATING A LISTING ON THE LAYERS PANEL

When the number of listings on the Layers panel grows long, it can be hard to locate a particular item. Organizing listings into sublayers can help, as does the Locate Object command. With the Selection tool, select the object in the document that you want to find the listing for, then choose Locate Object from the Layers panel menu. The list for the object's layer expands, if necessary, and a selection square appears for that item. (If "Locate Layer" is listed on the panel menu instead of "Locate Object," choose Panel Options from the panel menu and uncheck Show Layers Only; the Locate Object command will become available.)

On pages 94–95, you learned how to create, isolate, add a new object to, and ungroup a group. Here, you will select objects in a group by using the Layers panel.

To select a whole group via the Layers panel:

1. *Optional:* To put the group in isolation mode, double-click it in the document with the Selection tool ▶ (V).**A** Note: If this doesn't work, make sure Double Click to Isolate is checked in Illustrator/Edit > Preferences > General.

2. To select all the objects in the group (including any groups nested within it), click the selection area or the target circle ○ for the group listing on the right side of the Layers panel.

➤ To select a whole group when a document isn't in isolation mode, click an object in the group with the Selection tool (V). To select an object in a group (or to select individual anchor points or segments), use the Direct Selection tool (A). To turn on the bounding box feature (if you don't see the box around a selected object), press Cmd-Shift-B/Ctrl-Shift-B.

To select two or more objects in a group:

1. Deselect all (Cmd-Shift-A/Ctrl-Shift-A).

2. Do either of the following:

   The group can be in isolation mode for this method, or not. Expand the group list on the Layers panel, then Shift-click the selection area or the target circle ○ at the far right side of the panel for each object in the group that you want to select.**B**

   With the group in isolation mode, choose the **Selection** tool ▶ (V), click an object, then Shift-click additional objects.

➤ To deselect any selected item, Shift-click it again.

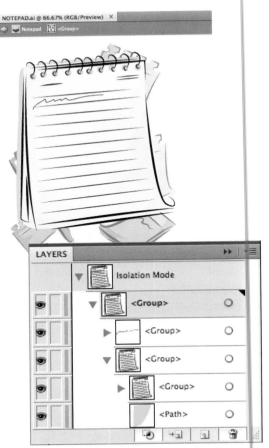

A *When a group is in isolation mode, the Layers panel lists only that group and its objects. The artwork in the image shown above is in isolation mode.*

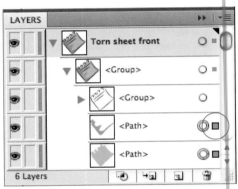

B *To select some objects in a group, expand the group list, then Shift-click the selection area for those objects.*

Restacking layers and objects

The order of objects (and layers) on the Layers panel matches the front-to-back order of objects (and layers) in the artwork. If you move a group, object, sublayer, or top-level layer upward or downward on the list, the artwork will redraw accordingly. You can restack objects and layers by dragging (see below) or by using a command (see the next page).

To restack a layer, group, or object via the Layers panel:

Drag a top-level layer, sublayer, group, or object upward or downward on the Layers panel, and while doing so, do either of the following:

Keep the listing within the same indent level (say, to restack a group within its own top-level layer).**A–C**

Move it to a different group or layer (release the mouse when the large black arrowheads point inward to the desired group or layer).

The document will redraw according to the new stacking position.**D**

➤ On page 95, you learned how to add an existing object to a group by using the Cut and Paste commands. You can also move an existing object into (or out of) a group by following the steps above.

➤ If you move an object that's part of a group or clipping mask to a different top-level layer, the object will be released from that group or mask.

A This is the original artwork.

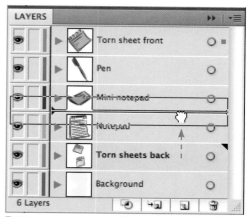

B We are dragging a layer listing upward to a new stacking position (the pointer is a hand icon).

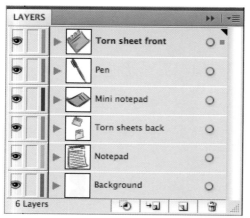

C The "Torn sheets back" layer is now in front of the Notepad layer.

D This is the result.

When the Layers panel contains many layers and a long list of objects, it can be tedious to expand and collapse layers each time you need to restack an object. In that case, the Send to Current Layer command, discussed below, is a faster method.

To move an object to a layer via a command:

1. Select one or more objects.

2. On the Layers panel, click the layer to which you want to move the selected object(s).

3. Right-click one of the selected objects in the document and choose Arrange > **Send to Current Layer** (or choose the command from the Object > Arrange submenu). Note: If the selected object was in a group, the entire group will be moved to the selected layer.

➤ To reverse the order of specific layers, groups, and objects on the Layers panel, Cmd-click/Ctrl-click nonconsecutive items (or click and then Shift-click a series of consecutive items), then choose Reverse Order from the panel menu.

Duplicating layers and objects

Duplicate objects appear in the same *x/y* location as, and directly on top of, the objects they are duplicated from. If you duplicate a layer or sublayer, the word "copy" is appended to the duplicate name.

To duplicate a layer, sublayer, group, or object:

Do one of the following:

On the Layers panel, click the layer, sublayer, group, or object to be duplicated, then choose **Duplicate** [layer or object name] from the Layers panel menu.

Drag a layer, sublayer, group, or object listing over the **New Layer** button .**A–B**

Click the selection area for a sublayer, group, or object (expand the listing if necessary), then Option-drag/Alt-drag the **selection square** upward or downward to the desired top-level layer or sublayer.**C–D** You can use this method to copy an object within a group. For a sublayer, only the objects are duplicated, not the sublayer listing.

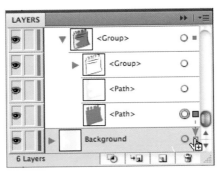

A *We are duplicating a layer by dragging it over the New Layer button. Note the plus sign in the pointer.*

B *A copy of the "Mini notepad" layer is made.*

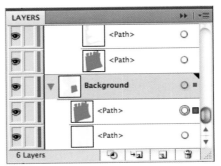

C *Duplicating an object a different way, we Option-drag/Alt-drag its selection square.*

D *A copy of the object appears in the layer named "Background."*

Locking layers and objects

Locked objects can't be selected or modified, but they do remain visible. When a whole layer is locked, none of the objects within it can be edited. When you save, close, and reopen a file that contains locked objects, the objects remain locked.

Note: As an alternative way to make some objects uneditable temporarily, you can isolate an object or group without locking it.

To lock or unlock layers or objects:

Do one of the following:

To lock a layer, on the Layers panel, click in the edit (second) column for a layer **A**, sublayer, group, or object. The lock icon 🔒 appears. Click the icon to unlock the item.

To lock multiple layers, sublayers, groups, or objects, drag upward or downward in the edit column. Drag back over the lock icons to unlock the items.

Option-click/Alt-click in the edit column for a top-level layer to lock or unlock all the other top-level layers except the one you click.

➤ If you lock an object and then lock its top-level layer, but later decide to unlock the object, you will have to unlock the top-level layer first.

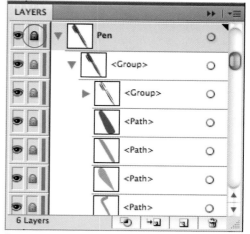

A When an entire layer is locked, none of the objects it contains can be selected or edited. Groups and individual objects can also be locked.

ONE-STOP SHOPPING FOR LAYER OPTIONS

➤ To open the Layer Options dialog, from which you can choose multiple options, double-click a top-level layer or sublayer. You can change the Name; choose a different Color for selections on the layer (say, if the current selection color is too similar to colors in the artwork); and check or uncheck any options, such as Lock, Show, Print, or Preview (view). Options chosen for a top-level layer apply to all the sublayers, groups, and objects within it. Layers for which printing is turned off are listed in italics on the panel.

Note: The Template option, in conjunction with the Dim Images To option, makes a layer that contains a placed image or object uneditable and dimmed so it can be traced manually. For an easier method, though, see Chapter 17, Live Trace.

Layer Options		
Name:	Elephants	OK
Color:	Blue	Cancel
☐ Template	☐ Lock	
☑ Show	☑ Print	
☑ Preview	☐ Dim Images to: 50 %	

➤ You can double-click a group or object to access the Name, Show, and Lock options in a simpler Options dialog.

Hiding layers and objects

When you hide the objects you're not working on, your artwork looks less complex, albeit temporarily, and the screen redraws faster. You can hide a top-level layer (with all its nested layers), a group, or an individual object. Hidden objects are invisible in both Outline and Preview views. When you save, close, and reopen a file that contains hidden objects, they remain hidden.

To hide or show layers or objects:

Do one of the following:

Click the **visibility** icon 👁 for a top-level layer, sublayer, group, or object.**A–C** To redisplay the hidden items, click in the same slot.

Drag upward or downward in the visibility column to hide multiple, consecutive top-level layers, sublayers, groups, or objects. To redisplay the hidden items, drag again.

Display all layers, then Option-click/Alt-click in the visibility column for a top-level layer to hide or show all the top-level layers except the one you click.

Note: If you want to redisplay a hidden object but its top-level layer is also hidden, you must redisplay its top-level layer first.

➤ To hide layers via a command, make sure all layers are visible (choose Show All Layers from the Layers panel menu if they're not), click a top-level layer or layers to remain visible, then choose Hide Others from the panel menu.

➤ To learn more about printing layers, see page 392.

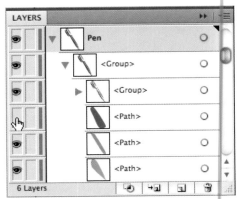

A *You can hide or show an individual object or group...*

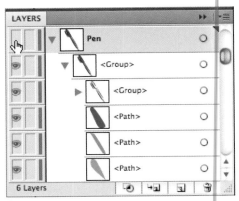

B *...or hide or show whole layers.*

C *The "Pen" objects in this artwork are hidden.*

Collecting objects into a new layer

The Collect in New Layer command collects all the currently highlighted top-level layers, sublayers, groups, or objects into a brand new layer.

To collect multiple layers, sublayers, groups, or objects into a new layer:

1. Cmd-click/Ctrl-click the listings for the layers, groups, or objects to be put on a new layer. **A** They must all be at the same indent level (e.g., all objects from the same sublayer or on consecutive sublayers). Don't click the selection area.

2. From the Layers panel menu, choose **Collect in New Layer**. If you selected sublayers, groups, or objects in the preceding step, they will now reside in a new sublayer within the same top-level layer; **B** or if you selected top-level layers, they will now be nested as sublayers within a newly named top-level layer.

➤ Quirky bug: To make the expand triangle appear for the new layer (for the first time), you have to either click its selection area or click another layer.

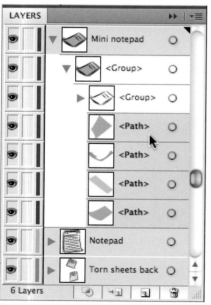

A We selected four path listings.

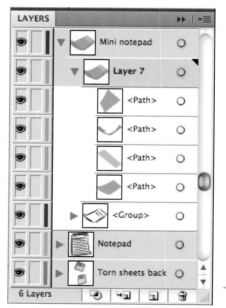

B The Collect in New Layer command gathered the four selected listings into a new sublayer (and labeled it Layer 7).

Releasing objects to layers

The two Release to Layers commands are useful when you need to prepare an Illustrator file for export to Adobe Flash Professional, to be used as the contents of an object or frame animation. The commands disperse all objects or groups residing within the currently selected top-level layer to new, separate layers within the same layer. After placing the file in Flash, you can convert the layers into separate objects or into a sequence.

Note: Illustrator (.ai) files can be imported directly into the Adobe Flash Catalyst application. ★ The layers in the file don't need to be released first. See page 418.

Read step 2 carefully before deciding which command to use.

To move objects to new, separate layers:

1. On the Layers panel, click a top-level layer, sublayer, or group (not an object). **A**

2. From the Layers panel menu, choose either of the following:

   Release to Layers (Sequence) to nest each object from the selected layer or group in a separate new layer within the original top-level layer. **B** Any former groups are nested in a new layer or sublayer. The original stacking order of the objects is preserved.

   Release to Layers (Build) if you're going to build a cumulative frame sequence in an animation program by adding objects in succession. **C** The bottommost layer will contain just the bottommost object; the next layer above that will contain the bottommost object plus the next object above it; the next layer above that will contain the two previous objects plus the next object above it, and so on.

➤ If you release a layer or sublayer that contains a clipping mask that you created via the Layers panel, the clipping mask will remain in effect.

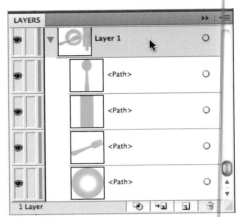

A *A top-level layer is selected on the Layers panel.*

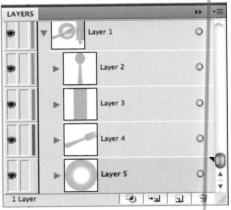

B *These are the results we got from the Release to Layers (Sequence) command...*

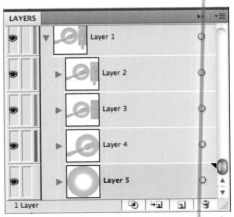

C *...versus the Release to Layers (Build) command.*

Merging layers and groups

If the layers and sublayers on your Layers panel grow to an unwieldy number, you can consolidate them at any time by using the Merge Selected command. Unlike the Flatten Artwork command, which flattens an entire document (see the next page), the Merge Selected command merges just the listings that you select.

In addition to merging layers (or sublayers) with one another, you can merge two or more groups, or merge a group with a sublayer, provided the selected listings reside within the same top-level layer. In the case of a group being merged with a sublayer, the objects will be ungrouped and will be placed on the selected sublayer. You can't merge objects with one another.

To merge layers, sublayers, or groups:

1. *Optional:* Use File > Save As to preserve a copy of your file, with its layers.

2. As you Cmd-click/Ctrl-click the listings for two or more layers, sublayers, or groups, click last on the listing that you want the selected items to merge into.**A** You can merge locked and/or hidden layers.

3. Choose **Merge Selected** from the Layers panel menu.**B**

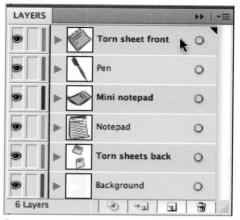

A *As you select the layers (or sublayers or groups) to be merged, click last on the layer you want the items to be merged into.*

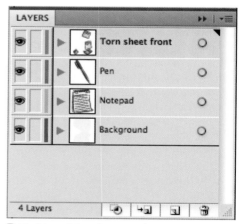

B *The Merge Selected command merged the three selected layers into one.*

Flattening layers

The Flatten Artwork command reduces a document to just one top-level layer, and nests all the sublayers and groups within it. Objects remain fully editable. If your document contains any hidden top-level layers when you choose this command, you can opt via an alert dialog to either keep the hidden artwork (by clicking No) or allow the hidden layers to be discarded (by clicking Yes).

To flatten all the layers in a document:

1. *Optional:* Use File > Save As to preserve a copy of your file, with its layers.

2. Redisplay any hidden top-level layers and objects that you want to preserve.

3. By default, if no layers are selected, the Flatten Artwork command merges all the currently visible layers into whichever top-level layer is displaying the Current Layer indicator. If you prefer to flatten the document into a layer of your choosing, click it now.

4. Choose **Flatten Artwork** from the Layers panel menu.

5. If the document contains artwork on hidden layers, an alert dialog will appear.**A–C** Click Yes to discard the hidden artwork, or click No to preserve it. If you click No, all the formerly hidden artwork will become visible, except for objects that you hid by clicking their individual visibility icon. Regardless of which button you click, the result will be a flattened file.

➤ The Flatten Artwork command can be undone if you choose Undo immediately.

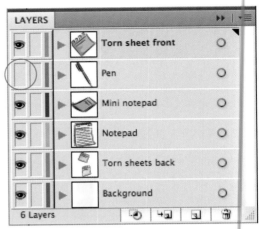

A *One of the layers in this file is hidden and contains artwork, so an alert dialog will appear when we choose the Flatten Artwork command.*

> The hidden layers contain artwork. Do you wish to discard the hidden art?
>
> No   Cancel   Yes

B *It's always nice to get a second chance.*

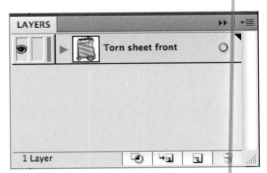

C *Because we clicked Yes, the Flatten Artwork command flattened the artwork into the selected layer ("Torn sheet front") and completely discarded the hidden layer.*

Appearance attributes are an object's fill, stroke, effect, and transparency settings. In this chapter, you'll learn how to use the Appearance panel ● to apply, edit, copy, and restack appearance attributes for a layer, sublayer, group, or object. Via in-panel links to a temporary Stroke, Swatches, Color, or Transparency panel, you can alter an object's appearance by adding additional fills and strokes, changing its opacity or blending mode, or applying effects. When an object is selected, its attributes are listed on the panel. **A–B**

Appearance attributes change how an object looks and prints, not its actual underlying path. You can save, close, and reopen a document, and the existing appearance attributes will remain editable and removable. Appearance attributes add speed and flexibility — but also some complexity — to object editing. When you're finished with this chapter, be sure to continue with the next two chapters, which are closely related: Chapter 15 (Effects) and Chapter 16 (Graphic Styles).

APPEARANCES

14

A *One of the circles in this artwork is selected.*

Link to a temporary Color or Swatches panel

Stroke Weight

An added Stroke attribute

Link to a temporary Stroke panel

Link to a temporary Transparency panel

APPEARANCE	▶▶ ▾≡
☐ Path	
👁 ▶ Stroke:	☐ ▼ ⬍ 4 pt ▼
👁 ▶ Stroke:	☐ 9 pt Outside
👁 ▶ Stroke:	▮ 15 pt Outside
👁 ▶ Fill:	☐
👁 Opacity:	Default

B *This Appearance panel is displaying the attributes for the object that is selected above.*

Add New Fill *Add New Effect* *Duplicate Selected Item* *Delete Selected Item*

Add New Stroke *Clear Appearance*

Applying appearance attributes

You can apply appearance attributes to individual objects one at a time, or you can target a whole top-level layer or group for appearance changes, in which case the attributes will apply to all the objects that are nested within the targeted layer or group. For example, if you target a layer and then change its opacity or blending mode, all the objects on that layer will adopt that opacity or blending mode. To edit an attribute at any time, you simply retarget the layer. When an object has more than just the basic fill and stroke attributes, its listing on the Layers panel will have a gray target circle. **A** Appearance attributes can be modified or removed at any time, even after you save, close, and reopen your file. Via convenient links and menus right on the Appearance panel, you can change an object's fill color, stroke attributes, opacity, blending mode, or brush stroke, and apply effects.

To apply appearance attributes via in-panel links:

1. Do either of the following:

   In the document window, select an object. **B**

   On the Layers panel, click the target circle ○ for a layer, group, or object. A ring appears around the circle, signifying that it's now an active target. If you click the target circle for a layer, all the objects on the layer will become selected, and the word "Layer" will appear at the top of the Appearance panel.

2. Show the Appearance panel. ◉

3. For a targeted object, do any of the following:

   Click the Stroke and/or Fill color square, then click it once more to open a temporary Swatches panel or Shift-click it to open a temporary Color panel (**A**, next page). Choose a color.

   To change other stroke attributes, click the underlined Stroke link, then choose a stroke weight, profile, or other settings on the temporary Stroke panel. For the new options that are available on this panel, see pages 120–122 and page 156. ★ Note: If the stroke has a variable width profile, an asterisk will display beside the stroke weight listing.

   To apply a brush stroke, click a Stroke listing, then choose a brush from the Brushes panel or from the Brush Definition menu on the Control panel.

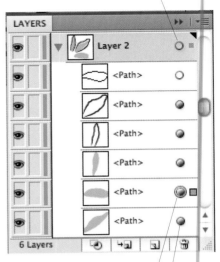

This layer is selected but not targeted, and it doesn't contain appearance attributes.

This object is targeted, and it contains appearance attributes.

This object contains appearance attributes, but it isn't targeted.

A *Learn to "read" the three different states of the target circles on the Layers panel.*

B *This is the original artwork.*

4. For a targeted object, group, or layer, do any of the following:

Click the Opacity link to open a temporary Transparency panel, then choose a different blending mode from the menu in the upper left corner and/or change the Opacity value via the arrowhead or slider.**B** To learn about the Transparency panel, see Chapter 27.

From the Add New Effect menu *fx,* at the bottom of the panel, choose an Illustrator effect, such as one of the effects on the Distort & Transform or Stylize submenu. Choose settings in the dialog, then click OK. The chosen command will be listed on the Appearance panel. (To learn about effects, see the next chapter.)

➤ To target multiple items, Cmd-click/Ctrl-click their target icons.

To untarget an object, group, or layer:

Either Shift-click the gray target circle ⬤ on the Layers panel or click a blank area of the artwork.

To choose default appearance settings for new objects:

If the **New Art Has Basic Appearance** command on the Appearance panel menu has a check mark, subsequently created objects will have just one fill and one stroke, in the current colors. If this option is unchecked, the appearance attributes currently displaying on the panel will apply to any new objects you create.

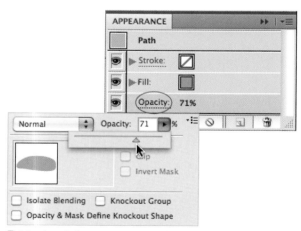

A *We selected the root of the veggie, Shift-clicked the highlighted Fill color square on the Appearance panel, then mixed a new fill color on the temporary Color panel (the carrot turned into a parsnip!).*

B *We selected the green area on one leaf, clicked the Opacity link on the Appearance panel, then lowered the opacity to 71%. We made the same change to the other leaves.*

Deciphering the Appearance panel

Depending on what entity (an object, group, or layer) is currently targeted and what attributes it has, you may see one or more of these icons in the upper portion of the Appearance panel:

➤ For a layer or group (not an object), this icon 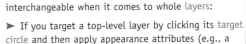 signifies that the item has an added stroke and/or fill attribute, and this icon ⊠ signifies that it has transparency edits.

➤ Effects are identified by this icon: *fx*.

The name for the currently targeted entity (e.g., a Layer, Group, **A** or Path **B–C**) is listed in boldface at the top of the Appearance panel. Note: If a type object is selected, the word "Type" will appear instead. Similarly, "Symbol" will appear for a symbol, and "Image" will appear for an image.

If you target an object that is nested within a layer and/or group to which appearance attributes have been applied, a "Layer" and/or "Group" listing will also appear above the "Path" listing at the top of the Appearance panel.

If you target a layer or group, a "Contents" listing will also appear on the Appearance panel. Double-click the Contents listing to display Path attributes, click a Layer listing to display attributes that apply to the whole layer, or click a Group listing to display attributes that apply to the group. (Yup, this can be mighty confusing!)

TARGETING LAYERS FOR APPEARANCE EDITS

Although both selecting and targeting cause objects to become selected in your document, they're not interchangeable when it comes to whole layers:

➤ If you target a top-level layer by clicking its target circle and then apply appearance attributes (e.g., a fill color, an effect, or an opacity setting), those attributes are applied to, and listed on, the Appearance panel for the whole layer.

➤ If you click the selection area for a top-level layer instead of the target circle and then apply appearance attributes, those attributes are applied separately to each object or group in that layer, not to the overall layer. When you click the selection area for the top-level layer next time, instead of an itemized list of attributes on the Appearance panel, you will see the words "Mixed Appearances." To edit the selected objects on that layer, use other panels in Illustrator.

Selecting and targeting do work interchangeably for an object or group. Clicking the selection area or target circle on the Layers panel for an object or group selects and also targets that item.

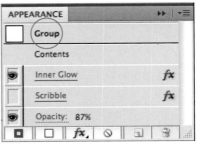

A When targeted, a group displays its own appearance attributes.

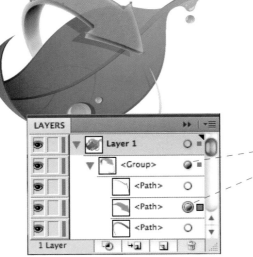

B The path we targeted is nested in a group, which has its own appearance attributes.

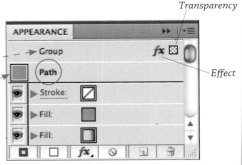

C The Appearance panel is listing the attributes for the path and its group.

To apply multiple stroke or fill attributes:

1. Target an object, group, or layer. **A**

2. Do either of the following:

   At the bottom of the Appearance panel, click the **Add New Stroke** button ■ (Cmd-Option-/; Ctrl-Alt-/) **B** or the **Add New Fill** button □ (Cmd-/;Ctrl-/).

   Click a Stroke or Fill listing on the Appearance panel, then click the **Duplicate Selected Item** button ▣ at the bottom of the panel.

3. A new Stroke or Fill listing appears on the panel. Click the new listing, then modify its attributes so it differs from the original one (or modify the original listing instead). Note: For multiple stroke attributes, make sure a narrower stroke is stacked above a wider one, **C–D** so the one on top doesn't obscure those on the bottom. Similarly, for multiple Fill listings, lower the opacity (or change the blending mode) of the topmost one.

➤ You can drag a Stroke or Fill listing upward or downward on the panel. Be aware that this will change the object's appearance in the document.

➤ When you select an object that contains multiple stroke attributes, an alert icon ⚠ may display next to its fill color on the Control panel. If you click the alert icon, the color for the topmost Stroke and/or Fill listing will display on the Control and Color panels.

A *The targeted object (the outer circle) has a gray fill and a green stroke.*

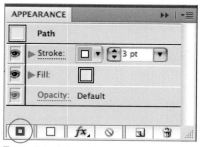

B *We clicked the Add New Stroke button twice.*

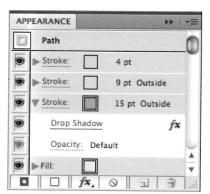

C *We edited the attributes for all three of the Stroke listings. We made the bottommost stroke the widest of the three and applied a Drop Shadow effect to it.*

D *This is how the edited attributes (listed in the Appearance panel at left) look on the object.*

Editing appearance attributes

You can use the same convenient in-panel links and menus on the Appearance panel to edit attributes as you did to apply them: the Stroke, Color, Swatches, and Transparency panels; the effect dialogs; and the Brush Definition menu.

To edit appearance attributes:

1. Do either of the following:

   In the document, select an object that contains appearance attributes.

   On the Layers panel, click the target circle for a layer, group, A or object.

2. On the Appearance panel, click any existing appearance listing to open a related panel (or a dialog, in the case of an effect). B If there are multiple Fill or Stroke listings, be sure to click the one you want to modify.

3. Using links or menus on the Appearance panel, make the desired edits C (see steps 3–4 on pages 190–191). For example, to modify the setting for a stroke attribute, click the underlined Stroke link to open a temporary Stroke panel and choose options. If the object contains a brush stroke, you can click a replacement brush on the Brush Definition menu ✶ or change the weight via the Stroke link.

   ➤ If you use the Brush Definition menu on the Appearance panel and then target or select a different object that doesn't have a brush stroke, the Brush Definition menu will still display. To redisplay the stroke Weight controls, deselect the Stroke listing, then reselect it. To learn more about brushes, see Chapter 23.

To add attributes to just an entity's stroke or fill:

1. On the Layers panel, click the target circle for a layer, group, or object.

2. On the Appearance panel, click a Stroke or Fill listing, then click the expand arrow. Do any of the following:

   Click the **Opacity** link to open a temporary Transparency panel, then change the Opacity value and/or blending mode.

   From the **Add New Effect** menu, fx. choose an effect.

   The newly applied attributes will be nested within the Stroke or Fill listing.

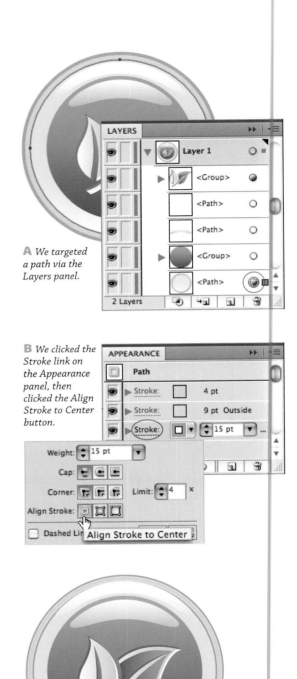

A We targeted a path via the Layers panel.

B We clicked the Stroke link on the Appearance panel, then clicked the Align Stroke to Center button.

C The new stroke alignment displays in the object.

Hiding and deleting appearance attributes

To hide an appearance attribute:

1. Target a layer, group, **A** or object.

2. On the Appearance panel, ● click in the visibility column to make the icon 👁 and the targeted entity disappear **B–C** or reappear.

To delete an appearance attribute:

1. Target a layer, group, or object.

2. On the Appearance panel, ● click the attribute to be deleted, then click the **Delete Selected Item** button 🗑 at the bottom of the panel.

➤ The sole remaining fill and stroke appearance attributes can't be removed. You can click the Delete Selected Item button for either of those appearance attributes to apply a color of None.

➤ To remove a brush stroke from a stroke attribute, click the Stroke listing on the Appearance panel, then click the Basic brush on the Brush Definition menu. ★

Next, you will learn how to remove all but the basic appearance attributes from a layer, group, or object. If you target a layer or group, both of the commands that are discussed below will remove only attributes that were applied to that layer or group, not attributes that were applied directly to paths nested within it. To remove attributes from a nested object, you must target that object specifically.

To delete all the appearance attributes from an entity:

1. Target an object, layer, or group.

2. Do either of the following:

   To remove all appearance attributes from the targeted entity and apply a stroke and fill of None, click the **Clear Appearance** button ⊘ on the Appearance panel (for type, the fill color becomes black and any stroke color is removed).

   To remove all the appearance attributes except the entity's original stroke and fill colors, choose **Reduce to Basic Appearance** from the Appearance panel menu.

   Regardless of which command you choose, all effects, brush strokes, and added fill and stroke attributes will be removed, and the transparency settings will be restored to a blending mode of Normal and an Opacity of 100%.

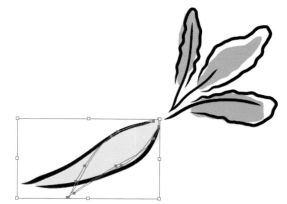

A *We targeted a group that contains an attribute we want to hide.*

B *On the Appearance panel, we clicked the visibility column for the Warp effect to hide that attribute.*

C *The Warp effect is now hidden (but it can redisplayed at any time).*

Copying appearance attributes

To copy appearance attributes from one object or layer to another:

Do either of the following:

On the Layers panel, Option-drag/Alt-drag the target circle from the item that contains the attributes you want to copy onto the target circle for another layer, group, or object.**A**

Choose the Selection tool (V), click an object that contains the attributes to be copied, then drag the square thumbnail from the upper left corner of the Appearance panel over an unselected object.**B–C** (Note: If you don't see the thumbnail, choose Show Thumbnail from the panel menu.)

➤ To remove the appearance attributes from one item and apply them to another, drag a target circle from one layer, group, or object to another one without holding down any modifier keys.

➤ To select objects in a document based on their matching appearance attributes, select one of the objects, then choose Select > Same > Appearance.

Expanding appearance attributes

When you expand an object's appearance attributes, the paths that were used to create the attributes are converted into (dozens of!) separate objects, which can be edited individually. When exporting an Illustrator file to a non-Adobe application that can't read appearance attributes, this command can be a necessity.

To expand an object's appearance attributes:

1. Select an object that contains the appearance attributes to be expanded.

2. Choose Object > **Expand Appearance**. On the Layers panel, you will now see a new <Group> (or a series of nested groups). The former effects or other attributes will be listed as individual path and/or image listings. Even the former fill and stroke attributes will be listed as separate paths.

A To copy appearance attributes, either Option/Alt drag the target circle from one listing to another...

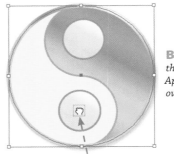

B ...or drag the thumbnail from the Appearance panel over an object.

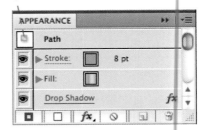

C The appearance attributes are copied to the object we dragged to.

Effects apply distortion, texture, artistic, shape, and stylistic changes to objects and imported images, with results that can range from subtle to marked. In this chapter, you will apply effects via the Appearance panel, the Effect menu, and the Effect Gallery, and explore a few effects in depth. (Effects can also be saved in and applied via graphic styles. See the next chapter.)

The effect commands change only the appearance of an object — not its underlying path. **A–B** Effects can be edited or deleted at any time without permanently affecting the object they're applied to, and without affecting other effects or appearance attributes in the same object. Moreover, if you reshape the path of the underlying object, the effects adjust accordingly. In other words, effects are live.

Applying Illustrator effects

The Effect menu offers a choice of Illustrator effects and Photoshop effects. Most of the Illustrator effects, which are in the top portion of the menu, are vector based, meaning they can be applied only to path shapes and output as vector objects. The following Illustrator effects can be applied to vector or raster objects and are rasterized upon output (are converted from vector

Continued on the following page

```
Twist
Angle:  16   °      ( OK )
☑ Preview          ( Cancel )
```

A *We chose this setting in the Twist dialog.*

B *The Twist effect was applied to the artwork shown at the top of the page, with these results (see page 205).*

to raster): all the effects on the 3D, SVG Filters, and Warp submenus; the Transform effect on the Distort & Transform submenu; and the Drop Shadow, Inner Glow, Outer Glow, and Feather effects on the Stylize submenu.

All the Photoshop effects (on the bottom part of the Effect menu) are pixel based, meaning they introduce painterly attributes, such as soft edges or transparency, and are rasterized upon output. They can be applied to both vector and raster objects.

An individual dialog opens when you choose an Illustrator effect or when you choose a Photoshop effect from the Blur, Pixelate, Sharpen, or Video submenu. When you choose any other Photoshop effect or choose Effect > Effect Gallery, a large dialog opens; the gallery provides access to most of the Photoshop effects and controls (see pages 207–208).

Keep these basic facts in mind as you apply effects:

➤ You can apply Illustrator and Photoshop effects to an object's fill or stroke (the object may have a brush stroke); to type; or to a group, layer, embedded bitmap image, symbol instance, blend, or compound shape.

➤ If you apply an effect to a targeted layer or group, it will affect all the current and future objects in the layer or group.

➤ If you apply an effect to editable type, the type and its attributes will remain editable.

➤ You can apply multiple effects to the same object. If you do so, the effects may preview more slowly in the dialog (a progress bar may display). Some effects and settings require more memory to process than others.

The Illustrator effects can be applied via the Effect menu **A** or via the Appearance panel. The effects that you have applied to the current selection of objects are listed individually as appearance attributes on the Appearance panel.

To apply an Illustrator effect:

1. Do either of the following:

On the Layers panel, click the target circle for a layer, group, or object (the circle should now have a double border), or click the selection area for a group or object. **B**

To limit the effect to just the stroke or fill of one or more ungrouped objects, select or isolate them. Display the Appearance panel, then click the Stroke or Fill listing.

Effect	
Apply Twist	⇧⌘E
Twist...	⌥⇧⌘E
Document Raster Effects Settings...	
Illustrator Effects	
3D	▶
Convert to Shape	▶
Crop Marks	
Distort & Transform	▶
Path	▶
Pathfinder	▶
Rasterize...	
Stylize	▶
SVG Filters	▶
Warp	▶
Photoshop Effects	
Effect Gallery...	
Artistic	▶
Blur	▶
Brush Strokes	▶
Distort	▶
Pixelate	▶
Sharpen	▶
Sketch	▶
Stylize	▶
Texture	▶
Video	▶

A *Most of the Illustrator effects on the Effect menu are vector effects (but a few are raster effects); the Photoshop Effects are all raster effects.*

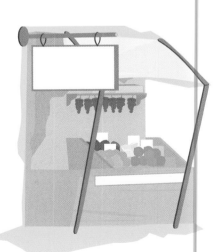

B *We targeted this entire group of objects.*

2. Choose one of the Illustrator effects from the top portion of the **Add New Effect** menu *fx.* on the Appearance panel, or from the **Effect** menu on the Illustrator menu bar.

3. Check Preview (if available), then choose settings and options.**A** After entering a value in a field, press Tab to update the preview.

4. Click OK.**B** The effect will be listed by name on the Appearance panel, either above or below the Stroke and/or Fill listings, or nested within one of those listings. Click the expand arrowhead to display it.**C–E**

➤ To apply effects to type, see pages 276–278.

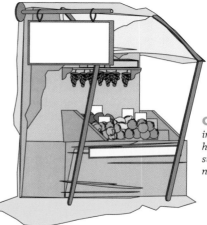

A *We chose these values in the Warp Options dialog.*

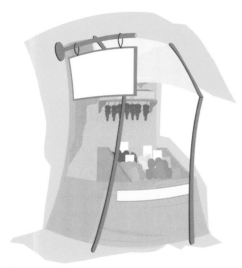

B *This is the result of the Warp > Squeeze effect (it reminds us a little of the artist Chaim Soutine).*

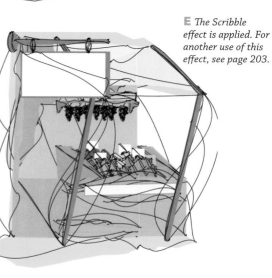

C *All the objects in this artwork have a black stroke. They're not in a group.*

E *The Scribble effect is applied. For another use of this effect, see page 203.*

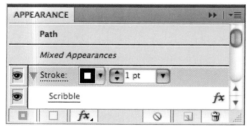

D *Because we clicked the Stroke listing on the Appearance panel before we applied the Stylize > Scribble effect, the effect nested within the Stroke listing.*

Editing, duplicating, and deleting effects

To edit an applied effect:

1. Do either of the following:

   Via the Layers panel,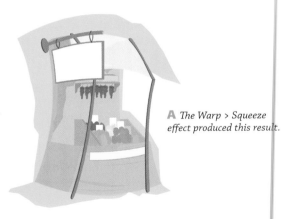 target the layer, group, or object that contains the effect you want to edit.**A**

   If you applied the effect to just an object's stroke or fill, select the object, then expand the Stroke or Fill listing on the Appearance panel.

2. Click the blue underlined effect listing on the Appearance panel.**B** The effect dialog reopens.

3. Make the desired adjustments, then click OK.**C**

➤ When multiple effects are applied to the same object or attribute, you can restack any individual effect by dragging it upward or downward. As a result, other effects may be enhanced or blocked out.

➤ To apply the last-used effect and settings to a selected object with no dialog opening, press Cmd-Shift-E/Ctrl-Shift-E. Or to reopen the last effects dialog or the Effect Gallery (if the gallery was used last), press Cmd-Option-Shift-E/Ctrl-Alt-Shift-E. If the object already contains the effect in question, an alert dialog will appear; click Cancel so you don't apply the same effect twice.

To remove an effect:

1. On the Layers panel, target the layer, group, or object that contains the effect to be removed.

2. On the Appearance panel, click next to the effect name, then click the **Delete Selected Item** button.

A *The Warp > Squeeze effect produced this result.*

B *After retargeting the group, we clicked the effect listing on the Appearance panel to reopen the dialog.*

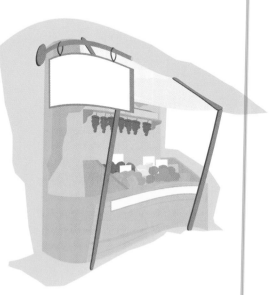

C *In the Warp Options dialog, we changed the Style from Squeeze to Fish.*

A few Illustrator effects up close

On this page and on the next four pages, we have illustrated uses for a few Illustrator effects, just to whet your appetite. In this first task, you will use a Convert to Shape effect to change an object's silhouette to a rectangle, rounded rectangle, or ellipse — without altering the actual underlying path.

To apply a Convert to Shape effect:

1. On the Layers panel, ✎ click the target circle for a layer, group, or object. **A** Or to limit the effect to a stroke or fill attribute, select or isolate an object, then on the Appearance panel, ◉ click the Stroke or Fill listing.

2. From the **Add New Effect** menu *fx.* on the Appearance panel or from the **Effect** menu on the Illustrator menu bar, under Illustrator Effects, choose Convert to Shape > **Rectangle, Rounded Rectangle,** or **Ellipse.** The Shape Options dialog opens. **B** (You can also choose one of those shapes from the Shape menu in the dialog.)

3. Check Preview.

4. Do either of the following:

   Click **Absolute,** then enter the total desired Width and Height values for the shape's appearance.

   Click **Relative,** then enter an Extra Width or Extra Height value to make the shape look larger or smaller than the actual path (enter a positive or negative value).

5. For the Rounded Rectangle shape, you can also change the **Corner Radius** value.

6. Click OK. **C–D**

➤ To round the corners of an object without converting its shape, use Effects > Stylize > Round Corners.

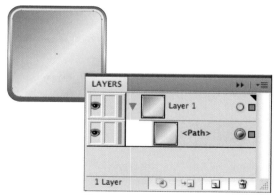

A *An object is targeted (this object contains a graphic style; see Chapter 16).*

B *We applied the Convert to Shape > Ellipse effect, choosing these options in the Shape Options dialog.*

C *Although the underlying path remains the same...*

D *...the outer shape looks like (and prints as if it were) an ellipse.*

The Inner Glow effect spreads a color from the edge of an object inward, whereas the Outer Glow effect spreads a color from the edge of an object outward.

To apply the Inner Glow or Outer Glow effect:

1. On the Layers panel,◔ click the target circle for a layer, group, or object. Or to limit the effect to a stroke or fill attribute, select or isolate the object, then on the Appearance panel,◉ click the Stroke or Fill listing.

2. From the **Add New Effect** menu _fx._ on the Appearance panel or from the **Effect** menu on the Illustrator menu bar, under Illustrator Effects, choose Stylize > **Inner Glow** or **Outer Glow**.

3. In the Inner Glow **B** or Outer Glow dialog, check Preview, then do any of the following:

   Click the color square next to the Mode menu, then choose a different spot or process color for the glow.

   Choose a blending **Mode** for the glow color.

   Choose an **Opacity** for the glow color.

   Click the **Blur** arrowhead, then move the slider in small increments to adjust how far the glow extends inward or outward. The higher the Blur value, the wider the glow area. If you choose the Center option (next), keep the Blur value low.

   For the Inner Glow effect, click **Center** to have the glow spread outward from the center of the object, or **Edge** to have it spread inward from the edge of the object toward the center.

4. Click OK.**C**

A _We targeted the papers in this group of objects._

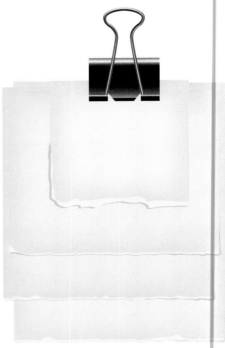

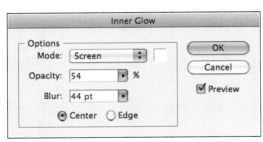

B _We chose these options in the Inner Glow dialog._

C _The Inner Glow effect is applied._

The Scribble effect makes an object's fill and stroke look as though they were sketched with a felt-tip marker or pen.

To apply the Scribble effect:

1. On the Layers panel, ◉ click the target circle for a layer, group, **A** or object. Or to limit the effect to a stroke or fill attribute, select or isolate the object, then on the Appearance panel, ◉ click the Stroke or Fill listing.

2. From the **Add New Effect** menu *fx.* on the Appearance panel or from the **Effect** menu on the Illustrator menu bar, under Illustrator Effects, choose Stylize > **Scribble**. The Scribble Options dialog opens. **B**

3. Check Preview. Begin by choosing a preset from the **Settings** menu. Follow the remaining steps if you want to choose custom settings for the preset, or if you're satisfied with the effect of the preset settings, click OK to exit the dialog.

4. To change the angle of the sketch lines, enter an **Angle** value or move the dial.

5. Drag the **Path Overlap** slider toward Outside to allow the sketch lines to extend beyond the edge of the path, or toward Inside to confine them to the interior of the path. Choose a high **Variation** value to produce random variations in line lengths and a wilder, more haphazard look, or a low Variation value for shorter and more uniform line lengths.

6. Under Line Options, do any of the following:

   Change the **Stroke Width** (thickness) of the lines.

   Change the **Curviness** value to control whether the lines angle sharply or loop widely where they change direction. The Variation slider controls the degree of random variation in changes of direction.

   Change the **Spacing** value to cluster the sketch lines more tightly or to spread them further apart. The Variation slider controls the degree of random variation in the spacing.

7. Click OK. **C**

➤ If you change the settings in the Scribble Options dialog and then choose a preset from the Settings menu, the preset values will be restored to the sliders. Unfortunately, custom Scribble settings can't be saved as a preset.

A *We targeted this group of bananas.*

B *We chose these setting in the Scribble Options dialog.*

C *The Scribble effect is applied.*

The Drop Shadow effect creates soft, naturalistic shadows.

To apply the Drop Shadow effect:

1. On the Layers panel, ✏ click the target circle for a layer, group, or object. **A** Or to limit the effect to a stroke or fill attribute, select or isolate the object, then on the Appearance panel, ◉ click the Stroke or Fill listing.

2. From the **Add New Effect** menu *fx.* on the Appearance panel or from the **Effect** menu on the Illustrator menu bar, under Illustrator Effects, choose Stylize > **Drop Shadow**. The Drop Shadow dialog opens. **B** Check Preview.

3. To customize the drop shadow, do any of the following:

   Change the blending **Mode**.

   Change the **Opacity** value for the shadow.

   Enter an **X Offset** for the horizontal distance between the object and the shadow and a **Y Offset** for the vertical distance between the object and the shadow.

   Change the **Blur** value for the width of the shadow (change this amount slowly).

   Click **Color**, click the color square, choose a different spot or process color for the shadow from the Color Picker, then click OK; or click **Darkness**, then enter a percentage of black to be added to the shadow.

4. Click OK. **C**

CHOOSING SPOT COLORS FOR EFFECTS

You can choose a spot color for the Stylize > Drop Shadow, Inner Glow, and Outer Glow effects. Load the desired swatch(es) onto the Swatches panel. In the effect dialog, click the color square to open the Color Picker. Click the Color Swatches button, if necessary, to display a list of the swatches that are currently on the Swatches panel, and click the desired spot color (then click OK twice to exit both dialogs).

A *We targeted just the outer shape in this group of objects.*

C *The Drop Shadow effect is applied.*

B *We chose these settings in the Drop Shadow dialog.*

The Roughen effect adds anchor points and then moves them. Use it to make an object look more irregular or hand drawn. This effect can be applied to whole objects or to just an object's stroke or fill.

To apply the Roughen effect:

1. On the Layers panel, ✪ click the target circle for a layer, group, A or object. Or to limit the effect to a stroke or fill attribute, select or isolate the object, then on the Appearance panel, ◉ click the Stroke or Fill listing.

   ➤ Choose View > Hide Edges (Cmd-H/Ctrl-H) to make the results easier to preview.

2. From the **Add New Effect** menu *fx.* on the Appearance panel or from the **Effect** menu on the Illustrator menu bar, under Illustrator Effects, choose Distort & Transform > **Roughen**. The Roughen dialog opens. B Check Preview.

3. Click **Relative** to move anchor points by a percentage of the object's size, or **Absolute** to move them by a specific amount, then choose a **Size** amount to specify how far the object's anchor points may move (try a low percentage first).

4. Choose a **Detail** amount for the number of points to be added to each inch of the path segments.

5. Click **Smooth** to produce curves, or click **Corner** to produce pointy angles.

6. Click OK. C

The Twist effect twists an object's overall shape. You can twist a single object or twist multiple objects together.

To apply the Twist effect:

1. For one or more objects, follow step 1 in the instructions above.

2. From the **Add New Effect** menu *fx.* on the Appearance panel or from the **Effect** menu (under Illustrator Effects), choose Distort & Transform > **Twist**. In the Twist dialog, check Preview.

3. Enter a positive **Angle** (press Tab) to twirl the path clockwise or a negative value to twirl it counterclockwise (–360 to 360).

4. Click OK (see A–B, page 197).

A *We targeted the green tile objects in this artwork.*

B *We chose these settings in the Roughen dialog.*

C *The Roughen effect is applied.*

Rasterizing objects

The Rasterize command converts vector objects to bitmap images. You can use the settings in the dialog to control, on a per-object basis, how an applied stroke, vector (Illustrator) effects, or bitmap (Photoshop) effects on an object are converted to pixels, to help prevent errors or surprises on output.

To rasterize a path object:

1. Select a path object or objects, or target them on the Layers panel.

2. Choose Object > **Rasterize.**

3. In the Rasterize dialog, choose a **Color Model** for the object. Depending on the current document color mode, you can choose CMYK for print output; RGB for video or onscreen output; Grayscale; or Bitmap to convert the object to black-and-white (Photoshop effects aren't available for an object in the Bitmap color model).

4. For the **Resolution,** choose Screen for Web or video output, Medium for desktop printing, or High for commercial printing; or enter a resolution in the Other field; or click Use Document Raster Effects Resolution to use the current global resolution settings in the Effect > Document Raster Effects Settings dialog (see page 409).

5. Click **Background: White** to make any transparent areas in the object opaque white, or **Transparent** to make the background transparent. We prefer the latter option (see the sidebar at right).

6. Under **Options:**

   For most kinds of objects, you can choose **Anti-aliasing:** Art Optimized (Supersampling) to allow Illustrator to soften the edges of the rasterized shape. Since this option can make type or thin lines look blurry, Type Optimized (Hinted) is a better option for type objects. If you choose a setting of None, object edges will be hard-edged and jagged. Note: The setting chosen for type on the Anti-aliasing menu on the Character panel (Sharp, Crisp, or Strong) is honored only for the Type Optimized option.

   If you clicked Background: White and you want a white border to be added around the object, enter a width for the border as the **Add [ ] Around Object** value.

Check **Preserve Spot Colors** (if available) to preserve spot colors in the object, if any.

7. Click OK.

➤ If the object contains a fill pattern and you want to preserve any transparency in the pattern, in the Rasterize dialog, click Background: Transparent and choose Anti-aliasing: Art Optimized.

➤ The Effect > Rasterize command has all the same options as the Object > Rasterize command except for the Preserve Spot Colors option. When applied as an effect, the rasterization isn't permanent, and you can edit the settings at any time. However, if you apply the Object > Expand Appearance command after applying the effect, the object will be rasterized permanently using the settings from the effect.

➤ If you save an Illustrator document to the TIFF, GIF, or JPEG format or export it to an application that doesn't read vector objects, the entire document will be rasterized.

➤ If you change the resolution setting in the Effect > Document Raster Settings dialog, all raster effects in the document will be recalculated, but you won't see a visual change in the objects.

TRANSPARENT VS. CLIPPING MASK OPTIONS

Both the Background: Transparent and Create Clipping Mask options in the Rasterize dialog remove an object's background, but they produce different results:

➤ The Transparent option removes the background by creating an alpha channel. Of the two options, this one does a better job of anti-aliasing. All the opacity settings are restored to the default value of 100%, but the look of semitransparency is preserved. All the blending modes are restored to the default setting of Normal, and their effect in the artwork is removed.

➤ The Create Clipping Mask option turns an object's path into a clipping path. Any existing transparency attributes are applied to the mask, and the transparency settings for the object are restored to Normal mode and 100% opacity. Any stroke or effects that extended beyond the object's path are clipped. If you click the Transparent option, there's no need to check this one.

Applying Photoshop effects via the Effect Gallery

The large Effect Gallery dialog provides access to most of the Photoshop effects and settings. Note: Unfortunately, the gallery lets you preview, apply, show, and hide only one individual effect at a time. If you want to apply multiple Photoshop effects, you have to reopen it for each one. To work around this limitation, after applying multiple effects, click the visibility icon 👁 on the Appearance panel for any effects that you want to hide or show.

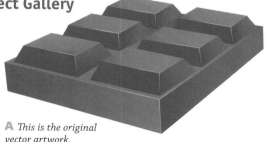

A *This is the original vector artwork.*

To use the Effect Gallery:

1. Select a path object, an embedded image, **A** or editable or outline type.

2. From the **Add New Effect** menu *fx.* on the Appearance panel or from the **Effect** menu (under Photoshop Effects), either choose **Effect Gallery** or choose an individual Photoshop effect from any submenu except Pixelate, Blur, Sharpen, or Video.

3. The resizable dialog opens. **B** It contains a preview window, effect thumbnails, and settings for the current effect. If you want to switch to a different effect, expand a category in the middle panel of the dialog, then click a thumbnail, or choose an effect name from the menu on the right side of the dialog.

Continued on the following page

Drag a magnified image in the preview window.

Click the arrowhead/chevron to hide the middle panel and expand the preview window; click it again to redisplay the middle panel.

Switch to a different effect either by clicking a thumbnail in the middle panel or by choosing from this menu.

Choose settings for the current effect.

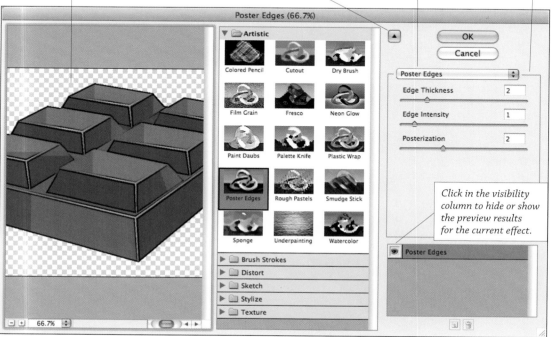

Click in the visibility column to hide or show the preview results for the current effect.

B *The Effect Gallery has three panels.*

4. Choose settings for the chosen effect.

➤ You can change the zoom level for the preview via the zoom buttons or menu at the bottom of the dialog, and you can drag a magnified preview in the window.

5. *Optional:* If you want to see the preview without the effect, click the visibility (eye) icon on the right side of the dialog. Remember to redisplay the effect before exiting the dialog.

6. For some effects, such as Artistic > Rough Pastels and Underpainting, you can choose a texture type from a **Texture** menu. Move the Scaling slider to scale the pattern; move the Relief slider, if there is one, to adjust the depth and prominence of the texture on the surface of the image; and choose a Light direction option.

7. Click OK.**A–E**

Note: All the Photoshop effects are rasterized upon output, as are these Illustrator effects: Stylize > Drop Shadow, Inner Glow, Outer Glow, and Feather. To control which settings Illustrator uses for this process, see page 409.

➤ In the Effect Gallery dialog, you can hold down Option/Alt and click Reset to restore the first effect that was applied when the dialog was opened, with its default settings (the Cancel button becomes a Reset button).

➤ To intensify the results of a Photoshop effect on a vector object, apply an Illustrator effect such as Stylize > Feather or Inner or Outer Glow first to add some variation to the fill color.

A *The Artistic > Plastic Wrap effect is applied.*

B *The Sketch > Stamp effect is applied.*

C *The Distort > Diffuse Glow effect is applied.*

D *The Texture > Grain effect is applied.*

E *The Sketch > Charcoal effect is applied.*

A graphic style is a collection of appearance attributes that is stored on the Graphic Styles panel and can be applied to an object, group, or layer. Any appearance attributes that can be applied to an object can be saved in a graphic style, such as fills and strokes, Stroke panel settings, Transparency panel settings (opacity and blending mode), and effects.**A**

In this chapter, you will learn how to load graphic styles from a library panel to the Graphic Styles panel; apply, remove, create, duplicate, redefine, and delete graphic styles; save custom graphic style libraries; and break the link between an object and a graphic style.

Graphic styles basics

To display the Graphic Styles panel, **B** choose Window > Graphic Styles. You can also display a temporary Graphic Styles panel by clicking the Style thumbnail or arrowhead on the Control panel.

Continued on the following page

A *These objects have the same underlying paths, but they contain different graphic styles.*

GRAPHIC STYLES

Graphic Styles Libraries menu   *Break Link to Graphic Style*   *New Graphic Style*   *Delete Graphic Style*

B *The Graphic Styles panel*

GRAPHIC STYLES

16

These are some of the benefits to using graphic styles:

➤ Using graphic styles, you can quickly apply many attributes at once.

➤ Graphic styles change the way an object looks without changing its underlying path.

➤ If you redefine a graphic style, the style will update instantly on any objects it's currently assigned to.

➤ At any time, you can apply a different graphic style to an object, apply additional styles, restore the default style (a 1-pt. black stroke and a solid white fill), or remove the style altogether.

If you're wondering if graphic styles are like paragraph and character styles, the answer is yes — except for one significant difference. If you modify an attribute directly on an object that a graphic style is linked to, that modification effectively breaks the link between the object and the style. So if you were to subsequently redefine that graphic style, it wouldn't update on that object.

You can apply a graphic style to a layer, group, or individual object.**A** When applied to a layer or group, the style will be linked to all the objects in the layer or group, as well as to any objects that you may subsequently add to it. When an object, group, or layer containing a graphic style is targeted, the name of the style and its individual attributes are listed on, and can be edited via, the Appearance panel.**B** The Graphic Styles and Appearance panels work hand in hand.

The original objects

Jiggle Outline
(Type Effects library)

Shirofuchi 2
(Type Effects library)

Chisel
(Artistic Effects library)

Thick Orange Neon
(Neon Effects library)

Yellow Glow
(Image Effects library)

A We applied a few Illustrator graphic styles to these objects, just to give you an inkling of what styles can do.

![Appearance panel screenshot]

APPEARANCE

Group: Yellow Glow

Fill:
Opacity: Default
Stroke: 2 pt
Opacity: Default

Contents

Fill:

B When an object or group containing a graphic style is targeted, the style name and its attributes are listed on the Appearance panel.

Loading graphic styles from a library

The default Graphic Styles panel contains only six styles, but there are many other predefined graphic styles that you can load onto the panel. The styles on the Graphic Styles panel save with the current document.

To load graphic styles from a library:

1. From the **Graphic Styles Libraries** menu at the bottom of the Graphic Styles panel, 🔲 choose a library name. A separate library panel opens. **A**

   Note: User libraries are opened from the User Defined submenu on the Graphic Styles Libraries menu (see page 218).

2. Do one of the following:

   To add a style to the Graphic Styles panel by applying it to an object, select an object, then click a style thumbnail in the library. Or drag a style thumbnail from the library over any selected or unselected object. The chosen style will appear on the Graphic Styles panel.

   To add a style to the Graphic Styles panel without styling an object, deselect, then click a style thumbnail in the library.

   To add multiple styles, click, then Shift-click a series of consecutive styles or Cmd-click/Ctrl-click multiple styles on the library panel, then choose **Add to Graphic Styles** from the library panel menu.

3. To scroll through other predefined libraries (in alphabetical order), click the Load Previous Graphic Styles Library button ◄ or Load Next Graphic Styles Library button ► on the library panel.

➤ If a style that you load onto the Graphic Styles panel contains a brush stroke, and the brush isn't already present on the document's Brushes panel, it will be added to the Brushes panel.

➤ To change the view for the Graphic Styles panel, from the panel menu, choose Thumbnail View, Small List View, or Large List View. Also choose the Use Square for Preview option (the default square shape) or the Use Text for Preview option (to have a "T" character display in each thumbnail).

➤ To load a graphic style library from another document, choose Other from the Graphic Styles Libraries menu, locate the desired file, then click Open.

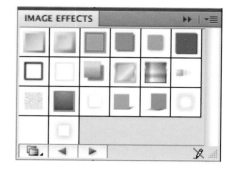

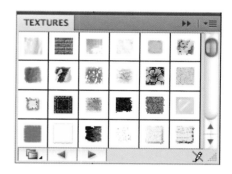

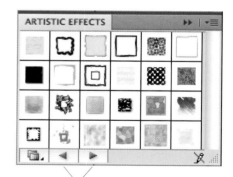

Click the Load Next or Load Previous button to cycle through the libraries.

A *Graphic style libraries display on a separate, free-floating panel.*

Applying graphic styles

When you apply a graphic style to an object, the attributes in the style completely replace the existing attributes in the object. On the preceding page, you learned that a graphic style is applied to a selected object automatically if you click a style on a library panel. In the steps below, you will apply a style via the Graphic Styles panel. The style will remain associated with the object unless you break the link intentionally (see page 218).

To apply a graphic style to an object:

1. Display the Graphic Styles panel, and load any styles onto it that you want to try out.

2. Do either of the following:

   With the Selection tool (V), select one or more objects in the document window.

   On the right side of the Layers panel, click the target circle for an object, layer, or group. **A**

   Remember, for a top-level layer, selecting and targeting have different functions (see the sidebar on page 178).

3. Do either of the following:

   Click a style name or thumbnail on the Graphic Styles panel. **B–C** The name of the graphic style that's linked to the currently selected object, group, or layer will be listed at the top of the Appearance panel. Some styles take a few moments to process (a progress bar displays).

   Click the **Styles** thumbnail on the Control panel to open a temporary Graphic Styles panel, then click a style on the panel.

   ➤ To view an enlarged thumbnail of a graphic style, Control-click/right-click and hold on any thumbnail on the panel.

➤ You can also apply a style by dragging from the Graphic Styles panel over any unselected object.

➤ If you apply a graphic style to a layer or group, **D** it will appear in all the current and subsequently created objects in that layer or group. You can also apply a different graphic style to individual objects that are nested within the layer or group (yes, this can lead to confusion!).

➤ To preserve the existing fill and stroke colors of type when applying graphic styles, make sure Override Character Color is checked on the Graphic Styles panel menu first.

A Via the Layers panel, we are targeting a text object for an appearance change.

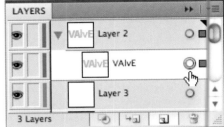

B We clicked a swatch on the Graphic Styles panel.

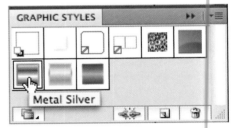

C The graphic style appears on the object (this style is Metal Silver, from the Type Effects library).

D We applied the Opal Inlay Normal graphic style from the Buttons and Rollovers library to these objects.

Removing graphic styles

To remove a graphic style that you have applied to an object, apply the Default Graphic Style, which consists of a solid white fill and a black stroke of 1 pt. (Note: If you need to break the link to a style without changing how the object looks, see page 218.)

To remove a graphic style from an object and apply the default style:

1. With the Selection tool ▶ (V), select the object to which you want to restore the default graphic style, or on the Layers panel,● click the object's target circle.**A**

2. On the Graphic Styles panel, click the **Default Graphic Style** (first) thumbnail. **B–C**

If you apply a graphic style to a layer or group and then subsequently decide to remove it, you need to click a different button than for an object.

To remove a graphic style from a layer or group:

1. Target the layer or group from which you want to remove a graphic style.

2. At the bottom of the Appearance panel, click the **Clear Appearance** button.●

If New Art Has Basic Appearance is checked on the Appearance panel menu, subsequently created objects will have one solid-color fill attribute and one stroke attribute but no graphic styles or effects. If this option is unchecked, the appearance attributes that are currently on the panel will be applied to new objects. Any time you want to specify the Default Graphic Style for an object you're about to create, follow these two simple steps.

To establish the default style for future objects:

1. Deselect all.

2. On the Graphic Styles panel, click the **Default Graphic Style** thumbnail.

A *This object has a graphic style. We want to restore the default style to it.*

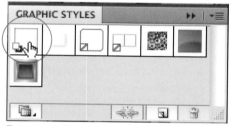

B *We are clicking the Default Graphic Style thumbnail on the Graphic Styles panel.*

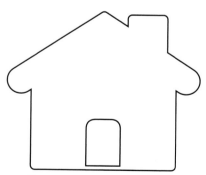

C *The default graphic style consists of a white fill and a black 1-pt. stroke.*

Adding graphic styles

Instead of letting a graphic style wipe out all the existing attributes on an object, you can add a graphic style to the existing attributes. Styles from the Additive and Additive for Blob Brush libraries must be applied this way, but any other graphic style can also be applied as an additive style.

To add a graphic style to an object's existing attributes:

1. With the Selection tool ➤ (V), click an object to which appearance attributes or a graphic style have been applied,**A** or target the object via the Layers panel.

2. *Optional:* Open the Additive graphic style library or another library (see page 211). The thumbnails for additive styles have a red slash.▨

3. On the Graphic Styles panel or on a library panel, Option-click/Alt-click a style thumbnail.**B–D** The new style will be added to the existing attributes.

4. If you didn't get the results you expected, it may be due to the stacking order of attributes on the Appearance panel. For example, a fully opaque fill attribute may be obscuring another fill attribute below it. To change the result, change the opacity and/or blending mode of the attributes that are listed first (see page 350), or restack them. To verify the effect of an attribute, hide and then show it by clicking in the visibility column.

➤ Graphic styles can be applied to symbol instances by using the Symbol Styler tool (see page 367).

A *The Floating with Shadow style (Image Effects library) is applied to these objects.*

B *We added the Yellow Glow style (Image Effects library) to the Floating with Shadow style.*

C *We added the Outer Glow style (Additive library) to the Floating with Shadow style.*

D *We added the Scribble 11 style (Scribble Effects library) to the Floating with Shadow style.*

Creating graphic styles

There are two ways to create a new graphic style. You can base it on an existing object that contains the desired attributes, or you can duplicate an existing style and then edit the duplicate. The first method will probably feel more natural and intuitive, especially if you want to experiment with various settings for the new style before you create it.

To create a graphic style from an object:

1. Target an object that contains the attributes to be saved as a graphic style. If desired, use the Appearance panel to apply attributes that you want the style to contain, such as effects, additional fills or strokes, or opacity settings. **A**

2. Do either of the following:

   On the Graphic Styles panel, Option-click/ Alt-click the **New Graphic Style** button, type a name for the style in the Graphic Style Options dialog, then click OK. **B** The new style will appear as the last thumbnail or listing on the panel. **C**

   Drag the thumbnail from the upper left corner of the Appearance panel onto the Graphic Styles panel, or with the Selection tool, drag the object onto the Graphic Styles panel. Double-click the new style swatch, type a name for it, then click OK.

To modify a duplicate graphic style:

1. On the Graphic Styles panel, click the style swatch or name to be duplicated, then click the **New Graphic Style** button. A numeral will be appended to the style name (e.g., the numeral "1" for the first duplicate of the style).

2. Double-click the duplicate style to open the Graphic Style Options dialog, type a name for the style, then click OK.

3. If you click the duplicate graphic style swatch or name, the attributes it contains will be listed on the Appearance panel. Edit the style by following the steps on the next page.

▶ To merge the attributes of two or more graphic styles into a new style (while keeping the original styles), Cmd-click/Ctrl-click the styles to be merged, choose Merge Graphic Styles from the panel menu, enter a name in the dialog, then click OK.

A *Click the object that contains the attributes to be saved as a graphic style.*

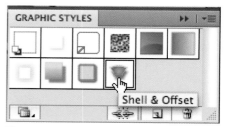

B *Enter a name for the new graphic style.*

C *The new style will appear as the last swatch on the Graphic Styles panel.*

Redefining graphic styles

Beware! If you redefine a graphic style, your edits will appear in all the objects the style is currently linked to. If you don't want this to happen, duplicate the style first (see "To modify a duplicate graphic style" on the preceding page), then edit the duplicate.

To redefine a graphic style:

1. Apply the graphic style to be redefined to an object, so you'll be able to preview your edits. Keep the object selected.**A–B**

2. Edit the object so it has the attributes you want in the redefined style. Via the Appearance panel,⬤ edit or restack the existing appearance attributes, add new attributes, or delete any unwanted ones (see Chapter 14).**C–D** For example, you could apply a different solid color, pattern, or gradient to an existing fill attribute; create an additional fill, stroke, or effect attribute; edit the settings for an existing effect by clicking the effect name; or change the blending mode or opacity via the Opacity link (see Chapter 27).

3. Do either of the following:

   On the Appearance panel menu, choose **Redefine Graphic Style** "[style name]."

   Option-drag/Alt-drag the square from the upper left corner of the Appearance panel over the original swatch on the Graphic Styles panel.

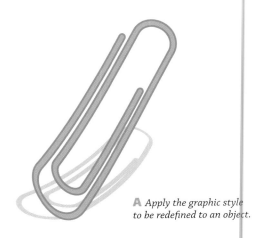

A *Apply the graphic style to be redefined to an object.*

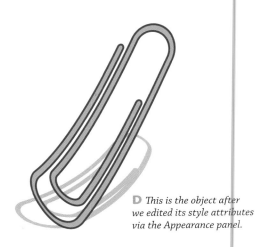

B *The Appearance panel displays the attributes for the Arc Lower graphic style (note the topmost listing).*

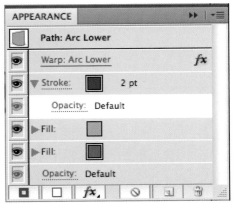

C *We modified the settings for the Warp effect and changed the color for the Stroke and lower Fill attributes.*

D *This is the object after we edited its style attributes via the Appearance panel.*

Regardless of which method you use, a progress bar may display temporarily, and the style swatch will update to reflect your edits.**A** Any objects to which the style is linked will update automatically.**B**

➤ While editing the settings for a graphic style, be careful not to click other styled objects or graphic style swatches, or your current appearance settings will be lost.

Deleting graphic styles from the panel

If you delete a graphic style that's linked to any objects in your document, the attributes from the style will remain on the objects, but of course the link will be broken.

To delete a style from the Graphic Styles panel:

1. On the Graphic Styles panel, click the style to be removed, or Cmd-click/Ctrl-click multiple styles.

2. Click the **Delete Graphic Style** button on the panel.

3. Click Yes in the alert dialog. (Oops! Change your mind? Choose Undo.)

➤ To delete a selected graphic style without an alert dialog opening, Option-click/Alt-click the Delete Graphic Style button.

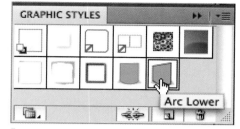

A *The style updates on the Graphic Styles panel…*

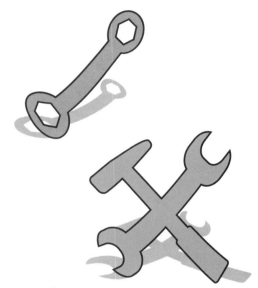

B *… and also updates on all the objects it's already linked to.*

Creating a custom graphic style library

If you save your favorite graphic styles to a custom library, you'll be able to use that library in any document. You can organize and name your libraries in any logical way, such as by theme or client name.

To create a graphic styles library:

1. Make sure the Graphic Styles panel contains only the styles to be saved in a library.

2. *Optional:* To remove all the styles from the Graphic Styles panel that aren't currently being used in the document, choose Select All Unused from the Graphic Styles panel menu, click the Delete Graphic Style button, 🗑 then click Yes in the alert dialog.

3. From the **Graphic Styles Libraries** menu 📑 on the Graphic Styles panel, choose **Save Graphic Styles**.

4. In the Save Graphic Styles as Library dialog, type a name for the library. Keep the extension and the default location, which in the Mac OS is /Users/[user name]/Library/Application Support/Adobe/Adobe Illustrator CS5/en_US/ Graphic Styles; and in Windows 7 is C:\Users\ [user name]\ AppData\Roaming\Adobe\Adobe Illustrator CS5 Settings\en_US\Graphic Styles. Click Save.

5. The new library will now be listed on, and can be opened from, the **User Defined** submenu on the Graphic Styles Libraries menu. **A**

Breaking the link to a graphic style

If you break the link between an object and a graphic style, the object won't change visually. However, if you subsequently redefine the style, the style won't update on that object (but it will update on any other objects it's still linked to).

To break the link to a graphic style:

1. Do one of the following:

   With the Selection tool (V), select one or more objects in the document.

   Click the target circle for an object on the Layers panel, or if the style was applied to a group, sublayer, or layer, click the target circle for that listing.

2. Do either of the following:

   Click the **Break Link to Graphic Style** button ⚒ at the bottom of the Graphic Styles panel. **B**

   Edit the appearance attributes of the selected item or items (e.g., apply a different fill color, stroke color or setting, pattern, gradient, transparency setting, or effect). Your edits will effectively break the link.

   Note: The graphic style name is no longer listed at the top of the Appearance panel for the selected or targeted object(s).

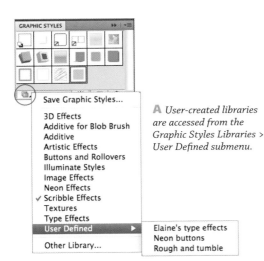

A *User-created libraries are accessed from the Graphic Styles Libraries > User Defined submenu.*

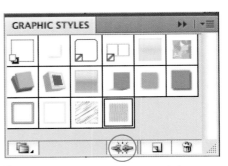

B *Click the Break Link to Graphic Style button on the Graphic Styles panel.*

If you have a digital photo or scanned graphic that you want to convert to editable vector art, you'll find the techniques you need in this chapter. You will learn how to apply custom tracing settings before and after tracing, create and manage custom tracing presets, release a tracing, expand a tracing into separate paths, and convert a tracing to a Live Paint group.

The tracing features in Illustrator

The Live Trace command can detect and trace the color and shade areas in any raster image that you open or place into Illustrator, such as a Photoshop EPS, TIFF, JPEG, or PSD image, or scanned artwork, such as a logo. You can choose from a wide array of tracing options prior to tracing—and because traced objects are "live," you can also fine-tune the tracing results via the Tracing Options dialog before converting them into editable paths or a Live Paint group. You can use a built-in tracing preset (a set of presaved settings) as a starting point, or create and save custom presets of your own. Among the numerous settings that you can specify are the precision with which the image is traced, the stroke weight and length, the number of colors, and a color palette.

With such a wide range of tracing controls at your fingertips, you can produce everything from a close simulation of your original artwork to a loose sketch. Regardless of the type of imagery you trace, the end result will be editable paths with a specific number of fill and/or stroke colors. Although the Live Trace command doesn't have the natural editing power of the human eye and brain, it does a decent job, and you may find the results useful—provided you're willing to do a little cleanup work afterward. When you need to create complex, nongeometric artwork, it's much faster to start with a tracing than it is to draw a gazillion intricate shapes by hand. **A–C**

LIVE TRACE

17

A *A portion of the original photo*

B *The photo traced*

C *The tracing displayed as path outlines*

Tracing a raster image

In these instructions, you'll trace a raster image using preset settings. In the instructions that begin on the next page, we'll show you how to choose custom settings for a new tracing and also apply custom settings to an existing tracing.

After tracing an image, you can either convert the results into editable paths via the Expand command or convert the artwork to a Live Paint group (see pages 225–226).

To trace a raster image:

1. Using File > **Open**, open a raster image, such as a TIFF, JPEG, or PSD file; or with an Illustrator document open, use File > **Place** to place a raster image. **A** (To learn about the Open and Place commands, see pages 288–291.)

   Note: If you open or place a PSD (Photoshop) file that contains layers with the Link option unchecked, the Photoshop Import Options dialog opens. Click Convert Layers to Objects to import the image as a series of objects on multiple layers, or click Flatten Layers to a Single Image to import the image as just one flattened layer.

2. With the Selection tool, ▸ click the image object to be traced, or select it via the Layers panel.

3. On the Control panel, do either of the following:

   To trace the object using preset settings, from the **Tracing Presets and Options** menu, ▾ **B–C** choose a preset based on how detailed you want the end result to be. You can try out a few different presets.

   To trace the object using the last-used settings (or the default settings), click **Live Trace**.

4. If an alert dialog appears, informing you that the tracing may proceed slowly, click OK. Some presets take longer to process than others. A progress bar may appear onscreen as Illustrator traces the object, and new options will display on the Control panel when the tracing is completed.

5. *Optional:* To customize the tracing results, see the instructions that begin on the next page.

A *Place a raster image into an Illustrator document…*

B *…then choose a tracing preset from the menu on the Control panel.*

C *The Color 6 tracing preset produced this yummy vector art.*

Applying tracing options

By choosing settings in the Tracing Options dialog or from the Control panel, you can make your tracing conform more closely to the colors and shapes in the original artwork, or do the opposite and simplify the tracing dramatically. And because tracings are live, you can choose these options before or after using the Live Trace command.

To apply tracing options:

1. *Optional:* To apply colors from a custom library to the resulting vector art, open that library via the Swatches Libraries menu 🗔. on the Swatches panel. If you click the Load Previous or Load Next Swatch Library button, the libraries you display will be listed on the Palette menu in the Tracing Options dialog (see step 5).

2. Select a Live Trace object in your document.

3. Click the **Tracing Options Dialog** button 🔠 on the Control panel. The Tracing Options dialog opens.**A** Check Preview (or to speed up processing, don't check it until you get to step 6).

Note: You can choose whichever options in steps 4 through 8 seem appropriate for your tracing.

4. Choose a different **Preset** (the choices here are the same as on the Preset menu on the Control panel).

5. Choose options in the **Adjustments** area to control how the image is prepared for retracing:

   From the **Mode** menu, choose Color, Grayscale, or Black and White, for the type of colors you want the final tracing to contain.

   For Black and White mode only, choose a **Threshold** value (0–255; the default value is 128). All pixels darker than this value will be converted to black; all pixels lighter than this value will be converted to white. (You can also change the Threshold value on the Control panel after exiting the dialog.)

   For Grayscale or Color mode, from the **Palette** menu, choose Automatic to have Illustrator use colors from the image in the tracing, or choose the name of any swatch library you opened in

Continued on the following page

CHOOSING OPTIONS BEFORE TRACING

To choose custom options prior to tracing, click an image object in your Illustrator document. From the Tracing Presets and Options menu ▼ on the Control panel, choose Tracing Options to open the dialog, then follow steps 4–9, beginning on this page.

A *Choose custom settings in the Tracing Options dialog.*

step 1 to allow the final tracing to contain colors just from that library (nifty feature!).

For just Grayscale or Color mode and the Palette menu choice of Automatic, choose a **Max Colors** value for the maximum number of colors the final tracing may contain (2–256; the default value is 6). For a hand-drawn or screen-printed look with fewer fill areas, keep this value low (say, 12 or less); this will also speed up the retracing. (You can also change the Max Colors value on the Control panel after exiting the dialog.**A**)

Click **Output to Swatches** (recommended) to save the colors in the resulting tracing as new global process color swatches on the Swatches panel.

Choose a **Blur** value (0–20 pixels) to reduce artifacts, noise, and extraneous marks. This option simplifies the image for retracing by diminishing its sharpness.

Check **Resample** and change the resolution for the tracing. The lower the resolution, the faster the retracing, but the fewer the resulting image details and the less precise the outlines.

6. Make sure **Preview** is checked, then in the **View** area, choose from the Vector menu, then from the Raster menu, to compare the source image to the tracing results:

The **Vector** options control how the tracing results are displayed: No Tracing Result hides the tracing so you can view your original or adjusted image; Tracing Result displays the tracing based on the current dialog settings; Outlines shows the tracing paths only, without any fills or strokes; and Outlines with Tracing displays the resulting paths on top of a dimmed version of the resulting fills and strokes.

The **Raster** options control how the underlying raster image displays (you won't see the raster image unless No Tracing Result or Outlines is chosen as the Vector preview option): No Image hides the original image; Original Image shows the original image unaltered; Adjusted Image shows how the image will be preprocessed for

tracing (e.g., by being resampled, or by having its colors or shades reduced); and Transparent Image dims the image so you can see the tracing results more clearly on top.

(You will also be able to choose these view settings via the Preview Different Views of Raster Image ▲ and Preview Different Views of Vector Result △ menus on the Control panel after exiting the dialog.**A**)

7. Choose **Trace Settings** options to control the resulting paths:

➤ As you choose Adjustments and Trace Settings, you can monitor the number of Paths, Anchors, Colors, and Areas in the resulting artwork via the readouts on the right side of the dialog.

For Black and White mode only, check **Fills** to create filled paths and/or **Strokes** to create stroked paths. If Strokes is checked, specify a Max Stroke Weight value (0–100 px; the default value is 10). Areas this wide or narrower will become strokes; wider areas will become outlined areas. If Strokes is checked, also specify a Min Stroke Length value (0–200 px; the default value is 20). Areas this long or longer will be defined as strokes; areas that are shorter than this length will be ignored.

Specify a **Path Fitting** value to control how closely traced paths will follow the edges of shapes in the image (0–10 px; the default value is 2). A low Path Fitting value results in a more accurate fit but also produces more anchor points.

Change the **Minimum Area** setting (the default is 10 px) to control the number of extraneous small paths that are created. Specify the smallest area that you will permit Illustrator to trace (0–3000 pixels square). For example, a 5 x 5-pixel object would occupy a 25-pixel area. For a medium-resolution image (200 ppi) using Grayscale or Color mode, a small Minimum Area value (10–60 px) produces a detailed tracing with a photographic look, whereas a larger area (144–300 px) produces a looser, more

A *These options are available on the Control panel when a color tracing object is selected.*

"hand-drawn" tracing. For a high-resolution image (300 ppi), a value of 600 px or greater would be needed to produce a loose tracing. Adjust the Max Colors and Minimum Area settings to control the tightness or looseness of the tracing. (You can also change the Min Area value on the Control panel after exiting the dialog.)

Choose a **Corner Angle** for the minimum angle a path must have to be defined by a corner anchor point instead of by a smooth point (0–180°; the default is 20°).

If you check **Ignore White**, a fill of None will be applied to any white areas in the tracing (in other words, those areas will be transparent).

8. If you save your settings as a preset, you'll be able to apply them to any image and use them as a starting point when choosing custom settings.

Click **Save Preset**, type a name for the preset in the Save Tracing Preset dialog, then click OK. (The Resample and View settings aren't saved.)

9. Click **Trace**. A–B A progress bar will appear onscreen while Illustrator traces the image (be patient!), then a "Tracing" listing for the traced object (possibly nested) will appear on the Layers panel. If you're happy with the results, you can either expand the tracing into editable paths or convert it into a Live Paint group (see pages 225–226).

➤ You can also create and edit a tracing preset by way of the Tracing Presets dialog. See the next page.

➤ Saved presets can be chosen from the Preset menu on the Control panel when a raster image or tracing object is selected, or from the Preset menu in the Tracing Options dialog.

A *After choosing the Detailed Drawing tracing preset, we changed the Threshold value to 135 and the Max Stroke Weight value to 2 px.*

B *For this tracing, we chose custom options of Max Colors 171, Path Fitting 5 px, and Minimum Area 404 px.*

Managing tracing presets

Use the Tracing Presets dialog to create, edit, delete, import, or export custom tracing presets.

To create, delete, edit, import, or export a tracing preset:

1. Choose Edit > **Tracing Presets**. The Tracing Presets dialog opens.**A**

2. To create a new preset based on an existing one, click a preset on the Presets scroll list, or to create a new preset based on the default tracing settings, click [Default]. Click **New** to open the Tracing Options dialog. Enter a Name, choose the desired settings, then click Done.

   To edit an existing preset, click the preset on the Presets scroll list, then click **Edit**. Choose settings in the Tracing Options dialog, then click Done.

   To delete a preset, click the preset name, then click **Delete**.

   The Import and Export options enable you to share presets with other users. To import a user-saved preset, click **Import**; in the Import Presets File dialog, locate and click the desired preset file, then click Open. To export the settings for the currently chosen preset as a file, click **Export**; in the Export Presets File As dialog, keep the default location, then click Save.

3. Click OK.

➤ To establish new settings for the [Default] preset, deselect all, choose Object > Live Trace > Tracing Options, choose settings in the Tracing Options dialog, then click Set Default.

➤ The Preview option isn't available when you create or edit a preset by way of the Tracing Presets dialog.

Releasing a tracing

To restore a tracing object to its virgin bitmap (pretraced) state, you must use the Release command.

To release a tracing object:

1. Select the tracing object.

2. Choose Object > Live Trace > **Release**. The listing on the Layers panel will change from Tracing to Image, or to the file name of the original image.

A *Use the Tracing Presets dialog to create, edit, delete, import, or export tracing presets, which are collections of settings.*

Converting a tracing to paths

The Expand command converts a tracing into standard paths, which can then be selected via the Layers panel and recolored, reshaped, or transformed, like any other paths. Once a tracing is expanded, it no longer has "live" properties, meaning its Tracing Options settings can't be altered.

To expand and recolor a live tracing:

1. Trace a placed image in your document, **A–B** and keep the Live Trace object selected.

2. On the Control panel, click **Expand**. On the Layers panel, you'll now see a group containing a gazillion paths — or possibly fewer, depending on the tracing settings used (**A**, next page).

3. Deselect. If you turn on Smart Guides (with the Object Highlighting preference checked) and pass the Selection tool over the former tracing,

you'll see that each area in the artwork is now a separate path.

4. *Optional:* Select the expanded group, then ungroup it (Cmd-Shift-G/Ctrl-Shift-G) (**B**, next page).

5. Select, isolate, then recolor, any of the resulting objects (**C–D**, next page).

To simplify color areas, unite multiple selected paths via the Unite button on the Pathfinder panel (under Shape Modes); see Chapter 25.

To delete extraneous paths, you can either select them with the Selection tool, then press Delete/Backspace; or multiple-select their listings on the Layers panel, then click the Delete Selection button. 🗑 If there are many paths, this can be painstaking work.

A *These custom Tracing Options settings produced the tracing at right.*

B *A low Max Colors value and a high Minimum Area value produced these simplified shapes.*

A *The tracing is expanded (here the objects are shown selected).*

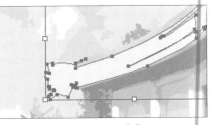

B *After ungrouping the expanded tracing, we put a section of the building into isolation mode.*

C *We used the Scissors tool to cut the object in two. We selected the left object, then with the Eyedropper tool, clicked an area of sky to apply that color to the selection.*

As an alternative to the Expand command, you can convert a Live Trace object to a Live Paint group. This is a good route to take if your tracing is relatively simple and you want to utilize Live Paint features, such as the ability to hide or recolor edges or quickly recolor faces (fill areas). To learn about the Live Paint features, see the next chapter.

To convert a Live Trace object to a Live Paint group:

1. Select a Live Trace object.

2. On the Control panel, click **Live Paint**. Ta-da!

D *This is the final result.*

The Live Paint feature provides a novel way to fill paths. To create an "armature" for a Live Paint group, you can either create some open or closed paths with a drawing tool, such as the Pencil or Blob Brush tool, then convert the whole drawing into a Live Paint group, **A** or you can convert a tracing into a Live Paint group and recolor it using Live Paint group features.

With the Live Paint Bucket tool, you simply click or drag across any area that is formed by intersecting lines (called a face), **B** and the current paint attributes are applied. Add to or reshape the Live Paint objects at any time, and the fill color flows into the new shape; that's what makes the whole process "live." Another unique feature of Live Paint groups is that you can recolor (or leave unpainted) individual line segments, called edges. **C** This method for recoloring sketches and tracings is flexible — and fun.

In this chapter, you will learn how to convert ordinary objects to a Live Paint group, apply colors to faces and edges in the group, reshape and move parts of the group, add new faces and edges, and finally, expand or release the group into standard paths.

LIVE PAINT

18

A *We converted this pencil sketch to a Live Paint group.*

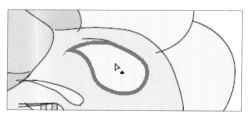

B *We selected a face in the group.*

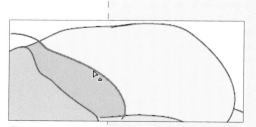

C *We selected an edge.*

Creating a Live Paint group

When drawing paths for a Live Paint group, you must allow your drawing lines to intersect. The Live Paint Bucket tool, which you'll use to color areas of the group, detects and fills only faces (areas that are bounded by intersecting lines).

To create a Live Paint group from your artwork, you can either click the paths with the Live Paint Bucket tool or choose the Live Paint command. Both methods preserve only the basic fill and stroke settings. Other attributes, such as transparency settings, brush strokes, and effects, are removed.

Note: Another way to create a Live Paint group, in addition to the two methods offered in step 3, is to trace an image via the Live Trace command, then with the tracing object selected, click Live Paint on the Control panel (see the preceding chapter).

To create a Live Paint group:

1. Draw some open or closed paths with any tool, such as the Pencil, Blob Brush, Pen, Line Segment, or Ellipse, and apply some stroke colors and weights. You may use the Paintbrush tool, but the Live Paint command will remove the brush stroke. As you create the sketch, be sure to let some or all of the segments intersect.**A**

2. Select all the paths.

3. Do either of the following:

   Choose the **Live Paint Bucket** tool (K), then click one of the selected objects.**B**

   Choose Object > **Live Paint** > **Make** (Cmd-Option-X/Ctrl-Alt-X).

   If an alert appears regarding object features that may be discarded, click OK. On the Layers panel, the paths will be nested within a Live Paint group.

   Note: If an alert illustrating the steps to create a Live Paint group appears, click OK. Make sure the objects are selected, then click with the Paint Bucket tool.

➤ To produce a Live Paint group from a symbol or a blend, you must apply Object > Expand first; to produce a Live Paint group from a clipping set, release the set first; or to produce a Live Paint group from type, convert it to outlines via Type > Create Outlines first.

➤ Some Illustrator commands aren't available for Live Paint groups, such as the Clipping Mask, Blend, Pathfinder, and Select > Same commands.

A *As you draw a picture, allow your line segments to intersect. This portrait was drawn with the Pencil tool.*

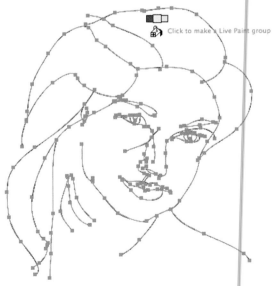

B *Click one of the selected paths or enclosed areas with the Live Paint Bucket tool to convert them all to a Live Paint group.*

Using the Live Paint Bucket tool

On the next page, you'll learn how to use the Live Paint Bucket tool to recolor a Live Paint group. Before doing that, use the Live Paint Bucket Options dialog to choose settings for the tool.

To choose options for the Live Paint Bucket tool:

1. Do either of the following:

   Double-click the **Live Paint Bucket** tool 🪣 (K).

   Select the Live Paint Bucket tool (K), then press Return/Enter.

2. The Live Paint Bucket Options dialog opens.**A** In the Options area:

   Click **Paint Fills** and/or **Paint Strokes**, depending on what parts of the group you want the tool to paint. Note: If you're going to follow the instructions on the next page, check only Paint Fills.

   ➤ If you check just one of these options, you can Shift-click with the tool to switch its function between painting fills (faces) and applying stroke (edge) colors and weights. We actually find this to be the easiest method, because when the tool has only one function, you can't inadvertently recolor a face when you intended to recolor an edge, or vice versa. If both Paint options are checked, you can hold down Shift to restrict the tool function to Paint Fills.

   Check **Cursor Swatch Preview** to display, in a tiny strip above the tool pointer, the current color (when using the Color panel), or the color of the last chosen swatch on the Swatches panel and the swatch to its left and right.**B–C** We keep this option checked, because we find the color strip to be helpful and unobtrusive.

3. *Optional:* If the current highlight color is too similar to colors in your artwork (or colors you're likely to apply), check Highlight, then, from the Color menu, choose a preset color for the faces and edges the tool will pass over, or click the color swatch and choose a color from the Colors dialog. You can also change the Width for the highlight.

4. Click OK. Now you're ready to use the tool, which we give instructions for on the next page.

   ➤ To avoid visual confusion, choose a different highlight color for the Live Paint Bucket tool than for the Live Paint Selection tool (see page 232).

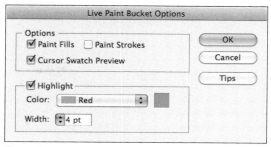

A *Use the Live Paint Bucket Options dialog to establish default settings for the tool.*

B *If the Cursor Swatch Preview option is on for the Live Paint Bucket tool and you mix a color via the Color panel, that color will display in the pointer.*

C *If the Cursor Swatch Preview option is on for the Live Paint Bucket tool and you click a swatch on the Swatches panel, that color and the two swatches adjacent to it will display above the pointer.*

When you apply fill or stroke attributes to a Live Paint group, faces or edges are recolored — not the actual paths. If you reshape a Live Paint group in any way, such as by editing the paths, colors in the group will reflow instantly into any newly created faces. In the steps below, you will recolor faces with the Live Paint Bucket tool. This technique reminds us of a drawing method we used as kids: We would draw a big swirly doodle on a piece of paper, then color in the shapes. It's so much faster in Illustrator!

Note: You can apply a solid color, pattern, or gradient to faces and edges in a Live Paint group. The term "color" in this chapter is a generic reference to all three kinds of swatches.

To recolor faces with the Live Paint Bucket tool:

1. Have a Live Paint group at the ready (you don't need to select it).**A** Double-click the **Live Paint Bucket** tool 🪣 to open the Live Paint Bucket Options dialog. Check Paint Fills, uncheck Paint Strokes, then click OK.

2. Set colors on the Swatches panel to be used for recoloring, preferably in groups. You can use the Recolor Artwork, Color Guide, or Kuler panel to create some color groups.

3. Click the Fill color square on the Tools or Color panel, then click a swatch or color group icon on the Swatches panel. If the Cursor Swatch Preview option is checked in the tool options dialog, as we recommend, the currently selected swatch will display as the middle color above the pointer.

   ➤ Press the left or right arrow key to select the previous or next swatch on the Swatches panel. Keep pressing the same key to proceed along the current row in the Swatches panel, or to cycle through the colors in a color group.

4. Do either of the following:

   Move the pointer over a face that you want to apply the color to (an area where two or more paths intersect), then click in the highlighted face.**B**

   Drag across multiple faces.

   ➤ Hold down Option/Alt to turn the Live Paint Bucket tool into a temporary Eyedropper tool, and use it to sample (by clicking) a fill color from anywhere in the document.

A *This Live Paint group was created from lines that were drawn with the Pencil tool.*

B *When the Live Paint Bucket tool is clicked on a face (an area where paths intersect) in a Live Paint group, the current fill color is applied (**B**, next page shows this face filled in).*

"FLOODING" FACES

➤ Double-click a face with the Live Paint Bucket tool to fill contiguous faces across all edges that have a stroke of None.

➤ Triple-click a face to recolor all faces that already have the same color as the one you click, whether they're contiguous or not.

You can also use the Live Paint Bucket tool to apply stroke colors and/or stroke settings. Each edge can have a different color, weight, and other stroke attributes, or a stroke color of None. A unique feature of Live Paint groups is that only the edges you click are modified — not the whole path.

To modify edges with the Live Paint Bucket tool:

1. Choose the **Live Paint Bucket** tool, and establish the same default settings as in step 1 on the preceding page.

2. Click the Stroke color square on the Tools or Color panel, then choose a stroke color. Also choose a stroke weight and other attributes via the Stroke panel, which you can access via the link on the Control or Appearance panel. ★ You can apply a color of None to effectively hide an edge.

3. Do either or both of the following:

   Hold down Shift to toggle the tool function to Paint Strokes, move the pointer over an edge in a Live Paint group (it becomes a brush icon), then click. **A–C**

   Starting with the pointer positioned over an edge, Shift-drag across or along multiple edges.

▶ To click an edge in a Live Paint group, position the very tip of the brush in the pointer on the edge (or press Caps Lock for a crosshairs pointer). Illustrator gives edges a narrower highlight than faces.

▶ You can also recolor a Live Paint group by using the Recolor Artwork dialog (see Chapter 29).

▶ You can apply transparency settings, brush strokes, and effects to an entire Live Paint group, but not to individual faces or edges within it. For instance, if you drag a brush from the Brushes panel over a Live Paint group, that brush will be applied to all the edges in the group.

"FLOODING" EDGES

▶ Double-click an edge with the Live Paint Bucket tool to apply the current stroke color and attributes to all edges that are connected to, and have the same stroke color and weight as, the one you click.

▶ Triple-click an edge to apply the current stroke color and attributes to all edges that have the same attributes as the one you click, contiguous and not.

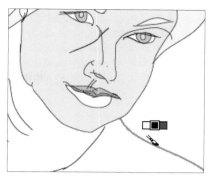

A We are applying stroke attributes to an edge with the Live Paint Bucket tool.

B To create more fillable faces, we drew additional paths on the neck, lips, and face.

C We used the Live Paint Bucket tool to fill the new faces, and also applied a stroke of None to edges on the neck, cheeks, and forehead.

Using the Live Paint Selection tool

With the Live Paint Selection tool, you can select edges and/or faces in a Live Paint group for editing or deletion. Choose options for the tool first.

To choose options for the Live Paint Selection tool:

1. Choose the **Live Paint Selection** tool 🔩 (Shift-L), then press Return/Enter (or double-click the tool).

2. In the Live Paint Selection Options dialog, check **Select Fills** and/or **Select Strokes**.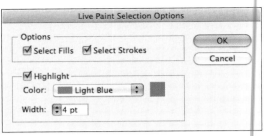 For example, if you want to select only faces, uncheck Select Strokes to prevent any edges from becoming selected inadvertently. You can also choose a different Highlight Color and/or Width for the selections, which we recommend. Click OK.

To select faces and/or edges with the Live Paint Selection tool:

1. Choose the **Live Paint Selection** tool 🔩 (Shift-L), and choose options for the tool (see the steps above).

2. Click an edge or face in a Live Paint group, then Shift-click additional edges and/or faces (depending on the current tool settings).**B** The selection displays as a gray pattern. (To deselect an individual edge or face, Shift-click it.)

3. Do any of the following:

   For **faces**, click the Fill color square on the Tools or Color panel, then choose a solid color,**C** gradient, or pattern. You can modify a gradient fill with the Gradient tool (see pages 323–324).

   For **edges**, click the Stroke color square on the Tools or Color panel, then choose a color. You can also change the stroke weight and other stroke attributes. Apply a stroke of None to any edges that you want to hide.

   To **delete** the currently selected edges or faces, press Delete/Backspace.

4. Click outside the Live Paint group to deselect it.

➤ We've found that if we delete an edge between two faces, the resulting area usually fills with the color from the larger of the former two faces.

➤ Select a face and/or an edge with the Live Paint Selection tool, then choose Select > Same > Fill Color, Stroke Color, or Stroke Weight to quickly select all the other faces and/or edges within the same group that have matching attributes.

A *Use the Live Paint Selection Options dialog to control what parts of a Live Paint group the tool may select. You can also change the Highlight color for selections.*

B *We selected three sections of the woman's hair with the Live Paint Selection tool.*

C *We applied a new fill color to the selected faces.*

COMPARE A LIVE PAINT GROUP CREATED FROM PENCIL TOOL STROKES...

A *When we drew a series of separate paths with the Pencil tool, we made sure the endpoints of each path overlapped another path, in order to create closed areas.*

B *With the Live Paint Bucket tool, we applied fill colors to the faces and stroke colors to individual edges. The fact that we were able to apply a different stroke color to each separate former Pencil tool path proves that those paths became separate edges when they were converted to a Live Paint group.*

...WITH A LIVE PAINT GROUP CREATED FROM BLOB BRUSH TOOL STROKES

C *We used the Blob Brush tool to create a series of separate strokes, which we connected with other strokes in order to create closed areas (faces). In this case, the result is one continuous closed path.*

D *With the Live Paint Bucket tool, we applied fill colors to faces, including one fill color to the entire former Blob Brush stroke outline. Because the Blob Brush drawing converted to just faces, we were able to apply stroke colors only to the entire perimeter of a face (orange to the outer edge of the stroke outline and yellow to the edge of the blue-green face). There are no separate edges to recolor or delete, as there are in Figure **B**, above.*

➤ *When drawing Pencil or Blob Brush artwork for a Live Paint group, try not to create overlapping shapes, which would produce extraneous faces in the resulting group. For a Pencil drawing, although you could apply a stroke of None to hide overlapping edges in the group, that would be extra work. For a Blob Brush drawing, although you could erase the overlapping lines, the erased areas would become separate, extraneous faces.*

Reshaping a Live Paint group

In this task, you will transform or move whole faces in a Live Paint group or manipulate the anchor points on any individual edges. Colors will reflow automatically into the newly modified shapes.

To reshape or move areas in a Live Paint group:

1. Choose the **Selection** tool ▸ (V), and make sure the Bounding Box feature is on (View menu).

2. To isolate a Live Paint group, double-click a face or edge in the group.

3. Do either or both of the following:

    With the **Selection** tool (V), either click a face that contains a fill color or click an edge. A bounding box displays, with star-filled selection handles. Drag the face or edge to move it, or drag a handle on an edge to transform it (see page 137).**A–B** If you want to delete the current selection, press Delete/Backspace.

    With the **Direct Selection** tool ▸ (A), click an edge to display its anchor points and direction handles, then reshape it by manipulating the points or handles (see Chapter 12).

    Fill colors will reflow automatically into any areas you reshape or transform, unless the Live Paint group was created exclusively from Blob Brush strokes.

4. To exit isolation mode, press Esc.

➤ To switch quickly between the Direct Selection tool for reshaping and the Live Paint Bucket tool for recoloring, press A for the former or K for the latter.

A *We selected an edge in a Live Paint group with the Selection tool, then lengthened it to make it intersect with another edge. A new face was created.*

B *With the Live Paint Bucket tool, we applied a fill color to the new face.*

Adding new faces and edges to a Live Paint group

To add new faces and edges to a Live Paint group:

Method 1 (via the Layers or Control panel)

1. Create a path on top of or next to a Live Paint group, or select an existing path.

2. Do either of the following:

   On the Layers panel, drag the new path listing into the **Live Paint Group** listing.

   Choose the Selection tool ▸ (V), marquee both the new path and the Live Paint group, then click **Merge Live Paint** on the Control panel. Click OK if an alert dialog appears.

Method 2 (in isolation mode)

1. Choose the Selection tool (V), then double-click the Live Paint group to put it in isolation mode.

2. With a drawing tool, such as the Pencil or Blob Brush, or a geometric tool, such as the Rectangle or Ellipse, draw the path to be added. **A** It will automatically be part of the Live Paint group.

3. To exit isolation mode, press Esc. **B–C**

➤ With a Live Paint group in isolation mode, if you create and then drag a new closed face over filled faces in the group, release the mouse, and then move the new face away from the group, any of the following may happen: Some faces may adopt the fill color of another face in the group, some faces may adopt the color of the new face, or the new face may be filled with an existing color from the group. If you don't like a result, undo it immediately.

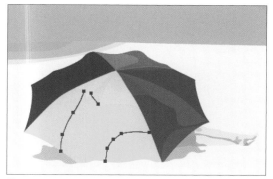

A *With the Live Paint group in isolation mode, we drew paths with the Pencil tool to create some new faces (then we exited isolation mode).*

B *Here we are using the Live Paint Bucket tool to apply fill colors to the new faces.*

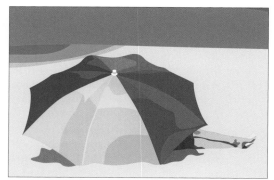

C *This is the final artwork.*

Choosing gap options for a Live Paint group

If you reshape an edge so as to create an opening (called a "gap") in a formerly closed area (face), any fill color in that face will leak or disappear, because in the world of Live Paint, fills can't be applied to open faces. Via the Gap Options dialog, you can specify a gap size setting that will stop fill colors from disappearing or leaking into other faces.

To choose gap options for a Live Paint group:

1. Choose the Selection tool (V), then click the Live Paint group that you want to choose options for.

2. Click the **Gap Options** button 🖼 on the Control panel. The Gap Options dialog opens.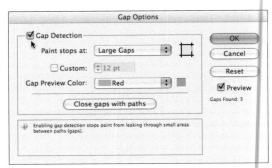

3. Check Preview, then do any of the following:

   Check **Gap Detection**, then to specify a gap size up to which the fill colors won't leak or disappear, from the **Paint Stops At** menu, choose Small Gaps, Medium Gaps, or Large Gaps, or check Custom and enter or choose an exact size (.01–72 pt).**B** The number of gaps in the artwork will be listed below the Preview check box.

   From the **Gap Preview Color** menu, choose a preview color for the invisible (and nonprinting) "lines" that Illustrator uses to bridge the gaps and prevent paint leakage. You can also click the color swatch and choose a color from the Colors dialog. The gap lines display onscreen in a selected Live Paint group when View > Show Live Paint Gaps is on or while the Gap Options dialog is open.

   Click the **Close Gaps with Paths** button to have Illustrator close up any existing gaps with edge segments (click Yes if an alert dialog appears). This may improve the processing time for further edits you make to the group.

4. Click OK. If you increased the gap size, try using the Live Paint Bucket tool to fill areas that couldn't be filled before.**C** Fill colors will still leak or disappear from open faces that have gaps that are larger than the current Paint Stops At size.

▶ The more you allow lines to intersect in the original objects, the fewer gaps will result when the objects are converted to a Live Paint group. To eliminate any overhanging edges, select them with the Live Paint Selection tool and delete them (or apply a stroke of None to hide them).

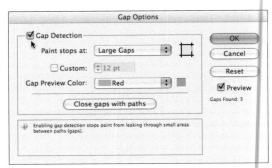

A *Choose Gap Options to control color leakage in a Live Paint group.*

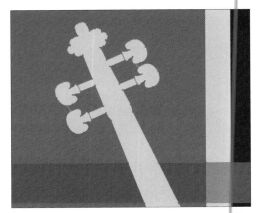

B *We chose the Paint Stops At: Large Gaps option. The gaps are previewing in the current Gap Preview Color.*

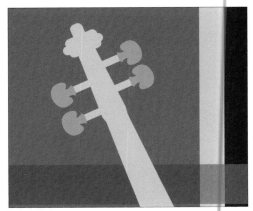

C *With the Large Gaps option chosen, we were able to fill the small- to medium-sized gaps in the open areas.*

Expanding and releasing Live Paint groups

You can't apply appearance attributes (such as brush strokes, transparency settings, or effects) selectively to individual parts of a Live Paint group; you would have to expand or release it into ordinary Illustrator objects first. A Live Paint group may also need to be expanded or released before it can be exported to a non-Adobe application. Use these commands only when you're sure you're done editing the group.

To expand or release a Live Paint group:

1. Using the Selection tool or the Layers panel, select a Live Paint group. *Optional:* Option-drag/ Alt-drag the selection square for the group to preserve a copy of it for future edits.

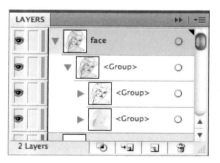

A *The Expand command produced these two nested groups.*

2. Do either of the following:

   On the Control panel, click **Expand** to convert the Live Paint group into two groups of standard paths, nested together within a group. **A** One group will contain filled paths from the former faces, **B** the other group will contain paths with stroke colors from the former edges.

   Choose Object > Live Paint > **Release** to convert the Live Paint group to separate paths, each with a .5-pt. black stroke and a fill of None, within one group. Use this option if, say, you want to start your sketch over with just line work, and you want to remove all the fill colors first.

➤ After applying the Expand or Release command, you can apply stroke or fill attributes, such as a brush stroke or an effect, to the single or multiple paths that result. **C**

B *After expanding the Live Paint group, we hid the <Group> layer that contains the stroked paths. Now only the filled paths are visible.*

C *Finally, we applied a .3-pt. brush stroke to the group of stroked paths to make the line work look more hand drawn.*

EXPANDING A LIVE PAINT GROUP: THE RESULTS FROM FORMER PENCIL PATHS COMPARED WITH FORMER BLOB BRUSH STROKES

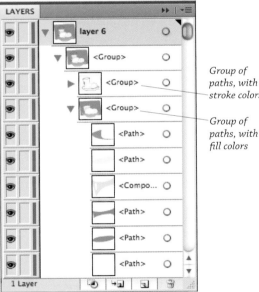

Group of paths, with stroke colors

Group of paths, with fill colors

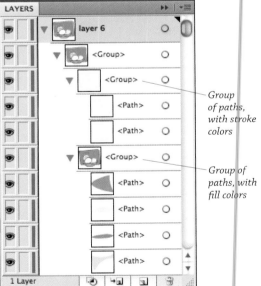

Group of paths, with stroke colors

Group of paths, with fill colors

When we applied the Expand command to a Live Paint group that we created from Pencil tool strokes, the result was two standard nested groups, one containing stroked paths (from the former edges), and the other containing filled paths (from the former faces).

When we applied the Expand command to a Live Paint group that we created from Blob Brush tool strokes, the result was also two nested groups. One contains the former faces, now filled paths; the other group contains only two stroked paths, because we had applied a color to only two edges in the Live Paint group.

The type controls in Illustrator are extensive, and worthy of the two chapters that we have devoted to them.
You will create four kinds of type in this chapter: point type, type in a rectangle, area type (inside an object), and type along a path. You will also copy type between objects, import type from another application, thread overflow type between objects, rotate type, and put type on a circle. In the next chapter, you will learn how to select type and change its attributes.

The type tools

There are three horizontal type tools: the Type tool, Area Type tool, and Type on a Path tool; and three vertical type tools: the Vertical Type tool, Vertical Area Type tool, and Vertical Type on a Path tool. With the exception of the versatile Type and Vertical Type tools, each tool has a specialized function.

➤ With the **Type** tool, T you can create a free-floating block of type that isn't associated with a path, **A** draw a rectangle with the tool and enter type inside the rectangle, enter type along the edge of an open path, or enter type inside a closed path.

➤ The **Area Type** tool T creates type inside an open or closed path. The lines of type that are created with this tool automatically wrap inside the path. **B**

➤ The **Type on a Path** tool creates a line of type along the outer edge of an open or closed path. **C**

➤ The **Vertical Type** tool |T has the same function as the Type tool, except that it creates vertical type.

➤ The **Vertical Area Type** tool T creates vertical type inside an open or closed path.

➤ The **Vertical Type on a Path** tool creates vertical type along the outer edge of an open or closed path. **D**

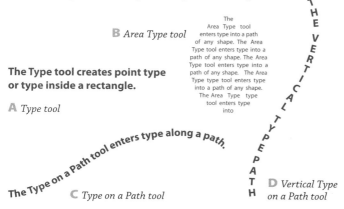

B *Area Type tool*

The Type tool creates point type or type inside a rectangle.

A *Type tool*

C *Type on a Path tool*

D *Vertical Type on a Path tool*

Choosing a font and font size for a type tool

In the next chapter, we'll show you how to use the extensive typographic controls in Illustrator to change the attributes of existing type. Here we offer the basic steps for choosing a font and font size for the type tools that you will use in this chapter.

To choose two basic attributes for a type tool:

1. Choose the Type T (T), Area Type, T Type on a Path, ✓ Vertical Type, T Vertical Area Type, T or Vertical Type on a Path ✓ tool.

2. Do either or both of the following:

   On the Control panel, A choose a font family from the **Font** menu and a style from the **Font Style** menu.

   On the Control panel, enter the desired size in the **Font Size** field (you don't need to reenter the unit of measure), or choose a preset size from the Font Size menu, or click the up or down arrow.

RECOLORING TYPE AFTER YOU CREATE IT

► When you enter type inside an object or along a path, a fill and stroke of None are applied to the object automatically. After entering type, if you want to apply fill and/or stroke colors to the type object, deselect it, click the edge of it with the Direct Selection tool, then choose the desired colors.

► To recolor the type itself, select it first with a type tool or a selection tool.

Creating point type

Point type stands by itself — it's neither inside an object nor along a path. This kind of type is most suitable for short passages, such as headlines, titles, or labels for Web buttons. For point type, line breaks are created manually.

To create point type:

1. Choose the **Type** tool T (T) or **Vertical Type** T tool.

2. *Optional:* Choose a font and/or a font size (see the steps at left).

3. Click a blank area of an artboard where you want the type to start (don't click an object). A flashing insertion marker appears.

4. Enter type. Press Return/Enter each time you want to start a new line.

5. To complete the type object, do either of the following: **B**

   Click a selection tool on the Tools panel (don't select the tool via a shortcut), then click outside the type block to deselect it.

   To keep the type tool selected so you can create another type object, either click the type tool or Cmd-click/Ctrl-click outside the type block to deselect it (the shortcut gives you a temporary selection tool).

► To align multiple separate blocks of point type, use the align buttons on the Control panel or the Align panel (see pages 105–106).

► If you open a file (into Illustrator CS5) that contains text from a pre-CS version of Illustrator, an alert dialog will appear, containing choices for updating the older, legacy text.

Character: Myriad Pro | Bold | 72 pt

A *From the menus on the Control panel, choose a font and a font style; also choose or enter a Font Size.*

I don't know the key to success, but the key to failure is trying to please everybody.

— Bill Cosby

B *This point type was created with the Type tool.*

Creating type in a rectangle

In this task, you'll draw a rectangle, then enter type inside it. The type will wrap within the edges of the object automatically. On the next page, you'll learn how to enter type inside an existing object of any shape.

To create type in a rectangle:

1. Choose the **Type** tool **T** (T) or **Vertical Type** ⏐**T** tool.

2. *Optional:* Choose a font and/or a font size (see the preceding page).

3. Drag to create a rectangle. When you release the mouse, a flashing insertion marker will appear.

4. Enter type.**A** The type will wrap automatically to fit into the rectangle. Press Return/Enter only when you need to create a new paragraph.

5. Do either of the following:

   Choose a selection tool on the Tools panel (don't use a keyboard shortcut to select the tool), then click outside the type block to deselect it.

   To keep the type tool selected so you can create another type object, either click the type tool or Cmd-click/Ctrl-click outside the type block to deselect it.

   Note: If you see an overflow symbol ⊞ on the edge of the rectangle, it's an indication that the rectangle isn't large enough to display all the type. If you want to reveal the hidden type, click the object with the Selection tool, then drag a handle on its bounding box (View > Show Bounding Box). The type will reflow to fit the new shape. Another option is to reshape the object with the Direct Selection tool.**B** A third option is to thread the overflow type into another object, as described on page 248.

➤ If you drag to define an area with the Vertical Type tool before entering type, the type will flow from top to bottom and from right to left.

➤ If you click in your document with a type tool unintentionally, an empty type object will be created. To delete the results of all such clicks, choose Object > Path > Clean Up. In the dialog, check Select Empty Text Paths, then click OK.

It spoils people's clothes to squeeze under a gate; the proper way to get in, is to climb down a pear tree.'

— *Beatrix Potter*

A *Drag with the Type tool to create a rectangle, then enter type. To reveal the edges of the rectangle, either choose Outline view or use the Object Highlighting feature of Smart Guides.*

'It spoils
people's
clothes to
squeeze
under a
gate; the
proper
way to
get in,
is to climb
down a
pear tree.'

B *We reshaped this type rectangle with the Direct Selection tool.*

Creating area type

When you use the Area Type or Vertical Area Type tool to place type inside a path of any shape or inside an open path, the object is converted to a type object. The type will wrap within the edges of the object automatically.

To enter type inside an object:

1. *Optional:* If you want to preserve the original object, drag-copy it (see the sidebar on this page).

2. To enter type inside a closed path, choose the **Area Type,** T **Vertical Area Type,** T **Type** T (T), or **Vertical Type** ⌊T tool. To enter type inside an open path, choose either one of the Area Type tools.

3. *Optional:* Choose a font and/or a font size (see page 240).

4. Click precisely on the edge of a path. A flashing insertion marker appears, and any fill, stroke, or brush stroke on the object is removed. On the Layers panel, the former <Path> object is now listed as a <Type> object.

5. Enter type inside the path, or copy and paste some type from a text-editing application into the path. The type will stay inside the object and conform to its shape.**A–B** (Vertical area type flows from top to bottom and from right to left.)

   ➤ To make the type fit symmetrically within the object, give it a relatively small point size. Also, on the Paragraph panel, check Hyphenate and click either the Align Center button or one of the Justify alignment buttons (see page 264).

6. Do either of the following:

   Choose a selection tool, then click outside the type object to deselect it.

   To keep the type tool selected (so you can continue using it), Cmd-click/Ctrl-click away from the type block to deselect it, release Cmd/Ctrl, then click the next type object.

   Note: To recolor the new type, see "Recoloring type after you create it" in the sidebar on page 240.

   ➤ To control the spacing between area type and the object it is contained in, see the next page.

   ➤ Type can't be entered into a compound path, a mask object, a mesh object, or a blend.

This is text in a copy of a light bulb shape. You can use the Area Type tool to place type into any shape you can create. When fitting type into a round shape, place small words at the top and the bottom. This is text in a copy of a light bulb shape. You can use the Area Type tool to place type into any

A *Area type*

The kiss of memory made pictures of love and light against the wall. Here was peace. She pulled in her horizon like a great fish-net. Pulled it from around the waist of the world and draped it over her shoulder. So much of life in its meshes! She called in her soul to come and see.
ZORA NEALE HURSTON

B *Type in a circle*

THERE'S NO GOIN' BACK

Once you place type inside or along a graphic object, it becomes a type object permanently (it can be converted back into a graphic object only if you choose the Undo command immediately). To preserve the original graphic object, Option-drag/Alt-drag it with the Selection tool to copy it before putting type into or along it.

Via the Area Type Options dialog, you can adjust the spacing between area type and the edge of its object by changing the Inset Spacing value, or reposition the first line of type by changing the First Baseline value.

To choose Inset Spacing and First Baseline options for area type:

1. Select an area type object with a selection tool, a type tool, or the Layers panel.**A**

2. Choose Type > **Area Type Options**. In the Area Type Options dialog,**B** check Preview.

3. In the Offset area, choose an **Inset Spacing** value to adjust the spacing between the type and the type object.**C**

4. To control the distance between the first line of type and the top of the object (or to the current inset, if the Inset Spacing value isn't zero), choose a **First Baseline** option. We usually use Ascent, Cap Height, or Fixed:

   Ascent to have the top of the tallest characters in the line touch the top of the object.

Cap Height to have the top of uppercase letters touch the top of the object.

Leading to make the distance between the first baseline of text and the top of the object equal to the leading value of the type.

x Height to have the top of the "x" character in the current font touch the top of the object.

Em Box Height to have the top of the em box in an Asian font touch the top of the object.

Fixed, then enter a Min (minimum) value for the location of the baseline of the first line of text.

Legacy to use the method from previous versions of Illustrator.

Optional: Change the minimum baseline offset value in the Min field. Illustrator will use either this value or the First Baseline value, whichever is greater.

5. Click OK.

➤ If you select an area type object and then reopen the Area Type Options dialog, you can view and edit the current settings for the object.

The human race has one really effective weapon, and that is laughter.

— *Mark Twain*

A *The type is touching the edges of this object.*

B *We are using the Inset Spacing control in the Area Type Options dialog to add space between the type and the edge of the object.*

The human race has one really effective weapon, and that is laughter.

— *Mark Twain*

C *Now this area type object has an Inset Spacing value of 6 pt. The type looks better with "breathing room" around it.*

Creating path type

Follow these steps to place type in a single line along the inner or outer edge of a path. Although you can't place type on both sides of the same path, you can move the line of type from one side of the path to the other after creating it.

To place type along an object's path:

1. *Optional:* Choose a font and/or a font size (see page 240).

2. Choose the **Type on a Path** ⤲ or **Vertical Type on a Path** tool, ⤲ then click the edge of a closed or open path.**A** Choose the **Type T** or **Vertical Type** ⌐T tool, then click an open path. The path doesn't have to be selected.

3. When the flashing insertion marker appears, enter type. Don't press Return/Enter. The type will appear along the edge of the object. The object will now have a fill and stroke of None and any brush stroke will be removed.**B**

4. Do either of the following:

   Choose a selection tool (or hold down Cmd/Ctrl), then click outside the type object to deselect it.

   If you want to use the same type tool on another path, click the tool again.

To reposition type on a path:

1. Choose the **Selection tool** ▶ or **Direct Selection tool.**▶

2. Click the type (not the path). Center, left, and right brackets appear.**C**

3. As you do any of the following, be sure to drag the bracket (the vertical bar) — not the little square. If your tool switches to a type tool, choose a selection tool and try again.

   To reposition the type block along the path, drag the center bracket to the left or right.

   To reposition the starting point of the type on the path, drag the left bracket.**D–E** You could also drag the right bracket back across the existing type (this will shorten the amount of type that's visible on the path and may produce a type overflow). For right-aligned type, do the opposite of the above.

   To flip the type to the opposite side of an open path, drag the center bracket perpendicularly across the path.

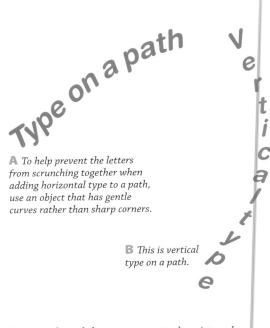

A *To help prevent the letters from scrunching together when adding horizontal type to a path, use an object that has gentle curves rather than sharp corners.*

B *This is vertical type on a path.*

The icons shown below appear next to the pointer when it's moved over a bracket on a selected type path.

Center bracket · Right bracket · Left bracket

C *The left, center, and right brackets display for path type when it's selected with the Selection or Direct Selection tool.*

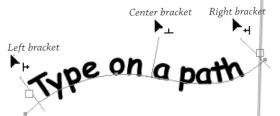

D *The left bracket is dragged to the right.*

E *The mouse is released.*

Via the Type on a Path Options dialog, you can quickly change the shape, orientation, and alignment of type on a path. The more curvy the path, the more obvious the changes. The dialog settings are editable and reversible.

To apply options to path type:

1. Do either of the following:

   Choose the Selection tool, then click the type on a path.

   On the Layers panel, click the selection area for a path type object.

2. Choose Type > Type on a Path > **Type on a Path Options**.

3. Check Preview in the dialog.

4. Do any of the following:

   From the **Effect** pop-up menu, choose Rainbow, Skew, 3D Ribbon, Stair Step, or Gravity.

   Choose **Align to Path**: Ascender, Descender, Center, or Baseline (the default setting) to specify which part of the type will touch the path. B

   Check (or uncheck) **Flip**.

   Choose or enter a positive or negative letter **Spacing** value. Change this value in small increments at first.

5. Click OK. To change or reverse any of the option settings at any time, reselect the object and reopen the dialog.

➤ To shift type from its baseline by a specific value, see page 272. To adjust the spacing between any pair of characters, see page 258.

➤ The type effects can also be applied individually via the Type > Type on a Path submenu.

Rainbow

Skew

3D Ribbon

Stair Step

Gravity

A *The Effect choices in the Type on a Path Option dialog change the shape and spacing of characters on a path.*

Ascender

Center

Descender

Baseline

B *The Align to Path options affect the position of the baseline of path type relative to the path.*

Copying or moving type characters

To copy or move type from one object to another:

1. Choose the **Type** tool T (T) or **Vertical Type** ⅼT tool.

2. Do either of the following:

   Select (drag across) the type characters to be moved.

   To move all the type from one or more threaded objects, click in one of the objects, then choose Select > **All** (Cmd-A/Ctrl-A).

3. Do either of the following:

   Choose Edit > **Cut** (Cmd-X/Ctrl-X). **A**

   Choose Edit > **Copy** (Cmd-C/Ctrl-C).

4. To create a text insertion point in an object, do one of the following:

   To put the type into an existing closed path (area type) or to put it onto an open path (path type), click the edge of a selected or unselected object. **B**

   To create a new type rectangle to contain the type, Cmd-click/Ctrl-click a blank area of the artwork to deselect, then drag to create a rectangle.

   To have the type appear on the outside of an object, Option-click/Alt-click the edge of a closed path.

5. Choose Edit > **Paste** (Cmd-V/Ctrl-V). **C**

A *We selected type, then chose Edit > Cut to put it onto the Clipboard.*

B *We clicked a path.*

C *We pressed Cmd-V/Ctrl-V. The contents of the Clipboard appeared on the path.*

COPYING A WHOLE TYPE OBJECT

► To copy a type object within the same document, use any method you would use to copy a path object: Option/Alt drag the object with the Selection tool, or Option/Alt drag the object's selection square upward or downward on the Layers panel (for the latter method, move the copy away from the original afterward).

► To copy a type object between Illustrator documents, use the drag-and-drop method (see page 102) or Clipboard commands (see page 103).

Note: When you copy a threaded text object, only that single object and the visible text within it are copied.

Importing text into Illustrator

The Place command lets you import text files in the following formats into an Illustrator document: plain text, ASCII (if it has the file name suffix .txt); Rich Text Format (.rtf); or Microsoft Word (.doc or .docx). The text will appear in a new rectangle.

Note: To enter text onto or into a custom path, first place it into an Illustrator document by following the steps below, then copy and paste it onto or into the path (as in the steps on the preceding page).

To import text into an Illustrator document:

1. Open or create an Illustrator document. Click an artboard in the document or on the Artboards panel.

2. Choose File > **Place**.

3. In the Place dialog, locate and click the text file to be imported, then click Place.

4. For a file in the Microsoft Word or RTF format, the Microsoft Word Options dialog opens. **A** Decide which options you want included. If you want to preserve any text styling, be sure to leave Remove Text Formatting unchecked.

   For a file in the plain text (.txt) format, the Text Import Options dialog opens. **B** Formatting and styling is removed from text in this format.

5. Click OK. The imported text will appear in a rectangle in the center of the current artboard. **C** To restyle it, see the next chapter. If the overflow symbol appears and you want to thread the type to another type object, see the next page.

DON'T SPACE OUT!

➤ If you press the Spacebar to access a temporary Hand tool when a type tool is selected and your cursor is blinking in a type block, you will add spaces to your text instead of moving your document in the window. Worse still, if type is selected, it will be replaced with spaces. Instead, to access a temporary Hand tool, press Cmd/Ctrl, add the Spacebar, move the mouse, release Cmd/Ctrl, then drag with the Spacebar still held down. Practice this until you get the hang of it.

➤ When editing type, keep track of where the pointer is. If it's in a panel field, you will wind up editing the panel values instead of your type characters.

A For text in the Microsoft Word or RTF format, you will choose settings in the Microsoft Word Options dialog.

B For text in the plain text format, you will choose settings in the Text Import Options dialog.

Let us spend one day as deliberately as Nature, and not be thrown off the track by every nutshell and mosquito's wing that falls on the rails. Let us rise early and fast, or break fast, gently and without perturbation; let company come and let company go, let the bells ring and the children cry,— determined to make a day of it. Why should we knock under and go with the stream? Let us not be upset and overwhelmed in that terrible rapid and whirlpool called a dinner, situated in the meridian shallows.

— Henry David Thoreau

C The placed text appears in a rectangle.

Threading type objects

Before you begin threading (linking) any overflow text between text objects, consider this simple solution: If your type object is almost — but not quite — large enough to display all the type that is on or inside it, you can enlarge the object to reveal the hidden type by doing either of the following:

➤ Click the type block with the Selection tool. If the bounding box isn't visible, choose View > Show Bounding Box. Drag a handle on the bounding box (the handles on a bounding box are hollow).

➤ Deselect the type object, click the edge of the rectangle — not the type — with the Direct Selection tool (use the Object Highlighting feature of Smart Guides to locate the rectangle), then Shift-drag a segment.

If your type overfloweth, you can spill, or thread, it into a different object or into a copy of the same object.

To thread a type object to another object:

Method 1 (by clicking)

1. With the **Selection** tool ➤ (V), select the original type object.

2. Click the **Out** port ⊞ on the selected object. The pointer becomes a Loaded Text pointer. ▦ **A**

3. Do either of the following:

   To create a new object to contain the overflow type, either click where you want a duplicate of the currently selected object to appear, or drag to create a rectangular type object. **B–C**

   Position the pointer over the edge of a second object (the pointer changes to ▦), then click that object's path. A fill and stroke of None will be applied to the path.

4. Overflow type flows from the first object into the second one. Cmd-click/Ctrl-click to deselect the objects.

➤ If you double-click an Out port with the Selection tool, the first object will be threaded to a linked copy of that object.

Method 2 (using a command)

1. Via the Selection tool ➤ or the Layers panel, select the original type object and a second object.

2. Choose Type > Threaded Text > **Create**.

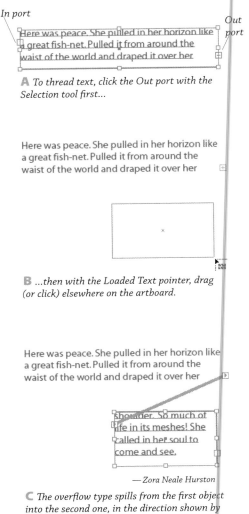

In port

Out port

A *To thread text, click the Out port with the Selection tool first...*

Here was peace. She pulled in her horizon like a great fish-net. Pulled it from around the waist of the world and draped it over her

B *...then with the Loaded Text pointer, drag (or click) elsewhere on the artboard.*

Here was peace. She pulled in her horizon like a great fish-net. Pulled it from around the waist of the world and draped it over her

shoulder. So much of life in its meshes! She called in her soul to come and see.

— Zora Neale Hurston

C *The overflow type spills from the first object into the second one, in the direction shown by the thread arrowheads.*

NOT ALL IS COPIED

If you click to duplicate a type object (step 3 on this page), only the object's shape will be copied, not its fill and stroke attributes. To copy the fill and stroke attributes afterward, choose the Direct Selection tool (A), Cmd-click/Ctrl-click the artboard to deselect, then click the edge of the duplicate object (the handles on the object should be hollow). Choose the Eyedropper tool (I), move the pointer over the background of the original type object (make sure the pointer doesn't have a little "t" in it), then click.

Are you curious to see what's threaded to what? Display the text threads (the nonprinting lines that reveal the links between text objects).

To reveal the text threads:

Select a linked type object via a selection tool or the Layers panel. If the thread lines aren't visible, choose View > **Show Text Threads** or press Cmd-Shift-Y/Ctrl-Shift-Y.

➤ The stacking order of type objects on the Layers panel has no effect on how text flows between objects.

When you unthread two objects, the chain is broken and the overflow text gets sucked back into the first object of the two. The path objects are preserved.

To unthread two type objects:

1. Choose the **Selection** tool ➤ (V), then click a threaded type object.

2. Do either of the following:

Double-click the object's In port or Out port. **A–B**

Click an In port or Out port, move the pointer slightly if you want to verify that it has become an unthreading cursor, then click the same port a second time to cut the thread.

Follow these steps if you want to keep the remaining links intact as you release just one object from a series of threaded objects. The type will reflow into the remaining objects.

To release an object from a thread while preserving the remaining threads:

1. Choose the **Selection** tool ➤ (V), then click the type object to be released. **C**

2. Do either of the following:

To unthread the object while preserving it, choose Type > Threaded Text > **Release Selection. D**

To unthread the type object by deleting it, press Delete/Backspace. (Too simple, right?)

➤ To disconnect all the objects in a text thread while keeping the type in its present objects, click one of the objects with the Selection tool, then choose Type > Threaded Text > Remove Threading. The threads disappear, and the type stays where it is.

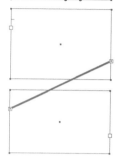

A When the Out port is double-clicked...

B ...that type object becomes unthreaded.

C Here the middle type object is selected...

D ...and then released from the thread.

Rotating type

To rotate type characters at a custom angle:

1. Select a type object with the Selection tool or via the Layers panel, or select one or more type characters with a type tool.

2. Show the Character panel  (Cmd-T/Ctrl-T). If the full options aren't showing, click the ⬥ on the panel tab.

3. Choose or enter a positive or negative **Character Rotation** value.⟳ A

➤ After rotating type, you may need to adjust the spacing between the characters (see page 258).

To make a whole horizontal type block vertical, or vice versa:

1. Select a type object with the Selection tool or via the Layers panel.

2. Choose Type > Type Orientation > **Horizontal** or **Vertical**.

A *We rotated the orange letter by 15°.*

> **SWITCHEROO**
>
> To rotate vertical area type characters, select only the characters to be rotated. On the Control panel, click Character, then from the panel menu, choose Standard Vertical Roman Alignment to uncheck that option.

TRANSFORMING TYPE

To rotate type, as in the numbers on the tickets below, use one of the rotation tricks you learned in Chapter 11 (e.g., manipulate the object's bounding box or use the Free Transform tool).

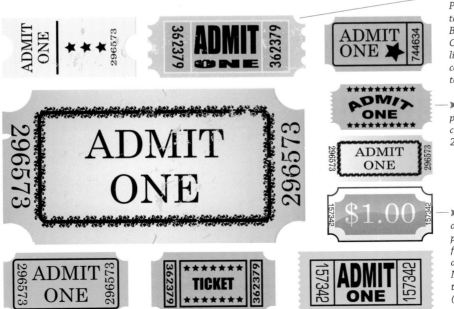

➤ *One way to create a "grunge" effect like this is by drawing strokes with the Paintbrush tool. For the tool, choose the Chalk Brush (in the Artistic_ ChalkCharcoalPencil library) and a stroke color that's similar to the background color.*

➤ *Use the Rainbow path option to produce curved type (see page 245).*

➤ *To carve the corners off a rectangle like this, place small circles in front of it, select all the objects, then click the Minus Front button on the Pathfinder panel (see page 333).*

EXERCISE: Putting type on a circle

Create the type

1. Deselect all, click Document Setup on the Control panel, choose Units: Inches, then click OK.

2. Using the Control panel, choose a fill color of None and a dark green as the stroke color.

3. Choose the Ellipse tool ⬭ (L), then click on an artboard to open the Ellipse dialog.

4. Enter "3" in the Width field, click the word "Height," then click OK.**A**

5. Double-click the Scale tool.⬚ Enter "68" in the Uniform: Scale field, then click Copy. Cmd-click/Ctrl-click to deselect.

6. Choose the Type on a Path tool.⤢

7. On the Control panel, click Character to open a temporary Character panel. Enter "28" in the Font Size field and choose the Stencil font from the Font menu. (Note: If you need to use the Stencil Std Bold font instead of the Stencil font, choose a Font Size of 25 pt.)

8. Click the top of the inner circle, then type the desired text (to copy our example, type "RECYCLED 100%"; press the Spacebar; to type an en dash in the Mac OS, press Option- – (hyphen), or in Windows, hold down Alt and enter 0150 on the number pad; then press the Spacebar again. Finally, enter the same type and dash again without the last space).**B** Don't deselect.

9. Click the Selection tool.⬉ Drag the center bracket (look for it near the bottom of the circle) along the outside of the small circle to reposition the type, so the dashes are positioned at the top and bottom of the circle.**C**

   Note that the left and right brackets are practically on top of each other near the starting point of the type. To avoid causing a text overflow, don't move the left bracket over the right bracket.

Continued on the following page

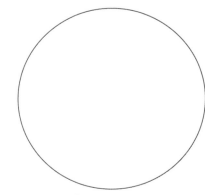

A *Create a circle.*

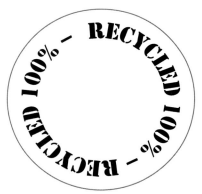

B *Create a smaller copy of the circle using the Scale dialog, then add path type along the edge of that circle (the circle now has a stroke of None).*

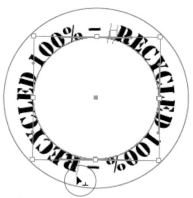

C *Drag the center bracket of the path type to position the dashes at the top and bottom of the circle.*

Refine the type

1. Choose the Direct Selection tool ♦ (A). Click the path for the larger circle. On the Appearance panel, click the Stroke listing, then click the up arrow to set the stroke weight to 3 pt.

2. Click the path of the smaller circle. Double-click the Stroke color square on the Appearance panel. On the temporary Swatches panel that opens, choose the same dark green as on the large circle. Click the up arrow to set the stroke weight to 3 pt.**A**

3. Choose the Selection tool and click the type. Display the Character panel.**A** Increase the Baseline Shift value to center the type in the space between the circles (we used a value of 8 pt).

4. If necessary, increase the Tracking value to space the type and the two dashes evenly,**B** then repeat step 9 from the preceding page to reposition the type on the circle.

5. On the Color panel, click the Fill color square, then on the Swatches panel, apply the same dark green to the type. (Don't apply a stroke color.)

6. Choose the Selection tool, marquee the two circles, then choose Object > Group (Cmd-G/Ctrl-G).

7. *Optional:* To produce the artwork shown in **C**, do as follows:

   On the Layers panel,◥ click the New Layer button to create a new layer.

   Display the Symbols panel.♣ From the Symbol Libraries menu at the bottom of the panel, choose Nature. From the library panel, drag the Trees 1 symbol into the center of the two circles.

   To scale the symbol to fit within the small circle, with the Selection tool, Shift-drag a corner handle of the bounding box for the symbol (if you don't see the bounding box, which has hollow handles, choose View > Show Bounding Box).

   On the Layers panel, click in the edit column for the symbol layer to lock it.

8. Cmd-click/Ctrl-click to deselect, then set both the Baseline Shift and the Tracking values on the Character panel back to the default value of 0 (for the next time you create type).

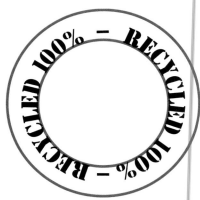

A *Apply the same green color and stroke weight to the smaller circle.*

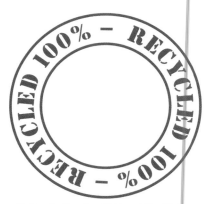

B *Use the Baseline Shift and Tracking controls to adjust the type, and apply the same green color to it.*

C *For the inner graphic, we dragged the Trees 1 symbol from the Nature library panel into the small circle, then scaled it to fit.*

In the preceding chapter, you learned how to create type. Now you will learn how to format and refine it. The first step is to learn how to select type, the type object, or both. Once you've mastered those skills, you will use the Character and Control panels to change typographic attributes; the Glyphs and OpenType panels to insert special characters; the Paragraph panel to apply paragraph settings; the Paragraph Styles and Character Styles panels to apply collections of attributes quickly; and the Tabs panel to align columns of text. Finally, you will learn how to convert type characters to paths; wrap type around an object; and apply appearance attributes to type, including multiple strokes and effects.

Selecting type

Before type can be modified, it must be selected. Use the selection method described on this page when you need to move, transform, restyle, or recolor all the type in or on a type object. To reshape or recolor a type object (but not the type), use the first selection method on the next page instead. Or to edit, restyle, or recolor just some of the type in a block, use the second method on the next page.

To select type and its object:

1. Choose the **Selection** tool ▶ (V).
2. Turn on the **Smart Guides** feature (Cmd-U/Ctrl-U).
3. Open the Illustrator/Edit > Preferences dialog, and do both of the following:

   In the Smart Guides panel, check Object Highlighting.

   In the Type panel, uncheck Type Object Selection by Path Only (the default setting is unchecked).
4. Do one of the following:

   For area type (inside an object), click a type character **A** or the outer path. **B** Or if the object has a fill color, you can click the fill.

Continued on the following page

If we shadows have offended,
Think but this—and all is mended—

A *To select type and its object, either click a type character…*

If we shadows have offended,
Think but this—and all is mended—
path

B *…or click the path of the type object.*

— *William Shakespeare*

20

IN THIS CHAPTER

For point type, click the type. **A**

For type on a path, click the type or the path.

For any kind of type, click the selection square for the type on the Layers panel.

Note: If the bounding box feature is on (View > Show Bounding Box), a bounding box will now surround the object.

➤ If the Type Object Selection by Path Only preference is on, you must click the path of the type object to select it. Use the Object Highlighting feature of Smart Guides to locate it.

Use this selection method if you want to recolor or reshape a type object but not the type.

To select a type object but not the type:

1. Choose the **Direct Selection** tool.
2. Cmd-click/Ctrl-click to deselect. Click the edge of an area or path type object (not point type). You can use the Object Highlighting feature of Smart Guides to locate it. **B** Any modifications you make now will affect only the type object. **C**

Use this selection method to select just the type — not the object — so you can copy-edit the text, or change its character or paragraph settings (Character or Paragraph panel) or its fill, stroke, or opacity settings (Appearance panel).

To select type but not the type object:

1. Choose a type tool.
2. Do any of the following:

   To highlight one or more words or a line of horizontal type, click and drag horizontally across them. **D** For vertical type, drag vertically.

   To select whole lines of horizontal type, drag vertically. Or for vertical type, drag horizontally.

   Double-click to select a word.

   Triple-click to select a paragraph.

   Click in a text block or on a text path, then choose Select > All (Cmd-A/Ctrl-A) to select all the type in the block or on the path, plus any overflow type.

   Click to start a selection, then Shift-click where you want the selection to end. Continue to Shift-click, if desired, to extend the selection.

3. When you're done editing the type, Cmd-click/Ctrl-click outside the type object to deselect it.

APPLYING COLORS TO TYPE CHARACTERS

When type is selected with the Selection tool or a Type tool, you can use the Color and Swatches panels to change its fill and stroke colors. Note: If type characters are highlighted with a type tool and you want to see how the new color looks, either deselect the object or choose a selection tool. For more creative effects, you will need to work with the Appearance panel; see pages 276–278.

INSERTING AND DELETING TYPE CHARACTERS

➤ To add characters to a existing type, choose a type tool, click to create an insertion point, then type away.

➤ To delete one character at a time, choose a type tool, click to the right of the character to be deleted, then press Delete/Backspace. Or to delete multiple characters, select them with a type tool before pressing Delete/Backspace.

---

*If we shadows have offended,
Think but this—and all is mended—*

A *Point type is selected with the Selection tool.*

*If we shadows have offended,
Think but this—and all is mended—*
path

B *With the Direct Selection tool, a type object is selected. The type characters are not selected.*

*If we shadows have offended,
Think but this—and all is
mended—*
anchor

C *The type object is reshaped and recolored.*

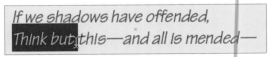

D *Two words are selected with a type tool.*

For a description of the Character and Paragraph panels, which you will use throughout this chapter, see pages 45 and 51, respectively. You can open either panel from the Type menu on the Window menu, or temporarily via a link on the Control panel. Once you become familiar with the type controls in Illustrator, be sure to learn how to use character and paragraph styles to apply collections of type attributes and formats quickly (see pages 266–269).

Note: To choose default formats for a type tool, before choosing settings, deselect instead of selecting type or a type object.

Changing the font

For an easy but dramatic change to the appearance of type, change its font and font style.

To change fonts:

1. Do either of the following:

   Select the type to be modified with a type tool.

   Select a type object with the Selection tool or the Layers panel.

2. Do either of the following:

   Right-click the type and choose a font and font style from either the **Font** submenu **A–B** or the **Recent Fonts** submenu on the context menu.

   On the Character panel **A C** or the Control panel, **D** choose a font from the **Font** menu and a style from the **Font Style** menu.

➤ To choose a font another way, press Cmd-Option-Shift-M/Ctrl-Alt-Shift-M to highlight the Font field on the Character panel, then type the first few characters of the desired font name. The name with the closest spelling match will appear in the field. Press Tab to proceed to the Font Style field, start typing the desired style name, then press Return/Enter to exit the panel. A lot of words to describe something that happens fast!

➤ To have font families display in the actual typeface (WYSIWYG) on the Font menus, see "Font Preview" on page 381.

If you create mock-ups for Web pages, you might find a use for the underline feature.

To apply underline or strikethrough styling:

1. Select the type to be modified with a type tool.

2. On the Character panel (with its full options displaying), click the **Underline** button or the **Strikethrough** button. (To remove the styling, click the same button again.)

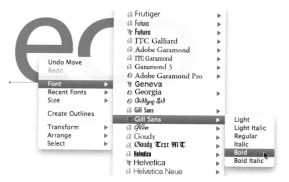

A *Select the type to be modified, then choose a font family and style from the context menu.*

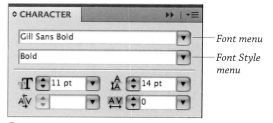

B *We changed the font family and font style from Myriad Pro Regular to Gill Sans Bold.*

C *The Character panel has two font controls.*

D *The Font and Font Style controls are also available on the Control panel.*

ANTI-ALIASING OPTIONS ★

To learn about the options on the new Anti-aliasing menu on the Character panel, see page 420.

Changing the font size

You can change the font (point) size of individual characters or words, or of all the type in an object.

To change the font size:

1. Do either of the following:

   Select the type to be modified with a type tool.

   Select a type object with the Selection tool or the Layers panel.

2. Do one of the following:

   On the Character panel **A** or the Control panel, enter the desired size in the **Font Size** field **A–B** (you don't need to reenter the unit of measure). You could also choose a preset size from the Font Size menu; or click the up or down arrow; or click in the Font Size field, then press the up or down arrow on the keyboard.

   ► If the type that you select is in more than one size, the Font Size field will be blank, but the new size you enter will apply to all the selected type. If you're using the Character or Control panel, you can press Return/Enter to apply the new value and exit the panel, or press Tab to apply the value and highlight the next field.

   Hold down Cmd-Shift/Ctrl-Shift and press > to enlarge the font size or < to reduce it. **C** The type will resize by the current Size/Leading increment, which is set in Illustrator/Edit > Preferences > Type (the default increment is 2 pt). To change the font size by five times the current Size/Leading value, hold down Cmd-Option-Shift/Ctrl-Alt-Shift and press > or <.

   Right-click the type and choose a preset size from the **Size** submenu on the context menu. (Choosing Other on the context menu highlights the Font Size field on the Character panel.)

   ► You can use the Horizontal Scale feature on the Character panel to make type wider (extend it) or narrower (condense it), or the Vertical Scale feature to make it taller or shorter. To keep the distortion to a minimum, raise or lower the percentage by just a few points (e.g., 104% or 98%). To reset the Horizontal Scale and Vertical Scale to the default value of 100%, select the type or type object, then press Cmd-Shift-X/Ctrl-Shift-X. Personally, we prefer to use a typeface that has the desired characteristics — and more balanced proportions — in its design, such as Helvetica Narrow or Gill Sans Condensed.

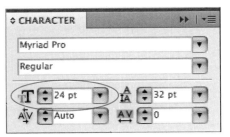

A *Change the size of type by using the Font Size controls on the Character panel...*

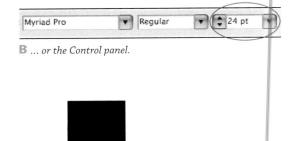

B *... or the Control panel.*

C *The font size can also be changed via a keyboard shortcut.*

SCALING TYPE INTERACTIVELY

To scale point or path type manually, select it first with the Selection tool, and make sure the bounding box feature is on (if it's not, press Cmd-Shift-B/Ctrl-Shift-B). Drag a handle on the box, or Shift-drag a handle to scale the type proportionally. You can also scale a type object with the Scale tool.

Changing the leading value

Leading is the distance between the baseline of each line of type and the line above it, and is traditionally measured in points. (To adjust the spacing between paragraphs, see page 265.)

Note: To change the vertical spacing in vertical type, change the horizontal tracking value (see the next page) instead of using leading. In vertical type, leading controls the horizontal spacing between vertical columns.

To change the leading value for horizontal type:

1. Do one of the following:

   To change the leading for an entire block of type, select it via the Selection tool or the Layers panel. (You can also select multiple threaded or nonthreaded type objects using either method.)

   To change the leading of all the lines in a paragraph, triple-click in the paragraph with a type tool.

   To change the leading of an entire line of type, drag across it with a type tool, making sure to include any spaces at the end of the line.

2. Do either of the following:

   On the Character panel, A enter a **Leading** value, A–C or choose a preset leading value from the Leading menu, or click the up or down arrow.

   Hold down Option/Alt and press the up arrow on the keyboard to decrease the leading or the down arrow to increase it by the Size/Leading increment, which is set in Illustrator/Edit > Preferences > Type (the default increment is 2 pt). To change the leading by five times the current Size/Leading increment, hold down Cmd-Option/Ctrl-Alt as you press an arrow.

➤ When Auto is the setting on the Leading menu, Illustrator calculates the leading as a percentage of the largest font size on each line (and the leading value is listed in parentheses). The default Auto Leading percentage of 120% can be changed in the Justification dialog, which opens from the Paragraph panel menu.

➤ If you change the leading for a threaded type object, only the leading in that object will change. To change the leading for a whole thread, select all the objects or use the Select > All command first.

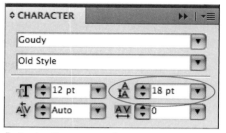

A On the Character panel, enter a Leading value, or click the up or down arrow, or choose a preset value from the menu.

> How can one conceive of a one-party system in a country that has over 200 varieties of cheese?

B This 12-pt. type has loose, 18-pt. leading.

> How can one conceive of a one-party system in a country that has over 200 varieties of cheese?
>
> — Charles de Gaulle

C This 12-pt. type has tight, 13-pt. leading.

SELECTING A TYPE TOOL QUICKLY

With the Selection or Direct Selection tool, double-click a character in a type object. The Type tool (or Vertical Type tool) becomes selected automatically, and an insertion point appears where you clicked.

Applying kerning and tracking

Kerning is the addition or removal of space between pairs of adjacent characters. All fonts have specific kerning values built into them to optimize the spacing between specific character pairs (e.g., between an uppercase "T" and a lowercase "a"). These built-in kerning values are adequate for small text, such as body type (see the sidebar on this page), but not for large type, such as headers and logos. To remedy any awkward spacing in large type, you can apply manual kerning values.

Tracking is the adjustment of spacing between three or more selected characters. It's best used sparingly, such as to spread out the characters in a single line of type (e.g., a header or subhead). Refrain from tracking whole paragraphs.

To apply manual kerning or tracking:

1. Do either of the following:

   Zoom in on the type that you want to kern or track. Choose a type tool, then either click to create an insertion point between two characters for kerning, or highlight a range of text for tracking.

   To track (not kern) all the type in an object, select it with the Selection tool or the Layers panel.

2. Do either of the following:

   In the **Kerning** or **Tracking** area on the Character panel, A A enter a positive value to add space between the characters or a negative value to remove space (or click in the field, then press the up or down arrow on the keyboard); B–D or choose a preset value from the menu; or click the up or down arrow.

   Hold down Option/Alt and press the right arrow on the keyboard to add space between letters or the left arrow to remove space, based on the current Tracking increment in Illustrator/Edit > Preferences > Type. To kern or track by a larger increment, hold down Cmd-Option/Ctrl-Alt as you press an arrow.

➤ The Tracking and Kerning features affect the vertical spacing of characters in vertical type.

➤ To undo manual kerning, click between a pair of characters, then reset the Kerning value on the Character panel to 0 (zero) or press Cmd-Option-Q/Ctrl-Alt-Q. To undo manual tracking, select the characters in question before resetting the Tracking value to 0.

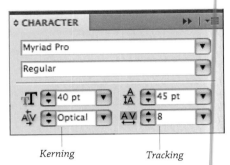

Kerning   Tracking

A Use the kerning and tracking controls to refine the spacing between characters.

Simone

B The original type contains no manual kerning or tracking.

Simone

C We tightened the spacing between the first two characters in this word via kerning...

Simone

D ...then tightened the spacing between the last five characters via tracking.

THE AUTO KERNING OPTIONS

On the Kerning menu on the Character panel, Illustrator offers a choice of three kinds of automatic (nonmanual) kerning:

➤ Auto (or "metrics" kerning), the default method, is applied to new or imported text based on the information that is built into each font for individual pairs of characters, such as To, Ta, We, Wo, and Yo.

➤ Optical adjusts the spacing between adjacent characters where needed. It's a good choice for type that is set in a font that has inadequate or no built-in kerning, or that contains multiple typefaces or font sizes.

➤ Metrics - Roman only also uses built-in kerning data, but is applicable only to type that is set in Roman (e.g., non-Asian) language fonts.

The Fit Headline command uses tracking values to fit a one-line paragraph of horizontal or vertical area type to the edges of the object.

To fit type to its container:

1. Choose a type tool.

2. Select or click in a single-line paragraph of area type (not point type or a line within a larger paragraph).**A**

3. Choose Type > **Fit Headline**.**B**

➤ If you scale a type object that you applied the Fit Headline command to, you will need to reapply the Fit Headline command afterward, because the tracking values won't readjust automatically.

A *Our text cursor is inserted into a line of type.*

B *The Fit Headline command added space between the characters to fit the line of type to the full width of the object.*

WORD AND LETTER SPACING OPTIONS

➤ To change the horizontal word or letter spacing for paragraphs that have a justified alignment setting, choose Justification from the Paragraph panel menu, then in the Justification dialog, change the Minimum, Desired, and Maximum values for Word Spacing or Letter Spacing. The Desired setting also affects nonjustified paragraphs. (We like to reduce the word spacing for subheads and headers, as part of a paragraph style.) Glyph Scaling (50%–200%) affects the width of the actual characters.

➤ If you are setting type for online viewing that is 20 pt. or smaller, you may want to turn the Fractional Widths feature off (Character panel menu). To learn about this feature, enter "Fractional character widths" in the search field in Illustrator Help.

Ocean
Body more immaculate than a wave,
salt washing away its own line,
and the brilliant bird
flying without ground roots.

Normal word and letter spacing

	Minimum	Desired	Maximum
Word Spacing:	80%	100%	133%
Letter Spacing:	0%	0%	0%
Glyph Scaling:	100%	100%	100%

Ocean
Body more immaculate than a wave,
salt washing away its own line,
and the brilliant bird
flying without ground roots.

Loose letter spacing

	Minimum	Desired	Maximum
Word Spacing:	80%	100%	133%
Letter Spacing:	5%	10%	20%
Glyph Scaling:	100%	100%	100%

Ocean
Body more immaculate than a wave,
salt washing away its own line,
and the brilliant bird
flying without ground roots.
— Pablo Neruda

Tight word spacing

	Minimum	Desired	Maximum
Word Spacing:	70%	70%	100%
Letter Spacing:	0%	0%	0%
Glyph Scaling:	100%	100%	100%

Using smart punctuation

The Smart Punctuation command converts applicable text (listed under "What to type" in the sidebar at right) to professional typesetting characters, when available in the current font. You can apply the command to just selected text or, even better, to the entire document. To set yourself apart from amateurs, use this feature (and also use typographers quotes, which are discussed next). Notes: The Smart Quotes option in the Smart Punctuation dialog overrides the current Double Quotes and Single Quotes settings in the Document Setup dialog. To set ligatures and expert fractions in an OpenType font, use the OpenType panel (see page 262).

To create smart punctuation:

1. To change all the type in your document, deselect;**A** or with a type tool, select the text to be smart punctuated.

2. Choose Type > **Smart Punctuation**.

3. In the dialog, check the desired options in the **Replace Punctuation** area,**B** and click Replace In: **Selected Text Only** or **Entire Document**.

4. *Optional:* Check Report Results to have a list of your changes appear onscreen after you click OK.

5. Click OK.**C**

To specify quotation marks and apostrophes for future type:

1. Deselect, then click **Document Setup** on the Control panel (Cmd-Option-P/Ctrl-Alt-P).

2. Under Type Options, check **Use Typographers Quotes** and choose the **Language** in which the text is going to be typeset. The standard Double Quotes and Single Quotes marks for the chosen language will display on both menus.

3. Click OK.

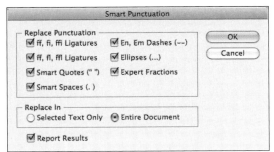

B *Check the desired Replace Punctuation options in the Smart Punctuation dialog.*

THE SMART PUNCTUATION OPTIONS		
Option in the Smart Punctuation dialog	What to type	The result
ff, fi, ffi Ligatures	ff, fi, ffi	ff, fi, ffi
ff, fl, ffl Ligatures	ff, fl, ffl	ff, fl, ffl
Smart Quotes	' "	' " " '
Smart Spaces (one space after a period)	. T	. T
En (dashes)	--	–
Em Dashes	---	—
Ellipses	...	...
Expert Fractions	1/2	½

"We are living in a world today where lemonade is made from artificial flavors and furniture polish is made from real lemons."

-- Alfred E. Newman

A *Dumb punctuation: Straight quotation marks, double hyphens instead of dashes, and no ligatures.*

"We are living in a world today where lemonade is made from artificial flavors and furniture polish is made from real lemons."

— Alfred E. Newman

C *Smart punctuation: Smart quotation marks, a single dash, and ligatures (the "fi" in "artificial" and the "fl" in "flavors"). For hanging punctuation, see page 270.*

Inserting alternate glyphs

The OpenType font format was developed jointly by Adobe and Microsoft to help prevent font substitution and text reflow problems in files that are transferred between platforms. Fonts labeled "Pro" have an expanded set of characters.**A** The OpenType format also allows for a wide range of stylistic variations, called glyphs, for any given character in a specific font (sounds like something in *The Hobbit!*). For each individual character in an OpenType font, you can choose from an assortment of alternate glyphs, such as ligatures, swashes, titling characters, stylistic alternates, ordinals, and fractions.

You can insert alternate glyphs manually by using the Glyphs panel (as in the steps below), or automatically by using the OpenType panel (as in the steps on the next page). The Glyphs panel isn't just used for OpenType fonts, though—you can also use it to locate and insert characters in a non-OpenType font.

To replace or insert a glyph using the Glyphs panel:

1. Choose a type tool, then select a character or click in the text to create an insertion point.

2. Display the Glyphs panel **Aa** (choose Glyphs from the Type menu or from the Window > Type submenu). If you selected a character in the prior step, it will be highlighted on the panel.

3. From the **Show** menu,**B** choose a category of glyphs to be displayed on the panel: Alternates for Current Selection,**C** Entire Font, Access All Alternates, or a specific category. Different options will be available depending on the current font and whether you selected a character or merely created an insertion point.

4. Double-click a glyph to be inserted in your text or to be used as a replacement for the selected character; or if the square containing the currently highlighted glyph has a mini arrowhead in the lower right corner, you can click the arrowhead and choose a glyph from the menu. The chosen glyph will appear in your text.

▶ You can choose a different font and font style from the menus at the bottom of the Glyphs panel.

▶ To change the display size of the glyphs on the Glyphs panel, click the Zoom Out or Zoom In button in the lower right corner.

SPOT THE IMPOSTORS!

To highlight all the text in which a glyph has been substituted throughout your document (due to the original font not being available), deselect, click Document Setup on the Control panel, then check Highlight Substituted Glyphs.

Adobe
OpenType
TrueType

A *When Font Preview is checked in the Type panel of the Preferences dialog, a specific symbol identifies each font type on the Font menu on the Character panel.*

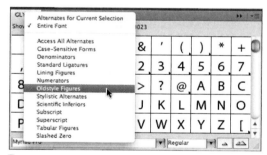

B *To control which categories of glyphs display on the Glyphs panel, choose an option from the Show menu.*

C *In this Glyphs panel, we clicked the letter "e" for our chosen font, then chose Alternates for Current Selection from the Show menu.*

By using the OpenType panel, you can control whether alternate glyphs in OpenType fonts will be substituted for standard characters automatically, where applicable (and if available in the current font). For example, you can choose to have a glyph for a properly formatted fraction be inserted automatically whenever you type the characters for a fraction, such as ½ for 1/2 or ¾ for 3/4. Other options include ligature glyphs for specific letter pairs (such as ff, ffl, and st), swash and titling characters, etc.

To specify or insert alternate glyphs for OpenType characters:

1. Display the OpenType panel (Cmd-Option-Shift-T/Ctrl-Alt-Shift-T). **A**

2. As you do either of the following, remember that the "Pro" fonts contain the most glyph options:

   To change all applicable occurrences in existing text, either select a type object with the Selection tool or the Layers panel or highlight one or more characters with a type tool, then choose an OpenType font on the Control or Character panel.

   To specify alternate glyph options for future text to be entered in a specific OpenType font, choose a type tool, then choose that font on the Control or Character panel.

3. Click any of the available buttons on the panel. **B–C** The choices will vary depending on the glyph set of the current font.

➤ The Figure menu on the OpenType panel controls the style and spacing of numerals. The Tabular options insert an equal amount of spacing between numerals, and are designed to align columns of numerals in a table. The Proportional options allow for variable spacing based on the actual width of each numeral character, and are designed to improve the appearance of nontabular numerals. Oldstyle numerals are beautiful, but because of their variable heights, are appropriate only in special design settings.

➤ If a font lacks a true superscript, superior, subscript, or inferior glyph, or doesn't contain nonstandard fractions (such as $^5/_{25}$), you can use options on the Position menu on the OpenType panel to produce the desired "faux" glyph. We used the Numerator and Denominator options to produce this fraction: $^5/_{25}$.

➤ To change the case for existing text (e.g., from all lowercase to sentence case), select the text, then choose from the Type > Change Case submenu.

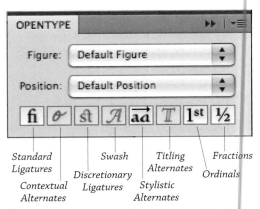

Standard Ligatures · Contextual Alternates · Discretionary Ligatures · Swash · Stylistic Alternates · Titling Alternates · Ordinals · Fractions

A Using the OpenType panel, you can control which categories of alternate glyphs will be used to replace standard characters in current or future text.

Swash — *Fluffy*

1st 2nd — Ordinal

Fraction — $^5/_8$ Fact — Discretionary ligature

Stylistic alternates — friend &

B The OpenType panel inserts alternate characters like these into your text.

1st — Available

1st — Selected

1st — Not available

C The buttons on the OpenType panel have three states.

Applying hyphenation

You can turn on auto hyphenation for whole selected paragraphs or as a default setting for future type.

To hyphenate text and choose hyphenation options:

1. *Optional:* To hyphenate or change the hyphenation settings for existing text, select it with a type tool or the Selection tool.

2. Display the Paragraph panel ¶ and its full set of options. Check **Hyphenate**.

3. If you want to choose hyphenation options, choose **Hyphenation** from the Paragraph panel menu. In the Hyphenation dialog, **A** check Preview.

4. In the **Words Longer Than** [ ] **Letters** field, enter the minimum number of characters a word must contain in order to be hyphenated (3–25). We usually enter a value of 6 or 7 here.

   In the **After First** [ ] **Letters** field, enter the minimum allowable number of characters that may precede a hyphen. We use a value of 3 or 4.

   In the **Before Last** [ ] **Letters** field, enter the minimum allowable number of characters that can be carried over to the next line following a hyphen. We use a value of 3.

   In the **Hyphen Limit** field, enter the maximum allowable number of hyphens in a row (0–25). We use a setting of 2. Oddly enough, a setting of 0 permits an unlimited number of hyphens in a row. **B**

   Or for a less calculated approach to achieving the desired number of line breaks (try this on existing text), simply move the **Hyphenation Zone** slider toward Better Spacing or Fewer Hyphens.

   Finally, decide whether you want Illustrator to **Hyphenate Capitalized Words** (preferably not).

5. Click OK.

▶ In Illustrator/Edit > Preferences > Hyphenation, you can choose a default language for hyphenation, enter Exceptions for words that you don't want Illustrator to hyphenate, and also enter words that you want hyphenated in a particular way (type a word in the New Entry field, then click Add).

▶ Regardless of the current hyphenation settings, you will need to "eyeball" your hyphenated text and, if necessary, correct any awkward breaks using a soft return or the No Break command.

OUR FAVORITE COMPOSER

On the Paragraph panel menu, you can choose either of the line-composer options for selected type — or for future type, if no type is selected:

▶ Adobe Every-line Composer (the option we prefer) examines all the lines in a paragraph and adjusts the line lengths and endings to optimize the overall appearance of the paragraph.

▶ Adobe Single-line Composer adjusts line breaks and the hyphenation for each line without regard to other lines or the appearance of the overall paragraph.

GIMME NO BREAK

To prevent a particular word from breaking at the end of a line, such as a compound word (e.g., "Single-line"), to reunite an awkwardly hyphenated word (e.g., "sextuplet"), or to keep related words together (e.g., "New York City"), select that word or those words, then from the Character panel menu, choose No Break.

A Set parameters for automatic hyphenation in the Hyphenation dialog.

AN
OVER-
ABUN-
DANCE
OF HY-
PHENS
MAKES
FOR TIR-
ING
READ-
ING.

B An excessive number of hyphens can make text hard to read, and it looks ugly, too. Granted, this is an extreme example, but it makes a point!

Changing paragraph alignment

Before learning how to apply alignment, indentation, and other paragraph formats, you need to know what a paragraph is, as far as Illustrator is concerned. To start a new paragraph as you enter a block of text (or to create a paragraph break where your cursor is inserted in existing text), press Return/Enter. Every paragraph ends with a hard return.

➤ To reveal the symbols for nonprinting characters, such as paragraph endings,¶ soft returns,↵ spaces,▪ and tabs,➡ choose Type > Show Hidden Characters (Cmd-Option-I/Ctrl-Alt-I).

Note: To create a soft return (line break) within a paragraph in nontabular text in order to bring the text to the right of the insertion point down to the next line, press Shift-Return/Shift-Enter.

To change paragraph alignment:

1. Do either of the following:

   Choose a type tool, then click in a paragraph or drag through one or more consecutive paragraphs.

   Select a type object with the Selection tool or the Layers panel.

2. Display the Paragraph panel ¶ (press Cmd-Option-T/Ctrl-Alt-T or click Paragraph on the Control panel).

3. Click an **alignment** button. **A–B** The first three alignment buttons (Align Left, Align Center, and Align Right) are also available on the Control panel.

   Use one of the keyboard shortcuts listed in the sidebar on this page.

➤ The justify alignment options have no effect on point type (type that's not inside an object), because point type doesn't have a container for the type to justify to.

SELECTING TYPE FOR EDITING: A SUMMARY

➤ To change character or paragraph attributes for all the text in a type object or on a path, select the object or path via the Selection tool or Layers panel.

➤ To change the attributes of one or more characters, words, or consecutive paragraphs, drag through them with a type tool.

SHORTCUTS FOR PARAGRAPH ALIGNMENT

	Mac OS	Windows
Left	Cmd-Shift-L	Ctrl-Shift-L
Center	Cmd-Shift-C	Ctrl-Shift-C
Right	Cmd-Shift-R	Ctrl-Shift-R
Justify Last Left	Cmd-Shift-J	Ctrl-Shift-J
Justify All (including the last line)	Cmd-Shift-F	Ctrl-Shift-F

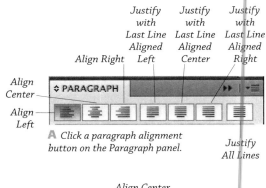

Justify with Last Line Aligned Left · *Justify with Last Line Aligned Center* · *Justify with Last Line Aligned Right*

Align Right · *Align Center* · *Align Left* · *Justify All Lines*

A *Click a paragraph alignment button on the Paragraph panel.*

Align Center

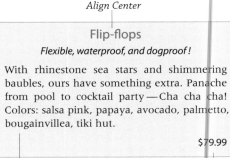

Flip-flops
Flexible, waterproof, and dogproof!

With rhinestone sea stars and shimmering baubles, ours have something extra. Panache from pool to cocktail party — Cha cha cha! Colors: salsa pink, papaya, avocado, palmetto, bougainvillea, tiki hut.

$79.99

Justify with Last Line Aligned Left · *Align Right*

B *A few paragraph alignment options are illustrated here.*

Changing paragraph indentation

You can apply left and first-line indentation values to area type or point type, and also apply a right indentation value to area type.

To change paragraph indentation:

1. Do either of the following:

   With a type tool, drag through the paragraphs to be modified or click in a paragraph.

   Select a type object with the Selection tool or via the Layers panel.

2. On the Paragraph panel,¶ do either of the following:

   Enter a **Left Indent** and/or **Right Indent** value, then press Return/Enter or Tab; A–B or click the up or down arrow; or click in the field, then press the up or down arrow on the keyboard.

   To indent only the first line of each paragraph, enter a positive **First-Line Left Indent** value.

Changing inter-paragraph spacing

Use the Space Before Paragraph or Space After Paragraph feature on the Paragraph panel to add or subtract space between paragraphs. (To adjust the spacing between lines of type within a paragraph, use leading; see page 257.)

To adjust the spacing between paragraphs:

1. Do either of the following:

   With a type tool, drag through the paragraphs to be modified or click in a paragraph that you want to adjust the spacing above.

   Select a type object with the Selection tool or the Layers panel.

2. In the **Space Before Paragraph** or **Space After Paragraph** field on the extended Paragraph panel,¶ enter a positive value to move the paragraphs farther apart or a negative value to bring them closer together (press Return/Enter or Tab to apply it); C you can also click the up or down arrow.

   ► Because the Space Before Paragraph value is combined with the Space After Paragraph value from the paragraph above, you could wind up with more space between paragraphs than you intend. We recommend that you enter a positive value for one of the two features, when needed, and keep the other value at zero.

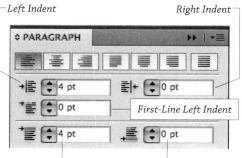

Left Indent — — Right Indent

First-Line Left Indent

Space Before Paragraph   Space After Paragraph

A *The Paragraph panel provides several indent and spacing options.*

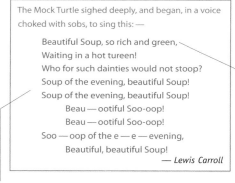

The Mock Turtle sighed deeply, and began, in a voice choked with sobs, to sing this: —

    Beautiful Soup, so rich and green,
    Waiting in a hot tureen!
    Who for such dainties would not stoop?
    Soup of the evening, beautiful Soup!
    Soup of the evening, beautiful Soup!
        Beau — ootiful Soo-oop!
        Beau — ootiful Soo-oop!
    Soo — oop of the e — e — evening,
    Beautiful, beautiful Soup!
            — Lewis Carroll

B *We increased the Left Indent value for these paragraphs.*

C *We also increased the Space Before Paragraph value for this paragraph.*

CREATING A HANGING INDENT

To create a hanging indent, enter a positive Left Indent value and a negative First-Line Left Indent value. Press Tab to align the second column of text.

Bene.: Pray thee, sweet Mistress Margaret, deserve well at my hands by helping me to the speech of Beatrice.

Marg.: Will you then write me a sonnet in praise of my beauty?

Bene.: In so high a style, Margaret, that no man living shall come over it; for, in most comely truth, thou deservest it.

Marg.: To have no man come over me? Why, shall I always keep below stairs?

Bene.: Thy wit is as quick as the greyhound's mouth; it catches.

            —William Shakespeare

Using paragraph and character styles

Now that you know how to style type manually by using the Paragraph and Character panels, you're ready to learn how to format type by using character and paragraph styles. They will enable you to reach the same goal with far less effort. In addition to making the job of typesetting easier, type styles also help ensure that your formatting remains consistent among multiple artboards and related documents. If you use a word processing or layout program, you may already be familiar with the general concept.

A paragraph style is a collection of paragraph formats, such as hyphenation and indentation, plus character attributes, such as the font, font style, and font size. When you click a paragraph style, all currently selected paragraphs are reformatted with the attributes in that style. **A**

A character style contains only character attributes, and is normally used to accentuate or reformat select characters or words within a paragraph (such as symbols in a bulleted list or boldfaced or italicized words) — not whole paragraphs. Character styles are applied in addition to paragraph styles — they're the icing on the cake. As with paragraph styles, when you click a character style, all currently selected characters are reformatted with the attributes in that style.

To create, modify, and apply type styles, you will use the Paragraph Styles and Character Styles panels. We'll show you the easiest way to create a style.

To create a paragraph or character style:

1. Display the Paragraph Styles ⬛ or Character Styles **A** panel (Window > Type submenu). **B** If this is your first foray into styles, we recommend working with paragraph styles first.

2. Apply all the attributes to be saved in the style to some text.

3. With a type tool, click in the type, then Option-click/Alt-click the **New Style** button ⬛ on the Paragraph Styles or Character Styles panel.

4. An options dialog opens. Change the default **Style Name** to a descriptive one that will help you remember the style's function (such as "Subheads" or "Body Indent").

5. Click OK. To apply the new style to some type, see the first task on the next page.

There is something that comes home to one now and perpetually ▲ It is not what is printed or preached or discussed…. ▲ It eludes discussion and print. ▲ It is not to be put in a book…. ▲ It is not in this book ▲ It is for you whoever you are ▲ It is no farther from you than your hearing and sight are from you ▲ It is hinted by nearest and commonest and readiest…. ▲ It is not them, though it is endlessly provoked by them…. ▲ What is there ready and near you now?

— *Walt Whitman*

A paragraph style   *A character style*

A *Use paragraph styles to format the main text (body, headers, subheads, etc.) and character styles to format special characters, bullets, or words within a paragraph.*

CHARACTER STYLES	PARAGRAPH STYLES	▶▶	▾≡
[Normal Character Style]			
Triangle symbols			
Italics			

B *Display the Character Styles and Paragraph Styles panel group.*

To apply a type style:

1. For paragraph styling, click in or select a type object, or drag through some paragraphs. Or to quickly select all the type objects in your document, choose Select > Object > Text Objects.

   For character styling, select one or more type characters (not a whole type object).

2. Click a style name on the Paragraph Styles 🔲 or Character Styles 🅰 panel. How easy was that?

   Note: If the text doesn't adopt all the attributes of the style sheet, see the next task.

▶ To choose a paragraph style before you create type, deselect, click the Normal character style on the Character Styles panel, then click a style on the Paragraph Styles panel.

If the text you have selected contains attributes (overrides) that are not found in the style definition, a + (plus) sign appears after the style name on the Paragraph Styles and/or Character Styles panel. This will occur, for example, if you style some text manually after applying a style. If you want to force the text to match the exact attributes in the applied style, you must clear the overrides, as in the steps below.

To remove overrides from styled text:

1. Select the characters or paragraphs that contain the overrides to be removed; 🅰 or to reset the whole object, select it with the Selection tool.

2. Hold down Option/Alt and click a name on the Paragraph Styles or Character Styles panel. 🅱 The manually applied attributes in your text will disappear, and the + sign will disappear from the style name on the panel.

▶ When you Option-click/Alt-click a paragraph style name to remove manual overrides, remember that to remove overrides from a character style, you have to Option-click/Alt-click that style name, too.

▶ If you unintentionally apply a character style to a whole type object and subsequently apply a paragraph style, only the formats from the paragraph style will be applied — not the character attributes — and the override symbol + won't display next to the paragraph style name. To force a paragraph style to override a character style completely, select the type object, then click [Normal Character Style] on the Character Styles panel.

When you edit a style, all the text in which it is being used in your document updates accordingly. There are two ways to edit a type style: by restyling a word or paragraph and then using it to redefine the style (as in the steps below), or by using the Paragraph or Character Style Options dialog (see the next page).

To edit a type style by redefining it:

1. Select a word or paragraph in which the style to be edited is being used. The style name becomes selected on the Paragraph Styles or Character Styles panel.

2. Change any attributes manually via the Paragraph, Character, Control, or Tabs panel.

   Note: Make sure all the type you have selected contains the style you are redefining and the new attributes. If you're redefining a paragraph style, also make sure the type doesn't have a character style applied to it.

3. Choose **Redefine Paragraph Style** from the Paragraph Styles panel menu or **Redefine Character Style** from the Character Styles panel menu. The style will update to reflect the custom styling in the selected text.

GEORGES BRAQUE (1882–1963)

There is only one **valuable** thing in art: the thing you cannot explain (as reported in *Saturday Review*, May 28, 1966).

A paragraph style   *A character style*

🅰 *The boldfacing for the word "valuable" was applied manually, so Illustrator considers it an override.*

GEORGES BRAQUE (1882–1963)

There is only one valuable thing in art: the thing you cannot explain (as reported in *Saturday Review*, May 28, 1966).

🅱 *We selected the main paragraph, then Option/Alt clicked the paragraph style on the Paragraph Styles panel. This removed the boldfacing override but not the character styling, which we used to format the words "Saturday Review."*

To edit a type style via an options dialog:

1. Deselect all, then double-click a style name on the Character Styles A or Paragraph Styles ¶ panel.

2. The Character Style Options or Paragraph Style Options dialog opens. A You can access an option set by clicking the set name on the left side. Check Preview to preview the changes in your document as you edit the style definition:

   Click **Basic Character Formats** to choose basic character attributes, such as the font (family), font style, size, kerning, leading, and tracking.

   Click **Advanced Character Formats** to choose horizontal and vertical scaling, baseline shift, or rotation values.

   In the Paragraph Style Options dialog, you also have access to the **Indents and Spacing**, **Tabs**, **Composition** (composer and hanging punctuation options), **Hyphenation**, and **Justification** option sets.

   Click **Character Color**, click the Fill or Stroke square, then choose a fill or stroke color for the type. Colors from the Swatches panel will be listed here. For a spot color, you can choose a Tint percentage. For the stroke, you can also change the Weight.

   Click **OpenType Features** to choose options to be applied if the style uses an OpenType font (see page 262).

   ➤ Click General at any time to view an expandable list of all the settings in the style.

3. Click OK. All the type in your document in which the style is being used will update instantly.

➤ To clear all the settings in the currently displayed option set (in the currently displayed style options dialog), click Reset Panel.

➤ A dash/blue background in a check box signifies that the option won't override any attributes that were applied manually to text in the document.

➤ To create a variation of an existing style, drag it to the New Style button. Click the duplicate style (labeled "copy"), then follow all the steps on this page. Neither of the Normal styles can be duplicated.

Paragraph Style Options

Style Name: Main Body Text

General	General
Basic Character Formats	
Advanced Character Formats	
Indents and Spacing	Style Settings: [Normal Paragraph Style] +
Tabs	
Composition	▼ Basic Character Formats
Hyphenation	Font Family:Tekton Pro
Justification	Font Style:Bold
Character Color	Size:12.5 pt
OpenType Features	▼ Advanced Character Formats
	Baseline Shift:0 pt
	▼ Indents and Spacing
	Left Indent:5 pt

☑ Preview   (Reset Panel)   (Cancel)   (OK)

A *The General option set of the Paragraph Style Options dialog lists all the attributes in the current style. Use features in any of the other option sets to edit the style.*

When you delete a paragraph or character style, the text attributes don't change in the document — the text merely ceases to be associated with the style (and, of course, that text won't update if the style is edited). Note that the deletion can't be undone, so proceed with caution.

To delete a character or paragraph style:

1. Deselect all.

2. Do either of the following:

   Click a style name (or Cmd-click/Ctrl-click multiple style names) on the Character Styles or Paragraph Styles panel, then click the **Delete Selected Styles** button.

   Drag a style name over the **Delete Selected Styles** button.

3. If the style is being used in your document, an alert dialog will appear. Click Yes.

➤ You can't delete the [Normal Paragraph Style] or [Normal Character Style].

➤ To delete all unused styles (those that aren't assigned to any text in your document), choose Select All Unused from the panel menu, then click the Delete Selected Styles button.

You can copy paragraph and character styles from one file to another. If you're working on a series of documents for the same client or project, using the same styles for all will produce consistently formatted type.

To load type styles from one Illustrator document to another:

1. From the Character Styles or Paragraph Styles panel menu, choose one of the following: **Load Character Styles**, **Load Paragraph Styles**, or **Load All Styles** (to load both character and paragraph styles).

2. In the Select a File to Import dialog, locate and click the Illustrator document that contains the styles you want to import, then click Open. Note: If an incoming style bears the same name as a style in the current document, it won't load, period.

Hanging punctuation

The Roman Hanging Punctuation command adds a professional typesetter's touch to your document by forcing punctuation marks that fall at the beginning and/or end of a line of area type to hang partially or fully outside the type block. This feature affects single and double quotation marks, hyphens, periods, commas, asterisks, ellipses, en dashes, em dashes, colons, semicolons, and tildes.

To hang punctuation:

1. Do one of the following:

   With a type tool, select a paragraph in an area type object.

   With a selection tool or the Layers panel, select a whole type object.

   To turn on hanging punctuation as a default setting for future type objects, deselect.

2. From the Paragraph panel menu, choose **Roman Hanging Punctuation.** A

➤ For a more visually pleasing alignment of letters and punctuation at the beginning and/or end of lines in a type object, such as the letters "W," "O," or "A," select the object, then choose Type > Optical Margin Alignment. This command may cause some letters to shift slightly outside the block, but they will print.

Setting tabs

The only way to align columns of text or numerals properly is by setting tabs — not by pressing the Spacebar! The default tab stops are half an inch apart. After inserting tabs in your text by following the steps below, you will need to use the Tabs panel to change their alignment style and/or location. You can also add an optional leader character (such as to create a dotted line in a table of contents).

To insert tabs into text:

1. Do either of the following:

   Press the Tab key once as you input copy, before typing each new column. The cursor will jump to the nearest default tab stop. B

   To insert a tab into existing text, click just to the left of the text that you want the tab to align, then press the Tab key (just once!). The text will move to the nearest default tab stop.

2. To customize the tab settings, follow the instructions on the next page.

"Dining is and always was a great artistic opportunity."

— Frank Lloyd Wright

A If you let it hang out — with Roman Hanging Punctuation, that is — your type will look more evenly aligned. This paragraph is left-aligned, so the punctuation is hanging in that direction.

	Front 9	Back 9	Total
Steve	34	34	68
Phil	38	44	82
Sergio	34	38	72
Tiger	35	38	73

B This text is aligned using tab stops. These nonprinting tab characters will display if you choose Type > Show Hidden Characters (Cmd-Option-I/Ctrl-Alt-I).

To set or modify custom tab stops:

1. After inserting tabs into your text (see the preceding page), do either of the following:

   Select a type object with the Selection tool or the Layers panel.

   Choose a type tool and select some text.

2. Display the Tabs panel ▦ (Window > Type > Tabs or Cmd-Shift-T/Ctrl-Shift-T).**A**

3. If the panel is floating (not docked), you can click the **Position Panel Above Text** button 🔒 to align the ruler with the left and right margins of the selected text for horizontal type, or with the top and bottom margins for vertical type.

4. Do any of the following:

   To add a marker, click in or just above the ruler (the selected text will align to that stop), then with the marker still selected, click an alignment button in the upper left corner of the panel. Repeat to add more markers.

   ▶ Option-click/Alt-click a selected marker to cycle through the alignment choices for it.

   To delete one marker, drag it off the ruler. Or to delete a marker and all markers to its right, Cmd-drag/Ctrl-drag it off the ruler.

   To move a tab marker, drag it to the left or right, or enter an exact location in the X field for horizontal type, or in the Y field for vertical type (or click in the field, then press the up or down arrow on the keyboard). Cmd-drag/Ctrl-drag a marker to move that marker and all the markers to its right by the same distance.

5. *Optional:* Click a tab marker in the ruler, then in the Leader field, enter a character (or up to eight characters), such as a period and a space, to be repeated between the tab and the succeeding text.**B**

6. *Optional:* For the Decimal-Justified tab alignment option, in the Align On field, enter a character for the numerals to align to (such as a period for a decimal point, or a dollar sign).**C** Unlike when you use the Leader option, the Align On character must be present (entered) in your text.

▶ To create a sequence of tab stops that are equidistant from one another, based on the spacing between a selected marker and the one to its left, choose Repeat Tab from the panel menu. *Beware!* This command deletes all existing markers to the right of the one you click before it inserts the new ones.

▶ Choose Snap to Unit from the Tabs panel menu to have tab markers snap to the nearest ruler tick mark as you insert or move them. (Or Shift-drag a marker to invoke the opposite behavior of the current Snap to Unit setting.)

▶ Drag the right edge of the panel to adjust the panel width.

▶ To clear all custom tabs, choose Clear All Tabs from the panel menu.

▶ To change the attributes of the leader characters in your text, use a character style.

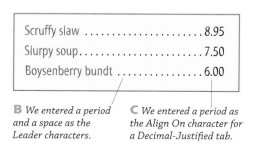

B *We entered a period and a space as the Leader characters.*

C *We entered a period as the Align On character for a Decimal-Justified tab.*

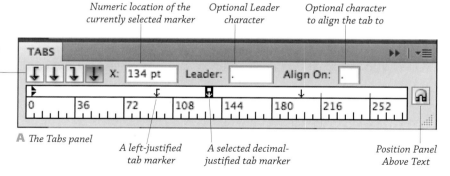

Numeric location of the currently selected marker

Optional Leader character

Optional character to align the tab to

Left-, Center-, Right-, and Decimal-Justified alignment buttons for horizontal type (or Top-, Center-, Bottom-, and Decimal-Justified buttons for vertical type)

A *The Tabs panel*

A left-justified tab marker

A selected decimal-justified tab marker

Position Panel Above Text

Changing the baseline shift value

By using the Baseline Shift feature, you can shift characters upward or downward from the baseline or, for path type, from a path. Note: To shift whole lines of type, use the leading feature instead (see page 257).

To shift type from its baseline:

1. With a type tool, select the type characters to be shifted.**A**

2. Do either of the following:

   On the Character panel **A** (with its full options displaying), enter or choose a positive **Baseline Shift** value to shift characters upward, or a negative value to shift them downward.**B–E**

   Hold down Option-Shift/Alt-Shift and press the up arrow on the keyboard to shift the selected characters upward or the down arrow to shift them downward by the current Baseline Shift increment in Illustrator/Edit > Preferences > Type (the default value is 2 pt). Or hold down Cmd-Option-Shift/Ctrl-Alt-Shift while pressing an arrow key to shift the type by five times that increment.

   ➤ To access superscript and subscript characters in an OpenType font, use the OpenType panel.

   ➤ To change the Baseline Shift value quickly, click in the field, then press the up or down arrow on the keyboard.

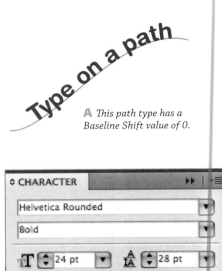

A This path type has a Baseline Shift value of 0.

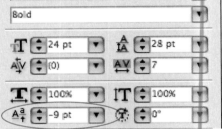

B We chose a Baseline Shift value of –9 to shift the type downward.

C Now the type is straddling the path.

D The original artwork contains some type on a path.

E To move the type closer to the inner circle, we shifted it downward by –7 pt.

Creating type outlines

The Create Outlines command converts each character in a type object into a separate graphic object. As outlines, the paths can then be reshaped, used in a compound or as a mask, or filled with a gradient, like other ordinary paths. You can use this feature to craft custom logos or insignia. Because the outlines are standard paths, they can be printed without your needing to make any printer fonts available.

To create type outlines:

1. Create type using any type tool. Note: All the characters in the object or on the path are going to be converted to outlines.

2. Style the type as desired, including scaling it to the desired size. Once the type is converted into outlines, you won't be able to change the font or other typographic attributes.

3. *Optional:* Type that is converted to outlines can't be converted back to type (unless you undo the conversion immediately), so we recommend that you duplicate the type object.

4. Select the type object with the Selection tool or the Layers panel.**A**

5. Do either of the following:

   Choose Type > **Create Outlines** (Cmd-Shift-O/Ctrl-Shift-O).**B**

Right-click the object and choose **Create Outlines** from the context menu.

6. Each former type character is converted to a separate compound path and is nested within a group on the Layers panel (see the last tip on page 339). If you want to reshape the points and segments on the resulting paths, you can double-click the group in the document window to put it into isolation mode first.**C**

Note: The fill and stroke attributes and any appearance attributes from the original type characters will be applied to the outlines. If the type was formerly along or inside an object, that object will be preserved as a separate path —unless it formerly had a stroke and fill of None, in which case it will be deleted.

➤ You should avoid creating outlines from small type, for the following reasons: The characters will no longer have the hinting information that preserves the shape of type characters for printing; second, outline shapes are slightly heavier than their editable type counterparts, so they can be hard to read (even more so if you give them a stroke color); and third, the outlines will increase the file size.

A *We selected a type object.*

B *We converted the type to outlines.*

C *Logos like these can be produced using type outlines as a starting point.*

Creating special effects with type

Type can be wrapped around an Illustrator path, an Illustrator type object, or a placed bitmap image.

To wrap text around an object:

1. Create area type (type inside an object). For the most even-looking wrap, apply one of the justify alignment options to the type (Paragraph panel).

2. Follow this step carefully, or the wrap isn't going to work: Make sure the object that the type is going to wrap around (we'll call it the "wrap object") is stacked in front of the type to be wrapped around it, within the same top-level layer, sublayer, or group. You can use the Layers panel to restack the object, if necessary. It can be a vector object, or a bitmap (placed) image that is surrounded by transparency.

3. Select the wrap object.**A**

4. Choose Object > **Text Wrap** > **Make**. If an alert dialog appears, click OK.

5. Choose Object > Text Wrap > **Text Wrap Options**. In the dialog,**B** check Preview, then enter or choose an **Offset** value for the distance between the wrap object and the type that is wrapping around it.

   Note: To prepare a Photoshop document for a text wrap in Illustrator, put the imagery on a layer that is surrounded by transparency, delete the Background, then save the file in the Photoshop (.psd) format. Import the image into an Illustrator document via the Place command (see page 289). The type should wrap around the opaque (or partially opaque) pixels in the image.

6. Click OK.**C** Try moving the wrap object slightly, and watch as the type rewraps around it.

➤ To prevent a text object from being affected by the wrap object, via the Layers panel, restack it above the wrap object or to a different top-level layer.

➤ To change the Offset for an existing wrap object, select it, then choose Object > Text Wrap > Text Wrap Options to reopen the dialog. (In case you're wondering, the Invert Wrap option forces text to wrap inside a path instead of outside it.)

To release a text wrap:

1. Select the wrap object (not the type).

2. Choose Object > **Text Wrap** > **Release**.

A *Select the object that you want the area type to wrap around.*

B *In the Text Wrap Options dialog, enter an Offset value and check Preview to see the effect in your document.*

Just picture a large sparrow cage made of bamboo grillwork and having a coconut-thatch roof, divided off into two parts by the curtains from my old studio. One of the two parts makes a bedroom, with very little light, so as to keep it cool. The other part, with a large window up high, is my studio. On the floor, some mats and my old Persian rug; and I've decorated the rest with fabrics, trinkets, and drawings. — *Paul Gauguin*

C *Here the type is wrapping around the palm tree.*

EXERCISE: Create a shadow for point type

A drop shadow that is created using the following method (unlike one that is produced via the Effect > Stylize > Drop Shadow command) will be an independent vector object, and can be modified via effects, the transform tools, or other methods.

1. Create some large point type, and select it with the Selection tool.

2. Apply a dark fill color and a stroke of None.

3. Option-drag/Alt-drag the type block slightly to the right and downward.

4. With the copy of the type block still selected, choose a lighter shade of the same fill color.

5. On the Layers panel, ⬛ drag the copy of the type below the original, **A** and make sure it's still selected (has a selection square).

6. Display the Appearance panel. From the Add New Effect menu **fx.** on the panel, choose Illustrator Effect > Stylize > Feather. Check Preview, choose a Radius value (try a low value of around 1–3 pt), then click OK. Next, click the Opacity link to open a temporary Transparency panel, and lower the opacity. **B**

Slant the shadow

1. Make sure the shadow type object is still selected.

2. Double-click the Shear tool ⬛ (it's on the Scale tool fly-out menu).

3. Enter 45 as the Shear Angle, click Axis: Horizontal, then click OK.

4. Use the arrow keys on the keyboard to align the baseline of the shadow text with the baseline of the original text. **C**

Reflect the shadow

1. With the shadow type still selected, double-click the Reflect tool ⬛ (it's on the Rotate tool fly-out menu), click Axis: Horizontal, then click OK.

2. Using the arrow keys again, drag the shadow type so its baseline meets the baseline of the original type. **D** You're done!

A Create a shadow, then via the Layers panel, stack it below the original type.

B Apply the Feather effect and lower the opacity of the shadow.

C Slant the shadow with the Shear tool.

D Reflect the shadow with the Reflect tool.

A DIFFERENT SLANT

After following steps 1–6 on this page, use the Layers panel to select the shadow object, choose the Free Transform tool, then vertically scale the object by dragging its top center handle upward. If you want to shear it, start dragging the top center handle downward, then hold down Cmd/Ctrl and continue to drag it downward and slightly to the right, all the way across the object. Cmd/Ctrl click away from the object to deselect it, then reposition it if needed.

Applying appearance attributes to type

When applying attributes to editable type, such as an added fill or stroke or editable effects, it's important to recognize the difference between selecting the type object and selecting the type characters. This can be made clear by studying the Appearance panel.

➤ When a type object is selected with the Selection tool or via the Layers panel, a **Type** label appears in boldface at the top of the Appearance panel. For newly created type, no Stroke or Fill listings display.**A** Any effects that you apply will affect the whole type object (both the fill and stroke) and will be listed on the panel when the type object is selected.**B**

➤ If you highlight some text characters with a type tool or double-click the word "Characters" on the Appearance panel, just the original Stroke, Fill, and Opacity attributes for those characters are listed on the panel.**C** (If you want to redisplay the attributes that apply specifically to the type object, click the word "Type" at the top.)

If you find this confusing, just remember that if the label next to the color square at the top of the panel is "Characters," your edits will affect just the selected characters, whereas if the label is "Type," your edits will affect all the type in the object.

➤ To apply transparency settings to the fill or stroke of type, see page 351.

A *Because we selected a type object with the Selection tool (above), a "Type" label appears next to the color square at the top of the Appearance panel (right).*

B *With the type object selected, we applied two effects: Bulge and Drop Shadow. (Effects can be applied to a type object, but not directly to type characters.)*

C *Here we selected type with a type tool, so a "Characters" label appears next to the color square on the Appearance panel, and the Stroke, Fill, and Opacity listings display (not the effect listings).*

Next, we'll show you two ways to embellish type, to build on the skills you learned in Chapter 14 (Appearances).

EXERCISE: Add multiple strokes to a character

1. Create a type character in a bold font of your choosing, approximately 230 pt. in size. Set the Horizontal Scale to 108%.

2. Select the type object with the Selection tool. **A** From the Swatches Libraries menu on the Swatches panel, ⊞ choose Gradients > Metals.

3. On the Appearance panel, ● click the Add New Fill button, ☐ then on the Metals library panel, click the Gold (first) swatch. On the Gradient panel, ▬ enter an Angle value of –90°.

4. On the Appearance panel, click the Stroke color square, then Shift-click it to open a temporary Color panel. Enter C18, M25, Y94, and K0

(press Tab to proceed from field to field). Choose 12 pt from the stroke Weight menu. **B–C**

5. Continuing on the Appearance panel, click the Add New Stroke button. ◼ Apply a color of C0, M7, Y51, and K8, and a stroke weight of 8 pt, as you did in the preceding step.

6. Click the Add New Stroke button once more. Apply a color of C20, M40, Y96, and K8, and a stroke weight of 2 pt.

7. Click the Opacity listing on the panel. From the Add New Effect menu, *fx,* choose Illustrator Effects > Stylize > Drop Shadow. Check Preview, choose settings to produce a nice-looking shadow, then click OK. **D–E**

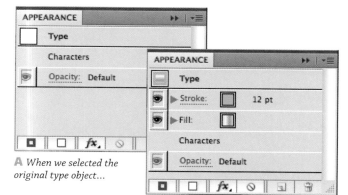

A When we selected the original type object...

B ...these listings displayed on the Appearance panel. We added new fill and stroke attributes to the type object.

C This is the type object after we applied the "Gold" gradient fill preset, a tan stroke color, and a stroke weight of 12 pt.

D The Appearance panel lists the two new stroke attributes and the effect that we applied to the type object.

E This is the final result.

EXERCISE: Use the Free Distort effect on type

1. Create a type character in an extra or ultra bold font,* approximately 230 pt. in size. Choose the Selection tool.

2. At the bottom of the Appearance panel,◉ click the Add New Fill button.☐

3. Click the Fill color square and choose a light brown color, or Shift-click the Fill color square to mix a color via the temporary Color panel.

4. Double-click the Stroke color square and click a dark brown swatch. Choose a value of 7 pt from the stroke Weight menu.**A**

5. Double-click the Characters appearance listing, then set both the Stroke and Fill listings to a color of None.

6. Click the Type appearance listing to view the appearance attributes for the type object. Click the Fill listing, then from the Add New Effect menu,***fx***, choose Distort & Transform > Free Distort.**B** In the Free Distort dialog, move the top left and right points downward and to the left to slant the fill, then click OK.**C**

➤ To edit the Free Distort settings at any time, expand the Fill listing, then click Free Distort.

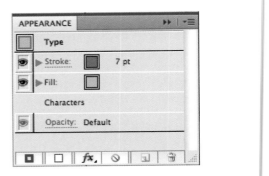

A We used the Appearance panel to add new fill and stroke attributes to this type object.

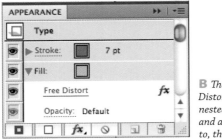

B The Free Distort effect is nested within, and applies only to, the Fill listing.

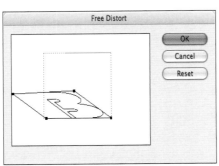

C The distortion was applied to the fill attribute for the type. (The point type on the bottom has a reddish-brown stroke color and a fill of None.)

*If you don't have that kind of font, choose a bold font, then on the Character panel, increase the Horizontal Scale to around 140%.

Mastering the Pen tool — Illustrator's most difficult tool — takes patience and practice. If you get accustomed to using it, refer to Chapter 12 to learn how to reshape the resulting paths. If you try using this tool but find it to be too difficult, remember that you can create shapes using other methods. For example, you can draw simple geometric shapes (Chapter 6) and then combine them (Chapter 25), or draw in a freehand style with the Blob Brush or Pencil tool (Chapter 7).

Drawing with the Pen tool

The Pen tool creates precise curved and straight segments that are connected by anchor points. You can either click with the tool to create corner points and straight segments without direction handles,**A** or drag with the tool to create smooth points and curve segments with direction handles (the handles look like antennae).**B** The initial shape of the curve segments is determined by the distance and direction in which you drag the mouse, but you can manipulate the direction handles afterward to reshape the curves. You can also use the Pen tool to create corner points, which join nonsmooth curves.**C**

In the instructions on the following pages, you'll learn how to draw straight segments, smooth curves, and nonsmooth curves. Once you master all three techniques, you'll naturally combine them without really thinking about it while drawing shapes: Drag-drag-click, drag, click-click-drag…

A *This corner point is joining two straight segments, and has no direction handles.*

B *A smooth point has a pair of direction handles that move in tandem. This is a smooth curve.*

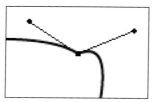

C *This corner point has direction handles that move independently. This is a nonsmooth curve.*

Before you tackle the challenge of drawing curves with the Pen tool, practice the easier task of clicking with the tool to create an open or closed polygon.

To draw a polygon with the Pen tool:

1. If the current fill choice is a solid color, a gradient, or a pattern (not None), your Pen path will be filled when you create the first three points. If you prefer to have the segments appear as lines only, choose a stroke color and a fill of None.

2. Choose the **Pen** tool 🖋 (P).

3. Turn on Smart Guides (Cmd-U/Ctrl-U), and in Illustrator/Edit > Preferences > Smart Guides, check all the boxes under Display Options.

4. Click to create the first anchor point, then click to create a second one. A straight segment will connect the two points.

5. Click to create additional anchor points. They will be connected by straight segments. You can use the Alignment Guides feature of Smart Guides to align new points and segments with existing ones or to the horizontal or vertical axis.**A** You can also hold down Shift to constrain the segments to an increment of 45°.

6. Do one of the following:

   To complete the object as an open path and keep it selected, click the Pen tool or any other tool.

   To complete the object as an open path by deselecting it, Cmd-click/Ctrl-click outside it or press Cmd-Shift-A/Ctrl-Shift-A.

   To complete the object as a closed path, position the pointer over the starting point (a tiny circle appears in the pointer and an "anchor" label displays next to the point), then click the point.**B–D**

➤ If the artboard starts to fill up with extraneous points as a result of numerous "false starts," choose Object > Path > Clean Up, check just Delete: Stray Points, then click OK.

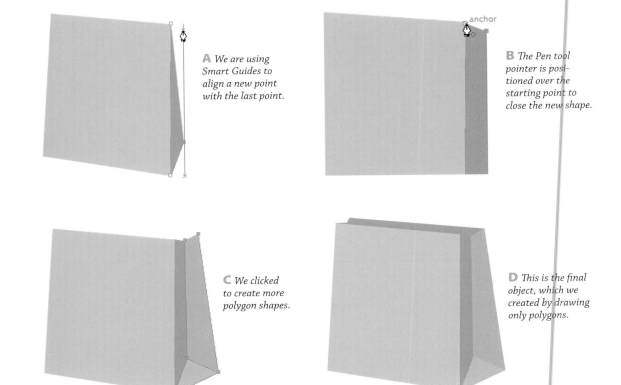

A *We are using Smart Guides to align a new point with the last point.*

B *The Pen tool pointer is positioned over the starting point to close the new shape.*

C *We clicked to create more polygon shapes.*

D *This is the final object, which we created by drawing only polygons.*

Follow these instructions to create smooth curves with the Pen tool. The smooth anchor points that connect curve segments always have a pair of direction handles that move in tandem. The longer the direction handles, the steeper or wider the curve.

To draw curves with the Pen tool:

1. Choose the **Pen** tool ✒ (P).

2. Turn on Smart Guides (Cmd-U/Ctrl-U), and in Illustrator/Edit > Preferences > Smart Guides, check all the boxes under Display Options.

3. Drag (don't click) to create the first anchor point.**A** The angle of the direction handles on the point will align with the direction you drag.

4. To create a second anchor point, release the mouse, move it away from the last anchor point, then drag a short distance in the direction you want the curve to follow.**B** A curve segment will connect the first and second anchor points, and the next pair of direction handles will appear.

5. Drag to create more anchor points and direction handles.**C–E** The points will be connected by curve segments.

    ➤ To produce smooth, symmetrical curves, place the points at the beginning and end of each arc rather than at the middle. You can use Smart Guides to align new points to existing ones.

6. Do one of the following:

    To complete the object as an open path and keep it selected, click the Pen tool or any other tool.

    To complete the object as an open path by deselecting it, Cmd-click/Ctrl-click outside it or press Cmd-Shift-A/Ctrl-Shift-A.

    To complete the object as a closed path, position the pointer over the starting point (a tiny circle appears in the pointer and an "anchor" label displays next to the point). Drag from that point, then release the mouse.

➤ To keep the curves from looking bumpy and irregular, use just the minimum number of anchor points necessary to define them. Also, drag short distances to produce relatively short direction handles — you can always lengthen them later.

➤ To practice drawing smooth curves, convert an object that has graceful curves to a guide (see page 108), then trace the guide with the Pen tool.

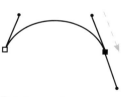

A *Drag to create the first anchor point.*

B *Release and reposition the mouse, then drag in the direction you want the curve to follow.*

C *Continue to reposition and drag the mouse.*

D *Continue to reposition and drag.*

E *The large curved shape in the background of this illustration is being used as a clipping mask (see Chapter 26).*

USING SMART GUIDES WHILE DRAWING A PATH WITH THE PEN TOOL

You can use Smart Guides to align new anchor points with existing points.

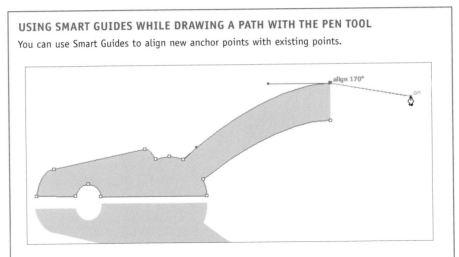

ADJUSTING POINTS WHILE DRAWING A PATH WITH THE PEN TOOL

► To reposition the last corner point, keep the mouse button down when you click to create the point, then hold down the Spacebar and drag the point (or do the same for the last smooth point, except drag the direction handle). Release the Spacebar, reposition the mouse, then continue to draw. Practice this; you sort of have to think ahead.

► If the last point you created was a corner point and you want to add a direction handle to it, position the Pen tool pointer over it, then drag; a direction handle appears. Release and reposition the mouse, then continue to draw.

► If the last anchor point you created was a smooth point (two direction handles) and you want to convert it to a corner point (one direction handle), click it with the Pen tool, release and reposition the mouse, then continue to draw. (See also the following page.)

YOU'RE A GENIUS!

If you get fed up with the Pen tool, create a cityscape like this one and maybe you'll feel better. Draw some rectangles with the Rectangle tool and fill them with a few different colors. Choose a black stroke and a fill color of None, then with the Pen tool, click, click, click to create the black lines — using Smart Guides to align them with the horizontal or vertical axis.

Converting anchor points on paths

Yet another use for the Pen tool is to create corner points that join nonsmooth curves — segments that jut out from the same side of an anchor point (unlike smooth curves, which extend from either side of a smooth anchor point). If you move one of the direction handles on a corner point, the contour of the curve changes on just that side of the point.

Note: Smooth points and corner points can be combined in the same path. You can convert smooth points into corner points (or vice versa) as you draw them (as in the instructions below) or after you draw them (as in the instructions on the next page).

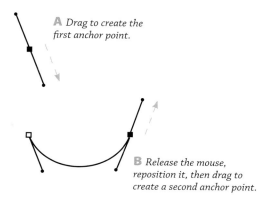

A *Drag to create the first anchor point.*

B *Release the mouse, reposition it, then drag to create a second anchor point.*

To convert smooth points into corner points as you draw them:

1. Choose the **Pen** tool ✍ (P).

2. Drag to create the first anchor point.**A**

3. Release the mouse, move it away from the last anchor point, then drag a short distance to create a second anchor point.**B** A curve segment will connect the first and second anchor points, and a second pair of direction handles will appear. The shape of the curve segment is controlled by the distance and direction in which you drag.

4. Do either of the following:

    Position the pointer over the last anchor point, Option-drag/Alt-drag from that point to drag one of the direction handles independently, release Option/Alt and the mouse, reposition the mouse, then drag the next point in the direction you want the curve to follow.**C** (So many words to describe a process that becomes intuitive with practice!)

    Click the last anchor point; one of the direction handles disappears from that point.

5. Repeat the last two steps to draw more anchor points and curves.

6. To close the shape, do either of the following: **D–E**

    Drag on the starting point to keep it as a smooth point.

    Click the starting point to convert it to a corner point with one direction handle.

C *Option-drag/Alt-drag from the last anchor point in the direction you want the new curve to follow. Both direction handles are now on the same side of the curve segment.*

D *Drag to create another anchor point, and so on.*

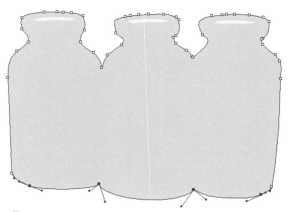

E *We used nonsmooth curves to define the bottom edges of these bottle shapes.*

To convert points on an existing path:

Method 1 (Control panel buttons)

1. Choose the **Direct Selection** tool ▸ (A).

2. Click a path, then click a point on the path to be converted.

3. On the Control panel, click the **Convert Selected Anchor Points to Corner** button ⌐ or the **Convert Selected Anchor Points to Smooth** button.

   ▶ Read about the Selection & Anchor Display Preferences on page 380. To make it easier to locate anchor points, we recommend checking the Highlight Anchors on Mouse Over preference.

Method 2 (Convert Anchor Point tool)

1. Choose the **Direct Selection** tool ▸ (A), then click a path.

2. Choose the **Convert Anchor Point** tool ▸ (Shift-C).

3. To help you locate the anchor points easily, turn on Smart Guides (Cmd-U/Ctrl-U) and in Illustrator/Edit > Preferences > Smart Guides, check Anchor/Path Labels.

4. Do any of the following:

   Drag new direction handles from a corner point to convert it to a smooth point. **A**

   To convert a smooth point to a corner point with a nonsmooth curve, rotate a direction handle from the point so it forms a V shape with the other direction handle. **B**

   Click a smooth point to convert it to a corner point with no direction handles. **C–D**

   ▶ To turn the Pen tool into a temporary Convert Anchor Point tool, hold down Option/Alt. To turn the Pen tool temporarily into the last-used selection tool, hold down Cmd/Ctrl.

   ▶ For more ways to reshape a path, see Chapter 12.

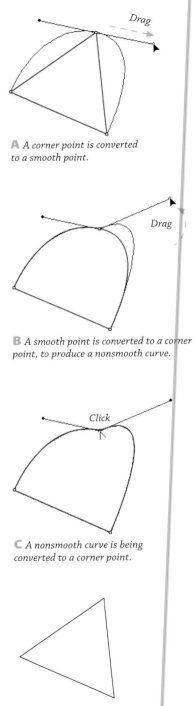

Drag

A *A corner point is converted to a smooth point.*

Drag

B *A smooth point is converted to a corner point, to produce a nonsmooth curve.*

Click

C *A nonsmooth curve is being converted to a corner point.*

D *The path has been restored to a triangle, with no direction handles.*

EXERCISE: Draw a knife with the Pen tool

Draw the knife blade

1. Turn on Smart Guides (Cmd-U/Ctrl-U) and in Illustrator/Edit > Preferences > Smart Guides, check Alignment Guides and Anchor/Path Labels.

2. Create a long horizontal artboard. Choose the Pen tool ✎ (P). Choose a light blue-gray solid fill color and a stroke of None.

3. Starting from the left side of the artboard, drag slightly downward and to the right to create the first anchor point. Reposition the pointer on the right side of the artboard and click, move the mouse upward, then click again to create a straight vertical edge.**A–B**

4. Complete the shape by clicking back on the starting point.**C** If necessary, choose the Direct Selection tool ▷ (A) and reposition the handle at the tip of the blade to reshape the blade. Cmd-click/Ctrl-click to deselect.

5. On the Color panel, choose white as the fill color, then add a touch of Cyan or Blue to it.

6. To create the narrow cutting edge of the blade, with the Pen tool (P), click the tip of the blade. Reposition the pointer over the curve of the blade, drag to create a curve that mimics the blade shape,**D** click twice to create a short, straight vertical edge,**E** drag to create a matching curve for the top of the edge of the blade, then click back on the starting point.**F** Reshape the new object, if necessary (as described in step 4).

Draw the knife handle

1. Deselect. Choose black as the fill color. With the Pen tool (P), drag over the top right edge of the blade. Working from left to right, drag to create four smooth curve points for the top and end of the handle.**G**

2. Wending your way back to the left, drag to create four smooth curve points to define the bottom of the handle.**H**

Continued on the following page

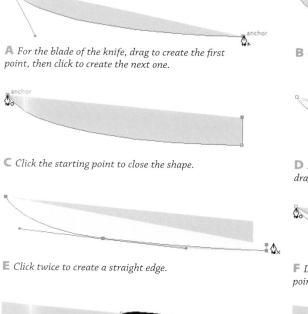

A *For the blade of the knife, drag to create the first point, then click to create the next one.*

C *Click the starting point to close the shape.*

E *Click twice to create a straight edge.*

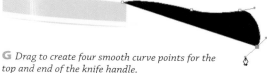

G *Drag to create four smooth curve points for the top and end of the knife handle.*

B *Click to create a straight edge.*

D *For the edge of the blade, click to create a point, then drag to create a curve.*

F *Drag to create a matching curve, then click the starting point to close the shape.*

H *Drag to create four smooth curve points to define the bottom of the handle.*

Finally, click near the bottom of the blade, then click the starting point for the handle shape.

Create a shadow for both parts of the knife

1. Choose the Selection tool ▸ (V). Option-drag/Alt-drag the larger blade object downward and slightly to the left. **B** On the Layers panel, drag the listing for the blade copy to the bottom of the layer.

2. Display the bounding box for the blade copy, then drag the bottom center handle upward slightly to make it more squat. Fill the object with a medium-dark color, and save the color as a swatch to the Swatches panel, if it hasn't already been saved. **C**

3. Option-drag/Alt-drag the handle object slightly downward and to the left. **D** On the Layers panel, drag the listing for the copy to the bottom of the layer.

4. Fill the handle copy with the shadow color that you saved to the Swatches panel in step 2.

5. Deselect. With the Direct Selection tool ▸ (A), move the bottom left corner point of the handle copy to smooth the contour between the two shadow shapes (it may help to isolate and zoom in on the object). **E**

6. Create a new layer, and stack it below the existing ones. With the Rectangle tool ▢ (M), draw a rectangle behind all the objects, and fill it with a lighter version of the color you chose for the shadows. Time to cook dinner!

A *Click to complete the bottom part of the handle, then click the starting point to close the path.*

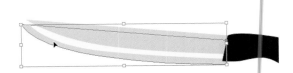

B *Option-drag/Alt-drag the blade object downward to copy it. Restack the copy to the bottom of the layer.*

C *To scale the shadow, drag the center handle on the bounding box of the copy upward, and fill the path with a medium-dark color.*

D *Option-drag/Alt-drag the handle object downward to copy it (shown tinted above, for clarity). Restack the copy to the bottom of the layer.*

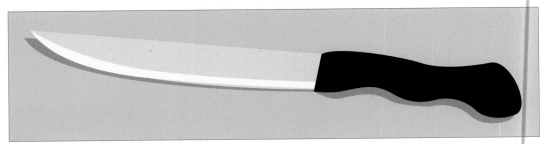

E *Fill the shadow for the knife handle with the same color that you used for the blade shadow. If necessary, with the Direct Selection tool, adjust the corner points on the shadow shapes to smooth the transition between them.*

If you want to incorporate a photo into your Illustrator design (say you want to place a photo behind some type for a book jacket, poster, or product label) or you need to import an image for tracing, you will gain the skills you need in this chapter. You will import images and graphics into an Illustrator document via the Open and Place commands and via the drag-and-drop method, and you will work with the Links and Control panels to edit, replace, locate, update, relink, and embed your linked images.

How images are acquired in Illustrator

The methods that can be used to acquire images from other applications include the Open command, the Place command, and drag-and-drop. Your choice will depend on what file formats are available for saving the file in its original application and how you plan to use the file in Illustrator.

When you open a document from another drawing (vector) application via the Open command, a new Illustrator file is created, and the acquired objects can be manipulated using Illustrator tools and commands. When you open a bitmap image via the Open command, the image isn't converted into separate vector objects, but rather is embedded in a new file as an object, in its own box.

Via the Place command, an image can be linked or embedded into your Illustrator file. For print output, the recommended formats for linked images — EPS, TIFF, and PDF — preserve the colors, detail, and resolution of the original image. When placing a layered Photoshop (.psd) file into Illustrator, you can choose (via a dialog) to have the image appear as a single flattened object or as separate objects on separate layers.

You can also acquire images by using the drag-and-drop method. When you drag an image from one Illustrator window into another or from a document window of another application (such as Photoshop) into an Illustrator document, a duplicate of the image appears in the target document.

A bitmap image that you acquire in Illustrator via the Open, Place, or drag-and-drop method can be moved, placed on a different layer, masked, modified using any transformation method, or modified using Photoshop effects. All three methods preserve the resolution of the original image.

The Clipboard commands (Cut, Copy, Paste) can also be used to acquire images in Illustrator. See page 103.

ACQUIRE IMAGES

22

Using the Open command

The Open command opens an image or graphics file as a separate Illustrator document. For a list of some of the formats that you can open in Illustrator, see the sidebar at right.

Note: To preserve the editability of appearances and text in an Adobe PDF file, use the Open command, as in the steps below, instead of the Place command, which is discussed on the next page.

To import a file into Illustrator via the Open command:

1. Do either of the following:

   In Bridge, click a file thumbnail, then choose File > **Open With** > **Adobe Illustrator CS5**.

   In Illustrator, choose File > **Open** (Cmd-O/ Ctrl-O). The Open dialog appears. In the Mac OS, choose Enable: All Readable Documents to dim any files that are in formats Illustrator can't read. In Windows, you can filter out files via the Files of Type menu, or choose All Formats (the default setting) to display files in all formats. Double-click a file name; or locate and click a file name, then click Open.

2. If you chose a multipage PDF file, the Open PDF dialog will appear. 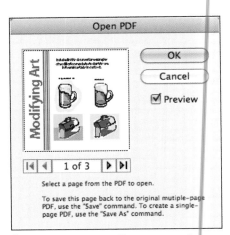 Check Preview, click an arrow to navigate to the desired page (or enter the desired page number in the field), then click OK. Respond to any alert dialogs that appear (see the sidebar on the following page and see also page 63).

   If you open a Photoshop PSD file that contains layers or layer comps, the Photoshop Import Options dialog will appear. See pages 290–291.

   Other formats may cause a different dialog to appear. Choose options, then click OK to proceed. B

   ➤ If you reduce the scale of a linked or embedded image in Illustrator, its resolution will increase accordingly; if you enlarge it, its resolution will decrease.

IMPORTABLE FILE FORMATS

Image and graphics files in a wide variety of formats can be opened or placed into Illustrator CS5. A few examples are BMP, CGM, CorelDRAW, DWG, EMF, EPS, FXG, GIF, JPEG, JPEG2000, PDF, PSD, SVG, SVGZ, TIFF, and WMF (but not SWF). You can also open or place text formats, such as TXT (plain text), RTF, and MS Word. To open native Illustrator files into Illustrator, see pages 55 and 62.

A For a multipage PDF file, navigate to the page that you want to open.

B To produce this artwork, we used editable type as a clipping path to partially mask an imported image. To learn about clipping masks, see Chapter 26. (We also added an object that has a solid white fill.)

Using the Place command

When you use the Place command, the chosen file appears in an existing Illustrator document. You can reposition it on the artboard, restack it via the Layers panel, use it in a mask, transform it, apply effects to it, or change its opacity or blending mode. When using the Place command in Illustrator, you can choose whether or not to link or embed the file into your document (you will learn how to manage linked files later in this chapter).

To import a file into an Illustrator document via the Place command:

Method 1 (from Illustrator)

1. Open an Illustrator file, and click a layer for the image to appear on.

2. Choose File > **Place**, then in the dialog, click a file to be placed. Next, indicate whether you want Illustrator to link or embed the image. Check **Link** to place just a screen version of the image into your Illustrator document, with a link to the original image file. The original image file won't be affected by your edits in Illustrator and won't be color-managed; and in order for it to print properly, it must be available on your hard disk. Or uncheck Link to embed a copy of the actual image into the Illustrator file and allow Illustrator to color-manage the image. The embedded image will increase the storage size of your Illustrator file. Click Place.

3. An options dialog may appear. For example, if you place a Photoshop PSD file that contains layers (with the Link option unchecked), or that contains layer comps (with the Link option checked or unchecked), the Photoshop Import Options dialog will appear. To learn about this dialog, see the next two pages.

Method 2 (from Bridge)

1. Open an Illustrator file, and click a layer for the image to appear on.

2. In Bridge, click a file thumbnail, then choose File > **Place** > **In Illustrator**. The image will appear in the Illustrator document and will be linked automatically.

➤ When selected, a linked image will have an X on top of it, in the selection color of the current layer. **A**

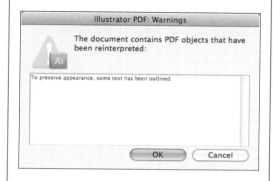

A *A linked image is selected in an Illustrator document.*

Importing Photoshop images into Illustrator

Choosing Photoshop import options

Importing a single-layer image

If you import a single-layer Photoshop PSD image into Illustrator via the **Open** or **Place** command, it will be listed on the Layers panel by its file name on the currently active layer, and no dialog will open (if any alerts appear, see the sidebar on the preceding page). No clipping mask will be generated by Illustrator.

Importing a multilayer image

If you place a PSD file that contains layers with the Link option unchecked, place a PSD file that contains layer comps with or without the Link option checked, or open a PSD file that contains layers or layer comps, the Photoshop Import Options dialog opens. Check **Show Preview** to display a thumbnail preview of the image. The other options are described below.

Importing layer comps

Choose from the **Layer Comp** menu to import a layer comp, if the file contains any. Any comments entered in Photoshop for the chosen comp will display in the Comments window. If you need to import additional layer comps from the same Photoshop image, you will have to use the Place command separately for each one.

If the image contains layer comps and you checked Link in the Place dialog, you can choose **When Updating Link: Keep Layer Visibility Overrides** to preserve the layer visibility (hide or show) state the layers were in when you originally placed the image, regardless of any visibility changes that are made to the file in Photoshop after it is imported; or choose **Use Photoshop's Layer Visibility** to have any subsequent layer visibility changes that are made to the image in Photoshop also appear in Illustrator.

Importing Photoshop layers

If you unchecked the Link option in the Place dialog, you now have the option to keep or flatten the layers. If you click **Convert Layers to Objects**, each object will be nested within an image group on the current layer.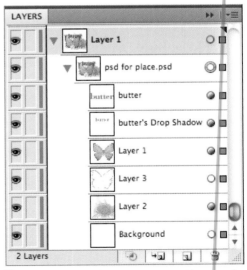 Transparency levels are listed as editable appearances in Illustrator. Blending modes that are also available in Illustrator (on the blending mode menu in the Transparency panel) are preserved and are listed as editable appearances. Layer groups are preserved, as are layer and vector masks. A vector mask is listed as a clipping path on the Layers panel, whereas a layer mask becomes an opacity mask

A When we imported a Photoshop PSD file containing layers into Illustrator, we unchecked the Link option in the Place dialog, and this Photoshop Import Options dialog opened.

B Because we checked Convert Layers to Objects in the Photoshop Import Options dialog, each Photoshop layer became a separate Illustrator object, nested within a group.

and displays on the Transparency panel, provided effects weren't applied to it in Photoshop. Plain type remains editable, when possible (see the last paragraph in this column). Each converted layer from the Photoshop file is listed separately on the Links panel.

If you click **Flatten Layers to a Single Image** instead, a flattened version of the image will be nested within the current layer. All transparency levels, blending modes, and layer mask effects will be applied to the flattened image but won't be listed as editable appearances in Illustrator.

Check **Import Hidden Layers** and/or **Import Slices**, if available (and if desired), to import those elements with the file.

Linked files are flattened automatically (that is, the Convert Layers to Objects option is dimmed).

If you click Convert Layers to Objects in the Photoshop Import Options dialog, the Background from the Photoshop file will become one of the nested objects within Illustrator, and will be opaque. You can change its opacity, hide it, or delete it via the Layers panel in Illustrator.

Other Photoshop issues

In Photoshop, the position of adjustment layers in the layer stack affects how image layers are converted to objects when the file is placed and embedded (not linked) into the Illustrator document. Any layers above an adjustment layer in the Photoshop file will be converted to separate objects in Illustrator. Any layers below an adjustment layer in the Photoshop file will be flattened, along with the adjustment layer, into one object in Illustrator, and the appearance of the adjustment will be preserved. You can delete or hide adjustment layers in Photoshop before placing an image into Illustrator. Hidden adjustment layers aren't imported.

When a Photoshop EPS file is placed or opened into Illustrator, any Photoshop shape layers become clipping masks, editable text becomes a clipping path or a compound clipping path, and all other Photoshop layers are flattened into one object below the shape layer(s). Each layer from a Photoshop PSD file, on the other hand, is converted to a separate object layer.

If you place a Photoshop file that contains editable type into Illustrator (with the Link option unchecked) and click Convert Layers to Objects, the type objects will remain editable, provided the type layer in Photoshop didn't contain effects and wasn't warped. If you want to import a type layer as vector outlines instead, in Photoshop, apply Layer > Type > Convert to Shape, save the file, then import it into Illustrator via the Open or Place command.

If the current layer in a Photoshop file contains pixels that extend outside the live canvas area, those pixels will be dropped when you import it into Illustrator, no matter which method you use — drag-and-drop, place, or open. Before acquiring an image from Photoshop, make sure the pixels that you want to import are visible within the live canvas area in the original file.

Importing a TIFF image

When you place a layered TIFF file into Illustrator, the TIFF Import Options dialog opens, offering the same options as in the Photoshop Import Options dialog. When saving a file in the Photoshop (.psd) format isn't an option for some reason, TIFF is an acceptable alternative.

CREATING AN OBJECT MOSAIC

To convert a bitmap image into a mosaic of colored vector squares, place an image into an Illustrator document with the Link option unchecked. Click the object, then choose Object > Create Object Mosaic. To approach this dialog simply, enter a Width value for the Number of Tiles, click Use Ratio, then click OK. Unfortunately, there is no Preview option in the dialog.

Managing linked images

When you place an image from another application into an Illustrator document, you can either embed a copy of the image into the file (and thereby increase the file size but allow Illustrator to color-manage it) or link the image to your document (and keep the file size smaller but require the original file to be available for print output). For the latter option, a screen version of each image serves as a placeholder in your document, but the actual image remains separate from the Illustrator file. To link a file, use the File > Place command with the Link option checked.

The Links panel A lists all the linked and embedded files in your Illustrator document, and provides controls for keeping track of those files. It lets you monitor the status of linked images, restore the link to a missing image (so it can be output properly), open a linked image in its original application (for editing), update a modified linked image, and convert a linked image to an embedded one.

Some Links panel commands are also available on the Control panel when a linked image is selected in your document. B–D In fact, you can open a temporary Links panel by clicking either the Linked File or Image link on the Control panel.

To edit a linked image in its original application:

1. Do either of the following:

   On the Links panel, ✎ click the image name, then click the **Edit Original** button. ✎

   Click the image in the document window, then click **Edit Original** on the Control panel.

   The application in which the linked image was created will launch, if it isn't already running, and the image will open.

2. Make your edits, resave the file, then return to Illustrator. If an alert dialog appears, E click Yes. The linked image will update in your document.

   Note: In Illustrator/Edit > Preferences > File Handling & Clipboard, under Files, you can choose preferences for linked images. For example, via the Update Links menu, you can specify whether linked images will update automatically if they are modified in their original application (see also "To update a modified linked image" on page 294, and learn more about the preferences on page 389).

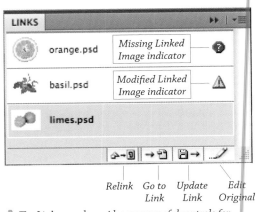

Relink   Go to   Update   Edit
         Link   Link   Original

A *The Links panel provides many useful controls for managing linked files.*

| Linked File | GARDEN.psd | CMYK | PPI: 300 |

B *When a linked image is selected in your document, you can click Linked File on the Control panel to open a temporary Links panel, or click the image name to access a menu of Links panel commands.*

| Image | limes.jpg | CMYK | PPI: 240 |

C *When an embedded JPEG image is selected in your document, you can click Image on the Control panel to open a temporary Links panel, or click the image name to access a menu of Links panel commands.*

| Group | Embedded | CMYK | PPI: 240 |

D *When any other type of embedded image is selected in your document, you can click Embedded on the Control panel to access a menu of Links panel commands.*

Some files are missing or modified in the Links panel. Would you like to update them now?

No   Yes

E *This prompt appears if you edit a linked file in its original application, then click back in the Illustrator document.*

If you replace one placed image with another, any effects, transparency settings, or transformations (e.g., scaling, rotation) that were applied to the original image in Illustrator will also be applied automatically to the replacement.

To replace a linked or embedded image:

1. Do either of the following:

   On the Links panel, click the name of the file to be replaced, then click the **Relink** button. A

   Click the image in the document window, then on the Control panel, click the image name or the **Embedded** link (not the Embed button) and choose **Relink** from the menu.

2. In the Place dialog, locate the desired replacement file, then click Place. B If another dialog opens, choose options, then click OK.

➤ To replace an image a different way, select a placed image in the document, choose File > Place, locate the replacement image, check Replace, then click Place.

The simple Go to Link command locates a placed image for you, selects it on its artboard, and centers it within the document window. This command may come in handy if your document contains many linked images.

To go to a linked or embedded image:

On the Links panel, click an image name, then click the **Go to Link** button.

➤ If you click the listing for a linked image on the Links panel, then choose Reveal in Bridge from the panel menu, Bridge will open, and the thumbnail for that image will be selected in the Bridge window. If necessary, click in the Bridge window to bring it forward.

LINKED VERSUS EMBEDDED IMAGES

➤ On the Layers panel, a linked image will be listed as <Linked File> or by the file name, within the currently active layer.

➤ An embedded image will be listed as an <Image> or by name on the current layer. A file in the EPS or TIFF format will be nested within a group; a PDF file will be nested within three groups, some of which will contain a clipping path.

➤ Photoshop effects on the Effect menu can be applied to both linked and embedded images and will remain editable.

➤ You can transform (e.g., move, scale, rotate, shear, or reflect) both linked and embedded images.

A *Click the linked image to be replaced, then click the Relink button.*

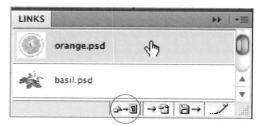

B *We replaced the "orange.psd" image with an image called "apples.psd."*

If this warning icon ⚠ appears on the Links panel, it means the original file was modified but the link wasn't updated. This will occur if you edit the file in its original application and Manually is the current setting on the Update Links menu in Illustrator/ Edit > Preferences > File Handling & Clipboard. To update the link, follow the steps below. Note: If the preference setting is Automatically, the image will update automatically; or if the setting is Ask When Modified, an alert will appear, offering you the option to update the file.

To update a modified linked image:

1. On the Links panel, 🔗 click the listing for the modified image. ⚠

2. Do either of the following:

   Click the **Update Link** button 🔄 at the bottom of the Links panel.

   Click the image in the document window, then click the image name on the Control panel and choose **Update Link** from the menu.

To locate or replace images upon opening an Illustrator document:

If you link an image to an Illustrator file, then move the actual image file from its original location or rename it, and finally reopen the Illustrator file, an alert dialog will appear. A Do either of the following:

To locate the missing file or substitute a different one, click **Replace**, locate the missing file or the desired replacement, then click Replace.

Click **Ignore**. The linked image won't display in the Illustrator document, but its bounding box will display if Smart Guides are on (with Object Highlighting) and you pass the cursor over it. A question mark icon will display for that listing on the Links panel. (To break the link completely and prevent an alert prompt from appearing for that image in the future, delete the bounding box and resave your document.)

Optional: Check Apply to All in the alert dialog to have whichever button you click be applied to any other missing images.

To locate or replace a missing linked image in an open Illustrator document:

1. Do either of the following:

   On the Links panel, click the name of the missing image, ❓ then click the **Relink** button. 🔄

   Click the image or the empty bounding box in the document window, then on the Control panel, click the image name or the Embedded link (not the Embed button) and choose **Relink** from the menu.

2. In the Place dialog, locate the missing file, then click Place.

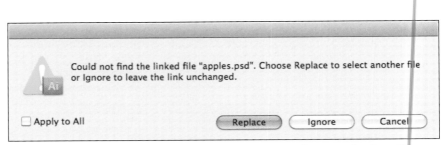

A *If Illustrator detects that a linked file is missing when you open a document, this alert will appear.*

To view information about a file:

1. Do either of the following:

   On the Links panel, ✎ double-click the listing for a linked or embedded file.

   Click the image in the document window, then click the image name on the Control panel and choose **Link Information**.

2. A dialog appears, listing data about the image, such as its file name, location, size, format, date created, date modified, and transformation settings. Click OK.

➤ To view metadata about a linked file, such as keywords, copyright info, and IPTC contact info, click its listing on the Links panel, then choose Link File Info from the panel menu.

The Embed Image command embeds a copy of the image into the Illustrator document (changes its status from linked to embedded) and breaks the link between the Illustrator file and the original image. Be aware that this will increase the file size of your document.

To change a file's status from linked to embedded:

Do either of the following:

On the Links panel, ✎ click the name of a linked image, **A** then choose **Embed Image** from the Links panel menu. **B**

Click a linked image in the document window, then click **Embed** on the Control panel.

When you embed a multilayer PSD image, the Photoshop Import Options dialog opens; for a TIFF image, the TIFF Import Options dialog opens. See pages 290–291.

➤ Although you can't convert an embedded image to a linked one, you can relink the original image to your Illustrator document. Click the image in the document or click its listing on the Links panel, then click the Relink button on the panel.

CHOOSING DISPLAY OPTIONS FOR THE LINKS PANEL

➤ To change the size of the image thumbnails on the Links panel, choose Panel Options from the panel menu, click the preferred size, then click OK.

➤ To change the sorting order of the listings, from the panel menu, choose Sort by Name (alphabetical order), Sort by Kind (by file format), or Sort by Status (missing, then modified, then embedded, then fully linked images).

➤ To control how many categories of links display on the panel, choose Show All, Show Missing, Show Modified, or Show Embedded from the panel menu.

A Click a listing on the Links panel, then choose Embed Image from the panel menu.

Embedded files have this icon

B Note that the file name will be listed for an embedded JPEG file, but not for embedded files in other formats.

Dragging and dropping images into Illustrator

Drag-and-drop is a quick method for duplicating imagery between applications or files; the copy is created instantly. You can drag and drop objects between Illustrator documents, as we showed you in Chapter 9, or between Illustrator and Adobe Dreamweaver, Adobe InDesign, or any other drag-aware application. You can also drag and drop a pixel selection or layer from Photoshop to Illustrator, as we describe in the steps below.

Note: When we need to acquire a Photoshop image for an Illustrator document that is going to be output to print, instead of using drag-and-drop, we convert the image to CMYK Color mode in Photoshop, save it in the Photoshop (.psd) format, then use the File > Place command in Illustrator to acquire it. The Photoshop Import Options dialog provides an option to convert layers to separate objects and preserve their editability, and the image stays in CMYK mode.

To drag and drop a selection or layer from a Photoshop document to an Illustrator document:

1. In Photoshop, click a pixel layer. *Optional:* Create a selection on the layer.

2. Open an Illustrator file. Arrange the Application frames in Illustrator and Photoshop so both document windows are visible.

3. In Photoshop, choose the Move tool ▸⊕ (V), then drag the selection or layer from the Photoshop document window into the Illustrator document window. A copy of the image appears in the target document.

   The selection or layer will be embedded at the resolution and color mode of the original image. In the Mac OS, the image will be nested within a group in the currently active layer; in Windows, it will be listed as <Image>.

➤ The drag-and-drop method doesn't use the Clipboard.

➤ A "dropped" Photoshop selection or layer will be assigned a transparency setting of 100%, regardless of its original opacity, but it may look lighter if its original opacity was less than 100%. You can lower the transparency in Illustrator, if desired. Photoshop blending modes will be ignored visually, and won't register on the Transparency panel in Illustrator.

➤ Layer masks and vector masks from Photoshop will be applied to the "dropped" image (meaning the image will be clipped), and then will be discarded. If necessary, you can create a clipping mask in Illustrator to mask the image further.

➤ If you drag and drop a selection, pixel layer, editable type layer, or shape layer from Photoshop into Illustrator with the Move tool, it will become rasterized (if it isn't already). Any transparent pixels will become opaque white. If you drag and drop a selected path or vector mask from Photoshop into Illustrator with the Path Selection tool, it will become a compound path in Illustrator and won't be rasterized.

➤ Yet another option is to copy a path from Photoshop and paste it into Illustrator, in which case the Paste Options dialog opens. Click Paste As: Compound Shape (fully editable) or Compound Path (faster). The Compound Shape option is recommended for multiple or overlapping paths.

To place an image into Illustrator by dragging it from Bridge:

1. Open or create an Illustrator document.

2. In Bridge, click an image thumbnail.

3. Do either of the following:

   To **link** the image, drag the thumbnail into an Illustrator document window.

   To **embed** the image, Shift-drag the thumbnail into an Illustrator document window.

You can embellish plain vanilla path edges with a brush stroke that looks like ink, paint, or chalk, or that contains a pattern or multiple vector objects. The five flavors of brushes — Calligraphic, Scatter, Art, Bristle, ★ and Pattern — are stored on and accessed from the Brushes panel.❦ A The default panel contains only a small handful of the brushes that are available in Illustrator; we'll show you how to add more.

Not only do Illustrator brushes have all the advantages of vector graphics (small file sizes, resizability, and crisp output), they're also live. If you edit a brush that's being used in your document, you'll be given the option via an alert dialog to update the paths in which the brush is being used. And if you reshape the path or increase the stroke weight or width, the brush stroke will conform automatically to the new contour.

In this chapter, you will embellish existing paths with brushes; remove and expand brush strokes; create and edit custom Calligraphic, Scatter, Art, and Bristle brushes; modify existing brush strokes; create and load brush libraries; and add, duplicate, and delete brushes from the Brushes panel.

There are two ways to produce brush strokes: You can choose the Paintbrush tool and a brush and draw a shape with a brush stroke built into it right off the bat, which we showed you how to do on page 85, or you can apply a brush stroke to an existing path of any kind, as described on the following page.

BRUSHES

23

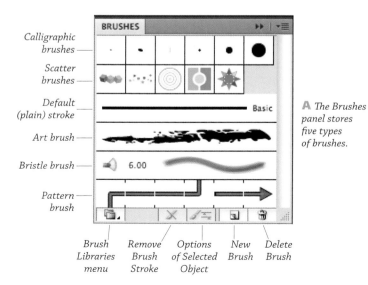

Calligraphic brushes

Scatter brushes

Default (plain) stroke

Art brush

Bristle brush

Pattern brush

A The Brushes panel stores five types of brushes.

Brush Libraries menu

Remove Brush Stroke

Options of Selected Object

New Brush

Delete Brush

Applying brushes to existing paths

In these steps, you will apply a brush stroke to an existing path. It doesn't matter which tool the path was created with (e.g., Star, Polygon, Ellipse, Type, Pencil, Blob Brush, Line Segment, or Pen tool).

To apply a brush to an existing path:

1. Do one of the following:

   Select an existing path of any kind using a selection tool or the Layers panel, **A** then click a brush on the Brushes panel 🖌 or on the Brush Definition menu on the Control panel. ★ **B–F**

   Drag a brush from the Brushes panel onto a path or onto type (the object doesn't have to be selected). Release the mouse when the pointer is over the object.

   Apply a brush from a library by following the instructions on the next page.

2. *Optional:* Change the stroke weight or color (a color change won't show up for a Pattern brush).

➤ What's the difference between a Pattern **G** and a Scatter brush? **H** For a Scatter brush, you can specify a degree of randomness for the size, spacing, and scatter variables; not so for a Pattern brush. Also, Pattern brushes are made from up to five tiles (Side, Outer Corner, Inner Corner, Start, and End). Unlike Scatter brushes, Pattern brushes are used for creating borders or frames. (To learn about Pattern brushes, see Illustrator Help; they are not covered in this book.)

A *We selected a path...*

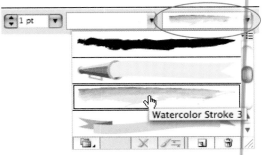

B *...and then clicked a brush on the Brush Definition menu on the Control panel.*

C *The Art brush we chose appeared on the path.*

D *Here a different Art brush is applied to the same path.*

E *A Calligraphic brush is applied.*

F *A Bristle brush is applied.*

G *A Pattern brush is applied.*

H *A Scatter brush is applied.*

Using the Brushes panel

After opening a brush library, you can either apply a brush from the library directly to any path in your document, or add brushes from the library to the Brushes panel for later use. Furthermore, you can use any brush from a library as the starting point for the creation of a custom brush. After adding a brush to your document's Brushes panel, you can duplicate it, if desired (see page 313), and then customize it to your liking. The brushes on the panel save with the current document.

To load brushes from a library:

1. From one of the submenus on the **Brush Libraries** menu 🗔. on the Brushes panel, choose a library name.

2. Deselect (Cmd-Shift-A/Ctrl-Shift-A).

3. Do one of the following:

   Click a brush in the library. It will appear on the Brushes panel.

   Click, then Shift-click, a consecutive series of brushes in the library, then choose **Add to Brushes** from the library menu. **A–B**

   Drag a brush directly from the library onto any object in the document (the object doesn't have to be selected). The brush will appear on the object and on the Brushes panel.

➤ To close a whole library panel, click its close button; to close a single library on the panel, right-click its tab and choose Close from the context menu.

➤ Once a library panel is open, you can cycle through other libraries by clicking the Load Next Brush Library ▶ or Load Previous Brush Library ◀ button at the bottom of the library panel.

➤ To force a library to display when you relaunch Illustrator, choose Persistent from the library menu.

➤ To access brushes from another document, for step 1 on this page, choose Other Library on the Brush Libraries menu. Locate the document that contains the desired brushes, click Open, then continue with steps 2 and 3.

WHICH BRUSH TYPES ARE WHICH?	
Type	Library
Calligraphic	Artistic_Calligraphic, 6D Art Pen Brushes
Scatter	Arrows_Standard, Artistic_Ink, Decorative_Scatter, 6D Art Pen Brushes
Art	Arrows_Special, Arrows_Standard, all the "Artistic" libraries except _Calligraphic, Decorative_Banners and Seals; Decorative_Text Dividers, Elegant Curl & Floral Brush Set, Grunge Brushes Vector Pack, Hand Drawn Brushes Vector Pack
Pattern	All the "Borders" libraries, Pattern Arrows, Elegant Curl & Floral Brush Set

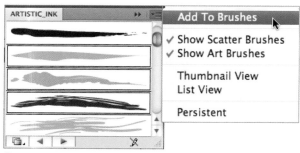

A To append multiple brushes to the Brushes panel for the current document, click, then Shift-click to select them, then choose Add to Brushes from the library panel menu.

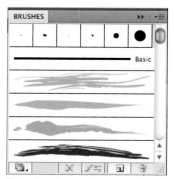

B The brushes we chose appeared on the Brushes panel for our document.

To choose display options for the Brushes panel:

From the Brushes panel menu:

Choose **List View** to have a small thumbnail, the brush name, and an icon for the brush type (Calligraphic, Scatter, Art, Bristle, or Pattern) display for each brush on the panel; 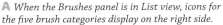 or choose **Thumbnail View** to display larger thumbnails without the names and icons.

To control which brush types (categories) display on the panel, choose **Show** [brush type] to check or uncheck that option.

➤ You can drag any brush upward or downward on the panel to a different location within its own category. To move a series of brushes, click, then Shift-click them first.

Removing brush strokes

When you remove a brush stroke from a path, you're left with a plain vanilla path. It will have the same color and uniform width as the former brush stroke.

To remove a brush stroke from an object, group, or layer:

1. Do either of the following:

   Select one or more objects that a brush is applied to. **B**

   Target a layer or group that a brush stroke is applied to.

2. Do either of the following:

   On the Brushes panel, click the **Remove Brush Stroke** button. **C**

   On the Brushes panel or on the Brush Definition menu (on the Control panel), click the **Basic** brush.

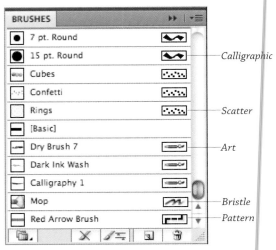

Calligraphic
Scatter
Art
Bristle
Pattern

A *When the Brushes panel is in List view, icons for the five brush categories display on the right side.*

B *A brush stroke is applied to this group of paths.*

C *We removed the brush stroke from the paths.*

Expanding brush strokes

When a brush stroke is expanded, it is converted into ordinary editable outlined paths (objects in the shape of the former brush strokes). The stroke will look the same, but will no longer be live, so you won't be able to replace it via the Brushes panel or edit it by editing the brush.

To expand a brush stroke into paths:

1. Select one or more objects that have a brush stroke. **A**

2. Choose Object > **Expand Appearance**. Each brush stroke (and fill, if any) is now a separate object or objects, nested (or double nested) within a group listing on the Layers panel. **B**

➤ To select all of the objects in your document that contain a brush stroke, from the Select > Object submenu, choose Brush Strokes.

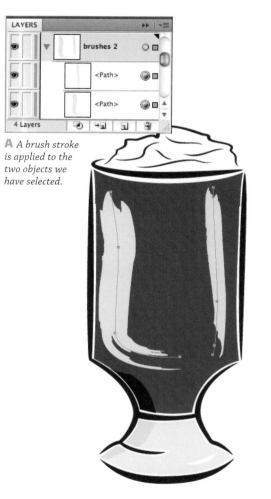

A *A brush stroke is applied to the two objects we have selected.*

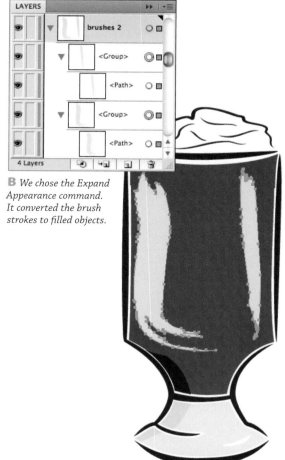

B *We chose the Expand Appearance command. It converted the brush strokes to filled objects.*

Next, we provide separate instructions for creating and modifying Calligraphic, Scatter, Art, and Bristle brushes.

Creating and editing Calligraphic brushes

Calligraphic brush strokes vary in thickness as you draw, as in traditional calligraphy.

To create or edit a Calligraphic brush:

1. Skip this step if you're going to edit an existing brush. To create a new brush, click the **New Brush** button on the Brushes panel. In the New Brush dialog, click **Calligraphic Brush**, then click OK. The Calligraphic Brush Options dialog opens. Enter a Name, click OK, then apply the new brush to a path.

   Note: You will reopen the options dialog in the next step; when you do, you can take advantage of the Preview option, which is available only for brushes that are in use.

2. Deselect, then on the Brushes panel, double-click the Calligraphic brush to be edited.**A–B** The Calligraphic Brush Options dialog opens.**C**

3. Check Preview to view the changes on paths where the brush is in use (this option is available only for a brush that is in use). The brush shape will also preview in the dialog.

4. For **Angle**, **Roundness**, and **Diameter**, choose one of the following variations from the menu:

   Fixed to keep the value constant.

A *The brush we're going to edit is in use on the heavier strokes in this artwork.*

B *On the Brushes panel, we are double-clicking the Calligraphic brush that we want to change the settings for.*

C *In the Calligraphic Brush Options dialog, we changed the Roundness value from 35% to 9% to make the brush very flat.*

Random, then move the Variation slider to define a range within which that brush attribute can vary. A stroke can range between the value specified for Angle, Roundness, or Diameter, plus or minus the Variation value. For example, a 50° angle with a Random Variation value of 10 could have an angle anywhere between 40° and 60°.

If you're using a graphics tablet, choose **Pressure**, **Stylus Wheel**, **Tilt**, **Bearing**, or **Rotation**. Move the Variation slider to define a range within which the brush attribute can respond to pressure from a stylus. Light pressure produces a brush attribute based on the Angle, Roundness, or Diameter value minus the Variation value, whereas heavy pressure produces a brush attribute based on the specified value plus the Variation value. To learn more about the stylus options, see Illustrator Help.

5. Enter an **Angle** (–180° to 180°) or drag the gray arrowhead on the circle. An angle of 0° produces a stroke that is thin when drawn horizontally and thick when drawn vertically; an angle of 90° produces the opposite result.

6. Enter a **Roundness** value (0–100%), or reshape the tip by dragging either of the two black dots inward or outward on the ellipse.

7. For the brush size, enter a **Diameter** value (0–1296 pt) or drag the slider.

8. Click OK. If the brush is already in use in the document, an alert dialog will appear.**A** Click **Apply to Strokes** to update the existing strokes with the revised brush,**B** or click **Leave Strokes** to leave the existing strokes unchanged.

A *When we exited the Calligraphic Brush Options dialog, this alert appeared because the brush we modified is in use in our document.*

B *We clicked Apply to Strokes in the alert dialog to allow the edited brush to update where it is being used in the artwork. The vertical parts of the revised brush strokes are thicker than the horizontal parts — just the calligraphic look we were aiming for.*

Creating and editing Scatter brushes

Objects in a Scatter brush are strewn evenly or randomly along the contour of a path. You can create a Scatter brush from an open or closed path, or from a type character, type outline, blend, or compound path. You can't create a Scatter brush from a bitmap image (placed or rasterized), mesh object, or clipping mask, or from an object that contains a gradient or pattern.

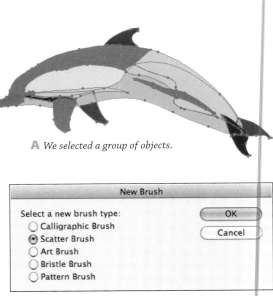

A *We selected a group of objects.*

To create or edit a Scatter brush:

1. Skip this step if you're going to edit an existing brush. To create a new brush, select one or more objects,**A** then click the **New Brush** button ![icon] on the Brushes panel. In the New Brush dialog,**B** click **Scatter Brush**, then click OK. The Scatter Brush Options dialog opens. Enter a name, click OK, then apply the new brush to any path.**C** (See the Note in step 1 on page 302.)

2. Deselect, then on the Brushes panel, double-click the Scatter brush to be edited. The Scatter Brush Options dialog opens.**D**

3. Check Preview so you will be able to view your edits on paths where the brush is in use.

4. For **Size**, **Spacing**, **Scatter**, and **Rotation**, choose one of the following variations from the menu:

   Fixed to use a single fixed value.

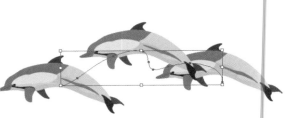

B *We clicked Scatter Brush in the New Brush dialog.*

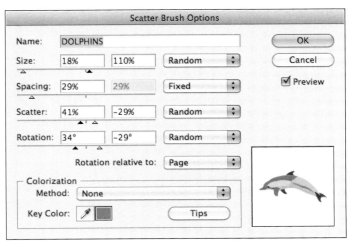

C *The new brush appeared on the path.*

D *Use the Scatter Brush Options dialog to adjust the settings for a new or existing brush. These settings produced the results shown on the next page.*

CREATING BRUSH VARIATIONS

To create a variation of an existing brush of any type, duplicate it first by following the instructions on page 313. To create a variation of a brush in a library, add the brush to the Brushes panel, then duplicate it.

Random, then move the sliders to define a range within which that property can vary.

If you're using a graphics tablet, choose **Pressure**, **Stylus Wheel**, **Tilt**, **Bearing**, or **Rotation**. Move the sliders (or enter different values in the two fields) to define a range within which that property can respond to stylus pressure. Light pressure uses the minimum property value from the field on the left; heavy pressure uses the maximum property value from the field on the right.

The following is a description of the properties:

Size controls the size of the scatter objects.

Spacing controls the spacing between the scatter objects.

Scatter controls the distance between the objects and the path. When Fixed is chosen as the Scatter setting, a positive value places all the objects on one side of the path, and a negative value places all the objects on the opposite side of the path. The further the Scatter value is from 0%, the less closely the objects will adhere to the path.

Rotation controls how much the scatter objects can rotate relative to the page or path. From the **Rotation Relative To** menu, choose **Page** or **Path** for the axis of rotation.

5. For the **Colorization** methods, see the sidebar on page 313.

6. Click OK. If the brush is in use in the document, an alert dialog will appear. **A** Click **Apply to Strokes** to update those objects with the revised brush, **B** or click **Leave Strokes** to leave the existing objects unchanged.

➤ Shift-drag a slider in the Scatter Brush Options dialog to also move its counterpart (if one is displaying) in the same direction. Option-drag/ Alt-drag a slider to simultaneously move the slider and its counterpart toward or away from each other.

➤ To orient scatter objects uniformly along a path, set Scatter and Rotation to Fixed, set Scatter to 0°, and choose Rotation Relative To: Path.

➤ To edit a Scatter brush on a path manually, see page 315.

Brush Change Alert

That brush is in use and some strokes may have overridden its options. Do you want to apply the changes to existing brush strokes?

[Apply to Strokes]   [Leave Strokes]   [Cancel]

A *This alert dialog appears if you modify a brush that's currently in use in your document.*

B *It took a considerable amount of fiddling with the sliders in the Scatter Brush Options dialog to get the look we wanted.*

Creating and editing Art brushes

An Art brush can be made from one or more paths (even a Blob Brush object or a compound path), but not from a gradient, mask, mesh, editable type, or bitmap image. When applied to a path, an Art brush stroke will conform to the path. If you reshape the path, the Art brush stroke will stretch or bend to fit the new path contour (fun!). If you browse through the predefined Art brushes, you'll see that some simulate art media brushes and some have recognizable shapes, such as arrows, banners, and ribbons.

To create or edit an Art brush: ★

1. Skip this step if you're going to edit an existing brush. To create a new brush, select one or more objects, **A** then click the **New Brush** button on the Brushes panel. In the New Brush dialog, click **Art Brush**, then click OK. The Art Brush Options dialog opens. Enter a Name, click OK, then apply the new brush to any path. (See the Note in step 1 on page 302.)

2. Deselect, then on the Brushes panel, double-click the Art brush to be edited. The Art Brush

Options dialog opens. **B** If you're creating a new brush based on an existing one, enter a new name; or to edit the brush, keep the name as is.

3. Check Preview to view the changes on paths where the brush is in use (this option is available only for brushes that are in use).

4. Click one of the Brush Scale Options: **Scale Proportionately** to preserve the original proportions of the art object (**A**, next page); **Stretch to Fit Stroke Length** to allow Illustrator to stretch (distort) parts of the brush to fit the path (**B**, next page); or **Stretch Between Guides**, then

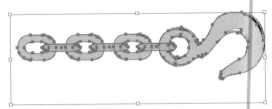

A We selected the objects to be used to create an Art brush.

B We applied the new brush to a path, then double-clicked the brush on the Brushes panel to open the Art Brush Options dialog.

move the guides in the preview to define which part of the brush Illustrator can stretch. ★ C

5. Do any of the following:

Click a **Direction** button to control the orientation of the brush relative to the path. The brush will be oriented in the direction the arrow is pointing (this option doesn't preview). The direction will be more obvious for a brush that has a distinct starting and ending shape.

Check **Flip Along** to flip the start and end of the brush and/or check **Flip Across** to flip the brush across the path. D

6. *Optional:* Change the brush Width setting. E If you're using a stylus and graphics tablet, you can choose an option from the Width menu. ★

7. *Optional:* Choose a Colorization method (see the sidebar on page 313). F

8. For the Overlap, click the **Do Not Adjust Corners and Folds** button ⟋⟍ to let the folds and joins in the object fall where they may on the object, with some possible overlap; or click the **Adjust Corners and Folds** button ⟋⟍ to prevent folds and joins from overlapping. ★

9. Click OK. If the brush is in use in the artwork, an alert dialog will appear. See step 6 on page 305.

➤ If you want to apply a different brush to a path using the same brush stroke settings that were chosen for the original brush, hold down Option/Alt while clicking the replacement brush. G–H

➤ To edit an Art brush on a path, see the following page and page 315.

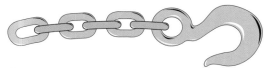

A *We applied the Art brush to a path, which we drew with the Paintbrush tool. Scale Proportionately is the current Brush Scale option.*

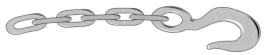

B *We chose Stretch to Fit Stroke Length as the Brush Scale option.*

C *We chose Stretch Between Guides as the Brush Scale option, and moved the guides in the preview to surround the chain (see Figure* B *on the preceding page). The chain stretches to fit the path, whereas the hook does not.*

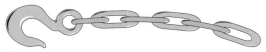

D *We checked the Flip Along option.*

E *We unchecked Flip Along, then changed the Width setting to 195%.*

F *We reset the Width to 100%, then chose Tints and Shades as the Colorization Method.*

G *We selected the path that is shown in figure* A *on this page, then clicked a replacement brush on the Brushes panel.*

H *Here we did the same thing as in Figure* G, *except we held down Option/Alt as we clicked the replacement brush to apply the settings from the original brush to the replacement.*

SCALING AN ART BRUSH STROKE USING THE WIDTH TOOL ★

If you want to scale a section of an art brush on a path, in addition to or instead of using the Stretch Between Guides option in the Art Brush Options dialog, try using the Width tool.✎ A–B

Note: If you use the Width tool on an Art brush stroke or you apply a variable width profile via the Control panel or Stroke panel, you can undo those edits at any time (make the stroke width uniform again). Select the path, then from the Variable Width Profile menu on the Control panel or the Profile menu on the Stroke panel, choose Uniform. If you used the Width tool, the largest width value that the tool produced will be applied to the brush stroke as a uniform value.

To restore the uniform stroke width another way, select the path, click the Options of Selected Object button ✐ on the Brushes panel to open the Stroke Options (Art Brush) dialog, and choose Fixed from the Width menu (change from the setting of Width Points/Profile).

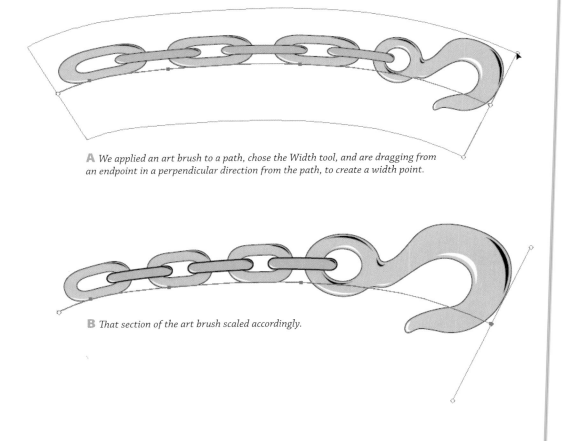

A *We applied an art brush to a path, chose the Width tool, and are dragging from an endpoint in a perpendicular direction from the path, to create a width point.*

B *That section of the art brush scaled accordingly.*

Creating and editing Bristle brushes

With the new Bristle brushes, you can mimic traditional art media, like oil paint or gouache. To produce the desired brush characteristics, you can choose from ten different shape presets (e.g., Flat Blunt, Round Fan) and adjust many variables, such as the bristle density, thickness, and stiffness. (To achieve the best results with Bristle brushes, Adobe recommends using a Wacom tablet and 6D pen.)

To explore the many options for Bristle brushes, you can start by customizing one of the brushes in the Bristle Brush library.

To create or edit a Bristle brush: ★

1. Deselect all, then from the **Brush Libraries** menu 🗔. on the Brushes panel, choose Bristle Brush > **Bristle Brush Library**.

2. Select one or more paths, then click a Bristle brush in the library panel. The brush will appear on the Brushes panel and on the selected paths.

3. Deselect (Cmd-Shift-A/Ctrl-Shift-A).

4. On the Brushes panel, double-click the Bristle brush that you applied to paths in your artwork. The Bristle Brush Options dialog opens.**A** If you're creating a new brush (a variation), enter

a new name; or if you want to edit the existing brush, keep the name as it is. (The brush will save with the current document.)

5. Check Preview so you will be able to view your edits on the paths where the brush is in use (this option is available only for brushes that are in use).

6. Choose a **Shape** preset for the brush.

7. Adjust any of the **Brush Options** settings: Size, Bristle Length, Bristle Density, Bristle Thickness, Paint Opacity, or Stiffness (**A–C**, next page).

8. Click OK. If the brush is in use in the document, an alert dialog will appear. Click **Apply to Strokes** to update those objects with the revised brush, or click **Leave Strokes** to leave the existing objects unchanged.

➤ Many good things come with a catch, and such is the case with Bristle brushes. A document that contains 30 or more Bristle brush paths could cause a printing error. When saving such a file, read the alert that displays. To learn about the Rasterize command, which helps to facilitate printing, see page 206.

A Use the Bristle Brush Options dialog to choose settings for a new or existing Bristle brush.

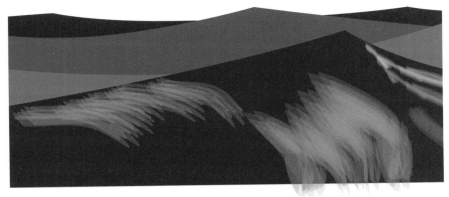

Short Bristle Length   *Long Bristle Length*

A *The Bristle Length controls the broadness of the flat, overlapping paths that form the paint stroke.*

Low Bristle Density   *High Bristle Density*

B *The Bristle Density controls how many overlapping paths pile up within each paint stroke.*

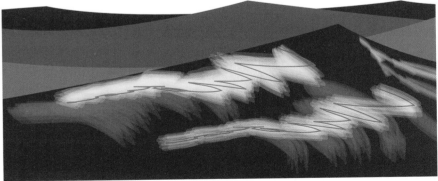

Flexible Bristle Stiffness   *Rigid Bristle Stiffness*

C *The Bristle Stiffness controls how rigidly the bristle paths adhere to the underlying path (here the path is shown in red).*

ENHANCING SOLID-COLOR OBJECTS WITH BRISTLE BRUSH STROKES ★

In addition to painting pictures with Bristle brushes, you can also draw Bristle brush strokes on top of flat vector shapes to add texture, shading, or depth. **A–B**

A *All the objects in the artwork above are crisp, flat vector shapes.*

B *To add shading and texture, we selected each cloud object individually, activated Draw Inside mode, then drew paths with the Paintbrush tool and a Bristle brush. Because we chose this mode, the Bristle brush paths were masked by the crisp vector edge of each object. (To learn about Draw Inside mode, see the next page and Chapter 26.) To create color highlights on the waves, we drew Bristle brush paths on a new layer above the wave objects.*

QUICKLY CHANGING THE SIZE OR OPACITY OF A BRISTLE BRUSH

Either select paths that have the same Bristle brush applied to them, or deselect to choose settings for paths you are about to draw. Choose the Paintbrush tool, then use either or both of the following shortcuts.

Change the brush size	Press [or]
Change the paint opacity percentage	Press a number between 0 and 9 (e.g., press 1 for 10%, 9 for 90%, 0 for 100%)

Painting brush strokes inside objects

In these steps, you will confine Bristle brush strokes to the interior of a vector object or editable type characters. You will put your document into Draw Inside mode, and as you draw strokes, they will be masked by the edges of a selected object. To learn more about clipping sets, see Chapter 26.

To paint brush strokes inside an object: ★

1. Choose the **Selection** tool ➤ (V) and select an object. It can be an editable type object.

2. From the Tools panel, choose **Draw Inside** mode.◉ Deselect.

3. Choose the **Paintbrush** tool ✎ (B). Click a Bristle brush on the Brushes panel and choose a stroke color from the Color or Swatches panel.

4. Paint brush strokes over the object or type characters.**A** Each time you release the mouse, the stroke will be masked by the object.**B**

5. To return to **Draw Normal** mode,◉ press Shift-D.

To edit brush strokes inside an object: ★

1. Choose the **Selection** tool ➤ (V), then double-click the group that contains the brush strokes you want to edit, to isolate it.

2. On the Layers panel, click the target circle or selection square for the brush stroke to be edited.**C**

3. Do any of the following: **D**

   Change the stroke color.

   On the Brushes panel,⊞ click the **Options of Selected Object** button ✐ to open the Stroke Options (Bristle Brush) dialog, then modify any of the brush options. This dialog contains the same options as the dialog shown on page 309. Click OK.

   Drag the brush path to reposition it within the object or type.

   To delete the selected object, press Delete/Backspace.

4. Press Esc to exit isolation mode.

➤ If you want to hide the object that is masking the strokes, on the Layers panel, expand the group, then click the visibility icon 👁 for the listing that has an underline (click again in the visibility column when you want to redisplay the object).**E**

A *We selected a type object, activated Draw Inside mode, chose a Bristle brush for the Paintbrush tool, then painted some brush strokes across the type.*

B *Each time we released the mouse, the stroke was masked by the edges of the type characters.*

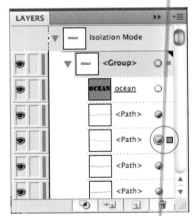

C *To edit a Bristle brush stroke, we put the group into isolation mode, and via the Layers panel, we selected a Bristle path.*

D *An individual brush stroke is edited in isolation mode.*

E *With the type hidden, we can edit, reposition, or delete individual paint strokes more easily.*

Duplicating brushes

Using the Duplicate Brush command as a starting point, you can create a variation of an existing brush, such as a slimmer or fatter version of it.

To duplicate a brush:

1. Deselect all objects.

   ➤ To duplicate a brush in a library, you must add it to the Brushes panel first.

2. Do either of the following:

   Click the brush to be duplicated, then choose **Duplicate Brush** from the panel menu.

   Drag the brush to be duplicated to the **New Brush** button ⬛. **A**

3. The word "copy" will be added to the brush name.**B** To modify the brush, follow the instructions for that specific brush type in this chapter.

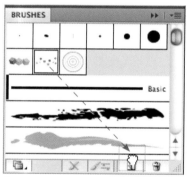

A *Drag the brush to be duplicated over the New Brush button.*

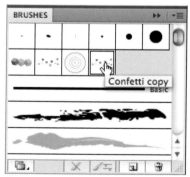

B *The duplicate brush appears after the last brush icon within its own category.*

CHOOSING A COLORIZATION METHOD

To change the way a brush applies color, from the Colorization Method menu in the Brush Options dialog for an Art or Scatter brush, choose one of the options listed below.

➤ None to keep the original brush colors as they are.

➤ Tints to change black areas in the brush stroke to the current stroke color at 100% and non-black areas to tints of the current stroke color. White areas stay white. Use for grayscale or spot colors.

➤ Tints and Shades to change colors in the brush stroke to tints of the current stroke color. Black and white areas stay the same.

➤ Hue Shift to apply the current stroke color to the most dominant color in a multicolor brush (the "key" color) and to change other colors in the brush to related colors. To change the key color, choose Hue Shift, click the Key Color eyedropper, 🖋 then click a color in the preview area of the dialog (not in the artwork). Unfortunately, a Key Color change won't display until you exit the dialog. (The Key Color eyedropper isn't available for the Options of Selected Object feature, which is discussed on page 315.)

To open the Colorization Tips dialog (shown below), click the Tips icon 💡 or the Tips button.

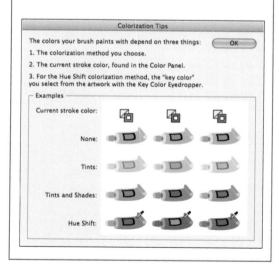

Editing brushes manually

You have already learned how to edit brushes via an options dialog. In these instructions, you will edit a Scatter or Art brush manually in a document.

To edit a Scatter or Art brush manually:

1. Deselect, then drag a brush from the Brushes panel 🖌 onto a blank area of the artboard. **A–B**

2. Edit the brush objects. To recolor or transform the entire brush, select it (Selection tool) or isolate it first. To recolor or transform individual objects in the brush, select them via the Direct Selection tool or the Layers panel first.

   ➤ You can recolor the brush objects by using the Recolor Artwork dialog. See Chapter 29.

3. Choose the **Selection** tool ▶ (V).

4. Do either of the following:

   To replace the existing brush with the edited one, Option-drag/Alt-drag the modified brush object or objects into the Brushes panel, and release the mouse when the pointer is over the original brush icon and the icon has a highlight border. **C**

   To make the object(s) into a new, separate brush, drag it (or them) onto the panel without holding down Option/Alt. The New Brush dialog opens. Click **Scatter Brush** or **Art Brush**, then click OK.

5. The Scatter Brush Options or Art Brush Options dialog opens. Keep or change the name, then click OK.

6. If you decided to replace the existing brush and it is currently in use in the document, an alert dialog will appear. Click **Apply to Strokes** to update the paths with the revised brush, **D** or click **Leave Strokes** to leave them be.

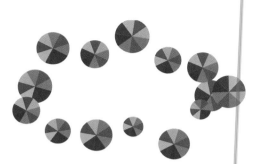

A *We applied a Scatter brush to a path.*

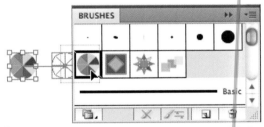

B *We dragged the brush from the Brushes panel onto an artboard.*

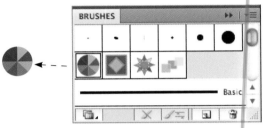

C *After recoloring the objects via the Recolor Artwork dialog, we are holding down Option/Alt and dragging them over the original brush on the Brushes panel.*

D *We clicked OK in the Scatter Brush Options dialog, then clicked Apply to Strokes in the alert dialog; the brush updated on the path.*

Editing brush strokes on objects

If you edit a brush, either manually or via the options dialog, all the objects in which that brush is being used will update to reflect your edits. If you would rather edit a brush stroke on an individual object—without changing the actual brush—follow these steps instead. You will use the same controls.

To edit a brush stroke on an individual object:

1. Select one or more objects to which the same brush is currently applied.

2. On the Brushes panel, click the **Options of Selected Object** button. The Stroke Options dialog for the brush type opens. Check Preview.

3. For a Calligraphic brush stroke, follow steps 4–7 on pages 302–303; for a Scatter brush stroke, follow steps 4–5 on pages 304–305; for an Art brush stroke, follow steps 4–8 on pages 306–307; or for a Bristle brush stroke, follow steps 6–7 on page 309.

4. Click OK. Your edits will affect only the selected object or objects, not the brush on the Brushes panel.

5. For a Calligraphic brush stroke, or for an Art or Scatter brush stroke that is set to any Colorization method except None, you can change the stroke color manually via the usual controls (e.g., Color, Color Guide, or Swatches panel). For an Art brush stroke, you can also change the stroke width profile.

   Beware! If you edit the actual brush after using the Options of Selected Object feature, your custom options will be removed.

▶ To restore the original brush stroke to the object, select the object, then click the original brush.

SCALING STROKES AND EFFECTS

If you scale an object that has a brush stroke and Scale Strokes & Effects is checked in the Scale dialog (which you open by double-clicking the Scale tool) or in Illustrator/Edit > Preferences > General, the brush stroke will also scale. With this option unchecked, a brush stroke stays the same size when the object it is applied to is scaled.

A *We selected some objects that contain brush strokes, clicked the Options of Selected Object button, then changed the brush Width.*

B *This is the result.*

C *After exiting the options dialog, we changed the stroke colors in the artwork via the Swatches panel.*

Deleting brushes

When you delete a brush that's being used in your document, you are given the option via an alert dialog to expand or remove the brush strokes.

To delete a brush from the Brushes panel:

1. Deselect.

2. Do either of the following:

   On the Brushes panel, click the brush to be deleted.

   To delete all the brushes that aren't being used in the document, choose **Select All Unused** from the Brushes panel menu.

3. Click the **Delete Brush** button 🗑 on the Brushes panel.

4. An alert dialog appears. If the brush is not currently in use in the document, click **Yes.A** If the brush is in use in the document, **B** click **Expand Strokes** to expand the brush strokes (they'll be converted into standard paths and will no longer be live), or click **Remove Strokes** to remove them from the objects. If the brush is being used in a graphic style, yet another alert will appear; follow the directions in the alert.**C**

➤ To restore a deleted brush to the Brushes panel, choose Undo immediately; or if the brush is in a library, you could add it to the Brushes panel again (see page 299).

Creating brush libraries

By saving your brushes in a library, you'll be able to access them easily and load them into any file.

To create a brush library:

1. Set up your Brushes panel so it contains only the brushes to be saved in a library. You can create new brushes or add them from a library panel. Delete any brushes you don't want saved in the library.

2. From the **Brush Libraries** menu 📷. at the bottom of the Brushes panel, choose **Save Brushes**.

3. In the Save Brushes as Library dialog, enter a name for the library. Keep the default location. In the Mac OS, that location is Users/[user name]/Library/Application Support/Adobe Illustrator CS5/en_US/Brushes. In Windows 7, the default location is C:\Users\[user name]\AppData\Roaming\Adobe\Adobe Illustrator CS5 Settings\en_US\Brushes.

4. Click Save. The library will now be listed on, and can be opened from, the **User Defined** submenu on the Brush Libraries menu.

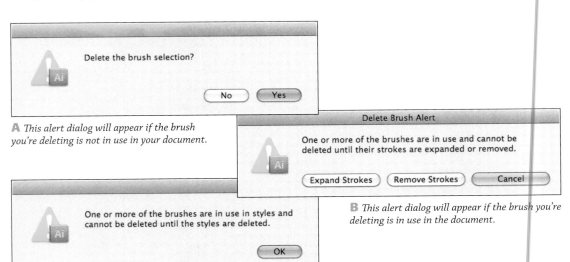

A *This alert dialog will appear if the brush you're deleting is not in use in your document.*

B *This alert dialog will appear if the brush you're deleting is in use in the document.*

C *This alert dialog will appear if the brush you're deleting is part of a graphic style that is on the Graphic Styles panel for the current document.*

A gradient fill is a soft, gradual blend between two or more solid colors. Gradients can be used to add shading or volume for a touch of realism, or to add depth to abstract shapes. In this chapter, you will load gradients from a library; fill one or more objects with a gradient; create a simple two-color gradient; add, delete, recolor, and change the opacity of colors in a gradient; save a gradient to the Swatches panel; change a gradient's position, length, shape, or angle interactively by using on-object controls (referred to collectively as the "annotator"); spread a gradient across multiple objects; and expand a gradient into paths.

Applying a gradient

A gradient can be composed of two solid colors (a starting and an ending color) or multiple colors; it can spread from one side of an object to another (linear) or outward from the center of an object (radial); **A** and it can be applied to individual objects or across multiple objects in one sweep.

Continued on the following page

A *The sun in this artwork contains a radial gradient, and the sky and water contain linear gradients.*

24

GRADIENTS

The first step is to load some predefined Illustrator gradients onto your document's Swatches panel.

To load gradients onto the Swatches panel:

1. Display the Swatches panel.⊞ From the Show Swatch Kinds menu, choose Show Gradient Swatches, and from the panel menu, choose Large Thumbnail View.

2. From the **Swatch Libraries** menu 🗂 at the bottom of the Swatches panel, on the Gradients submenu, choose a library.

3. A separate library panel opens.**A** Do either of the following:

   Click a gradient on the panel. It will appear on the Swatches panel.

   Cmd-click/Ctrl-click (or click, then Shift-click) to select multiple gradients, then choose **Add to Swatches** from the panel menu.

➤ To view the other gradient libraries, click the Load Next Swatch Library 📄 or Load Previous Swatch Library ◀ button on the library panel.

Now you're ready to apply a gradient to an object.

To fill an object with a gradient:

Do one of the following:

Select one or more objects, then click a gradient swatch on the Swatches panel ⊞ (which you can access quickly via the Control panel) or on an open gradient library panel.

Select one or more objects,**B** and display the Gradient panel.▢ Click the arrowhead next to the Gradient Fill square ▯ to open the gradient menu,**C** then click a gradient. The gradients that are on your document's Swatches panel are listed on this menu.**D**

Drag a gradient swatch from the Swatches panel, from any open gradient library panel, or from the Gradient Fill square on the Gradient panel over any selected or unselected object.

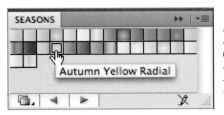

A *The gradient library opens as a floating panel (the Seasons, Brights, Foliage, and Simple Radial libraries contain simple gradients).*

B *A plain vanilla rectangle is selected.*

Gradient menu

Gradient Fill square

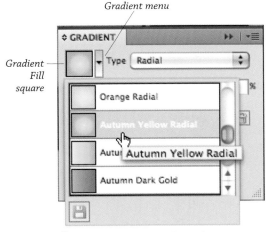

C *We click a gradient on the gradient menu (Gradient panel).*

D *The object fills with the soft radial gradient.*

Creating a two-color gradient

A custom gradient can contain all CMYK colors, all RGB process colors, tints of the same spot color, or multiple spot colors. In these steps, you will change the colors in a simple, two-color gradient.

To create and save a two-color gradient:

1. *Optional:* Select one or more objects.

2. On the **Swatch Libraries** menu ▣ at the bottom of the Swatches panel, from the Gradients submenu, choose Simple Radial. In the library panel that opens, click any gradient swatch.

3. Display the Gradient panel.▭

4. Double-click the left color stop below the gradient slider to display a temporary coloring panel.**A** You can click the ✎ button to display an abridged Color panel or the ▦ button to display an abridged Swatches panel.**B** Click a swatch or mix a color, then click outside the temporary panel to close it.

5. Repeat the preceding step for the right color stop.

6. From the Type menu, choose **Radial** or **Linear**.

7. *Optional:* Move the midpoint diamond to the right to produce more of the starting color than the ending color, or to the left to do the opposite (the results will be evident if you selected an object in step 1).**C** The diamond marks the location where two color stops are mixed in equal amounts.

   Note: Although you could add colors or change the opacity of colors via this panel, we think it's easier to use the annotator, which is discussed on the next two pages.

8. If you select another object or swatch now, the new gradient will be lost — unless you save it to the Swatches panel by doing either of the following and then resave your document:

   At the bottom of the gradient menu ⌐ on the Gradient panel, click the **Add to Swatches** button.▣

   To name the gradient as you save it, click the **New Swatch** button ▣ on the Swatches panel, enter a name, then click OK.

➤ To swap the starting and ending colors (or any other two colors) in a gradient, Option-drag/Alt-drag one stop on top of the other. To reverse the order of all the colors in a gradient, click the Reverse Gradient button.▣

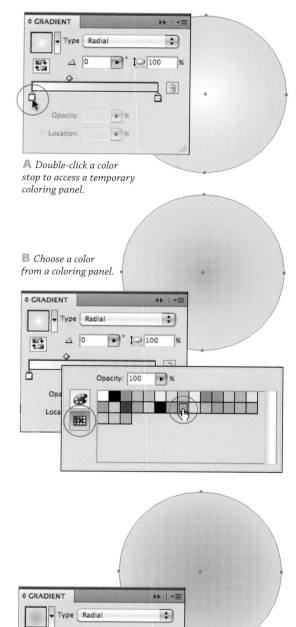

A *Double-click a color stop to access a temporary coloring panel.*

B *Choose a color from a coloring panel.*

C *To display more of one color than the other, drag the midpoint diamond.*

Editing gradient colors via on-object controls

Sometimes it's hard to predict how a gradient is going to look until you actually see it in an object. Using the interactive controls known as the annotator, you can replace, add, move, remove, or change the opacity or spread of any color in a gradient right on the object it's applied to. For other on-object controls, see pages 323–324.

To edit the colors in a gradient via on-object controls:

1. Display the full Gradient panel ▨ (click the double arrows on the panel tab, if necessary).

2. Apply a gradient to an object, and keep the object selected.

3. Choose the **Gradient** tool ▨ (G). The gradient annotator bar should display on the object. If it doesn't, press Cmd-Option-G/Ctrl-Alt-G or choose View > **Show Gradient Annotator**.

4. Position the pointer over the annotator to expand it; color stops will display below the annotator. **A** To **recolor** an existing stop, double-click it. A temporary coloring panel appears. You can click the ✎ button to display an abridged Color panel **B** or the ▦ button to display an abridged Swatches panel. Click a swatch or mix a color, then click outside the panel to close it.

5. To **add** a color to the gradient, click below the annotator; a new color stop appears. **C** Recolor the new stop as in the preceding step.

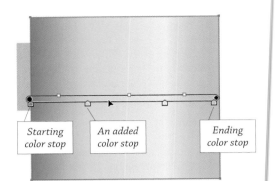

Starting color stop An added color stop Ending color stop

A *To display the annotator, select an object that contains a gradient fill, and select the Gradient tool.*

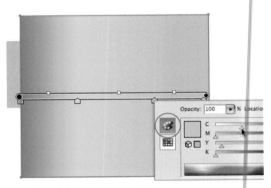

B *Double-click a color stop on the annotator to open a temporary coloring panel. We clicked the Color panel button so we could mix a custom color.*

APPLYING A GRADIENT TO TYPE

To apply a gradient to type, select the type with the Selection tool. Create a new fill attribute first by clicking the Add New Fill button ☐ on the Appearance panel or by pressing Cmd-/ (Mac OS) or Ctrl-/ (Windows), then apply a gradient.

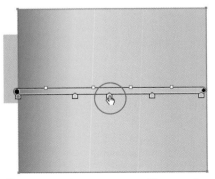

C *Click below the annotator to add a new color stop at that location.*

6. On the annotator, do any of the following:

To change how abruptly a color **spreads** into adjacent colors, move the stop to the left or right.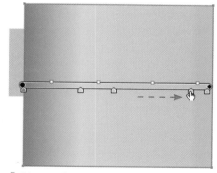

To adjust how colors are **distributed**, move one of the midpoint markers (located above the annotator) to the left or right. This marker denotes where two adjacent colors are mixed equally (are 50% each).

To **duplicate** a color stop, Option-drag/Alt-drag it to the left or right.

To **remove** a color stop, drag it downward off the annotator.**B**

To change the **opacity** of a color stop, double-click the stop, then change the Opacity value via the temporary coloring panel.**C**

➤ Edits made via the on-object controls also register on the Gradient panel. To learn more about the panel, including three controls for which there are no equivalent features on the annotator, see page 325.

7. To save your edits either to the original swatch or as a new swatch, follow the steps on the next page.

A *Move a color stop toward or away from an adjacent one to control how abruptly that color spreads into the adjacent one.*

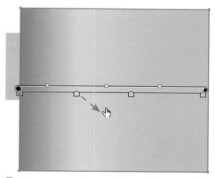

B *To remove a color stop, drag it downward off the annotator bar.*

C *To adjust the opacity of a color stop, double-click the stop, then use the Opacity control on the temporary panel. Underlying objects will be visible below any partially or fully transparent areas in the gradient.*

Saving a gradient as a swatch

To save an edited gradient as a swatch:

1. Edit a gradient by following the instructions on the preceding two pages or in the sidebar on page 325.

2. Read the two methods below before deciding which one to perform:

   To update the existing swatch with your edits, Option-drag/Alt-drag the **Gradient Fill** square from the Gradient panel to the swatch on the Swatches panel. **A–B** *Beware!* This method will cause the gradient to update in all objects in which it is being used, whether those objects are selected or not.

   To save the modified gradient as a new swatch, from the bottom of the gradient menu on the Gradient panel, click the **Add to Swatches** button **C** or drag the **Gradient Fill** square from the Gradient panel to the Swatches panel. The gradient won't update in any unselected objects.

➤ To save gradient swatches as a library, see "To save a library of swatches" on page 127. User-defined libraries are listed on, and can be chosen from, the User Defined submenu on the Swatch Libraries menu.

REAPPLYING THE LAST GRADIENT

To apply the last gradient to any selected object after applying a solid color or a fill color of None, do one of the following:

➤ Click the Gradient Fill square in the upper left corner of the Gradient panel.

➤ Press . (period).

➤ Click the Gradient button on the Tools panel.

APPLYING A GRADIENT TO AN OBJECT'S "STROKE"

Normally, you can't fill an object's stroke with a gradient, but there is a workaround to this limitation. Make the stroke fairly wide, then apply Object > Path > Outline Stroke to convert it to a closed object. Double-click the object to put it into isolation mode, click the converted object, then apply a gradient. Exit isolation mode.

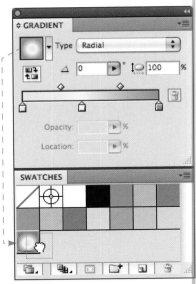

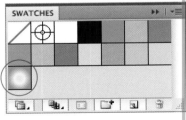

A *To replace an existing gradient swatch with your edited one, Option-drag/ Alt-drag the Gradient Fill square over a swatch on the Swatches panel.*

B *The swatch updates on the Swatches panel.*

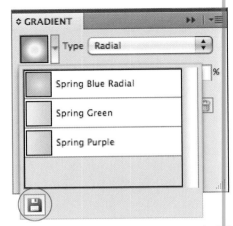

C *To save an edited gradient as a new swatch, click the Add to Swatches button on the gradient menu.*

Changing the position, length, or angle of a gradient in an object

In these instructions, you will use on-object controls to change the origin, length, or angle of a linear gradient in a selected object. In the steps on the next page, you will make similar changes to a radial gradient.

To change the position, length, or angle of a linear gradient in an object:

1. Select an object that contains a linear gradient fill.

2. Choose the **Gradient** tool 🔲 (G). The annotator should display on the object. **A** If it doesn't, press Cmd-Option-G/Ctrl-Alt-G.

3. On the annotator, do any of the following:

   To **reposition** the gradient in the object, drag the round endpoint in a perpendicular direction to the color bands in the gradient. The annotator for a linear gradient always crosses through the center of the object. If you try moving it away from the center (parallel to the color bands), it will snap back.

   To **lengthen** the overall gradient to make the transitions between colors more gradual, **B** or to **shorten** it to make the transitions more abrupt, drag the diamond-shaped endpoint outward or inward.

   To change the **angle** of the gradient, position the pointer just outside the diamond-shaped endpoint, then when the rotation pointer appears, ⟳ drag in a circular direction. **C**

   To change both the **length** and **angle** of the gradient simultaneously, hold down Option/Alt as you drag the diamond-shaped endpoint.

➤ If you change the position, length, or angle of the annotator on an object and then apply a different gradient fill of the same type (radial or linear) to the object, those custom position, length, and angle settings will be applied to your new gradient choice.

➤ If you scale an object that contains a gradient, the gradient will scale by the same amount.

A *To display the gradient annotator, select an object that contains a gradient fill and choose the Gradient tool.*

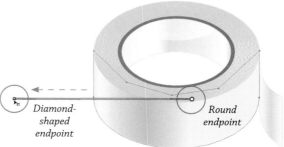

Diamond-shaped endpoint　　　*Round endpoint*

B *To reposition the gradient, we dragged the round endpoint to the left, and to lengthen it, we dragged the diamond-shaped endpoint. Now the color transitions are more gradual, and the gradient extends beyond the object (although it displays only within it).*

C *To change the gradient angle, we are rotating the diamond-shaped endpoint.*

To change the position, length, shape, or angle of a radial gradient in an object:

1. Select an object that contains a radial gradient fill.

2. Choose the **Gradient** tool ▢ (G).**A** The annotator should display on the object. If it doesn't, press Cmd-Option-G/Ctrl-Alt-G.

3. On the annotator, do any of the following:

   To **reposition** the gradient, drag either the bar or the larger of the two round endpoints.**B** The annotator for a radial gradient doesn't have to remain centered on the object.

   To lengthen or shorten the **radius** of the gradient (to scale the gradient ellipse), drag either the diamond-shaped endpoint or the smaller of the two black circles (on the edge of the ellipse) inward or outward.**C** The smaller the ellipse

(and the shorter the radius), the more abrupt the color transitions, and vice versa.

To change the **aspect ratio** of the ellipse to make the gradient more oval or more round, drag the larger of the two black circles (on the edge of the ellipse) inward or outward.**D**

To change the **gradient angle**, position the pointer on the edge of the ellipse, then when you see the rotation pointer, drag in any direction. An angle change in a radial gradient will be visible only if the gradient is oval shaped.

➤ To move the center of the radial gradient fill without scaling the ellipse, drag the smaller round endpoint on the annotator away from the larger one.

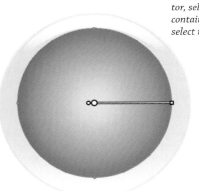

A *To display the annotator, select an object that contains a gradient fill and select the Gradient tool.*

B *To reposition the gradient, drag the large round endpoint.*

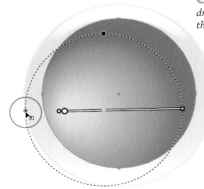

C *To scale the gradient, drag the smaller circle on the edge of the ellipse.*

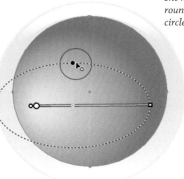

D *To make the gradient more oval or more round, drag the larger circle on the ellipse.*

Spreading a single gradient across multiple objects

Normally, when you fill multiple selected objects with a gradient, the gradient fill starts anew in each object.A With the Gradient tool, you can spread a single gradient across multiple objects.

To spread a gradient across multiple objects:

1. Select two or more objects, and put them in a group (press Cmd-G/Ctrl-G). Keep the group selected.

2. On the Appearance panel,⬤ click the **Add New Fill** button.☐ Click the color square for the new Fill listing, then click a gradient swatch on the temporary Swatches panel. Now the gradient is applied to the group as a whole, not to the individual objects.B

3. *Optional:* Choose the Gradient tool ▦ (G). The annotator for the entire group displays. Use the controls or color stops on the annotator to edit the gradient.

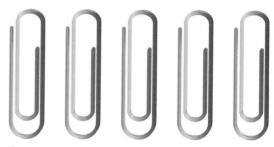

A *A gradient fill is applied individually to each one of these objects.*

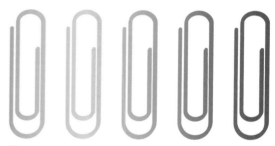

B *We grouped the objects, then, via the Appearance panel, applied a gradient to the entire group. Now a single gradient extends all the way from the first object to the last one.*

EDITING A GRADIENT VIA THE GRADIENT PANEL

The Gradient panel ▦ provides three options that aren't available on the annotator (noted with asterisks in the figure below), as well as some equivalent controls. To use this panel, either select an object or group that contains the gradient to be edited, or deselect all objects and then click the gradient swatch to be edited. To display the full Gradient panel, click the double arrows on the panel tab.

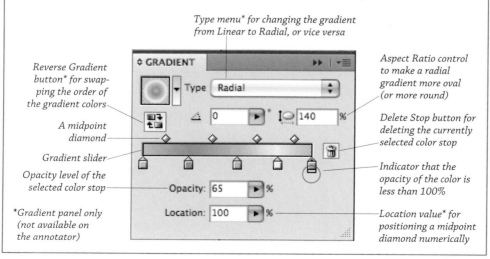

Type menu* for changing the gradient from Linear to Radial, or vice versa

Reverse Gradient button* for swapping the order of the gradient colors

Aspect Ratio control to make a radial gradient more oval (or more round)

A midpoint diamond

Delete Stop button for deleting the currently selected color stop

Gradient slider

Opacity level of the selected color stop

Indicator that the opacity of the color is less than 100%

*Gradient panel only (not available on the annotator)

Location value* for positioning a midpoint diamond numerically

Expanding a gradient into paths

The Expand command lets you expand the colors in a gradient fill into a collection of individual paths. One practical reason for doing this might be if a gradient is causing a printing error and has to be simplified.

To expand a gradient fill into separate objects:

1. Select an object that contains a gradient fill.

2. Choose Object > **Expand**. The Expand dialog opens.

3. Check Expand: **Fill**.

4. Click Expand Gradient To: **Specify**, then enter the desired number of Objects to be created.**B** To print the expanded gradient successfully, this number must be high enough to produce smooth color transitions (say, over 100). Or if you want to expand it into obvious bands of color intentionally, enter a value below 20.

5. Click OK.**C** Note: If the original gradient contained fewer colors than you specified, the resulting number of objects may not match the number of objects that you specified in the dialog.

   If you look on the Layers panel, you will see a group containing a clipping path (from the object that contained the gradient fill) and the resulting paths.

➤ To expand a gradient using the current Specify [ ] Objects setting without opening the dialog, hold down Option/Alt while choosing Object > Expand.

➤ To learn about color-separating gradients, see the sidebar on page 397.

A *The original object contains a linear gradient fill.*

B *In the Expand dialog, we are specifying the number of objects to be produced from the gradient.*

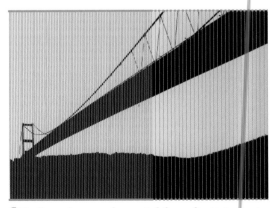

C *The Expand command converted the gradient into a series of separate rectangles, containing different tints, within a group. The outer rectangle became a clipping path.*

All the commands discussed in this chapter form a new shape by combining two or more objects. You will learn about the new Shape Builder tool, which unites multiple objects by dragging; the Shape Mode commands, which create one or more standard paths or an editable compound shape from multiple objects; the Pathfinder commands and effects, which produce either a flattened, closed object or a compound path; and the Compound Path command, which joins two or more objects into one object, creating a "hole" where the original objects overlapped. In addition, you will learn how to add objects to, reverse an object's fill in, and release a compound path.

Using the Shape Builder tool ★

The new Shape Builder tool can be used to unite overlapping closed paths, open filled paths, compound paths, or outline type into one shape.**A–B** With this tool, you drag across objects to unite them, in an intuitive way. You can also use it to divide areas that are formed by overlapping objects and to extract (cut out) parts of objects.

Before using the Shape Builder tool, you need to choose options for it, as described on the next page.

Continued on the following page

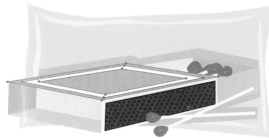

A *We selected three objects.*

B *With the Shape Builder tool, we are dragging across the selected objects. The final, united shape is shown above right.*

COMBINE PATHS

25

IN THIS CHAPTER

ANOTHER WAY TO WORK WITH INTERSECTING SHAPES

Hide or recolor intersecting faces or edges in a Live Paint group. The result will look similar to some of the Pathfinder commands, but will be easier to edit. See Chapter 18.

To choose options for the Shape Builder tool: ★

1. Double-click the **Shape Builder** tool 🦐 to open the Shape Builder Tool Options dialog.**A**

2. *Optional:* Check Gap Detection and choose a Gap Length option that best describes the gaps that you see between objects in your artwork. Where the tool detects gaps of this length between selected objects, it will treat areas on either side of the gap as separate, unconnected shapes.**B**

3. Under Options, do the following:

   Check **Consider Open Filled Path as Closed** to have the tool treat filled open paths as separate shapes.**C–D**

   Optional: Check In Merge Mode, Clicking Stroke Splits the Path to allow the tool to split a path when you click it on a segment that is created by overlapping shapes. We keep this option off unless we intentionally want to divide a path into separate segments (see **A–B**, page 331).

   From the **Pick Color From** menu, choose **Artwork** to have the final shape adopt the fill and stroke attributes from the object you either click first or start dragging from; or choose **Color Swatches** and check **Cursor Swatch Preview** to display, in a tiny strip above the tool pointer, either the current fill or stroke color (if you are using the Color panel) or the color of the most recently chosen swatch on the Swatches panel and the two swatches that are adjacent to it.

4. Under Highlight, do any of the following:

   Check **Fill** to have a gray highlight texture display temporarily within overlapping areas of selected objects as you roll or drag across them, marking the areas that the tool will alter.

   Check **Highlight Stroke When Editable** to have the current highlight color display temporarily on the segments of selected paths you roll or drag across, marking the areas that the tool will alter.

   Optional: From the Color menu, choose a different preset color for the highlights, or click the color swatch and choose a custom color.

5. Click OK.

➤ With Artwork as the current Pick Color From setting, if the first object you drag across has a fill and stroke of None, the colors from the last object you drag across (where you release the mouse) will appear in the united shape.

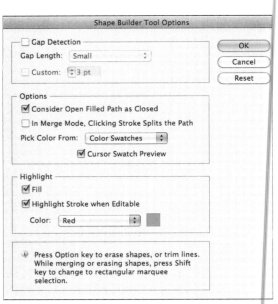

A *Choose settings in the Shape Builder Tool Options dialog.*

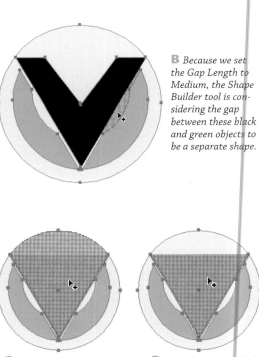

B *Because we set the Gap Length to Medium, the Shape Builder tool is considering the gap between these black and green objects to be a separate shape.*

C *Consider Open Filled Path as Closed off: The tool is ignoring the fill area and selecting a larger shape.*

D *Consider Open Filled Path as Closed on: The tool is recognizing the open fill area as a shape.*

To unite, extract, and divide objects with the Shape Builder tool: ★

1. Arrange the objects to be united so they partially overlap, and select them all. **A** Note: This tool doesn't work with editable type, blend objects, or Live Paint groups.

2. Choose the **Shape Builder** tool 🔩 (Shift-M).

3. If the current Pick Color From setting in the tool options dialog is Artwork, position the tool over an object that has the fill and stroke colors that you want to appear in the final shape; or if Color Swatches is the current setting, choose a fill color for the final shape.

   ➤ For the Color Swatches option, after clicking in the Swatches panel, you can press the left or right arrow key to cycle through other swatches (this shortcut works even when the Cursor Swatch Preview option is off).

4. Do any of the following:

   To **unite** some shapes, either drag across the objects to be united **B** or Shift-drag a marquee around them. A closed shape will be created.

   To **extract** a shape, Option-click/Alt-click a non-overlapping area to eliminate it, or Option-click/Alt-click an overlapping area to exclude it (create a cutout).**C–E** Note: If the overlapping area is completely contained within a larger shape (as in a donut), the result will be a compound path; see pages 338–339.

   Continued on the following page

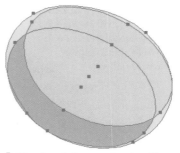

A *We selected three overlapping ellipses, chose the Shape Builder tool, and in the Shape Builder Tool Options dialog, set the Pick Color From menu to Artwork.*

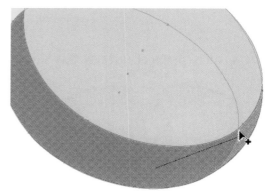

B *As we drag the tool across an area where two selected objects overlap, a gray highlight texture appears in the shapes, indicating that they will be united.*

C *Each final, united shape adopted the color of the first object we dragged across. Next, we held down Option/Alt and clicked an overlapping area...*

D *... to extract it, in order to make the center of the ring blank.*

E *Finally, we added an ellipse (and converted its stroke to an outlined path), and applied gradients to all the shapes.*

To **divide** shapes, click an area that is formed by overlapping paths; that area will become a separate shape.**A–B** The current Pick Color From option will control which fill color is applied to the newly divided shape.

A *With the Shape Builder tool, we clicked the bottom part of the circle to divide it.*

B *We dragged the newly divided bottom shape away from the black V shape.*

CREATING AN ILLUSION OF INTERLOCKING SHAPES WITH THE SHAPE BUILDER TOOL ★

C *With the Reflect tool, we produced a symmetrical copy of the ring (the copy appeared on the left side).*

D *We dragged with the Shape Builder tool across overlapping areas that were formed by the two rings, to unite them.*

E *We united a section of the ring on the left with a larger section of the ring on the right. Now it looks as though the rings are linked.*

USING THE "IN MERGE MODE, CLICKING STROKE SPLITS THE PATH" OPTION OF THE SHAPE BUILDER TOOL ★

The Shape Builder tool can also be used to split path segments where they touch overlapping objects. To enable this function, in the options dialog for the tool, check In Merge Mode, Clicking Stroke Splits the Path (and while you're at it, also choose Pick Color From: Color Swatches). **A–B**

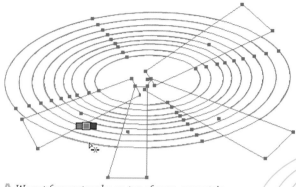

A *We put four rectangles on top of some concentric circles, selected all the objects, then started clicking segments to divide them. The red highlight shows which segment the pointer is currently over, and the green stroke color that we chose from the Swatches panel displays in the center of the Cursor Swatch Preview strip, above the pointer.*

B *When we clicked the segment, it became a separate object, and the tool applied the green stroke color. To complete the artwork, we continued to divide the circles by clicking segments, each time with the desired stroke color selected.*

Applying the Shape Mode commands

When you click a Shape Mode button on the Pathfinder panel, ▪ selected, overlapping objects are combined into one or more standard paths, and the result is permanent.

When you Option-click/Alt-click a Shape Mode button, selected, overlapping objects are combined into a compound shape. The objects are nested within a Compound Shape listing on the Layers panel. If you move or reshape an individual object within a compound shape, the overall shape adjusts accordingly. And this method is reversible: If you release the compound shape, the objects regain their original attributes.

Here are a few guidelines to bear in mind as you use the Shape Mode commands:

➤ The Shape Mode commands can be applied to multiple standard paths, groups, compound paths, and outline type. When the Option/Alt key is used, an editable type object or objects in a blend can be combined with other objects into a compound shape.

➤ The Shape Mode commands can't be applied to placed images, rasterized images, or mesh objects.

➤ The original objects can contain gradients, patterns, brush strokes, transparency, effects, and graphic styles.

➤ The Unite, Intersect, and Exclude commands apply the color, stroke, and transparency attributes (and any effects) from the topmost object to the resulting path or shape and remove all other color attributes, whereas the Minus Front command applies those attributes from the backmost object. To achieve the desired results, remember to put the objects in the necessary stacking position before applying the command.

Continued on the following page

To combine objects into a path by using a Shape Mode command:

1. *Optional:* Duplicate the objects to be combined, to preserve a copy of them.

2. Select two or more overlapping objects.

3. On the Pathfinder panel, 🔳 click one of the **Shape Mode** buttons: **A**

   Unite joins the perimeter of the selection into one path, deletes the segments where paths intersect, and closes any open paths (see also page 167).**B**

   Minus Front subtracts the objects in front from the backmost object, preserving the color attributes of only the backmost object. The result is one path or multiple nonoverlapping paths.**C**

   Intersect preserves areas where objects overlap and deletes the nonoverlapping areas. The result is one path.**D** Note: If an alert dialog appears, make sure every object overlaps all the other objects.

   Exclude deletes areas where the objects overlap, preserving only the nonoverlapping areas. The result is multiple nonoverlapping paths nested within a group layer.**E**

➤ You can apply new color or appearance attributes to the combined path.

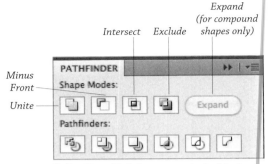

Expand (for compound shapes only)

Intersect   *Exclude*

Minus Front

Unite

A *The Shape Mode buttons on the Pathfinder panel combine multiple selected objects into a path if you click the button without holding down any keys, or into a compound shape if you hold down Option/Alt while clicking the button.*

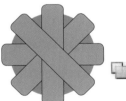

B *These are the original objects.*

Unite joined the perimeter of the selection to produce one path.

C *These are the original objects.*

Minus Front used the frontmost objects like a cookie cutter on the object behind it.

D *These are the original objects.*

Intersect preserved only the area where the original objects overlapped.

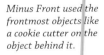

E *These are the original objects.*

Exclude removed the areas from where the original objects overlapped.

When you Option-click/Alt-click a Shape Mode button, a compound shape is produced. Unlike the result that simply clicking the button produces (as on the preceding page), this method preserves all of the original objects, although this won't be evident unless you view the Appearance panel for a selected object in the shape, or release the compound shape.

To combine objects into a compound shape by using a Shape Mode command:

1. Select two or more overlapping objects.

2. On the Pathfinder panel, Option-click/Alt-click a **Shape Mode** button (**A**, previous page):

   Unite joins the perimeter of the selection into one compound shape, applies the attributes of the frontmost object to the result, and hides the object edges in the interior of the shape. **A–B**

   Minus Front subtracts the objects in front from the backmost object, preserving the color attributes of only the backmost object. The subtracted objects are hidden.

   Intersect applies the color attributes of the frontmost object only to the areas where all the selected objects overlap, and hides all nonoverlapping areas.

   Exclude turns areas where objects overlap into fully transparent cutouts, through which any underlying objects will be visible.

3. *Optional:* Double-click the compound shape to isolate it, then change its color attributes, or move or transform individual objects within it to alter its contour. **C**

When you expand a compound shape, it looks the same onscreen, but the individual objects that it formerly was composed of are eliminated. If you expand a compound shape that contains an interior cutout or separate shapes, the result is a compound path (see pages 338–339), whereas if you expand a single shape that doesn't have a cutout, the result is one path.

To expand a compound shape:

1. Select the compound shape.

2. Click **Expand** on the Pathfinder panel.

The Release Compound Shape command restores the original objects and their attributes.

To release a compound shape:

1. Select the compound shape.

2. Choose **Release Compound Shape** from the Pathfinder panel menu. **D**

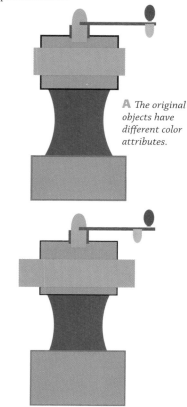

A *The original objects have different color attributes.*

B *We Option/Alt clicked the Unite button to produce a compound shape.*

C *In isolation mode, we used the Selection tool to reshape and move objects within the compound shape.*

D *The Release Compound Shape command restored the original object colors.*

Applying the Pathfinder commands

Next, you will use the Pathfinder commands on the Pathfinder panel to divide, trim, merge, crop, outline, or subtract areas from selected overlapping paths. The result will be separate, nonoverlapping closed paths or lines, nested within a group. (To learn how the Pathfinder effects on the Effect menu differ from these commands, see page 340.)

Keep the following guidelines in mind as you use the Pathfinder commands:

➤ The objects that you apply the command to may contain patterns, gradients, brush strokes, transparency, or effects.

➤ Editable type must be converted to outlines first.

➤ Illustrator may take the liberty of closing any open paths for you as it performs the command, so we also recommend closing all open paths first. See the steps for converting a stroke or an open path into a filled object on page 336.

➤ The original objects can't be restored after you apply the command (unless you choose Undo immediately), so be sure to duplicate the objects first.

➤ Transparency settings are preserved.

➤ For the Trim, Merge, and Crop commands, the original stroke colors are deleted, except from objects that contain an effect or a brush stroke.

To apply a Pathfinder command:

1. Select two or more overlapping objects, and duplicate them.

2. On the Pathfinder panel, click a **Pathfinder** button. A

   Divide turns each overlapping area into a separate, nonoverlapping object. B–C (Read about the Divide and Outline option in the sidebar at right.)

   ➤ After applying the Divide command, you can double-click the group to isolate it, then apply new fill colors or effects to the individual objects or a fill of None; lower an object's transparency; or remove an object to create a cutout effect. You can also reposition any individual object with the Selection tool.

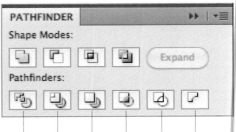

Divide   Trim   Merge   Crop   Outline   Minus Back

A *The Pathfinder buttons on the Pathfinder panel produce separate closed paths or lines.*

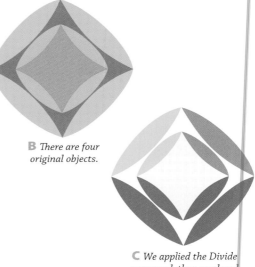

B *There are four original objects.*

C *We applied the Divide command, then recolored the resulting shapes.*

CHOOSING PATHFINDER OPTIONS

To open the Pathfinder Options dialog, from which you can choose the following preferences for the Pathfinder commands, choose Pathfinder Options from the Pathfinder panel menu:

➤ The higher the Precision value (.001–100 pt), the more precisely the commands are applied, and the longer they take to process.

➤ With Remove Redundant Points checked, duplicate anchor points in the same *x/y* location are deleted.

➤ With Divide and Outline Will Remove Unpainted Artwork checked, the Divide and Outline commands will delete any nonoverlapping areas of selected paths that have a fill of None.

Trim preserves the frontmost object shape but deletes sections of objects that are behind it and overlap it. **A** Adjacent or overlapping objects of the same color or shade remain separate (the opposite result of the Merge command). Stroke colors are deleted, except from objects that contain an effect or a brush stroke.

Merge unites adjacent or overlapping objects that contain the same fill attributes into one object or into nonoverlapping objects. (The original objects can contain the same or different stroke attributes.) **B** Stroke colors are deleted, except from objects that contain an effect or a brush stroke.

Crop crops away (deletes) areas of objects that extend beyond the edges of the frontmost object, and removes the fill and stroke from the frontmost object. **C**

Outline converts all the objects into segments with a stroke setting of 0 pt. and converts the fill colors to stroke colors. **D** The resulting strokes can be transformed, reshaped, and recolored individually. (Read about the setting for Divide and Outline in the sidebar on the preceding page.)

Minus Back subtracts the objects in back from the frontmost object, leaving only portions of the frontmost object. **E** The color attributes and appearances of the frontmost object are applied to the resulting path. For this command to produce a result, make sure the frontmost object only partially overlaps the backmost one.

3. To edit the resulting paths, put the group into isolation mode first by double-clicking it with the Selection tool.

➤ To apply the last-used Pathfinder command to any selected objects, press Cmd-4/Ctrl-4.

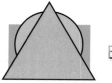

A There are three original objects.

The Trim command was applied (the resulting objects were pulled apart).

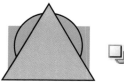

B There are three original objects.

The Merge command was applied (the resulting objects were pulled apart).

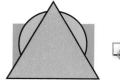

C There are three original objects.

The Crop command was applied.

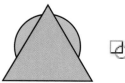

D There are two original objects.

The Outline command was applied (the resulting objects were pulled apart).

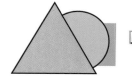

E There are three original objects.

The Minus Back command was applied (the objects in back cut through the topmost one).

Instead of letting a Pathfinder command close any open paths for you, consider using the Outline Stroke command to turn the stroke on a path into a filled object first. Other reasons you may need to convert a line or a stroke into a closed path are to enable it to be filled with a gradient, or to prepare it for trapping.

To convert a stroke or an open path to a filled object:

1. Select an open or closed object. Choose a stroke weight (it will be the width of the final object). **A**

2. Choose Object > Path > **Outline Stroke**. The original stroke and fill areas are now separate objects within a group. The former stroke color is applied as a fill color to the converted stroke. **B–C**

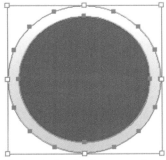

A *Select an object that contains a stroke in the desired weight.*

B *The Outline Stroke command converted the stroke to a compound path, to which we applied a gradient fill.*

C *In the final art, a gray stroke color is applied to the compound path.*

HOW COMPOUND SHAPES...	...DIFFER FROM COMPOUND PATHS	AND HOW THEY'RE ALIKE
Option-click/Alt-click a Shape Mode button on the Pathfinder panel to produce a compound shape.	Apply the Object > Compound Path > Make command to subtract overlapping areas from the backmost object.	With the Selection tool, you can select or transform a whole compound shape or a whole compound path; or double-click it to isolate it, then click to select and edit any subpath within it.
Subpaths are nested as separate objects within a Compound Shape listing on the Layers panel.	Subpaths become part of one compound path object and listing. The original objects are no longer listed separately.	Stroke attributes that are applied to a compound shape or compound path will display on the outer edge of the overall shape and on any interior cutout shapes.
The Release Compound Shape command restores the original objects and their appearances (see page 333).	Released objects adopt the appearance attributes of the compound path, not their original attributes (see page 339).	

Using the Compound Path command

The Make Compound Path command joins two or more objects into one object. A transparent hole is created where the objects originally overlapped, through which underlying objects are revealed. Regardless of their original attributes (e.g., color, gradient, pattern, brush stroke, transparency, effects), all the objects in a compound path are given the attributes of the backmost object, and form one unit. A compound path can be released at any time, at which point the original object shapes (but not their original attributes) are restored.

To create a compound path:

1. Arrange the objects to be made "see-through" in front of a larger shape. **A**

2. Select all the objects.

3. Press Cmd-8/Ctrl-8 or choose Object > **Compound Path** > **Make**. Or if the objects aren't in a group, you can right-click in the document and choose **Make Compound Path** from the context menu.

   The frontmost objects will cut through the backmost object like cookie cutters. **B–C** A Compound Path listing appears on the Layers panel; the original objects are no longer listed individually.

   The attributes of the backmost object (e.g., fill, stroke, transparency, brush stroke, effects) are applied to sections of all the selected objects. If the see-through holes didn't result, follow the second set of instructions on the next page.

   Note: You can isolate a compound path using the Selection tool, then reshape any of the paths within it using the Direct Selection tool. You can apply different fill, stroke, and other attributes to the whole compound path, but not to any of the individual paths within it.

➤ When combined into a compound path, all the objects are moved to the layer of the frontmost object.

➤ To help prevent a printing error, avoid creating a compound path from very complex shapes, and also avoid creating multiple compound paths in the same file.

➤ Compare this command with the Divide Objects Below command, which is discussed on page 169.

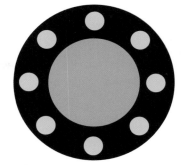

A *Place smaller objects on top of a larger one, select all the objects, then right-click in the document and choose Make Compound Path.*

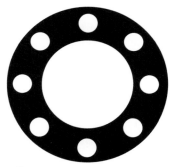

B *The objects are converted to a compound path.*

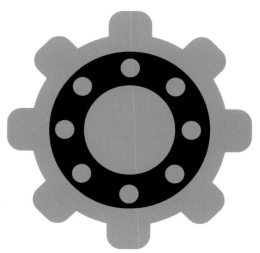

C *We placed an object behind the compound path.*

Working with compound paths

To add an object to a compound path:

1. Move the object to be added in front of the compound path. (If it's in back, its attributes will be applied to the compound path.) You can restack it by dragging its selection square upward on the Layers panel.

2. Select both the compound path and the object to be added to it.

3. Press Cmd-8/Ctrl-8 or choose Object > **Compound Path** > **Make**.

By flipping the Reverse Path Direction switch on the Attributes panel, you can remove the fill color of any shape in a compound path, and thereby make that object transparent, or vice versa.

To make a filled area in a compound path transparent, or vice versa:

1. Deselect the compound path.

2. Choose the **Direct Selection** tool (A).

3. Click the edge of the object in the compound path that you want to reverse the color of.**A** Only that path should be selected.

4. Show the Attributes panel.

5. Click the **Reverse Path Direction Off** button or the **Reverse Path Direction On** button (the one that isn't currently highlighted).**B–C**

   Note: If the Reverse Path buttons are dimmed, make sure the Use Non-Zero Winding Fill Rule button on the right side of the panel is activated.

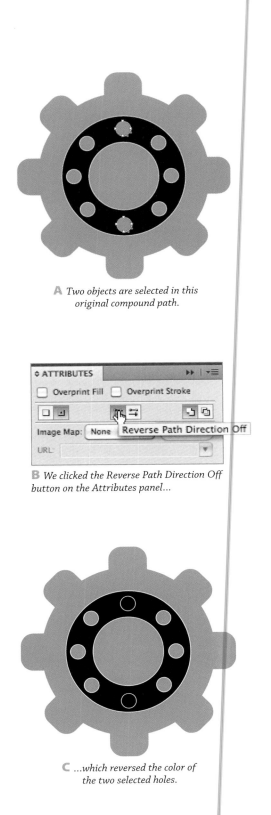

A *Two objects are selected in this original compound path.*

B *We clicked the Reverse Path Direction Off button on the Attributes panel...*

C *...which reversed the color of the two selected holes.*

You can release a compound path at any time to restore the original, individual paths (but not their original attributes).

To release a compound path:

1. Select a compound path. **A**

2. Do either of the following:

   Right-click the artboard and choose **Release Compound Path** from the context menu.

   Press Cmd-Option-Shift-8/Ctrl-Alt-Shift-8 or choose Object > **Compound Path** > **Release**.

   All the objects will be selected and will adopt the colors, effects, and other appearance attributes from the compound path — not their original, precompound attributes. **B** You can use the Object Highlighting feature of Smart Guides to help you figure out which shape is which.

➤ All the released objects will be nested within the top-level layer that the former compound path resided in.

➤ The Type > Create Outlines command always produces a compound path. If the former character had a counter (an interior shape, such as in the letters P, A, O, R, or D) and you release the compound path, the counter will be a separate path and will have the same color attributes and appearances as the outer part of the letterform. **C–D**

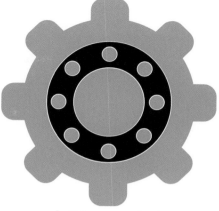

A *Click a compound path.*

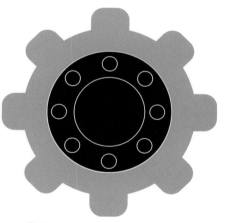

B *We released the compound path, so the holes are no longer transparent.*

C *All type outlines are compound paths.*

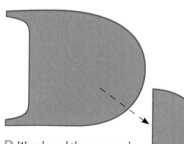

D *We released the compound path into separate objects. (Then we repositioned the counter of the "D.")*

Applying Pathfinder effects

The Pathfinder effects function like the commands on the Pathfinder panel, with the following exceptions:

➤ Unlike the Pathfinder panel commands, the Pathfinder effects modify an object's appearance but not its actual path (until the file is flattened for output). For example, the Divide, Trim, and Merge effects don't break up overlapping areas into separate objects (as the commands on the Pathfinder panel do) until the file is flattened.

➤ The effects don't create compound shapes or compound paths.

➤ You can easily delete the effect at any time, because it is listed on the Appearance panel as an attribute (see page 195).

To apply a Pathfinder effect:

1. Collect two or more objects into a separate layer or group, then target the layer or group (we do mean target — not select). If you don't do this, an alert dialog may appear when you choose the effect.**A** The objects can be path or type objects, groups, or objects in a blend, and they can contain gradients, patterns, brush strokes, and transparency. They cannot be placed or rasterized images. Remove any Stylize or Photoshop effects.

2. Display the Appearance panel. ● From the **Pathfinder** submenu on the **Add New Effect** menu,*fx*, choose an effect.**B–C**

➤ To move an object into or out of a group that a Pathfinder effect is applied to, move the object's selection square upward or downward on the Layers panel. Reposition the object, if necessary.

➤ To learn more about effects, see Chapter 15.

➤ If you apply a Pathfinder effect to an object and then apply the Object > Expand Appearance command, the results of the effect will be converted to one or more standard paths.

To replace one Pathfinder effect with another:

1. Target the layer or group that the Pathfinder effect is applied to.

2. On the Appearance panel, click the Pathfinder effect listing. The Pathfinder Options dialog opens. Check Preview.

3. From the **Operation** menu, choose a different **Pathfinder** option, then click OK.

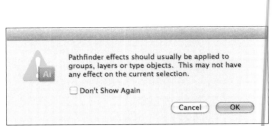

Pathfinder effects should usually be applied to groups, layers or type objects. This may not have any effect on the current selection.

☐ Don't Show Again

Cancel | OK

A *This alert dialog may appear if you fail to target a layer or group before applying a Pathfinder effect.*

B *We applied the Add Pathfinder effect (via the Appearance panel) to unite the objects in this group.*

C *When we hid the effect on the Appearance panel, the individual paths redisplayed.*

When objects are put in a clipping set, the topmost object (called the "clipping path") crops the objects or images that are below it, like a picture frame or mat. Parts of objects that extend outside the clipping path object are hidden and don't print. This mechanism allows you to fit multiple objects within the confines of a shape without having to spend time cropping and reshaping them. The clipping path and the masked objects are referred to collectively as a "clipping set." The masked objects can be moved, reshaped, or recolored, and can be restacked within the set. A clipping set can be released at any time.

Creating a clipping set

You can create a clipping set from all the objects on a given layer, in which case it is called a "layer-level" set, or from multiple selected objects on one or more layers, in which case it is called an "object-level" set. The methods for creating these two types of clipping sets differ, as do the methods used to select objects within them, but in all other respects they function in the same way.

Before creating a clipping set, review these general guidelines:

➤ If you need to restack an object before creating a clipping set, drag its listing upward or downward on the Layers panel.

➤ The clipping path object (the one that works like a frame) can be an open or closed path, editable type, a compound shape, or a closed object that was produced by the Unite command (Pathfinder panel).

➤ To help prevent a printing error, avoid using very complex objects in a clipping set.

➤ When you create a clipping set, the clipping path object is listed on the Layers panel as "<Clipping Path>" with an underline (unless editable type is used as the clipping path, in which case the type characters are listed instead). When you create an object-level clipping set, the objects are moved into a new group automatically.

Continued on the following page

CLIPPING MASKS

26

IN THIS CHAPTER

When you use the Make Clipping Mask command, the objects to be put into a clipping set can be on any layer. The command moves the objects into a new group within the layer that contains the clipping path.

To create an object-level clipping set from existing objects:

1. Arrange the object or objects to be masked.**A** They can be grouped, or not. Using the Layers panel, stack the clipping path object so it's in front of the objects to be masked.

2. With the Selection tool ▶ (V), draw a marquee around the clipping path and the objects to be masked.

3. Press Cmd-7/Ctrl-7 (Object > Clipping Mask > Make), or right-click in the document and choose **Make Clipping Mask**. The masked objects will be moved into a new group on the same top-level layer as the clipping path.**B–C** The clipping path is assigned a fill and stroke of None.

A *We positioned a rectangle in front of the objects to be clipped, then selected all the objects.*

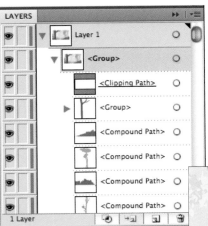

B *We chose the Make Clipping Mask command, which put the objects into a clipping set within a <Group>.*

C *Sections of objects that extend beyond the bounds of the rectangle (the clipping path) are now hidden.*

The new Draw Inside mode offers a novel approach to creating clipping sets. When this mode is activated, new objects that you draw, or existing objects that you paste, are clipped automatically by an object that you designate as a clipping path. The original stroke and fill attributes of the clipping path object are preserved.

To create an object-level clipping set using Draw Inside mode: ★

1. With the Selection tool ▶ (V) or via the Layers panel, select an object to become the clipping path object.

2. On the Tools panel, choose **Draw Inside** ◯ as the drawing mode. A dashed border appears around the corners of the object.**A** Deselect.

3. Choose a drawing tool (such as the Paintbrush, Pencil, Rectangle, or Ellipse tool) and the desired fill and stroke attributes, then draw new objects that intersect with the clipping path object.**B**

   The object that you selected in step 1 is now functioning as a clipping path. That object, along with the masked objects, are nested within a group on the Layers panel. If you need to reselect a masked object or the clipping path, click its selection square on the Layers panel.

4. *Optional:* You can also paste an object into the clipping set. With Draw Inside mode still active, copy an existing object on the artboard, then press Cmd-V/Ctrl-V to paste it. It will automatically be centered within the clipping path, but you can move it with the Selection tool.

5. When you're done drawing or pasting inside the clipping path, double-click in the artboard with a Selection tool or press Shift-D to return to **Draw Normal** mode.◻ The dashed border disappears.**C**

➤ To reactivate Draw Inside mode for an object-level clipping set, select the clipping path via the Layers panel (or click its edge with the Direct Selection tool), then on the Tools panel, choose Draw Inside ◯ mode. The dashed border reappears. Deselect, then repeat steps 3–5 above.

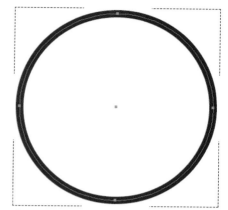

A *We chose the Draw Inside option. A dashed border appeared around our selected object.*

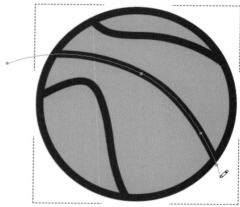

B *We drew an orange ellipse and lines to define the seams. Only sections of the objects that fall within the bounds of the black ellipse are visible.*

C *We put Illustrator in Draw Normal mode.*

The Make/Release Clipping Mask button on the Layers panel clips all the objects and groups on the currently active layer (whether the objects are selected or not) and uses the topmost object in the layer or group as the clipping path.

To create a layer-level clipping set:

1. Put all the objects for the clipping set on the same layer, and make sure they're the only objects on that layer. Stack the object to be used as the clipping path so it's the topmost listing on the layer.**A** Click the layer listing.

2. Click the **Make/Release Clipping Mask** button on the Layers panel.**B–C** The clipping path is assigned a fill and stroke of None.

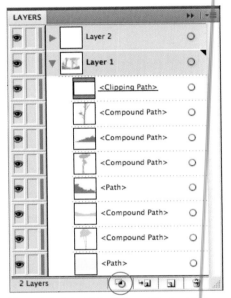

B *We clicked the Make/Release Clipping Mask button on the Layers panel, which created a clipping set from all the objects in the currently active layer. The topmost object (the rectangle) became a clipping path.*

A *These are the original objects.*

C *This is the artwork after we clicked the Make/Release Clipping Mask button. Sections of objects that lie outside the bounds of the clipping path object are hidden.*

Selecting objects in a clipping set

When objects are in a clipping set, only the areas of masked objects that are positioned within the confines of the clipping path are visible (whether the set is selected or not). Follow these instructions to select a whole clipping set, which includes the clipping path and the masked objects.

To select a whole clipping set:

Do either of the following:

On the Layers panel, ✏ click the selection area for the clipping set (the group or layer).

For an object-level clipping set (a group), choose the Selection tool ▶ (V), then click a visible part of any masked object in the document window.

➤ The bounding box (View > Show Bounding Box) for a selected set will surround the clipping path, not the outermost edges of the masked objects.

You need to use a different method to select objects in an object-level clipping set than to select objects in a layer-level set. (To select objects in a layer-level clipping set, see the next page.)

To select objects in an object-level clipping set:

Method 1 (isolation mode)

1. Choose the Selection tool ▶ (V). In the document, double-click a visible part of one of the masked objects to put the group into isolation mode.

2. Use the Selection tool to move or transform the clipping path or any other object in the clipping set, or to select any of them for recoloring. **A** Use the Direct Selection tool ▶ (A) to reshape them.

3. To exit isolation mode, press Esc.

Method 2 (buttons on the Control panel)

1. Choose the Selection tool ▶ (V).

2. To select all the masked objects but not the clipping path (perhaps to move or transform all the masked objects as a unit), click any visible object within the set, then click the **Edit Contents** button ▣ on the Control panel. **B–C**

   To select just the clipping path (perhaps to change its color attributes), click any object within the clipping set, then click the **Edit Clipping Path** button ▣ on the Control panel.

➤ You can also select the clipping path or a masked object in a clipping set by clicking its selection area on the Layers panel.

A With a clipping set in isolation mode, you can edit individual objects as you would objects in an ordinary group.

B We clicked the Edit Contents button on the Control panel to select all the masked objects, so we could move them.

C We moved the masked objects downward within the "frame" of the clipping path.

To select objects in a layer-level clipping set:

1. Choose the Selection tool ► (V), then click an object in the clipping set (either a clipped object or the clipping path). You can use the Object Highlighting feature of Smart Guides to locate it.

2. Do any of the following:

   Use the Selection tool to move or transform any object in the clipping set.

   Use the Direct Selection tool ► (A) to reshape a selected object, or the Color or Appearance panel to recolor it.

To isolate an individual object, double-click it. On the isolation mode bar, click the layer name to access and edit other objects. Press Esc to exit isolation mode.

➤ You can also select the clipping path or a masked object in a clipping set by clicking its selection area on the Layers panel.

RECOLORING A CLIPPING PATH

To apply a fill or stroke color to a clipping path, click its selection area on the Layers panel first. **A–B** The stroke color will be visible no matter what, whereas the fill color will be visible only if there are gaps between the masked objects. **C**

A This is the original clipping set.

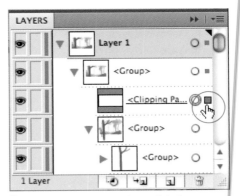

B To select the clipping path, we clicked its selection area on the Layers panel.

C We applied a stroke color (dark green) and a fill color (midnight blue).

Adding objects to, and deleting them from, a clipping set

To add a new object to a clipping set: ★

Method 1 (for object-level and layer-level sets)

1. On the Layers panel, click the selection square for the Clipping Path listing.

2. From the Tools panel, choose **Draw Inside** ◔ as the drawing mode. Deselect.

3. Do either of the following:

    Draw a new object, making sure the pointer intersects with the set as you do so.

    Copy and paste an object.

4. Press Shift-D to return to **Draw Normal** mode. ◔

Method 2 (for object-level sets)

1. With the Selection tool ▶ (V), double-click a masked object in an object-level clipping set to put the group into isolation mode.

2. Draw a new object, making sure the pointer intersects with the set as you do so. To exit isolation mode, press Esc.

To add an existing object to a clipping set:

1. With the Selection tool ▶ (V), move the object to be added over the set. **A**

2. On the Layers panel, ◔ expand the list for the clipping set, then restack the listing for the object to be added to the set group or layer, below the Clipping Path listing. **B–C**

➤ To restack an object within a clipping set, on the Layers panel, drag the object listing upward or downward within its group or layer. Be sure to stack it below the Clipping Path listing.

You can take an object out of a clipping set while preserving the object.

To take an object out of a clipping set:

1. Expand the list for the clipping set on the Layers panel.

2. Create a new, blank layer, if necessary, to hold the object you will take out of the clipping set.

3. Drag the listing for a clipped object upward or downward to a different top-level layer.

➤ To remove an object from a clipping set by deleting it from the document, click its selection square on the Layers panel, then press Delete/Backspace.

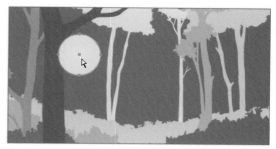

A *A new circle is moved over the clipping set.*

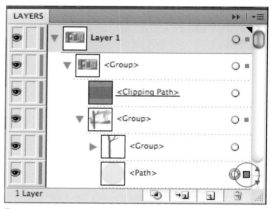

B *We moved the new path to the desired stacking position within the clipping set group.*

C *Once in a blue moon?*

Releasing a clipping set

When you release a clipping set, the masked objects regain their original attributes. The former clipping path is listed again as a standard path on the Layers panel, but it will have a stroke and fill of None (not its former attributes), unless you applied a color to it while it was a clipping path. If the clipping path was editable type, it is given a black fill and a stroke of None. The steps for releasing a clipping set differ depending on how it was created (whether it is object-level or layer-level).

To release an object-level clipping set:

1. Do either of the following:

   With the Selection tool ▶ (V), click any visible part of the clipping set.

   On the Layers panel, click the selection area for the group that contains the clipping set.

2. Do either of the following:

   Press Cmd-Option-7/Ctrl-Alt-7 (Object > Clipping Mask > Release).**A–B**

   Right-click in the document window and choose **Release Clipping Mask**.

   The group listing for the clipping set disappears from the Layers panel.

To release a layer-level clipping set:

1. On the Layers panel, ● click the layer that contains the clipping set to be released.

2. Click the **Make/Release Clipping Mask** button ⬚ at the bottom of the Layers panel.

A *This is the original clipping set. The large blue rectangle is functioning as a clipping path.*

B *This is the result after we released the clipping set. The blue rectangle has been restored to a standard object.*

The objects in your environment have various densities depending on the type of material they're made of and may also look different depending on how much light is filtering through or reflecting off them. Take a minute to study the shade on a lamp. You might say "The shade is white" when you describe it simply, but upon closer inspection, you may notice that rather than being a dense, uniform color, it contains several permutations of white. And if the bulb is switched on, the shade will look semitransparent rather than opaque.

By using Illustrator's transparency controls, you can add a touch of realism to your drawings. If you were to draw a window, for example, you could add a tinted, semisheer, diaphanous curtain on top of it. Draw some autumn leaves, and you could lower their opacity to make them look semitransparent. Abstract designs can be enhanced by opacity changes, too.

Changing an object's opacity or blending mode

You can change the opacity of any kind of object, even editable type. You can also choose a blending mode for any object to control how its colors blend with the colors in the underlying objects. Objects that you add to a group or layer adopt the transparency settings of that group or layer. The opacity and blending mode controls in Illustrator are chosen from the Transparency panel. A You can open this panel via the Window menu, or access it temporarily via the Opacity link on the Control panel or Appearance panel.

Continued on the following page

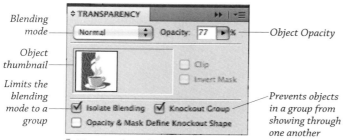

Blending mode —
Object thumbnail —
Limits the blending mode to a group —

Object Opacity
Prevents objects in a group from showing through one another

A *The controls on the Transparency panel*

To change the opacity or blending mode of an object, group, or layer:

1. Do one of the following:

   On the Layers panel, click the selection area or the target circle for an object, type, or placed image that you want to change the transparency settings for. **A–B** To edit the attributes of all the objects in a group or layer, click the target circle for that entity.

   With the Selection tool, select or isolate one or more objects in the document.

   Select some type characters with a type tool. (To change the opacity of just the fill or stroke of type, see the second task on the next page.)

2. Do either of the following:

   To change the opacity, enter or choose an **Opacity** percentage on the Control panel.

   To change the opacity and/or blending mode, click the Opacity link on the Control or Appearance panel to open a temporary Transparency panel. The contents of the selected or targeted layer, group, or object display in the thumbnail on the panel. Choose from the **Blending Mode** menu and/or move the **Opacity** slider. **C–D**

A This is the original artwork.

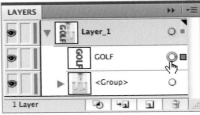

B On the Layers panel, we are clicking the target circle for the type object.

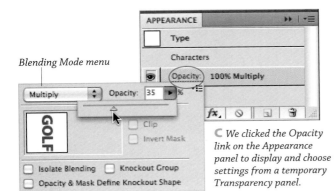

Blending Mode menu

C We clicked the Opacity link on the Appearance panel to display and choose settings from a temporary Transparency panel.

D We changed the opacity of the type object to 35% and chose a blending mode of Multiply.

To change the opacity or blending mode of an object's fill or stroke:

1. On the Layers panel, click the target circle for an object. (For a type object, follow the next set of instructions instead.)

2. On the Appearance panel,● expand the Fill or Stroke listing, then click Opacity to open a temporary Transparency panel. Move the **Opacity** slider **B** or choose from the **Blending Mode** menu.

If you want to change the opacity of the stroke on a type object separately from the fill, or vice versa (while keeping the type editable), follow these steps.

To change the opacity or blending mode of the fill or stroke in type:

1. Select an editable type object using the Selection tool or the Layers panel.**C** You're going to add an extra fill and stroke attribute, so make sure the type is large enough for both of those attributes to be visible.

2. At the bottom of the Appearance panel, click the **Add New Fill** button □ or press Cmd-/;Ctrl-/. A new fill attribute and stroke attribute are created.

3. Click the Fill color square and choose a fill color. Double-click the Stroke color square and choose a stroke color; also use the controls on the panel to adjust the stroke weight.

4. Double-click **Characters** on the Appearance panel. All the characters in the object will become selected.

5. Click the **Fill** listing on the Appearance panel, then click the Delete Selected Item button 🗑 on the panel; do the same for the Stroke listing. Now the fill and stroke of the Characters have a setting of None.

6. Click the **Type** listing at the top of the Appearance panel.

7. Expand the new Fill or Stroke listing, click the Opacity link, then choose from the **Blending Mode** menu and/or move the **Opacity** slider.**D**

EXPORTING TRANSPARENCY

To export a file that contains nondefault transparency or blending mode settings to another application, keep it in the Adobe Illustrator (.ai) format if the target application supports that format or, if it doesn't, save a copy of it in the PDF format (see pages 414–417).

A *We selected an object.*

B *We lowered the opacity of the object's fill, but not of its stroke.*

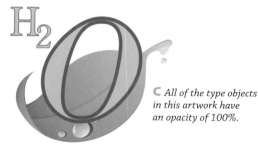

C *All of the type objects in this artwork have an opacity of 100%.*

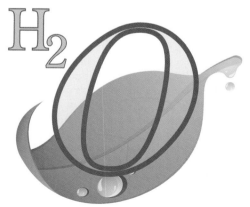

D *We reduced the fill opacity of the "0" to 30%, but left the opacity of the stroke at 100%.*

Controlling which objects the transparency settings affect

If you apply a blending mode to multiple selected objects, that mode becomes an appearance attribute for each object. In other words, the objects blend with one another and with any objects that are stacked below them. By applying the Isolate Blending option to a group, as in the instructions below, you can seal a collection of objects so they blend with one another but not with any underlying objects.

Note: The Isolate Blending option affects blending, not opacity. Whether this option is on or off, underlying objects will show through any objects in the artwork that aren't fully opaque.

To restrict a blending mode to specific objects:

1. On the Layers panel, ❧ expand the listing for a group of objects. Apply different blending modes (other than Normal) to all or some of the objects. **A** Click the target circle for the group.

2. On the Transparency panel, ❧ check **Isolate Blending. B** (If this option isn't visible, click the double arrowhead on the panel tab.) Nested objects within the targeted group will now blend with one another, but not with any objects below them. To view the effect of this setting, move the targeted group over other objects.

   Note: To reverse the effect, retarget the group, then uncheck Isolate Blending on the Transparency panel.

➤ This option can also be applied to a targeted layer.

➤ If Isolate Blending is checked for a group of objects and you export the Illustrator file to Photoshop (via File > Export, with the Photoshop .psd format chosen and the Write Layers option clicked), those objects will be converted to separate nested layers within a group in Photoshop, and their blending mode settings will be assigned to, and preserved in, the Photoshop layers.

➤ To learn about the opacity mask options on the Transparency panel, enter "opacity mask" in the search field in Illustrator Help.

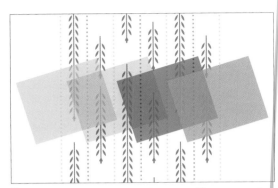

A *The original objects consist of a pattern fill in a rectangle, stacked below a group of rectangles. The blending mode and opacity setting of each rectangle are interacting with all the underlying layers.*

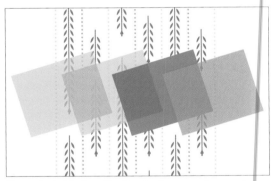

B *We checked Isolate Blending for the group of rectangles. Now the blending modes are affecting only the objects within that group. (Note that where objects in the group don't overlap one another, you can still see through them to the underlying pattern.)*

The Knockout Group option on the Transparency panel controls whether objects in a group or layer will show through (knock out) one another in the areas where they overlap. This option affects only objects within the same targeted group or layer.

To knock out objects:

1. Nest some objects within the same group or layer and arrange them so they partially overlap one another.

2. So you will be able to see how the Knockout Group option works, to some or all of the nested objects, apply opacity values below 100% and/or apply different blending modes (not Normal mode).

3. On the Layers panel, ● target the group or layer that the objects are nested within. **A**

4. On the Transparency panel, ● click the **Knockout Group** box once or twice, until a check mark displays. **B** With this option checked, objects nested in the group won't show through one another, but you will still be able to see through any semitransparent objects in the group to underlying objects.

   Note: To turn off the Knockout Group option at any time, target the group or layer that the option is applied to, then click the Knockout Group box once or twice until the check mark disappears.

➤ To select all the objects in your artwork that have the same blending mode or opacity, select an object that contains the attribute you're looking for, then choose Select > Same > Blending Mode or Opacity.

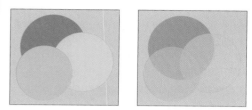

SELECTING INDIVIDUAL OBJECTS VERSUS TARGETING A GROUP OR LAYER

We selected multiple ungrouped objects in a layer (above left), then chose an Opacity setting of 65% (above right).* The opacity levels are compounded in the areas where the objects overlap (it's as though we piled up sheets of colored acetate). If we were to select one of the objects individually, the Transparency and Appearance panels would list its Opacity level as 65%.

Above, we targeted a group, then chose an Opacity setting of 65%.* The opacity levels aren't compounded in the overlapping areas. If we were to target an individual object in the group, its Opacity would be listed as 100%. (We would have gotten the same result had we targeted a layer.)

*This information also applies to blending modes.

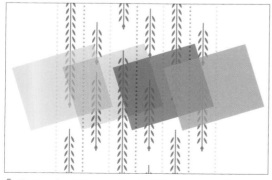

A *The Knockout Group option is off for the group of rectangles (and Isolate Blending is also unchecked).*

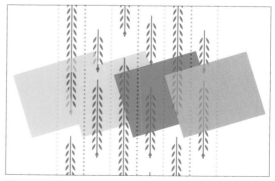

B *We checked the Knockout Group option. The rectangles are no longer transparent to one another or blend with one another (but they still blend with the underlying pattern).*

Using the transparency grid

Once you start changing the opacity settings for objects, you may find it hard to distinguish among those that have a light but solid tint and those that are semitransparent (have an opacity below 100%). With the transparency grid on, you will be able to see the gray-and-white checkerboard through semitransparent objects.

To show or hide the transparency grid:

Choose View > **Show Transparency Grid** (Cmd-Shift-D/Ctrl-Shift-D). A Repeat to hide the grid.

You can change the colors or size of the transparency grid to make it contrast better with the colors in your artwork.

To choose preferences for the transparency grid:

1. Deselect, then click **Document Setup** on the Control panel.

2. In the **Transparency** area, do either or both of the following: B

   Choose a **Grid Size** of Small, Medium, or Large.

   From the **Grid Colors** menu, choose Light, Medium, or Dark for a grayscale grid, or choose one of the preset colors. (Or to choose custom colors, click the top color swatch, choose a color in the Colors dialog, then click OK. Repeat for the second swatch.)

3. *Optional:* Check Simulate Colored Paper to have objects and placed images in your document look as though they're printed on colored paper. The object color will blend with the "colored paper," which will display as the background on all the artboards. The color in the top swatch (on the right side of the dialog) will be used as the paper color. You will need to hide the transparency grid to view the effect of this option (see the preceding task).

4. Click OK.

A semitransparent object

A light-colored, fully opaque object

A With the transparency grid showing, it's easy to see which objects are fully opaque and which are not.

B Use the Document Setup dialog to control how Illustrator represents transparency onscreen.

Objects that are stored on the Symbols panel can be placed singly or in multiples into any document. With symbols, you can create complex art quickly and easily. Illustrator supplies hundreds of predefined symbols, and you can also create symbols from your Illustrator artwork. They are stored on and accessed from the Symbols panel ♣.A

To place a single instance of a symbol onto the artboard, you drag it out of the panel or click the Place Symbol Instance button. To place multiple instances of a symbol (into what is called a symbol set), you either drag with the Symbol Sprayer tool or hold the tool down in one spot. To create a flowering forest and meadow, for example, you could create a few tree and flower instances by dragging symbols into your document and create a set of grass symbols by spraying.

In this chapter, in addition to learning how to create symbol instances and sets, you will learn how to replace, create, delete, and edit symbols, as well as expand symbol instances. And by using the Symbol Shifter, Scruncher, Sizer, Spinner, Stainer, Screener, and Styler tools (that's a tongue-twister!), you will change the stacking order, position, size, rotation angle, color tint, transparency, and style, respectively, of multiple symbol instances in a selected symbol set. These tools merely alter the way the instances look without breaking their link to the original symbol.

Continued on the following page

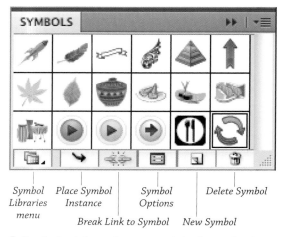

Symbol Libraries menu   Place Symbol Instance   Symbol Options   Delete Symbol

Break Link to Symbol   New Symbol

A *Use the Symbols panel to store symbols, place and replace symbol instances into your artwork, access symbol libraries, and open an options dialog for the symbolism tools.*

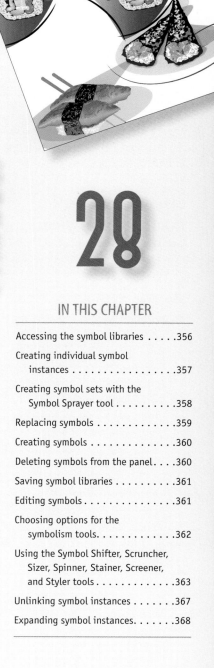

SYMBOLS

28

IN THIS CHAPTER

The reverse is also true: If you edit the original symbol that some instances are linked to, your changes will appear instantly in all those instances.

Another advantage of using symbols is efficient storage. For example, say you add a dozen instances of a parking symbol to a map design. Although all the multiple parking symbols will be visible in your document, Illustrator defines the object only once in the document code. This helps reduce the file size and speeds up printing and downloading. File size is especially critical when outputting to the Web in the SVG (Scalable Vector Graphics) or SWF (Flash) format. Because each symbol is defined only once in the exported SVG image or Flash animation, the size of the export file is kept relatively small and the download time is minimized.

Accessing the symbol libraries

The default assortment of symbols on the panel is limited. In these steps, you will learn how to access the Adobe symbol libraries and add some of those symbols to the Symbols panel for the current document.

To access symbols from other libraries:

1. Display the Symbols panel.

2. From the **Symbol Libraries** menu 🗂 at the bottom of the Symbols panel, choose a library. A separate library panel opens.**A**

3. Do any of the following:

   Click a symbol on the library panel. It will appear on the Symbols panel.

   To add multiple symbols from a library to the Symbols panel, click, then Shift-click a series of consecutive symbols or Cmd-click/Ctrl-click nonconsecutive ones, then choose **Add to Symbols** from the library panel menu.

   Drag a symbol from a library panel into your document; the symbol will also appear on the Symbols panel.

4. To browse through other libraries, click the Load Next Symbol Library button ▶ or Load Previous Symbol Library button ◀ at the bottom of the library panel.

➤ To change the Symbols panel display, from the Symbols panel menu, choose Thumbnail View, Small List View, or Large List View. When the panel is in Thumbnail View, you can identify symbol names via tool tips.

A *These are two of the many predefined symbol libraries that are available in Adobe Illustrator.*

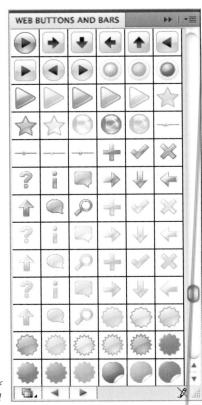

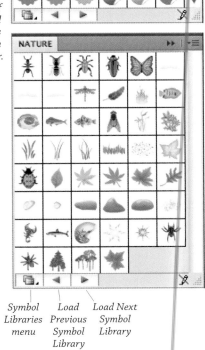

Symbol Libraries menu *Load Previous Symbol Library* *Load Next Symbol Library*

- To sort the symbols alphabetically by name, choose Sort by Name from the Symbols panel menu. You can also rearrange the symbols manually by dragging them.

- To control whether a library panel reappears when you relaunch Illustrator, check or uncheck Persistent on the library panel menu.

- To import symbols from another Illustrator file, from the Symbol Libraries menu ▦ on the Symbols panel, choose Other Library. Click the file that you want to import symbols from, then click Open. The symbols will appear in a symbol library panel; follow step 3 on the preceding page.

Creating individual symbol instances

In the steps below, you will create individual symbol instances. On page 358, you will place multiple instances of a symbol into a document quickly by using the Symbol Sprayer tool.

To create individual symbol instances:

1. Display the Symbols panel.🍀

2. Do either of the following:

   Drag a symbol from the Symbols panel onto an artboard.**A**

   Click a symbol on the Symbols panel, then click the **Place Symbol Instance** button ↘ on the panel. The instance appears in the center of the document window. When selected, its registration point displays (see the sidebar on page 359).★

3. Repeat the preceding step if you want to add more instances.**B**

- To demonstrate the fact that each instance is linked to the original symbol, place instances of a few different symbols into your document. Click one of the instances, then look at the Symbols panel. The thumbnail for that symbol becomes selected on the panel.

- To duplicate an instance (along with any transformations or other edits that you have applied to it), Option-drag/Alt-drag it in your document. The duplicate instance will be linked to the same symbol on the Symbols panel.

- If the View > Smart Guides feature is on (with the Alignment Guides preference enabled) and you drag an object near a symbol instance, Smart Guides will display for shapes within the instance.★ (In Illustrator CS4, Smart Guides would display only for the outer bounding box.)

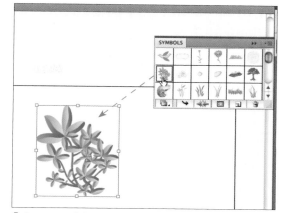

A *Drag a symbol from the Symbols panel onto an artboard.*

B *This artwork was created from symbols in the Nature library, which is shown on the preceding page.*

APPLYING ILLUSTRATOR COMMANDS TO SYMBOL INSTANCES AND SETS

- You can transform a symbol instance or set by manipulating its bounding box with the Free Transform or Selection tool.

- To undo all the transformations you have applied to a selected symbol instance or set, click Reset on the Control panel.★

- You can apply Appearance and Transparency panel settings to symbol instances and sets.

- Although you can apply effects (Effect menu) to symbol instances and sets, you'll achieve a smaller file size if you apply them to the original symbol instead.

Creating symbol sets with the Symbol Sprayer tool

The Symbol Sprayer tool sprays multiple instances of a symbol into a symbol set; it can also be used to delete instances from a set. It's easy and fun to use. You can choose from a slew of options for the tool (as we show you on page 362), but first do a bit of spraying with it, just to get the hang of it.

To create a symbol set with the Symbol Sprayer tool:

1. Choose the **Symbol Sprayer** tool (Shift-S).
2. On the Symbols panel, click a symbol.
3. Click to create one instance per click, or click-and-hold or drag to create multiple instances quickly. **A** The instances will appear in a set, within one bounding box.
4. *Optional:* To create another set, hold down Cmd/Ctrl and click outside the bounding box for the current set to deselect it, then click, or click-and-hold or drag to create the set.

To add more instances to an existing set, you must use the Symbol Sprayer tool (not the Place Symbol Instance button).

To add instances to a symbol set:

1. Do either of the following:

   Choose the Selection tool (V), then click an instance in a symbol set.

   Select a symbol set via the Layers panel.
2. Click a symbol on the Symbols panel. It can be a different symbol than those already in the set.
3. Use the **Symbol Sprayer** tool. **B**

To delete instances from a symbol set:

1. Select a symbol set with the Selection tool (click an instance in the set) or via the Layers panel.
2. If the set contains instances of more than one symbol, do either of the following:

   To restrict the deletion to instances of a particular symbol, click that symbol on the Symbols panel (or Cmd-click/Ctrl-click multiple symbols).

   To allow instances of any symbol to be deleted, click a blank area of the Symbols panel.
3. Choose the **Symbol Sprayer** tool.
4. With Option/Alt held down, click or drag within the set.

A *Create a symbol set with the Symbol Sprayer tool.*

B *To add instances of a different symbol to a set, select the set, choose the Symbol Sprayer tool, click the desired symbol on the Symbols panel, then drag within the set.*

Replacing symbols

When you replace a symbol in a solo instance or in a symbol set with a different symbol, any transformations, transparency changes, or edits made by a symbolism tool (e.g., by the Symbol Shifter or Sizer tool) that were applied to the original instance or set will appear automatically in the replacements.

To replace one symbol with another in an instance:

1. With the Selection tool ▶ (V), click an individual symbol instance in your document. A

2. On the Control panel, click the **Replace** thumbnail or arrowhead to open a temporary Symbols panel, then click a replacement symbol. B–C

When you apply a replacement symbol to a set, all the instances in the set are replaced with the new one, even if they originated from different symbols.

To replace the symbols in a symbol set:

1. Via the Selection tool ▶ (V) or the Layers panel, select a symbol set in your document.

2. Click a replacement symbol on the Symbols panel, then choose **Replace Symbol** on the panel menu.

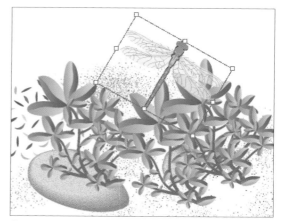

A *Click a symbol instance in your document.*

B *Click the Replace thumbnail or arrowhead on the Control panel, then click a replacement symbol on the temporary Symbols panel that opens.*

REGISTRATION POINT OR REFERENCE POINT ★

By default, the transformation of an individual symbol instance is calculated from its registration point. To have Illustrator calculate transformations from the point chosen on the Reference Point locator on the panel instead, uncheck Use Registration Point for Symbol on the Transform panel menu.

ALIGNING SYMBOLS TO THE PIXEL GRID ★

To align an individual instance or all the instances in a set to the pixel grid (for Web output), select the instance or set or select the symbol it is linked to on the Symbols panel. Choose Symbol Options from the panel menu, then check Align to Pixel Grid. Any new instances that you add to the set will also align to the grid. Note also that even when aligned to the grid, instances that have been scaled may not output crisply.

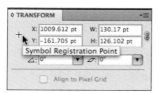

C *We replaced the dragonfly symbol with a fish symbol.*

Creating symbols

Now that you're acquainted with the Symbols panel, you're ready to create your own symbols. Any Illustrator object (or group of objects) can be made into a symbol: a standard path, a compound path, an embedded raster image, type — even another symbol. Well...within reason. If you're planning to spray the symbol densely all over a document, try to avoid creating it from complex artwork.

The object that you create a symbol from can contain a brush stroke, blend, effect, or graphic style. Those elements won't be editable in the symbol instances, but you can edit the original symbol at any time (see "Editing symbols" on the next page).

To create a symbol from artwork:

1. Create one or more objects, or a group of objects. Color and scale them as desired, and keep them selected.**A**

2. Choose the Selection tool ▶ (V), then Shift-click the **New Symbol** button ▣ on the Symbols panel (the Shift key prevents the original object from becoming an instance).

3. The Symbol Options dialog opens.**B** Enter a name for the new symbol, choose Type: **Movie Clip**, click a **Registration** point to establish a reference point (for transformations to be calculated from), check **Align to Pixel Grid** if the symbol will be used for Web output, then click OK.★ The symbol appears on the Symbols panel.**C**

Deleting symbols from the panel

If you try to delete a symbol from the Symbols panel that is in use in your document, you will be given a choice via an alert dialog to expand or delete the instances that were created from it.

To delete symbols from the Symbols panel:

1. Click a symbol on the Symbols panel, then click the **Delete Symbol** button 🗑 on the panel.

2. If there are no instances of the deleted symbol in your document, click **Yes** in the alert dialog.

   If the document does contain instances of the symbol, a different alert dialog appears. Click **Expand Instances** to expand the linked instances into standard objects, or click **Delete Instances** to delete the linked instances (or click Cancel to call the whole thing off).

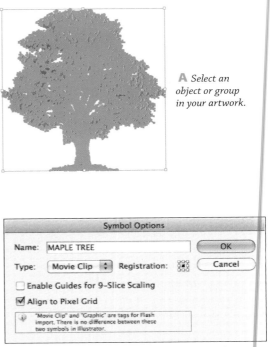

A Select an object or group in your artwork.

B In the Symbol Options dialog, enter a name for the new symbol, choose Type: Movie Clip, click a Registration point, and if desired, check Align to Pixel Grid.

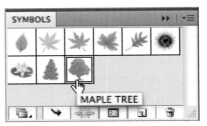

C The new symbol appears on the panel.

RENAMING SYMBOLS AND INSTANCES

► To rename a symbol, click the symbol on the panel, click the Symbol Options button ▦ at the bottom of the panel, then change the name in the dialog.

► If you're going to export your symbol artwork to the Flash (.swf) format, you can assign names to individual instances. Click an instance, then enter a new name in the Instance Name field on the Control panel.

Saving symbol libraries

If you save the symbols currently on the Symbols panel as a library, you'll be able to access them quickly at any time via the Symbol Libraries menu.

To save a symbol library:

1. Make sure the Symbols panel contains only the symbols to be saved in a library. From the Symbol Libraries menu ⬛ at the bottom of the Symbols panel, choose **Save Symbols**.

2. In the Save Symbols as Library dialog, type a name for the library, keep the default location (the Symbols folder), then click Save.

3. The new library (and other user-saved libraries) can be opened from the **User Defined** submenu on the Symbol Libraries menu. ⬛

Editing symbols

In these instructions, you will edit a symbol in the Symbols panel. When you do so — *beware!* — the edits will be applied to any and all instances in the document that the symbol is linked to.

To edit a symbol:

1. Do either of the following:

   Double-click a symbol on the Symbols panel. A temporary instance of the symbol appears in your document, in isolation mode.**A**

   Click an individual symbol instance in your document, click **Edit Symbol** on the Control panel, then click OK if an alert dialog appears. The instance is now in isolation mode.

2. Select and modify the object(s).**B**

3. Exit isolation mode by clicking the gray bar at the top of the document window. Your edits will be applied to the original symbol on the Symbols panel **C** and to any instances that are currently linked to that symbol. Any transformations that were applied to those instances before the symbol was edited will be preserved.

▶ To create a variation of a symbol, click the symbol on the Symbols panel, then choose Duplicate Symbol from the panel menu. Double-click the duplicate, then follow steps 2–3, above.

▶ To reposition the registration point for a symbol, after step 1 above, drag the instance relative to the stationary registration point. ★ When you exit isolation mode, all instances of that symbol will be repositioned automatically.

A *When we double-clicked a symbol, a temporary instance of it appeared in the document window, in isolation mode.*

B *We edited the temporary instance.*

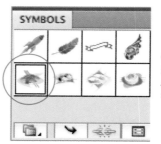

C *When we exited isolation mode, the symbol updated on the Symbols panel.*

REDEFINING A SYMBOL

To replace an existing symbol with one or more entirely different objects, hold down Option/Alt and drag the nonsymbol object over the symbol on the Symbols panel to be replaced (or select the object, click the symbol to be replaced on the panel, then choose Redefine Symbol from the panel menu). Any instances that are linked to that symbol will update accordingly.

Choosing options for the symbolism tools

In the Symbolism Tools Options dialog, you can choose global settings that apply to all the symbolism tools, as well as settings that apply just to individual tools. The global settings and the settings that apply to just the Symbol Sprayer are discussed below and in the sidebar on this page; the settings that are unique to other symbolism tools are mentioned on pages 364–367. Note: We recommend opening the tearoff toolbar for the symbolism tools, to keep them readily accessible.

To choose options for the symbolism tools:

1. *Optional:* If you want to change the density for an existing set or sets in your document, select them now via the Selection tool or Layers panel.

2. Double-click any symbolism tool to open the Symbolism Tools Options dialog.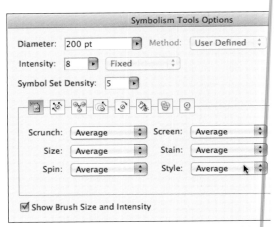

3. To specify a default size for all the symbolism tools, choose or enter a **Diameter** value.

4. The current choice on the **Method** menu applies to all the symbolism tools except the Symbol Sprayer and Symbol Shifter: **User Defined** modifies instances based on how the mouse is used, **Random** applies random values, and **Average** gradually equalizes the edits made by the tool.

5. To adjust the rate at which the sprayer creates instances or the tools produce changes, choose an **Intensity** value (1–10). Or to allow a stylus to control the intensity instead, choose any option from the menu except Fixed.

   ➤ To adjust the Diameter and Intensity values "on the fly," see the sidebar on the next page.

6. To specify how tightly all the instances will be packed within the set when the Symbol Sprayer tool is used, choose a **Symbol Set Density** value (1–10). Changes to this value will also affect the instances within any currently selected sets.

7. Check **Show Brush Size and Intensity** (as we do) to have a change to the current Diameter setting be represented by a ring around the tool icon, and a change to the Intensity setting be represented by a shade of that ring (black for high intensity, gray for medium intensity, and light gray for low intensity). With this option off, only the tool icon will display (no ring).

8. Click OK.

A *Use the Symbolism Tools Options dialog to choose global and individual properties for the eight symbolism tools. The menus in the lower portion of the dialog appear only when the Symbol Sprayer tool icon is clicked.*

USER DEFINED, DEFINED (FOR THE SPRAYER)

For each property of the Symbol Sprayer tool (Scrunch, Size, Spin, Screen, Stain, and Style), you can choose either Average or User Defined:

With Average chosen, the tool adds each new instance based on an average sampling of neighboring instances already in the set, within the current diameter of the brush cursor.

With User Defined chosen, the properties will be based on the following values:

➤ Scrunch (density) uses the original symbol density, not the current density values in the set.

➤ Size uses the original symbol size, not modified sizes in the set.

➤ Spin is controlled by the direction in which the mouse is moved.

➤ Screen applies instances at an opacity of 100%, not based on modified opacity values in the set.

➤ Stain applies the current fill color at a tint of 100%.

➤ Style applies the graphic style that is currently selected on the Graphic Styles panel.

Note: The settings chosen from the six individual tool menus are unrelated to the Method setting, which applies to all the symbolism tools except the Sprayer and the Shifter.

Using the Symbol Shifter, Scruncher, Sizer, Spinner, Stainer, Screener, and Styler tools

The tools discussed in this section modify the attributes of individual instances or instances within a set, such as their stacking position, location, size, orientation, color, transparency, or graphic style. Generic instructions for using the tools are given here. On the next four pages, you will find separate instructions for each tool.

To use the Symbol Shifter, Scruncher, Sizer, Spinner, Stainer, Screener, or Styler tool:

1. With the Selection tool ▶ (V), click a symbol instance or set.

2. Choose the **Symbol Shifter, Scruncher, Sizer, Spinner, Stainer, Screener,** or **Styler** tool. A

3. *Optional:* Choose settings via the Symbolism Tools Options dialog (see the preceding page) or use the shortcuts listed in the sidebar at right.

4. Do any of the following:

   Click an instance.

   Drag within a symbol set.

   Hold the mouse button down within a set.

   Note: If a selected set contains instances from more than one symbol, and one of those symbols is selected on the Symbols panel, modifications made by a symbolism tool will be limited to instances of that symbol. To remove this restriction so you can modify instances of different symbols, deselect all symbols first by clicking a blank area of the Symbols panel. Or to modify instances of multiple symbols, Cmd-click/Ctrl-click those symbols on the panel first.

➤ Although the symbolism tools affect all the instances in a set, by choosing a small brush diameter and by positioning your pointer carefully, you can control where a tool has the most impact. The effect is strongest in the center of the brush and diminishes gradually toward its perimeter.

➤ When using a symbolism tool (such as the Symbol Shifter, Scruncher, or Sizer) to modify a set, keep these two seemingly conflicting tendencies in mind: The tool will shift or scale the instances while also trying to maintain the existing density of the set. Yin and yang.

A *The Symbol Sprayer tool creates symbol instances; the other symbolism tools modify symbol instances in different ways.*

Symbol Sprayer | Symbol Scruncher | Symbol Spinner | Symbol Screener

Symbol Shifter | Symbol Sizer | Symbol Stainer | Symbol Styler

---

THE SHORTCUTS FOR QUICK DIAMETER AND INTENSITY CHANGES

When using a symbolism tool, you can quickly change the tool Diameter or Intensity without opening the Symbolism Tool Options dialog:

Increase or decrease the brush Diameter	Press or hold down] (right bracket) or [(left bracket)
Increase or decrease the brush Intensity	Press or hold down Shift-] or Shift-[

THE NEW REGISTRATION POINT ★

When you select symbol instances or edit them with a symbolism tool, a registration point displays in the center of each instance. If you want to move the registration point from the default location (the center), see the last tip on page 361.

The Symbol Shifter tool ✎

The Symbol Shifter tool has two functions. It either shifts instances in a set on the same plane, based on the direction in which the mouse is dragged, or changes their stacking order from front to back depending on where you click. Having the ability to bring instances forward or behind other instances would be useful, for instance (pun intended), in a set in which trees are obscuring some figures: You could move the trees closer together to create a forest, then bring the figures forward, in front of the trees.

➤ Drag within a symbol set to move instances sideways.

➤ Shift-click an instance within a symbol set to bring it in front of adjacent instances, or Option-Shift-click/Alt-Shift-click an instance to send it behind adjacent instances. **A–B**

The Symbol Scruncher tool ✎

The Symbol Scruncher tool either pulls symbol instances closer together or spreads them farther apart. You could use this tool on a symbol set of clouds or fish, for example, to pack the instances more densely or to pull them apart.

➤ For the most predictable results, double-click the Symbol Scruncher tool, and in the options dialog, choose Method: User Defined.

➤ To bring instances closer together, either drag with the tool or hold the mouse button down in one spot. To spread instances apart, hold down Option/Alt while dragging. **C**

A *We selected the symbol for the plant on the Symbols panel, and with the Symbol Shifter tool, we're dragging to the right.*

B *Some of the plants moved to the right, while the other instances stayed in place.*

C *With the same plant symbol selected on the Symbols panel, we're using the Symbol Scruncher tool (Method: User Defined) with Option/Alt held down to move the plants apart in all directions from the center of the cursor.*

The Symbol Sizer tool ⊘

Although you can't create instances of variable sizes with the Symbol Sprayer tool, you can scale existing instances by variable amounts with the Symbol Sizer tool.

The Method options for this tool are as follows: User Defined scales instances based on how you use the mouse, Average gradually makes variably scaled instances more uniform in size, and Random enlarges or shrinks instances by random amounts.

➤ With User Defined chosen as the Method for this tool, click on or drag across instances to enlarge them, **A–B** or hold down Option/Alt and click or drag to shrink them. Instances closest to the center of the tool cursor will scale the most.

The options dialog offers two extra features for this tool:

➤ Proportional Resizing prevents instances from being distorted as they are resized.

➤ Resizing Affects Density allows instances to move apart when they're enlarged or move closer together when they're scaled down. With this option off, the Sizer tries to preserve the existing density of the set. If the Resizing Affects Density option is on, you can disable it temporarily by holding down Shift as you drag with the tool.

The Symbol Spinner tool ⊘

The Symbol Spinner tool rotates instances (changes their orientation).

The Method options for this tool are as follows: User Defined rotates symbol instances in the direction in which the mouse is dragged, **C** Average gradually makes the orientation of all rotated instances within the brush diameter more uniform, and Random varies their orientation at random angles.

As you use this tool, temporary arrows appear in the direction the instances are being rotated. If the arrows are hard to see against your artwork, change the selection color for the layer the set resides in to a more contrasting color (double-click next to the layer name to open the Layer Options dialog).

A *This is the original symbol set.*

B *This is after we selected the plant symbol on the Symbols panel, then used the Symbol Sizer tool (Method: User Defined) to enlarge the plants in the foreground.*

C *And this is after we used the Symbol Spinner tool to rotate the plant instances (or was it a tropical wind?).*

The Symbol Stainer tool

The Symbol Stainer tool colorizes solid-color fills, patterns, and gradients in symbol instances with variable tints of the current fill color, while preserving existing luminosity values. This is a useful tool because you can't recolor instances via the usual Illustrator color controls. You could use the Stainer to vary the shades of green in foliage, the shades of blue-green in water, etc.

➤ Before using this tool, choose a fill color to be used for staining. Click on, or drag across, an instance or within a set to apply a tint of the current fill color. Continue clicking or dragging to increase the amount of colorization, up to the maximum amount.**A–B** Black and white aren't stained, and dark and light colors are stained the least.

➤ Hold down Option/Alt and click or drag to decrease the amount of colorization and restore more of the original symbol colors.

➤ To apply a new stain color only to instances that have already been stained without changing the existing levels of staining, choose a new fill color, then Shift-click or Shift-drag with the tool.

The Method options for this tool are as follows: User Defined gradually applies the current fill color, Average evens out the amount of any existing staining without applying more, and Random applies multiple stain colors.

Note: The results of the Symbol Stainer tool (and the Symbol Styler tool, which is discussed on the next page) increase the file size and diminish Illustrator's performance. Avoid using them if you're going to export your file in the Flash (.swf) format or if you're having problems with system memory.

The Symbol Screener tool

Use the Symbol Screener tool to fade instances and make them more transparent. The Method options for this tool are as follows: User Defined gradually increases or decreases the transparency of instances, Average gradually makes nonuniform transparency more uniform, and Random varies the transparency by random amounts (for a naturalistic look).

➤ With User Defined chosen as the Method for the tool, click and hold on or drag across instances to make them more transparent,**C** or hold down Option/Alt and click or drag across instances to restore their opacity.

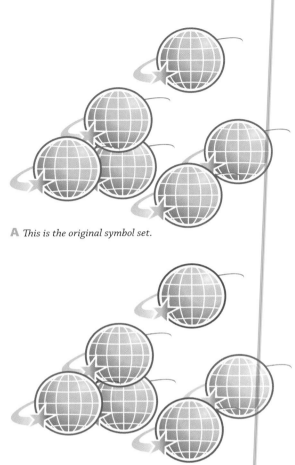

A *This is the original symbol set.*

B *We chose a blue as the fill color, then dragged the Symbol Stainer tool (Method: User Defined) across the set.*

C *With the Symbol Screener tool (Method: User Defined), we dragged across the original set (shown in* **A***, above).*

The Symbol Styler tool ⊘

The Symbol Styler tool applies the graphic style that is currently selected on the Graphic Styles panel to symbol instances. You can apply more than one style to the same symbol set.

➤ Use the Symbol Styler tool in this sequence: Select a symbol instance or set; choose the Symbol Styler tool; click a graphic style on the Graphic Styles panel or choose a style from the Style preset picker on the Control panel; then finally, click and hold on or drag across the instance or set to apply the style. **A–B** The longer you hold down the mouse, the more completely the style settings are applied. Pause to allow the results to process. This can take some time, even on a speedy machine.

➤ Shift-click or Shift-drag with the tool to gradually apply more of the same graphic style or a different style only to instances that have already been styled.

➤ With Option/Alt held down, click or drag to remove styling that you have applied.

The Method options for this tool are as follows: User Defined gradually increases or decreases the amount of styling; Average evens out the amount of styling that has already been applied without applying any new styling; and Random doesn't seem to make any difference, at least in our testing.

Unlinking symbol instances

When you break the link between an instance or set and the original symbol, the instance is converted to a normal object or group of objects.

To break the link between instances and a symbol:

1. With the Selection tool ▸ (V), click a symbol instance or set.

2. Do either of the following:

   Click the **Break Link to Symbol** button ⌗ at the bottom of the Symbols panel. You must use this method when breaking the link for a set.

   Click **Break Link** on the Control panel.

➤ To select all the instances of a particular symbol in your document, click the symbol on the Symbols panel, then choose Select All Instances from the panel menu.

A *This is the original symbol set.*

B *And this is the set after we applied a few different graphic styles with the Symbol Styler tool.*

Expanding symbol instances

When applied to a symbol set, the Expand command breaks the set apart into individual instances without breaking the link to the original symbol, and nests the resulting instances within a group on the Layers panel. When the command is applied to an individual symbol instance, it produces a very different result: It breaks the link to the original symbol and nests the resulting paths within a group and sublayer on the Layers panel.

To expand a symbol instance or set:

1. Select a symbol instance, multiple instances, or a symbol set. **A** Note that individual instances are listed by their symbol name on the Layers panel, whereas sets have the generic name "Symbol Set."

2. Choose Object > **Expand** (or choose Object > Expand Appearance if you applied an effect or graphic style to the symbol instance or set).

3. In the Expand dialog, **B** check **Object** and **Fill**, then click OK.

4. If you expanded a symbol set, **C** you can now use the Direct Selection tool ▹ to move the individual instances apart, or double-click the group with the Selection tool ▸ to isolate it, then modify the instances. In either case, they will remain linked to the original symbol.

   If you expanded an individual instance, **D** it will now be a group of paths within a sublayer (bearing the name of the former symbol), ★ and will be unlinked from the original symbol. **E** You can edit the group in isolation mode.

➤ If you use the Symbol Stainer tool on a symbol set and then expand the set, the instances that were modified by the tool will be given a numeric listing on the Layers panel.

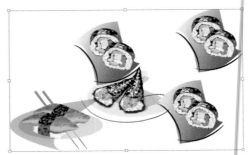

A *We selected a symbol set.*

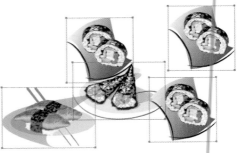

B *We checked Object and Fill in the Expand dialog.*

C *The Expand command divided the set into individual instances.*

D *We selected an individual symbol instance.*

E *We applied the Expand command to the individual symbol instance. (And then we moved the resulting paths apart.)*

Now that you know how to use the basic color controls in Illustrator, you're ready to explore the Recolor Artwork dialog. Using this complex and powerful feature, you can generate color schemes based on a new harmony rule or other variables, reassign specific colors in your artwork, save color groups to the Swatches panel, and, should the need arise, reduce the number of colors in your artwork. The practical applications for this dialog are wide-ranging, from improvising to see how your artwork might look in a different range of hues or tints or in a new group of coordinated colors to assigning colors that have been specified for a particular project.

Creating color groups via the Recolor Artwork dialog

There are so many features in the Recolor Artwork dialog, we have divided the instructions into four manageable tasks. In this first task, you will save the existing colors in your artwork as a group (to revert to, if necessary), then change all the colors in the artwork in various ways based on those original colors.

To create a color group via the Recolor Artwork dialog:

1. Select the objects to be recolored.**A**

2. Do either of the following:

   Click the **Edit or Apply Colors** button 🎨 at the bottom of the Color Guide panel.📑 The current color group on the panel is applied instantly to the objects, as a preview.

   Click the **Recolor Artwork** button 🎨 on the Control panel. The colors in the selected objects won't change yet.

3. At the bottom of the Recolor Artwork dialog, check **Recolor Art**.

Continued on the following page

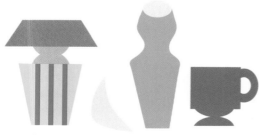

A *These are the original objects.*

4. If the list of Color Groups isn't displaying on the right side of the dialog, click the **Show Color Group Storage** button.**A**

5. To create a color group from the selected objects, click the **Get Colors from Selected Art** button ☞ at the top of the dialog, and enter a descriptive name in the adjacent field. Click the **New Color Group** button.☐⁺

   ➤ To restore the original object colors at any time, click the original color group or click the Get Colors from Selected Art button. This is useful because you can't undo individual editing steps while the dialog is open.

6. To try out some new colors on the selected objects, do any of the following:

   Choose a rule from the **Harmony Rules** menu at the top of the dialog. You may recognize the rules from the Color Guide panel.

From the **Color Mode** menu, choose **Global Adjust**, then move the Saturation, Brightness, Temperature,**B** and Luminosity sliders.

Click (and continue clicking) the **Randomly Change Color Order** button 🔀 or **Randomly Change Saturation and Brightness** button.🔀

7. Click the **New Color Group** button ☐⁺ to save the active color group to the list of Color Groups. (The colors also appear on the Color Guide panel.)

8. Continue to create as many new groups as you like by repeating the last two steps. You can also recolor your artwork at any time by clicking any group on the list of Color Groups.

9. Do either of the following:

   To save all new color groups to the Swatches panel and recolor the selected objects, click OK.

   To save all new color groups to the Swatches panel without recoloring the selected objects, uncheck Recolor Art, then click OK.

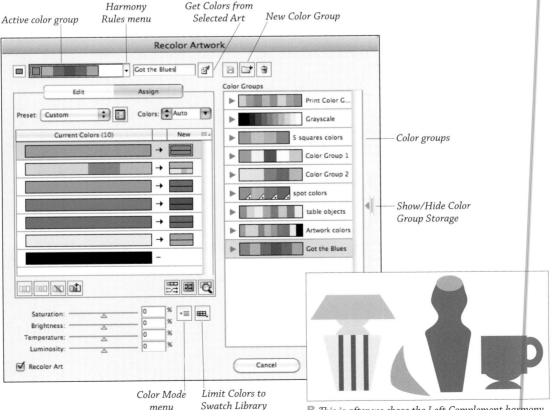

Active color group   *Harmony Rules menu*   *Get Colors from Selected Art*   *New Color Group*

Color groups

Show/Hide Color Group Storage

Color Mode menu   *Limit Colors to Swatch Library*

A *The Recolor Artwork dialog is complex — and powerful.*

B *This is after we chose the Left Complement harmony rule and reduced the Temperature value to a chilly −74.*

Using the color wheel in the Recolor Artwork dialog

Next, you will use the color wheel in the Recolor Artwork dialog to adjust the hue, saturation, and brightness of the colors in your artwork.

To use the color wheel in the Recolor Artwork dialog:

1. Select the objects to be recolored.**A**

2. On the Control panel, click the **Recolor Artwork** button.

3. In the Recolor Artwork dialog, check **Recolor Art**, then click the **Edit** tab.

4. If you don't see a color wheel, click the **Display Smooth Color Wheel** button.

5. Edits you make to the color wheel will affect the active color group. To choose that group, either click the **Get Colors from Selected Art** button at the top of the dialog or click a group in the list of **Color Groups**. If desired, you can also choose a new rule from the **Harmony Rules** menu.

   Each round marker on the color wheel represents a color in the current group, except for the largest marker, which represents the current base color.**B** The arrangement of the markers is based either on the colors in the selected artwork or on the current harmony rule.

6. When the dialog is first opened (or when the Get Colors from Selected Art button is clicked), the lines connecting the markers to the hub are dashed and the color markers can be moved independently of one another. If you click a color group or choose a harmony rule, the connecting lines become solid, the color relationships are preserved, and the color markers can be moved only as a unit. Depending on how you want to edit the artwork colors in the next step, click the **Unlink Harmony Colors** button to unlink the markers, or click the **Link Harmony Colors** button to link them.

7. From the **Color Mode** menu, choose **HSB**.

8. To adjust the colors, do any of the following:

   Drag a color marker around the wheel to shift it to a different **hue**. The Hue (H) slider moves accordingly. Drag a color marker inward or outward to adjust the **saturation** or **brightness**, depending on the current status of the Show

A *This is the original artwork.*

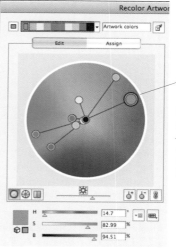

Base color

B *In this view of the Recolor Artwork dialog, the colors on the wheel are linked (the lines are solid).*

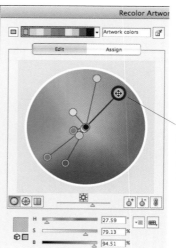

C *To shift all the hues, we're Shift-dragging the base color marker in a circular direction.*

Continued on the following page

Saturation/Brightness and Hue button. ☀ ☼ Hold down Shift while dragging to confine the adjustment to only the saturation, brightness, or hue (**C**, preceding page and **A**, this page).

Use the tool tip to find out whether the slider below the color wheel says "**Adjust brightness**" or "**Adjust saturation**." Click the button if you want to switch modes, then move the slider to adjust the overall color lightness or purity.

To edit a color or all colors (depending on whether they are linked), click a color marker in the wheel, then adjust the **Hue**, **Saturation**, or **Brightness** sliders at the bottom of the dialog. **B–C**

To add a new color (and marker) to the group, click the **Add Color** tool, ● then click a color area somewhere in the wheel.

To remove a color, right-click the marker to be removed and choose **Remove Color**.

To choose a replacement color, either double-click a color marker or right-click a marker and choose **Color Picker**. Click Color Swatches to view the colors that are currently on the Swatches panel, or click Color Models to display the process color controls. Choose a color, then click OK. **D** Another option is to right-click a marker and choose **Select Shade**, choose a shade, then click outside the shade box to close it.

9. Modify the group name, then click the **New Color Group** button. ⬚⁺ The new group displays on the list, but your original group colors are preserved.

10. Do either of the following:

   To save all new color groups to the Swatches panel and recolor the selected objects, click OK.

   To save all new color groups to the Swatches panel without recoloring the selected objects, uncheck Recolor Art, then click OK.

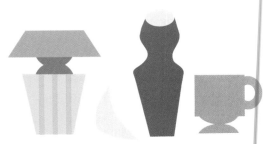

A *This is after we changed the hues.*

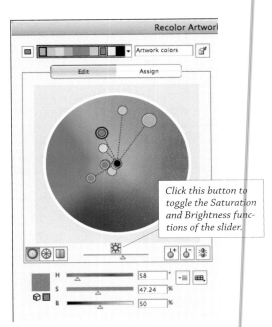

Click this button to toggle the Saturation and Brightness functions of the slider.

B *We clicked the Unlink Harmony Colors button, clicked the marker for the purple color, changed its hue to olive green, and lowered its Brightness value via the B slider.*

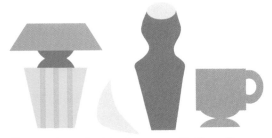

C *This is the result of the changes noted in Figure* **B**.

D *And this is after we replaced a few more colors.*

Assigning colors to artwork via the Recolor Artwork dialog

By using the Assign tab of the Recolor Artwork dialog, you can control which colors in a group will replace specific colors in your artwork. The features in this tab can be confusing, so it may take you a few tries to get the hang of using them. We will discuss the key features.

To assign colors to artwork via the Recolor Artwork dialog:

1. Select the objects to be recolored. 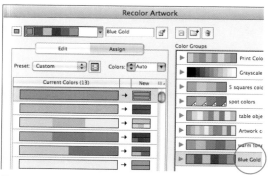A

2. On the Control panel, click the **Recolor Artwork** button. In the Recolor Artwork dialog, check **Recolor Art**.

3. Click the **Assign** tab. B Colors from the currently selected objects display in the Current Colors column, and colors from the active color group display in the New column.

4. To change the active color group, click a group on the **Color Groups** list on the right side of

the dialog and/or choose a new rule from the **Harmony Rules** menu at the top of the dialog. C

5. If the new active color group contains fewer colors than the number of current colors, the current colors that are closest in hue, shade, or tint to one another will be grouped in the same row and will be assigned the same New color (the total number of colors is thereby reduced). The solid colors and tints that are assigned to each row display in the New column. D

Click a color in the **New** column. A white border displays around it, and the row becomes selected. To edit the color, move the sliders at the bottom of the dialog; or double-click the color, then choose a color in the Color Picker; or click Color Swatches in the picker to choose from the colors that are on the Swatches panel.

Continued on the following page

A *This is the original artwork.*

Active color group

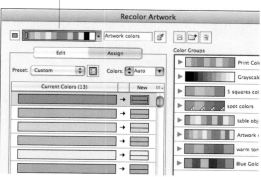

B *In the Assign tab of the Recolor Artwork dialog, colors from the selected artwork display in the Current Colors column and replacement colors display in the New column.*

C *We clicked the "Blue Gold" color group. Because that group contains fewer colors than the original artwork, Illustrator combined similar colors into multicolor rows in the Current Colors column.*

D *The new color group is assigned to the artwork.*

6. Do any of the following:

To reassign a color to a different New color, drag a block from the **Current Colors** column upward or downward to a different row. 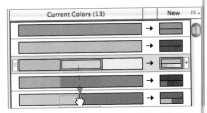A–B

To reassign a whole multicolor row to a different New color, drag the selector bar (located at the left edge of the row) upward or downward to a different row.**C**

To reassign a New color to a different Current Colors row, drag it upward or downward in the **New** column.

> ➤ To prevent a row of Current Colors from being reassigned to a New color, click the arrow between the two columns;**D–E** it becomes a dash. (To permit the colors to be assigned, click the dash.) To prevent an individual color from being reassigned, right-click it and choose Exclude Colors from the context menu.

7. *Optional but recommended:* Click the New Color Group button ▭⁺ to save the active color group to the Color Groups list (it will also appear on the Swatches panel when you exit the dialog).

8. Click OK.

> ➤ Although you could click the Save Changes to Color Group button 💾 to save your changes to the existing group, we prefer and recommend saving edited colors as a new group instead (as in step 7).

> ➤ To delete a color group, click the group, then click the Delete Color Group button. 🗑 To remove a color from a color group, you can expand the color group by clicking the arrowhead, if desired, then right-click the color to be removed and choose Remove Color. Like other individual edits in the dialog, this cannot be undone.

A *We are dragging a Current Color block to another row to assign it to a different New color.*

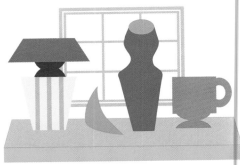

B *The tabletop and window are now blue-green.*

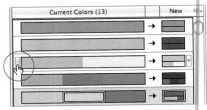

C *If you want to relocate a whole row, drag the selector bar upward or downward.*

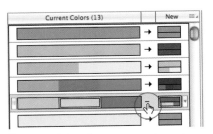

D *We are clicking between two columns to remove the arrow, and thereby prevent the colors in that row from being reassigned.*

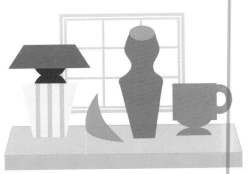

E *Because we removed the arrow, the original colors for that row are now redisplaying in the artwork.*

Reducing colors via the Recolor Artwork dialog

Yet another use for the Recolor Artwork dialog is to reduce the number of colors in your artwork. You may need to do this if you're planning to print your document using one, two, or three spot colors instead of the usual four process colors.

To reduce colors in artwork via the Recolor Artwork dialog:

1. *Optional:* If you're going to reduce the colors in your artwork to specific process or spot colors, make sure those colors are in your document's Swatches panel. Deselect your artwork, select the desired colors, then on the Swatches panel, click the New Color Group button.☐⁺

2. Copy your document using File > Save As.

3. Select the objects that you want to reduce the colors in.**A**

4. On the Control panel, click the **Recolor Artwork** button.

5. In the Recolor Artwork dialog, click the **Assign** tab. Also check **Recolor Art** to preview changes in your artwork (and to allow your changes to apply to the artwork when you exit the dialog).

6. Do either of the following:

   From the **Colors** menu, choose the desired number of colors.**B–C** That number of colors

Continued on the following page

A *The original artwork contains 13 colors.*

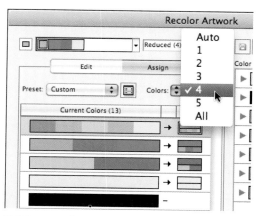

B *When you select a value from the Colors menu, the Current Colors are reduced to that number.*

EDITING DOCUMENT SWATCHES

Deselect your artwork, then double-click the icon for a color group on the Swatches panel to edit those colors in the Edit Colors dialog.

LIMITING COLORS TO A LIBRARY

To limit the colors on the color wheel and Harmony Rules menu to colors in a library, from the Limit Color Group to Swatch Library menu ▦ in the dialog, choose a library name (e.g., Color Books > PANTONE Solid Coated). The library name will now be listed above the menu button. To remove the restriction at any time, choose None from the same menu.

USING KULER SWATCHES

To recolor your artwork using color groups from the Kuler panel, add them to your document's Swatches panel (see page 131). The color groups will appear on the list of Color Groups in the Recolor Artwork dialog.

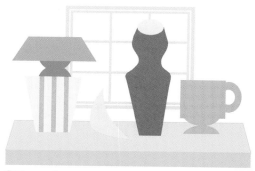

C *The number of Current Colors in the artwork was reduced to four colors in the original color group.*

from the active color group will be applied to your artwork. If you created a color group (in step 1), you can click that group now; if not, you can click a different color group or choose a new harmony rule.

From the **Preset** menu, choose **1**-, **2**-, or **3 Color Job**.**A** From the Library menu ▦, in the dialog that opens, choose a matching system library or choose None, then click OK. If you chose a library, the active color group will now be limited to colors from that library.**B–C**

➤ To reset the artwork colors to the active color group at any time, choose Auto on the Colors menu or choose Color Harmony on the Preset menu. Or to restore the original colors to your artwork, click the Get Colors from Selected Art button.🖌

7. Follow steps 5–6 on pages 373–374 to reassign and edit the New colors.

8. *Optional:* Click the New Color Group button 🗀⁺ to add the reduced color group (now the active color group) to the Swatches panel.

9. Click OK.

➤ To control whether black is recolored in your artwork or preserved, click the Color Reduction Options button 🔲 next to the Preset menu in the Recolor Artwork dialog. In the Recolor Options dialog,**D** check or uncheck Preserve: Black. This dialog contains the same Preset and Colors menus as the Recolor Artwork dialog, plus some Colorize Methods. To learn more about these options, enter "Reduce colors in artwork" in the search field in Illustrator Help.

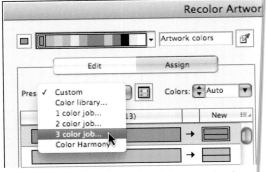

A *You can also reduce the number of Current Colors by choosing a Color Job option from the Preset menu.*

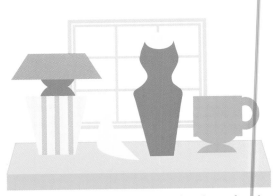

B *We chose the 3 Color Job preset to reduce the number of colors in the artwork to three.*

C *Here, we chose the 1 Color Job preset, with a more minimal result. We also changed the sole color in the New column to blue.*

D *In the Recolor Options dialog, you can specify whether instances of black in your artwork will be recolored or preserved.*

The preferences are default settings for various Illustrator features that apply to the current and future documents. Use this chapter as a reference guide to the options in the 12 panels of the Preferences dialog.

Opening the Preferences dialog

To open the Preferences dialog:

1. Do one of the following:

   Press Cmd-K/Ctrl-K.

   Deselect, then click **Preferences** on the Control panel.

   Choose a panel name from the **Preferences** submenu on the Illustrator/Edit menu.

2. To switch panels in the dialog, choose from the menu at the top of the dialog, or click Next or Previous.

RESETTING THE ILLUSTRATOR PREFERENCES

To restore all the default settings to the Illustrator preferences, quit/exit Illustrator, then relaunch the program while holding down Cmd-Option-Shift/Ctrl-Alt-Shift.

PREFERENCES

30

IN THIS CHAPTER

General Preferences

Keyboard Increment
This value is the distance by which a selected object moves when an arrow key is pressed on the keyboard. To move a selected object by 10 times this increment, press Shift-arrow.

Constrain Angle
This sets the angle (−360° to 360°) for the x and y axes. The default setting is 0°, which is parallel to the edges of the document window. Edits such as transformations, dialog and panel measurements, the construction of new objects, Smart Guides, and the grid are calculated relative to this angle. See the sidebar on the next page.

Corner Radius
This value controls the degree of curvature in the corners of objects drawn with the Rounded Rectangle tool. The default value is 12 pt. A value of 0 (zero) produces a right angle. This value can also be set in the Rounded Rectangle dialog.

Disable Auto Add/Delete
Checking this option disables the ability of the Pen tool to switch to a temporary Add Anchor Point tool when moved over a path segment on a selected path, or to a temporary Delete Anchor Point tool when moved over an anchor point on a selected path. You can hold down Shift to enable or disable this option.

Use Precise Cursors
When this option is checked, the drawing and editing tool pointers display as crosshairs instead of as the tool icon. To turn this option on temporarily when the preference is off, press Caps Lock.

Show Tool Tips
If this option is checked and you rest the pointer on an application feature, such as a tool, swatch, panel button, or icon, a brief description of that feature pops up onscreen. For some features, such as tools, the shortcut is also listed.

Anti-Aliased Artwork
When this option is checked, the edges of existing and future vector objects (not placed images) look smoother onscreen. It doesn't affect print output.

Select Same Tint %
When this option is checked, the Select > Same > Fill Color and Stroke Color commands select only objects that contain the same spot color and exact tint percentage as the currently selected object. When this option is off, the tint percentage is ignored as a criterion.

Append [Converted] Upon Opening Legacy Files
If this option is checked and you open a file that was created in Illustrator version 10 or earlier into a CS version of the application, Illustrator will append the word "[Converted]" to the file name.

Double Click To Isolate
If this option is checked and you double-click an object or group, the object or group is put into isolation mode and other objects become temporarily uneditable. To exit isolation mode, click the gray bar at the top of the document window or press Esc. This is a great feature, so we recommend keeping this option checked. To put an object (or group) into isolation mode when this option is off, select the object, then click the Isolate Selected Object button ⯐ on the Control panel.

Use Japanese Crop Marks
Check this box to have Illustrator use Japanese-style crop marks when outputting color separations.

Transform Pattern Tiles
If this option is checked and you use a transformation tool (such as the Scale tool) on an object that contains a pattern, the pattern will also transform. This option can also be turned on or off in the Move dialog, on the Transform panel menu, and in the dialog of any individual transformation tool.

Scale Strokes & Effects
Check this box to allow an object's stroke weight and effects to be scaled when you scale an object, such as via its bounding box, the Scale tool, the Free Transform tool, or the Transform panel. This option can also be turned on or off in the Scale dialog and on the Transform panel menu.

Use Preview Bounds
If this option is checked, an object's stroke weight and any applied effects are included as part of the object's height and width dimensions. It affects the Align commands, calculations on the Transform panel, and the dimensions of the bounding box. (If you were to select an object, apply a command on the Effect > Distort & Transform submenu, and then turn this feature on and then off, you would see a change in the size of the bounding box.)

Reset All Warning Dialogs
Click this button to allow warnings in which you checked "Don't Show Again" to redisplay when editing operations cause them to appear.

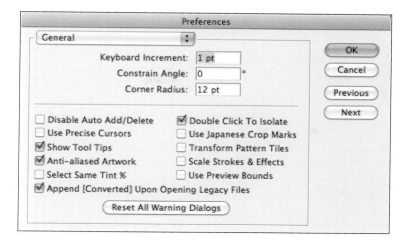

WHAT THE CONSTRAIN ANGLE AFFECTS

➤ Type tools, when creating a type object

➤ The Rectangle, Ellipse, and Graph tools (see the figure below)

➤ Some transformation tool dialogs (Scale, Reflect, and Shear, but not Rotate or Blend)

➤ The Gradient tool and the Pen tool (with the Shift key held down)

➤ Objects that are moved or duplicated with the Shift key held down or by pressing an arrow key

➤ The grid

➤ Smart Guides (Construction Guides and Transform Tools options)

➤ Readouts on the Info panel

As we draw an object, it conforms to the nondefault Constrain Angle of 25° that we specified in the Preferences dialog.

To establish a constrain angle based on an object that you have just rotated with the Rotate tool or the Free Transform tool, keep the object selected, note the Angle ⧍ readout on the Info panel, and enter that number as the new Constrain Angle value.

Selection & Anchor Display Preferences

Selection

Tolerance
Specify the range within which an anchor point becomes selected when you click near it with the Direct Selection tool. The default setting is 3 px.

Object Selection by Path Only
With this option checked, in order to select an object with the Selection or Direct Selection tool, you must click a path segment or anchor point. With this option unchecked, you can select a filled object in Preview view by clicking the fill area with a selection tool. We keep this option off.

Snap to Point
With this option checked, as you drag, draw, or scale an object, the pointer will snap to a nearby anchor point or guide within the range of pixels that you specify in the adjacent field (the default setting is 2 px). This option can also be turned on or off via the View menu.

Command/Ctrl Click to Select Objects Behind ★
With this option checked, you can Cmd-click/Ctrl-click to select objects in succession below the currently selected object, under the pointer.

Anchor Point and Handle Display

Anchors
Choose a display style for anchor points: small selected and unselected points, large selected points and small unselected points, or large selected and unselected points. We prefer the third option.

Handles
Choose a display style for the direction points on direction handles: small solid, large solid, or hollow.

Highlight Anchors on Mouse Over
If this option is checked and you move the Direct Selection tool over an anchor point, the point will become highlighted (enlarged) temporarily. We recommend checking this option, because it makes it easier to locate anchor points on a path.

Show Handles When Multiple Anchors Are Selected
Check this option to allow direction handles to display on multiple curve anchor points when they are selected with the Direct Selection tool, or uncheck it to prevent direction handles from displaying when multiple curve anchor points are selected.

➤ When multiple curve anchor points are selected with the Direct Selection tool, you can control the display of direction handles by clicking the Handles: Show Handles for Multiple Selected Anchor Points button ▗ or Hide Handles for Multiple Selected Anchor Points button ▪ on the Control panel.

Type Preferences

Size/Leading, Baseline Shift, and Tracking
Selected text is modified by this increment each time a keyboard shortcut is executed for the Size/Leading, Baseline Shift, or Tracking feature.

Type Object Selection by Path Only
When this option is checked, in order to select a type object with a selection tool, you have to click precisely on the type baseline. With this option unchecked, you can select a type object by clicking anywhere on or near it. Unless your artwork is very complex, we recommend keeping this option off.

Show Asian Options
Check this option to have options for Chinese, Japanese, and Korean language characters display on the Character, Paragraph, and OpenType panels, and on the Type menu.

Show Font Names in English
When this option is checked, Chinese, Japanese, and Korean font names display in English on the Font menus. When this option is off, two-byte font names display in their native characters.

Number of Recent Fonts
Choose the maximum number of recently chosen fonts (1–15) that you will permit Illustrator to list on the Type > Recent Fonts submenu.

Font Preview
Check this option to have font family names display in their actual fonts, along with the icon for the font type (e.g., TrueType, OpenType) for easy identification on the Type > Font menu (and, in the Mac OS,

also in the Find Font dialog and on the Character panel). Choose a Size for the font display of Small, Medium, or Large.

Enable Missing Glyph Protection
Check this option to enable Illustrator to preserve a glyph that's being used in your artwork if you switch to a font that doesn't support that glyph.

Use Inline Input for Non-Latin Text
Check this option to allow non-Latin characters to be typed directly into Illustrator (instead of having to use a separate dialog outside Illustrator).

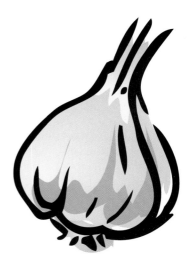

Units Preferences

To open this panel of the dialog quickly in the Mac OS, press Cmd-, (comma).

General
This unit of measure is used in entry fields in most panels and dialog boxes, and for the rulers in the document window. (See also the instructions below right.)

Stroke
This unit of measure is used on the Stroke panel and in the Stroke Weight field on the Control and Appearances panels.

Type
This unit of measure is used on the Character and Paragraph panels. (We use points.)

Asian Type
This unit of measure is used for Asian type. This menu is available only if Show Asian Options is checked in the Type panel of this Preferences dialog.

➤ When entering values in a dialog or panel, you can use any unit listed in the sidebar below, regardless of the current default units. A value entered in a nondefault unit will be converted to the default unit when you press Tab or Return/ Enter.

Numbers Without Units Are Points
If Picas is the current Units: General setting and this option is checked, a value entered in a field will be listed in points instead of picas and points. For example, if you enter "99", it will stay that way instead of being translated to "8p3".

➤ To enter a combination of picas and points in a field, separate the two numbers with a "p". For example, 4p2 equals 4 picas plus 2 points, or 50 pt. (for your information, 12 points = 1 pica; 6 picas = 1 inch).

Identify Objects By
Using the Variables panel, you can make objects dynamic by associating them with XML-based variables. Here you can specify whether dynamic objects are identified by their Object Name or an XML ID number. Consult with your Web developer regarding this option.

The measurement unit that you specify for a document in the Document Setup dialog (as described below) overrides the General unit that is specified for Illustrator in the Units panel of the Preferences dialog.

To change the measurement unit for the current document:

Do either of the following:

If the rulers aren't showing, press Cmd-R/Ctrl-R. Right-click either ruler and choose a unit from the context menu.

Cmd-click/Ctrl-click an artboard to deselect, then click **Document Setup** on the Control panel. Choose a unit from the **Units** menu, then click OK.

ABBREVIATIONS TO ENTER FOR UNITS	
Unit	Symbol
Points	pt
Picas	p
Inches	" or in
Millimeters	mm
Centimeters	cm
Q (a type unit)	q
Pixels	px

Guides & Grid Preferences

Guides

Color

For ruler guides, choose a color from the Color menu; or choose Other or double-click the color square to open the Colors/Color dialog, then choose a custom color. See page 107.

Style

For ruler guides, choose a Style of Lines or Dots.

Grid

Color

For the grid (View > Show Grid), choose a color from the Color menu; or choose Other or double-click the color square to open the Colors/Color dialog, then choose a custom color. See page 110.

Style

Choose a Style of Lines or Dots for the grid. Subdivision lines don't display for the Dots Style.

Gridline Every

Enter the distance between gridlines.

Subdivisions

Enter the number of subdivisions to be drawn between the main (darker) gridlines when the Lines Style is chosen for the grid. **A–B**

Grids in Back

Check Grids in Back (the default and recommended setting) to have the grid display behind all objects, or uncheck this option to have the grid display in front of all objects.

Show Pixel Grid (Above 600% Zoom) ★

To see a representation of the pixel grid onscreen to make it easier to position objects for Web output, check this option, turn on View > Pixel Preview, and choose a zoom level of 600% or higher for your document.

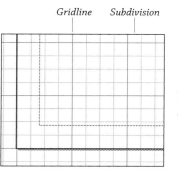

A *These gridlines have four subdivisions.*

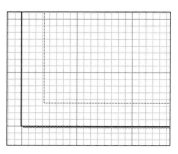

B *These gridlines have eight subdivisions.*

Smart Guides Preferences

To use Smart Guides, choose View > Smart Guides or press Cmd-U/Ctrl-U, and also turn off View > Snap to Grid and View > Pixel Preview.

Display Options

Color

Choose a color for Smart Guides from the menu; or choose Other from the menu to open the Colors/Color dialog, then choose a custom color. (This color can be different from the color that is specified for ruler guides in the Guides & Grid panel.)

Alignment Guides

If this option is on and you create, drag, or transform an object, straight lines will appear when the object's center point or edge meets the center, edge, or bounding box of another object, or the edge of the artboard or bleed region. Alignment guides also appear when you use the Artboard tool to create or move an artboard.

Anchor/Path Labels

Check this option to allow a "path," "anchor," or "center" label to display as you pass the pointer over that part of an object. And if the Alignment Guides option is also checked, an "intersect" label will display where two alignment guides intersect.

Object Highlighting

Check this option to have an object's path become highlighted as you pass the pointer over it. **A** This is helpful for locating paths that have a fill and stroke of None (e.g., clipping mask objects) or paths that are stacked behind other paths. The highlight color matches the selection color of the object's layer.

Measurement Labels

If this option is checked and you move the pointer (with the mouse button up) over an anchor point or the center point of a stationary object, the x/y location of that point displays in a gray label. When an object is moved, the label displays the x/y distance between the object and its original location. When a geometric drawing tool (e.g., the Rectangle tool) is used or a type tool is dragged to create a rectangle, a label displays the current width and height dimensions of the object. When a transformation tool is used, a label displays those transformation values (e.g., the angle of rotation or shear). When the Pen tool is used, a label displays the distance between the pointer and the last anchor point. And if you press Shift before clicking or dragging with a drawing tool, the starting location is listed.

Transform Tools

Check this option to have angle lines display as you transform an object with the Scale, Rotate, Reflect, or Shear tool. **B** Choose or create an angles set for the lines in the Angles area (see below).

Construction Guides

With this option checked, if you pass the mouse across an anchor point on a stationary object while drawing a new object or transforming an existing one, a diagonal angle line emerges from that anchor point. **C** To choose or create an angles set for construction guides, see below.

Angles

Choose a preset set of angles from the Angles menu or enter custom angles in one or more of the six fields (press Tab to update the schematic preview). If you enter custom angles, then choose a predefined set, and later choose "Custom Angles" on the menu, the last custom angles will redisplay in the fields.

Snapping Tolerance

The Snapping Tolerance is the distance (0–10 pt) within which the pointer must be from an object for a Smart Guide to appear. The default value is 4 pt. Activate the "snap" and specify a snap distance in the Selection & Anchor Display panel of this dialog.

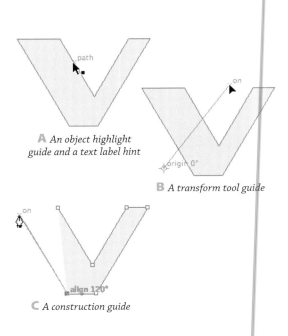

A An object highlight guide and a text label hint

B A transform tool guide

C A construction guide

Preferences

Smart Guides

Display Options

Color: ▭ Green

☑ Alignment Guides   ☑ Anchor/Path Labels
☑ Object Highlighting   ☑ Measurement Labels
☑ Transform Tools

☑ Construction Guides: 90° & 45° Angles

0   45   90
135

Snapping Tolerance: 4 pt

OK
Cancel
Previous
Next

Slices Preferences

These preferences apply to creating slices for Web output, a topic that is not covered in this book.

Show Slice Numbers
Check this option to have slice numbers display onscreen.

Line Color
From the Line Color menu, choose a color for slice numbers and for the lines that surround each slice.

Preferences

Slices

☑ Show Slice Numbers
Line Color: ▭ Light Red

OK
Cancel
Previous
Next

Hyphenation Preferences

Default Language

Choose the language dictionary for Illustrator to refer to when it inserts hyphen breaks.

Note: From the Language menu on the Character panel, you can choose a different hyphenation language dictionary for the current document.

Exceptions

Enter words that you want Illustrator to hyphenate in a particular way. Type the word in the New Entry field, inserting hyphens where you would want them to appear (or enter a word with no hyphens to prevent Illustrator from hyphenating it), then click Add. To remove a word from the list, click it, then click Delete.

Plug-ins & Scratch Disks Preferences

Note: For changes in this dialog to take effect, you must relaunch Illustrator.

Additional Plug-ins Folder

The core and add-on plug-ins that are supplied with Illustrator provide additional functionality to the main application, and are installed automatically in the Plug-ins folder inside the Adobe Illustrator CS5 folder.

If you have additional plug-ins that you want to use with Illustrator but want to store in a separate folder, you must use this Preferences dialog to tell Illustrator where that folder is located. Check Additional Plug-ins Folder, then click Choose. In the New Additional Plug-ins Folder dialog, locate and click the name of the desired plug-ins folder, then click Open. The new location will be listed in this panel.

Scratch Disks

Primary

Illustrator uses the Primary scratch disk as virtual memory when the amount of currently available RAM is insufficient for processing. From the Primary menu, choose an available hard disk, preferably your largest and fastest one. The default Primary scratch disk is Startup.

Secondary

As an optional step, choose an alternate Secondary hard disk to be used for extra virtual memory when needed. If you have only one hard disk, of course, you can have only one scratch disk.

User Interface Preferences

Brightness
Choose a gray value between Dark and Light for the background of the Illustrator panels, Application frame, Application bar, Control panel, and document tab.

Auto-Collapse Icon Panels
If this option is checked and you expand a panel that was collapsed to an icon, then click away from the panel, the panel will collapse back to an icon automatically. If this option is unchecked, panels that you expand will remain expanded.

Open Documents As Tabs
If this option is checked (the setting we recommend), multiple documents will dock as tabs into the same window when opened. If this option is unchecked, documents will open into separate floating windows.

File Handling & Clipboard Preferences

Files

If you work with a lot of linked files, you can enhance Illustrator's performance by checking **Use Low Resolution Proxy for Linked EPS**. Placed images will display as low-resolution bitmap proxies (screen previews, in plain English). With this preference unchecked, linked EPS images will display at their full resolution. (We keep this option off.)

The **Update Links** options control whether the link to image files that you have imported into an Illustrator document are updated automatically if you modify them in their original application (and then click back in your Illustrator document). From the Update Links menu, choose one of the following:

Automatically to have Illustrator update the linked images automatically, with no dialog opening.

Manually to leave the links unchanged. You can update individual links at any time via the Links panel.

Ask When Modified to have a dialog open, giving you the option to update the links (click Yes) or not (click No).

Clipboard on Quit

These options affect how Illustrator copies artwork to the Clipboard for transfer to other Adobe Creative Suite applications, such as Photoshop, Dreamweaver, or InDesign. Artwork is copied in the PDF and/or AICB format, depending on the current **Copy As** setting:

PDF preserves transparency information in the selection and is designed for use with Adobe programs, such as Photoshop.

AICB (No Transparency Support), a PostScript format, preserves the appearance of transparency (not transparency values) by flattening objects (dividing them into nonoverlapping objects). Click **Preserve Paths** to copy a selection as a collection of paths, or click **Preserve Appearance and Overprints** to preserve the appearance of the selection and any objects that are set to overprint.

Note: It is recommended that both PDF and AICB be checked to allow the receiving application to choose between the two and to allow the Paste dialog to display. The copying time is slightly longer and the memory requirements higher, but the likelihood that such elements as fills and effects will copy and paste accurately increases.

Appearance of Black Preferences

For added depth, black areas in a document can be printed using a combination of CMYK inks, rather than just black (K) ink. The first menu in this preferences panel controls how black areas in a document are displayed onscreen; the second menu controls how those areas print on an RGB or grayscale device.

Options for Black on RGB and Grayscale Devices

On Screen

Choose Display All Blacks Accurately to display blacks onscreen based on their actual values (pure CMYK black will display as dark gray), or choose Display All Blacks as Rich Black to display all blacks as rich blacks regardless of their actual CMYK values.

Printing/Exporting

Choose Output All Blacks Accurately to print blacks on RGB and grayscale devices using their actual K or CMYK values, or choose Output All Blacks as Rich Black to print all black areas as a mixture of CMYK values on those devices. This setting affects print output (not color separations), and it doesn't alter any values in the document. The Output All Blacks as Rich Black setting produces the darkest possible black on an RGB printer.

Description

To learn about any option in this panel, rest the pointer on it with the mouse button up, and read the pertinent information in the Description area.

Preferences

Appearance of Black

Options for Black on RGB and Grayscale Devices

On Screen: Display All Blacks as Rich Black

Printing / Exporting: Output All Blacks as Rich Black

Example of 100K Black ▪Aa   Example of Rich Black ■Aa

OK
Cancel
Previous
Next

Description

Displaying all blacks as rich black will show both pure blacks (100K) and rich blacks (blacks with mixed CMYK values) as rich black. This will not change color values in the document, but all blacks will appear as dark as possible.

Output tasks are divided into two chapters in this book: print output in this chapter, and export from Illustrator to other applications in the next. The tasks you will learn here include how to print using basic settings, print multiple artboards, specify a bleed region for objects that extend beyond an artboard, prepare a file for color separation, choose flatness settings, choose settings for downloading fonts, use color management in printing, choose overprint options, create and edit print presets, create crop marks, choose a resolution for outputting effects, and use the Document Info panel to get information about a file.

Using the Separations Preview panel, you will preview how the C, M, Y, and K color components in a CMYK document will separate to individual printing plates during the commercial printing process, check if a particular color is properly set to knock out or overprint other colors, and find out whether a specific black is a rich black (made from a mix of C, M, Y, and K) or a simple black containing only the K component.

Although Illustrator objects are described and stored as mathematical commands, when printed, they're rendered as dots. The higher the resolution of the output device, the more smoothly and sharply the lines, curves, gradients, and continuous-tone images in your artwork are rendered. The Print dialog contains all the controls needed for outputting a color proof on a desktop printer, and for preparing and printing color separations. To begin, you can output a document using just the basic settings in the dialog, as we show you on the following page. After that, you can delve into the many specialized and advanced controls that are offered.

PRINT

31

IN THIS CHAPTER

Print dialog: General options

There are seven option sets in the Print dialog. We'll show you how to print a document on a desktop color or grayscale printer using basic settings first.

To print a document on a black-and-white or color printer:

1. For printing on a desktop inkjet printer, choose File > Document Color Mode > RGB Color; for printing on a desktop color laser printer, check your printer documentation to verify the correct document color mode; for a grayscale printer, choose either CMYK Color or RGB Color mode.

2. Choose File > **Print** (Cmd-P/Ctrl-P). The Print dialog opens (**A**, next page). The settings you choose in this dialog will apply to all the artboards in the document.

3. From the **Printer** menu, choose from the list of printers that are available in your system.

   If you choose a PostScript printer, the PPD menu will display the default PPD (PostScript printer description) file for that printer. If your commercial printer supplied (and you installed) a custom PPD file for the chosen printer, you should choose that file name from the menu.

4. On the list of option sets on the left side of the dialog, click **General**.

5. In the **Copies** field, enter the desired number of print copies.

   Click **All** to print all the artboards in the document; or click **Range** and enter an artboard number or a range of numbers (separate consecutive numbers with a hyphen, or non-consecutive numbers with a comma). Each artboard will print on a separate sheet of paper.

   ➤ Use the navigation arrows below the preview to display a different artboard.

6. In the **Media** area, from the **Size** menu, choose **Defined by Driver** or a specific paper size.

   Click one of the orientation buttons to print the artboards vertically or horizontally on their respective pages, or check Auto Rotate ★ to let Illustrator orient any landscape artboards automatically to the longest dimension (usually the vertical dimension) of the current paper size.

7. *Optional:* If you need to change the position of the artboards relative to the paper, in the Options area, do any of the following:

   Click a different point on the Placement icon.

   Enter X and Y values to specify the position of the upper left corner of all the artboards.

   Drag an artboard in the preview area. Note that this will reposition the page borders for all the artboards. Only objects that display within the page area of an artboard will print.

8. For scaling, click **Do Not Scale** to print each artboard at its current size, even if it exceeds or is smaller than the paper size; or **Fit to Page** to scale each artboard to the current paper size; or **Custom Scale**, then enter a W (width) or H (height) value to scale all the artboards proportionally. (For nonproportional scaling, deactivate the Constrain Proportions button,⊌ then enter separate width and height values.) The default Scale value is 100.

   For oversized artboards, read about the tile options in the sidebar on the next page.

9. From the **Print Layers** menu, choose which layers are to be printed:

   Visible & Printable Layers to print only the visible layers for which the Print option is checked in the Layer Options dialog (which opens from the Layers panel menu). Note: To prevent an object from printing, you have to uncheck the Print option for its top-level layer before opening the Print dialog.

   Visible Layers to print only those layers that display a visibility icon on the Layers panel, regardless of their current Print option setting.

   All Layers to print all layers, regardless of the current Layers panel visibility and Print settings.

10. Click **Print** to print the artboards you selected in the Copies area using the current settings (or if you want to save the current settings with your document without printing it, click Done, then save the file). Each artboard prints on a separate piece of paper.

    ➤ Adobe recommends choosing all print settings from the Print dialog and bypassing the system options that display when you click the Page Setup or Printer button (in the Print dialog) in the Mac OS, or the Setup button in Windows.

    ➤ To save a file containing multiple artboards as a multipage PDF file, see page 414.

A *In the General option set in the Print dialog, choose basic print settings.*

PRINTING OVERSIZED ARTWORK AS TILED PAGES

To print oversized artwork onto multiple sheets of paper, in the General option set, check Ignore Artboards, then under Options, click Tile to tile the artwork based on the printer media size. From the menu, choose Full Pages to divide the artwork into whole pages (and choose an Overlap value, to overlap pages to account for the page margins), or choose Imageable Areas to divide the artwork onto a grid of pages. See the figures at right. Additional options are as follows:

► Drag in the preview to reposition the artwork relative to the tile breaks. To recenter the artwork at any time, click the center point on the Placement icon.

► Check Scale, then enter W and H values to scale the artwork to fit the tiles.

► To print select tiled pages, check Tile Range, then enter the desired range of pages.

Full Pages

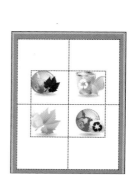

Imageable Areas

Next, we'll explore settings in the six other option sets of the Print dialog.

Marks and Bleed options

Use the Marks and Bleed set in the Print dialog to create marks at the edges of each artboard or the overall printable area (for use by a commercial printer), or to set parameters for objects that extend beyond that area, into the bleed region.

To include printer's marks in your printout:

1. To ensure that the printer's marks you opt for will fit within the respective page sizes for the artboards, in the General option set, do either of the following:

   Make sure the chosen output **Media: Size** is large enough to accommodate printer's marks for the largest artboard in the document.

   Click **Fit to Page** to allow the artwork and artboards to be scaled down, if necessary.

2. Click **Marks and Bleed** on the left side of the Print dialog (**A**, next page).

3. Under Marks, check **All Printer's Marks**, then keep checked or uncheck any of these options:

   Trim Marks adds thin lines that designate where the printed paper is to be trimmed. The trim marks align with the horizontal and vertical edges of each artboard or, if Ignore Artboards is checked in the General option set, with the tiled artwork.

   Registration Marks adds small circles that a commercial printer uses to align the printing plates. They are placed outside the corner of each artboard or, if Ignore Artboards is checked, outside the corner of the bounding box of the tiled artwork.

   Color Bars adds color swatches that a commercial printer uses to judge the density of inks. They are placed outside each artboard or, for tiled artwork, outside the sides of the bounding box.

   Page Information adds a text label, containing specs for the print shop, at the top of the printout.

4. From the **Printer Mark Type** menu, choose a style for printer's marks of Roman or Japanese.

5. *Optional:* Via the Trim Mark Weight menu, change the thickness for trim marks. You can also enter an Offset value (0–72 pt) for the distance between the trim marks (and other printer's marks) and the edge of each artboard

or the bounding box of the tiled artwork. If Fit to Page is checked, the artwork and artboards will be reduced in scale to accommodate a larger offset value.

If you position objects on any artboard so they extend into the bleed region (the area just beyond the edge of the artboard), they will print to the very edge of the final trimmed page. The bleed settings are set initially in the New Document dialog, and can be changed in the File > Document Setup dialog. For commercial printing, you should ask your print shop what bleed values to enter for their specific output device, either in one of the above-mentioned dialogs or here in the Print dialog.

To choose bleed values:

1. Follow steps 1–2 in the instructions at left.

2. If you have already set the bleed values for the document, in the **Bleeds** area, check **Use Document Bleed Settings** and skip the next step. If you haven't set bleed values yet, uncheck this option and follow the next two steps.

3. Do either of the following:

   With the link icon activated,🔗 enter a single bleed value (then press Tab) to use that value for all four sides of each artboard.

   To specify asymmetrical bleed values, deactivate the link icon,🔗 then enter separate **Top**, **Left**, **Bottom**, and **Right** values.

   Enter a low bleed value (or values) to move the edge of each artboard and its trim marks closer to the edges of the page; or enter a higher bleed value to move the edge of each artboard farther away from the edge of the page, and thereby print more of the objects that extend into the bleed region. If you chose Fit to Page in the General option set, this change will be reflected in the preview. If Ignore Artboards is checked and Tile: Imageable Areas is chosen in the General options, more tile pages may be added to accommodate a wide bleed region.

4. Choose any other print settings, then click **Print** to print the document; or to save the current settings with the document without printing, click Done, then save your file.

Print

Print Preset:	Custom
Printer:	HP LaserJet 4050
PPD:	Default (HP LaserJet 4050 Series)

Marks and Bleed

General
Marks and Bleed
Output
Graphics
Color Management
Advanced
Summary

Marks
☑ All Printer's Marks
  ☑ Trim Marks   Printer Mark Type: Roman
  ☑ Registration Marks Trim Mark Weight: 0.25 pt
  ☑ Color Bars   Offset: 0.0833 in
  ☑ Page Information

Bleeds
☑ Use Document Bleed Settings
  Top: 0 in   Left: 0 in
  Bottom: 0 in   Right: 0 in

Document: 8.83 in x 7 in
Paper: 8.5 in x 11 in

1 of 2 (1)

Page Setup...   Printer...   Cancel   Print   Done

A *In the Marks and Bleed option set in the Print dialog, choose marks for commercial printing and set values for the bleed region.*

Output options

During color separation, each color prints to a separate plate or piece of film. The settings in the Output option set of the Print dialog are used primarily by prepress operators to produce color separations for commercial printing (a separate plate is made for each process and spot color in the file), but some settings also apply to composite printing.

To output a composite print or color separations:

1. *Optional:* To preview how colors in your artwork are going to overprint and/or separate onto individual plates, click Done to exit the Print dialog, then follow the instructions for the Separations Preview panel on pages 402–403.

2. Make sure your file is in CMYK Color mode.

3. In the Print dialog, show the **Output** option set. A

4. On the **Printer** menu, choose a PostScript color or grayscale device that's available in your system.

   Before choosing other settings (steps 5–6), consult with your commercial printer.

5. From the **Mode** menu, choose one of the following:

   Composite to print all the colors on one sheet (from a desktop printer).

   Separations (Host-Based) to allow Illustrator to prepare the separations data and send it to the printing device.

   In-RIP Separations to have Illustrator send PostScript data to the printer's RIP* to allow that device to perform the separations. (Available options will vary depending on the type of printer you chose in step 4.)

6. For color separations, do all of the following:

   Choose **Emulsion: Up (Right Reading)** or **Down (Right Reading)**.

   Choose **Image: Positive** or **Negative**.

   From the **Printer Resolution** menu, choose the halftone screen ruling (lpi)/device resolution (dpi), that your commercial printer recommends.

   For more Output options, see the next page.

A *Use the Output option set in the Print dialog to choose settings for color separations.*

*The RIP (short for "raster image processor") converts vector data into printable dots.

You can also use the Output option set to turn printing on or off for individual colors or to convert individual spot colors, which normally print from a separate plate, to process colors, which print using the standard four plates.

To change the print setting for, or convert, individual colors in a document:

1. Display the **Output** option set of the Print dialog, then choose a separations option from the **Mode** menu.

2. The colors being used in the document are listed in the Document Ink Options area. **A** To prevent a particular process or spot color from outputting, click to remove its printer icon 🖨 in the left column.

3. Do either of the following:

   Check **Convert All Spot Colors to Process** to convert all spot colors in the document to process colors.

   To convert any specific spot colors to process colors, uncheck **Convert All Spot Colors to Process**, then click the spot color icon ⦿ on the list; it will change to a process color icon. ☒

4. *Optional:* To allow black fills and strokes to overprint any underlying colors, check Overprint Black. To learn more about overprinting, see page 403.

5. Choose settings in other option sets.

▶ Don't change the Frequency, Angle, or Dot Shape settings unless your commercial printer advises you to do so. You can click Reset to Defaults at any time to restore all the default ink settings.

▶ The Adobe Illustrator (.ai), Illustrator EPS (.eps), and Adobe PDF (1.4 and later) file formats preserve spot colors and apply overprinting correctly. Spot colors that are applied to objects, raster effects, and grayscale images will appear on separate plates, whether the document is output from InDesign or directly from Illustrator.

COLOR-SEPARATING A GRADIENT

▶ To color-separate a gradient containing one spot color and white onto one plate, use the spot color as the starting color in the gradient and use a 0% tint of the same spot color as the ending color.

▶ To color-separate a gradient that contains one spot color as the starting color and another spot color as the ending color, uncheck Convert All Spot Colors to Process (see step 3 at left), and ask your output service provider to assign screen angles to those colors.

▶ To convert a spot color in a gradient to a process color, click that color stop on the Gradient panel, then on the Color panel, click the Spot Color button. ⦿ The color will convert to the current document color mode of RGB or CMYK. Repeat for the other color stops.

Printer Resolution:	106 lpi /600 dpi ⧖

☐ Convert All Spot Colors to Process

☐ Overprint Black

Document Ink Options   (Reset to Defaults)

🖨		Document Ink	Frequency	Angle	Dot Shape
🖨	☒	Process Cyan	94.8683 lpi	71.5651°	Dot
🖨	☒	Process Magenta	94.8683 lpi	18.4349°	Dot
🖨	☒	Process Yellow	100 lpi	0°	Dot
🖨	☒	Process Black	106.066 lpi	45°	Dot
	⦿	C=42 M=82 Y=100 K=0	106.066 lpi	45°	Dot
🖨	☒	PANTONE 3275 C	106.066 lpi	45°	Dot
🖨	⦿	PANTONE Orange 021 U	106.066 lpi	45°	Dot

This spot color won't output because we removed its printing icon.

This spot color will output as a process color.

A *Using the Output option set in the Print dialog, you can prevent individual colors from outputting or convert specific spot colors to process colors.*

Graphics options

The Flatness setting in the Graphics option set of the Print dialog controls how precisely all the objects in a document are going to print on a PostScript printer. If your document doesn't print, one possible solution is to increase the Flatness setting.

To change the Flatness setting for a file, to facilitate printing:

1. Open a file that stubbornly refuses to print, choose File > **Print**, then display the **Graphics** option set (**A**, next page).

2. If **Automatic** is checked (under Paths), Illustrator will choose an optimal Flatness value for the chosen printing device. If you have encountered a printing error, uncheck Automatic, drag the **Flatness** slider a notch or two to the right (toward Speed), then try printing the file. If it prints, but with noticeably jagged curve segments, the Flatness value is too high. Lower it slightly by dragging the slider to the left (toward Quality), then print the file again.

➤ To display a numeric readout of the current Flatness setting, with Automatic unchecked, rest the pointer on the slider.

➤ If your document contains 30 or more Bristle brush paths, you will encounter an alert dialog when you try to print it. One solution is to select some of the offending paths and rasterize them via the Object > Rasterize command. ★

To choose settings for downloading fonts:

1. To manage how fonts are downloaded to the printer, open the Print dialog and display the **Graphics** option set.

2. From the **Download** menu in the **Fonts** area, choose one of the following options:

   None to have no fonts download. This is the preferred setting in a scenario where fonts are permanently stored in the printer.

   Subset to download only the characters (glyphs) that are being used in the document.

   Complete to have all the fonts being used in the document be downloaded at the beginning of the print job. This is effective if you are printing multiple artboards that use the same fonts.

3. Click **Print** to print the document; or to save your settings with the document without printing, click Done, then save the file.

FLATTENING VERSUS FLATNESS

Upon output, Illustrator flattens overlapping shapes in order to preserve the look of transparency. This is a different process from setting a Flatness value (as in the steps at left) to control how precisely the curve segments in a document will print; the higher the Flatness value, the less precisely the curves are printed.

OTHER GRAPHICS OPTIONS

Normally, Illustrator sets the PostScript (LanguageLevel 2 or 3) and Data Format (Binary or ASCII) options in the Graphics option set of the Print dialog based on what features the chosen printer supports, so you can ignore them. However, if your printer supports multiple options for those features, you will need to choose settings (decisions, decisions!). For PostScript, we recommend choosing LanguageLevel 3, because it contains the latest definitions for printing transparency and facilitates smooth shading (which helps prevent banding in gradients).

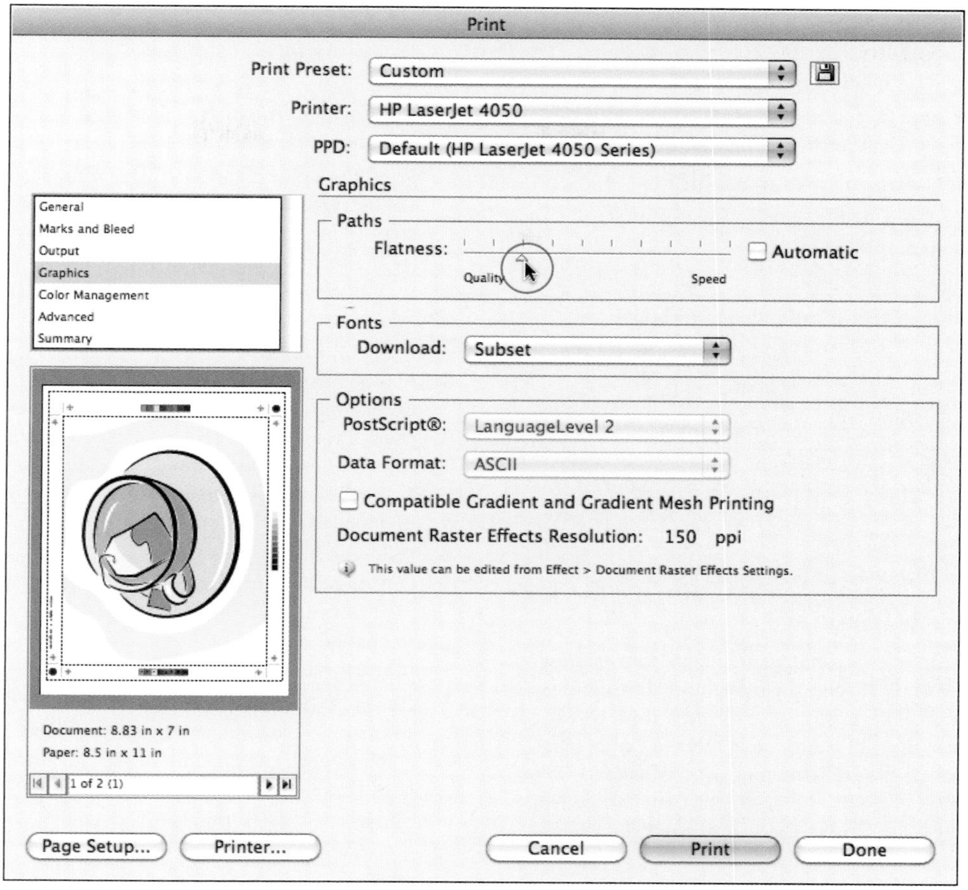

A *In the Graphics option set of the Print dialog, choose a Flatness setting and an option for how fonts are to be downloaded.*

Color Management options

Use the Color Management option set of the Print dialog to control how color conversions will be handled. Note: If you haven't learned about profiles and color settings yet, read Chapter 2 first.

To print using color management:

1. In the **Print** dialog, display the **Color Management** option set.**A**

2. Do one of the following:

   From the Color Handling menu, choose **Let Illustrator Determine Colors** (the preferred choice) to let Illustrator convert document colors to the printer gamut based on the chosen printer profile and send the converted data to the printer. The quality of the conversion will depend on the accuracy of the chosen printer profile. From the Printer Profile menu, be sure to choose the correct ICC profile for your printer, ink, and paper. Click Printer/Setup, then turn off color management for the printer driver. (See also Illustrator Help.)

   To turn off color management for your printer in the Mac OS, click Printer. If an alert dialog appears, click Continue. From the third menu (which you will need to expand the dialog to access), depending on your printer, choose Color Options or Color Management, then choose None or Off. Click Print to return to the Print dialog.

To turn off color management for your printer in Windows, see "Let your application manage colors when printing" in Illustrator Help, and refer to your printer manual.

From the Color Handling menu, choose **Let PostScript Printer Determine Colors** (if available) to send the color data to the printer and let the printer convert the colors to its gamut. If your printing device requires it, click Printer/Setup, then locate and turn on color management for the printer driver.

3. If you chose Let PostScript Printer Determine Colors and the document color mode is CMYK, check **Preserve CMYK Numbers** to preserve the color values of native objects and type in your artwork. For RGB documents, Adobe recommends keeping this option unchecked.

4. Leave the **Rendering Intent** on the default setting of Relative Colorimetric unless you or your output specialist have a specific reason to change it. (To learn more about the rendering intents, see the sidebar on page 22.)

5. Choose other print options, then click **Print** to print the document; or to save the current settings with the document without printing, click Done, then save your file.

A *Use the Color Management option set in the Print dialog to control whether Illustrator or your PostScript printer will handle the color conversion.*

Advanced options

In the Advanced option set of the Print dialog, you can choose overprint settings for fills and strokes in your artwork, to be used for color separations or composite printing.

To choose overprint and flattening options for output:

1. In the **Print** dialog, display the **Advanced** option set.**A**

2. Choose an option from the **Overprints** menu:

   Preserve to keep the file's overprint settings, for color separations.

   Discard to have the output device ignore the overprint settings.

   Simulate to create the visual effect of overprinting on a composite printer, for the purpose of proofing the document.

   Note: The Overprints setting chosen here doesn't override the current Overprint Fill or Stroke settings on the Attributes panel.

3. To specify how transparent objects will be flattened for printing, choose a resolution preset from the **Preset** menu (see step 2 on page 404), or click Custom, then choose settings in the Custom Transparency Flattener Options dialog (see page 405).

4. Choose other print settings, then click **Print** or **Done**.

Summary options

Finally, in the Summary option set, you can read a summary of the current Print dialog settings.

To view a summary of the current print settings:

1. In the Print dialog, display the **Summary** option set.**B**

2. Expand any listings in the Options window to view the settings, and read any pertinent alerts that display in the Warnings window.

3. *Optional:* Click Save Summary to save the current settings to a separate file (choose a location, then click Save).

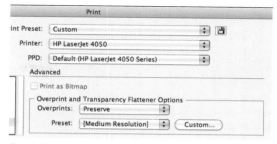

A *Use the Advanced option set in the Print dialog to choose overprint settings.*

B *In the Summary option set in the Print dialog, you can view a listing of the current print settings.*

ARE YOU USING A NON-POSTSCRIPT PRINTER?

If your document contains complex objects (such as gradients or soft-edged effects) and it generates a printing error from a non-PostScript or low-resolution printer, instead of printing the file as vectors, in the Advanced option set in the Print dialog, check Print as Bitmap. All the artwork in the document will be rasterized upon output. Note that the driver for the chosen printer controls whether this option is available, and most Macintosh printer drivers don't offer it.

Using the Separations Preview panel

The Separations Preview panel lets you see how the C, M, Y, and K color components in a CMYK document will separate to individual printing plates for commercial printing. You can use the panel to check that a color is properly set to knock out colors beneath it in the artwork, or to check whether a color is properly set to overprint on top of the other colors. You can monitor the use of spot colors in the artwork and verify that any spot color is set to knock out colors beneath it. And you can determine whether a specific black is a rich black (a mixture of C, M, Y, and K inks) or a simple black containing only the K component.

To view individual color plates in a CMYK document:

1. Open a CMYK document, **A** and display the Window > **Separations Preview** panel.

2. Check **Overprint Preview** at the top of the panel to make the list of process and spot colors accessible. With this option on, knockouts and overprints are simulated onscreen.

3. To view a single color plate, Option-click/Alt-click the visibility icon for a color listing. **B** Only the objects in which that color will print are now visible in the document. If an object contains 0% of that particular color, it will display as white.

   To redisplay all the process and spot color plates, Option-click/Alt-click the same visibility icon.

4. To restore the normal view of your artwork, uncheck Overprint Preview.

➤ The Separations Preview panel lists all the spot colors that are currently on the Swatches panel, whether they are being used in your document or not.

➤ If you want to reduce the number of colors in your document to, say, two or three colors, use the Recolor Artwork dialog (see pages 375–376).

➤ There is no set recipe for a rich black; each print shop uses their own formula to produce a warm, cool, or neutral black. Ideally, the shop will adapt the formula to the content of the artwork.

➤ A rich black should not be used for small type. The multiple inks could cause registration problems.

A *We will preview color separations for this artwork.*

SEPARATIONS PREVIEW

☑ Overprint Preview

- ☒ CMYK
- 👁 ☐ Cyan
- 👁 ☐ Magenta
- ☐ Yellow
- ☐ Black
- ☐ PAN

B *On the Separations Preview panel, we checked Overprint Preview and used the visibility controls to display just the Cyan and Magenta color plates.*

By default, when color-separating a CMYK document for commercial printing, Illustrator knocks out the colors below an object so its colors won't mix on press with the colors it overlaps. Because black ink is opaque (and normally is printed last), it may be preferable to set black fills or strokes to overprint on top of other inks instead. This will help prevent any potential gaps from showing due to the misregistration of printing plates. Note: Colors overprint on a commercial press but not on a composite print (proof) that you output from a PostScript color printer.

To preview and change black knockouts to overprints:

1. Open a CMYK document.

2. Display the Separations Preview panel,  and check **Overprint Preview**.

3. Click the visibility icon 👁 for **Black** to hide that color plate.

4. In Overprint Preview view, if a black object is previewing as white, it means that object is set to knock out any colors below it and that black won't mix with other inks on press. **A** Any black objects that aren't previewing as white are going to overprint on top of other colors, meaning their colors will mix with other inks. Note: If any black objects preview as gray, see the steps at right.

5. To make a black object overprint instead of knock out, with the Selection tool (V), click the white knockout area or the hidden object (use the Object Highlighting feature of Smart Guides to locate its path). Display the Attributes panel, then check **Overprint Fill** or **Overprint Stroke** (whichever part of the object you want to enable overprinting for). **B**

➤ Any object that is set to overprint will display differently in Overprint Preview view if it contains 0% of at least one of the four process colors.

➤ Checking Overprint Preview on the Separations Preview panel also causes the View > Overprint Preview command to be checked, and vice versa. When this feature is on, "Overprint Preview" is listed in the document window tab.

➤ In an RGB document, only spot colors can be set to overprint.

➤ To learn more about trapping and overprinting, see Illustrator Help, and be sure to consult with your output service provider.

To identify which objects contain rich or 100% K black:

1. Display the Separations Preview panel, and check **Overprint Preview**.

2. Click the visibility icon 👁 for **Black** to hide that color plate. Objects containing 100% K (black) ink will now be hidden; objects containing a rich black (made from a mixture of C, M, Y and K) will display as a shade of gray. If you want to confirm this, click a gray object with the Selection tool and view the CMYK settings on the Color panel.

3. Click in the visibility column for Black to redisplay that plate.

A *With the Black color plate hidden, black objects preview as white. They will knock out the colors beneath them.*

B *Overprint Fill is checked for the black objects and the Black plate is hidden. Those objects will overprint other colors, so they don't preview as a white knockout.*

Printing and exporting semitransparent objects

Any nondefault transparency settings* in objects, groups, and layers are preserved when a document is saved in a native Adobe Illustrator (ai) format (CS through CS5) or in the Adobe PDF (pdf) format if saved with a Compatibility setting of Acrobat 5 or higher.

When you print a file that contains nondefault transparency settings or when you export it in a nonnative format, Illustrator uses the current transparency flattener settings to determine how objects will be flattened and rasterized, in an effort to preserve the appearance of semitransparency.

During the course of flattening, if Illustrator detects a semitransparent object that overlaps an underlying object, it converts the overlapping area into a separate flat, opaque shape and leaves the remaining, nonoverlapping parts of the original objects as they are.

Although Illustrator tries to keep flattened shapes as vector objects, if the look of the current transparency settings can't be preserved in the flattened vector object, the program will rasterize those shapes instead. This happens, for instance, when two gradient objects containing nondefault transparency settings overlap; the resulting flattened shape is rasterized in order to preserve the complex appearance of transparency.

To control how transparency in a document will be flattened:

1. Deselect, then check **Document Setup** on the Control panel.

2. Do either of the following:

   In the Transparency area, **A** choose from the **Preset** menu: [High Resolution] for high-quality color separations or color proofs, [Medium Resolution] for desktop PostScript color prints or proofs, or [Low Resolution] for black-and-white desktop printing or Web output. Click OK.

   Click **Custom** to create a custom preset that will save with the file, then follow steps 2–8, starting on the next page.

TRANSPARENCY TO ADOBE INDESIGN

When saving artwork for InDesign CS5, use the native Adobe Illustrator (ai) format, which keeps transparency settings editable. Illustrator objects that contain nondefault transparency settings will interact correctly with the content of, and any transparency in, the InDesign layout, and InDesign will perform transparency flattening, if needed, during printing.

A *Using the Transparency controls in the Document Setup dialog, you can either choose an existing transparency flattener preset or create a custom one.*

*A blending mode other than Normal and/or an opacity level below 100%.

To choose custom transparency flattener options:

1. To open the Custom Transparency Flattener Options dialog, click **Custom** in the Transparency area of the Document Setup dialog or in the Advanced option set of the Print dialog.**A** Perform any of the following steps.

2. Move the **Raster/Vector Balance** slider to control the percentage of flattened shapes that will remain as vector shapes versus those that will be rasterized. Vector shapes print with cleaner, higher-quality color and crisper edges. This setting applies only to flattened shapes that represent transparency.

   If you choose a higher value (move the slider toward "Vectors"), more shapes will be flattened as vectors, although complex flattened areas may still be rasterized. Also, output processing will be slower and will require more memory. With the slider moved toward "Rasters," the file will output more quickly at a lower resolution. If a document is very complex and contains a lot of transparency effects, you may need to choose a low setting in order to achieve acceptable (not necessarily poor) quality output.

3. During the rasterization process, the output quality is calculated based on two resolution settings. To specify the resolution for rasterized line art and text, choose or enter a **Line Art and Text Resolution** value. For most purposes, the default resolution setting of 300 ppi is adequate, but for small text or thin lines, you should increase it to 600 ppi. Transparent type is flattened and preserved as type objects. Clipping and masking are used to preserve the look of transparency.

4. For the **Gradient and Mesh Resolution**, choose or enter the resolution for rasterized gradients and mesh objects. Gradients and meshes, like continuous-tone imagery, don't contain sharp details. The default value of 150 ppi is usually adequate; a value of 300 ppi would be considered high.

   When an EPS image is overlapped by an object that contains transparency, to ensure an accurate printout of the image and to preserve the look of transparency, embed the image into the Illustrator document by clicking the **Embed** button on the Control panel.

5. With the Raster/Vector Balance slider at a setting between 10 and 90, portions of type that are overlapped by an object that is semitransparent will be rasterized or converted to outlines, and may be thickened slightly. If those areas look noticeably different from type that isn't overlapped by semitransparency, try checking **Convert All Text to Outlines** to make all the type within a given font print in the same width, or move the type into its own layer above the semitransparent object.

6. With the Raster/Vector Balance slider at a setting between 10 and 90, any strokes that are overlapped by a semitransparent object will convert to outlines. As a result, very thin strokes may be thickened slightly and may look noticeably different from parts of strokes that don't overlap semitransparent objects. If you check **Convert All Strokes to Outlines**, the look of each stroke will be preserved for its entire

Continued on the following page

A Choose custom settings for your file in the Custom Transparency Flattener Options dialog.

length, but this option will also increase the number of paths in the file. An alternative to this option is to apply Object > Path > Outline Stroke to selected strokes in the artwork.

7. When a file is sent to print, any areas of semi-transparent objects that overlap other objects are flattened and rasterized. The flattened areas, however, won't match the exact path shapes of the objects. Also, the resulting flattened object may contain a combination of pixel and vector areas, and color discrepancies (called "stitching") between adjacent pixel and vector areas may result. If you check **Clip Complex Regions**, boundaries between raster and vector flattened shapes will fall exactly on object paths. This helps eliminate the signs of stitching but also slows down printing because the resulting paths are more complex. (Note: If an entire document is rasterized, no stitching occurs.)

8. Click OK.

Via the Flattener Preview panel, you can see in advance which semitransparent areas of a document are going to be flattened and which are not.

To preview the flattening settings for a document:

1. Display the Flattener Preview panel. ☑ A

2. From the panel menu, choose Show Options, and also check Detailed Preview. On the panel, click Refresh.

3. From the **Highlight** menu, choose what type of objects you want the highlight color to display on.

4. Move the **Rasters/Vectors** slider, if desired; check the appropriate options; then click Refresh again.

5. *Optional:* To save your settings as a preset, choose Save Transparency Flattener Preset from the panel menu, enter a name, then click OK.

➤ To learn more about flattening, enter "transparency flattener options" in the search field in Illustrator Help.

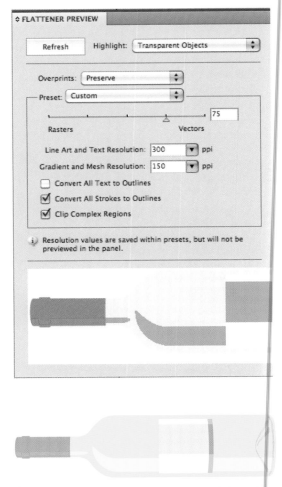

A *Use the Flattener Preview panel to preview different flattening settings for semitransparent objects in your document.*

FLATTENING OBJECTS SELECTIVELY

In addition to setting flattening options for an entire document, you can also set them for individual objects. When your document is ready to be output, save a copy of it. Select a semitransparent object and any objects that it overlaps in the artwork, choose Object > Flatten Transparency, then follow our steps on the preceding two pages. The command will flatten (divide) the areas where selected objects overlap into separate, nonoverlapping objects. Although the objects will still look semitransparent, the transparency settings will no longer be editable. (To learn about the "Preserve Alpha..." and "Preserve Overprints..." options, enter "Preserve alpha transparency" in the search field in Illustrator Help.)

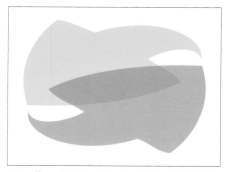

The yellow object in this artwork has a fill color and a stroke of None; the green object has a semitransparent fill and a stroke of None.

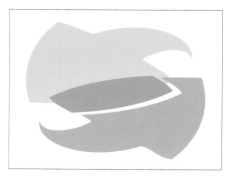

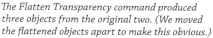

The Flatten Transparency command produced three objects from the original two. (We moved the flattened objects apart to make this obvious.)

Creating and editing presets

By creating a preset for your custom transparency flattener or Print dialog settings, you'll be able to apply the same settings to multiple files quickly. For example, instead of having to tediously choose custom flattener settings via the Print dialog (in the Advanced option set) or the Document Setup dialog (in the Transparency area) for individual files, you can create presets for different printing scenarios, and use them with any file. Presets can also be exported as files for use by other users.

To create or edit a transparency flattener, tracing, print, or PDF preset:

1. From the Edit menu, choose **Transparency Flattener Presets, Tracing Presets, Print Presets,** or **Adobe PDF Presets.** A preset dialog opens.

2. *Optional:* Click New to create a new preset; or click an existing preset, then click New to create a variation (copy) of it.

3. Enter a descriptive Name.

4. Choose settings. For the Transparency Flattener Preset Options dialog, follow the instructions on the preceding two pages; for the Tracing Options dialog, see pages 221–223; for the Print Preset Options dialog, see pages 392–401; or for the Adobe PDF Preset dialog, see pages 414–417. Click OK.

5. To edit an existing user-created preset (one that is not listed in brackets), click the preset name, click Edit, change any of the settings, then click OK. Note: You can also edit the settings for the [Default] print preset, but not for the predefined transparency flattener, tracing, or Adobe PDF presets.

6. Do any of the following optional steps:

   To view a summary of the settings in a preset, click the preset name, then view the information in the **Preset Settings** window.

   Click **Delete** to delete the currently selected user-created preset.

   Click **Export** to save the settings for the currently selected preset as a separate text file.

   Click **Import** to locate and open a settings file that was previously exported.

7. Click OK.

Producing crop and trim marks

Both the Crop Marks effect and the Create Trim Marks command place four pairs of crop marks around a selected object or group. Print shops use these marks as guides to trim the paper. If you move or transform an object that the Crop Marks effect is applied to, the marks will move accordingly, whereas if you do the same for an object that the Create Trim Marks command was applied to, the actual trim marks will stay where they are.

To produce crop marks for an object or group:

1. Select an object or a group.

2. From the Add New Effect menu *fx.* at the bottom of the Appearance panel or from the Effect menu on the Illustrator menu bar, choose **Crop Marks**. Crop marks will appear at the four corners of the selection.**A–B**

▶ To delete a set of crop marks, select or target the object or group the effect is applied to. On the Appearance panel, click the Crop Marks effect listing, then click the Delete Selected Item button.

▶ You can apply the Crop Marks effect to a selection of multiple groups (such as a series of business cards), but bear in mind that the effect will produce a separate set of crop marks around each group.

To produce trim marks for one or more objects or a group:

1. Select one or more objects or groups. The Create Trim Marks command will produce one set of trim marks around the entire selection.

2. Choose Object > **Create Trim Marks.** ★ Trim marks will appear at the four corners of the overall selection. The trim marks will be listed as a group (containing eight separate lines) on the Layers panel.**C**

▶ To delete a set of trim marks, delete its group listing from the Layers panel.

▶ Marks that are produced by the Trim Marks option in the Marks and Bleed option set of the Print dialog will align with the edges of each artboard or the tiled artwork, and are independent of any marks that are produced by the Crop Marks effect or Create Trim Marks command.

A We applied the Crop Marks effect to this group of objects.

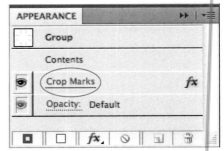

B The Crop Marks effect appeared as a listing on the Appearance panel.

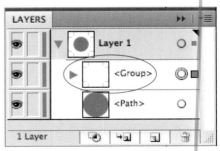

C The Create Trim Marks command produced a group listing on the Layers panel.

THE REGISTRATION COLOR

The [Registration] color is used for crop marks and other marks that a commercial printer uses to align the printing plates. Objects in this color will output to all the separation plates.

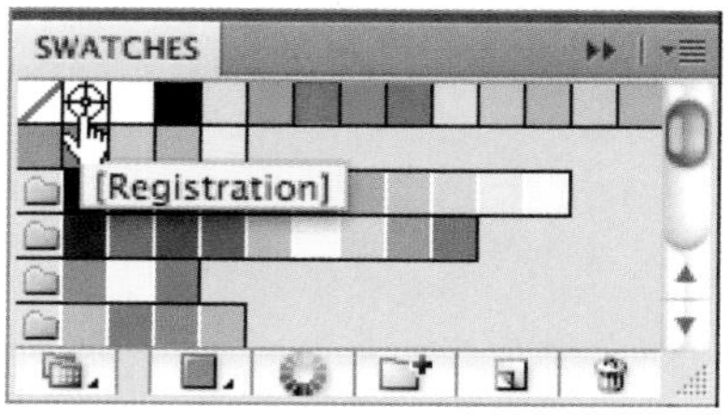

The [Registration] color appears on every plate when a file is color-separated.

Choosing a resolution for effects

All the Photoshop effects in the lower half of the Effect menu will rasterize automatically upon export or output, as will the following effects on the Illustrator Effects > Stylize submenu: Drop Shadow, Inner Glow, Outer Glow, and Feather. By following these steps, you can specify a resolution value for all the raster effects in a document.

To choose a resolution for raster effects:

1. With your Illustrator file open, choose Effect > **Document Raster Effects Settings**.A

2. In the dialog, click another **Resolution** option, or click **Other** and enter a custom resolution value. Choose the resolution needed for output — 72 ppi for onscreen or Web output, or 300 ppi (usually) for print output. The higher the resolution, the slower the output processing time, but the higher the quality of the rasterized effects.

➤ To learn more about the options in this dialog, see page 206.

➤ The resolution value from this dialog is also listed in the Graphics panel of the Print dialog.

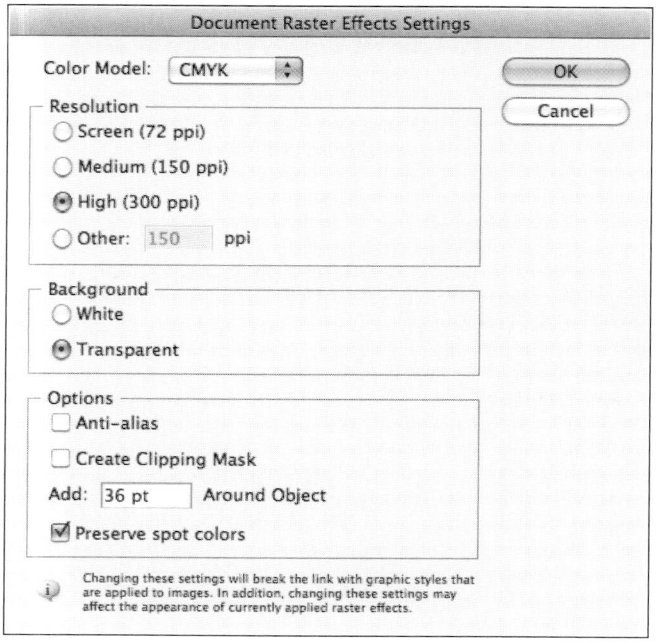

A *In the Document Raster Effects Settings dialog, choose a Resolution setting for raster effects.*

Using the Document Info panel

On the Document Info panel, you can view data about the entire document or about just a selected object or objects.

To display information about an object or a whole document:

1. *Optional:* Select the object (or objects) that you want to read info about.

2. Display the Document Info panel. 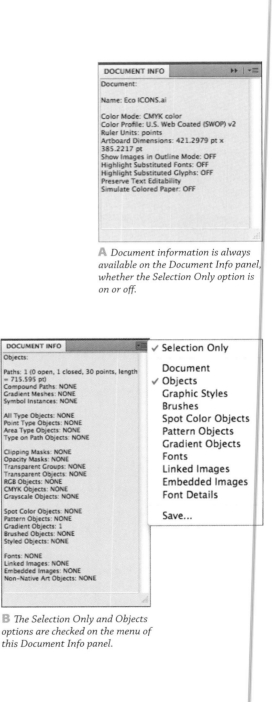 A

3. To display information about a currently selected object, on the panel menu, make sure Selection Only has a check mark, B or uncheck that option to display information pertaining to all the objects in the document.

4. Do either of the following:

   Choose **Objects** from the panel menu to view a tally of various kinds of items in the document, such as paths, compound paths, clipping masks, opacity masks, transparent objects, gradients, etc., as well as the number of colors, fonts, and linked images used.

   Choose another category from the panel menu to view data about such document features as graphic styles; brushes; objects containing spot colors, patterns, or gradients; fonts; linked or embedded images; or font details (PostScript name, font file name, language, etc.).

5. *Optional:* If Selection Only is checked on the panel menu, you can click another object in the document to view data about that object in the currently chosen category.

6. *Optional:* Choose Save from the panel menu to save the currently displayed information as a text document. Choose a location in which to save the text file, rename the file, if desired, then click Save. Use the system's default text editor to open the text document. You can print this file and refer to it when preparing the document for output, such as high-resolution printing.

A *Document information is always available on the Document Info panel, whether the Selection Only option is on or off.*

B *The Selection Only and Objects options are checked on the menu of this Document Info panel.*

In this chapter, you will learn how to save files in various formats for export to other applications. You can save your file in the Illustrator EPS format for a layout or drawing application, the Adobe PDF format for a wide variety of output media, or the GIF or JPEG format for a Web layout application. For export to Adobe Photoshop, you can keep it in the Adobe Illustrator (ai) format to be opened as a Smart Object, or save a copy of it in the Photoshop (psd) format, among other options.

To export a document to a CS version of InDesign, we recommend keeping it in the native Adobe Illustrator (ai) format. In the Illustrator Options dialog, which opens from the File > Save As dialog, check Create PDF Compatible File so the file will include both Illustrator and PDF data. The Adobe Illustrator (ai) format preserves transparency and live features, such as effects.

To prepare an Illustrator file for a drawing or page layout application that doesn't read native Adobe Illustrator files, save it in either the Illustrator EPS format (as in the steps below) or the PDF format (see pages 414–417).

Saving files in the EPS format

The EPS (Encapsulated PostScript) format saves both vector and bitmap objects and is supported by most illustration and page layout programs. Files saved in the Illustrator EPS format can be reopened and edited in Illustrator.

To save a file in the EPS format:

1. With a file open in Illustrator, choose File > Save As (Cmd-Shift-S/Ctrl-Shift-S) or Save a Copy (Cmd-Option-S/Ctrl-Alt-S).

2. From the Format/Save as Type menu, choose **Illustrator EPS (eps)**. Choose a location for the file. If the document contains multiple artboards that you want to save as separate files, check **Use Artboards**, then click **All** (to save each artboard as an EPS file labeled with the artboard name, ★ plus a master EPS file containing all the artboards) or click **Range** and enter a range of artboards. Or to combine all the artboards into one file, uncheck Use Artboards. Click Save.

Continued on the following page

EXPORT

32

If the file contains spot colors that aren't fully opaque, an alert dialog will appear (**A**, next page). If you allow those spot colors to be converted to process colors by another application, you may get unpredictable results. Either click Cancel and convert the spot colors in Illustrator, or click Continue if you know that the color conversion won't be an issue.

3. The EPS Options dialog opens (**B**, next page). Keep the Version setting as **Illustrator CS5 EPS**. (Or to save the file in an earlier version of the program, read the sidebar on the next page.)

4. Under Preview, choose a **Format**:

   None for no preview. The image won't display onscreen in any other application, but it will print.

   TIFF (Black & White) for a black-and-white preview.

   TIFF (8-Bit Color) for a color preview.

   Note: Regardless of which preview option you choose, color information will be saved with the file, and it will print normally from Illustrator or any other application that it is imported into.

   If you chose the TIFF (8-Bit Color) format, click **Transparent** to save the file with a transparent background, or **Opaque** to save it with a solid background.

5. If the artwork contains overprints (applied via the Attributes panel), from the **Overprints** menu under Transparency, choose **Preserve** to record the overprint information into the EPS file, or **Discard** to save the EPS file without the overprint information.

   If the artwork uses blending modes or contains transparency, those areas will be flattened. From the **Preset** menu, choose [High Resolution], [Medium Resolution], or [Low Resolution] as the preset to be used for flattening transparency (see page 404). The [High Resolution] preset produces the best-quality printout.

   Take a moment to read any messages ⓘ that display in the **Warnings** area regarding the current settings. For example, you may learn that the document contains transparency, which requires flattening, or learn how overprinting in transparent areas will be handled.

6. Under Fonts, check **Embed Fonts (for Other Applications)** to embed any fonts being used in the artwork into the file so they'll display and print properly on any system, even where they aren't installed. Check this option if your Illustrator file contains type and will be imported into a layout application.

7. Check any of these optional boxes, if available:

   Include Linked Files to embed a copy of any linked images being used in the artwork into the Illustrator EPS file. This option increases the file size but allows you to print the EPS file from other programs without the original (linked) images. (In any case, don't discard the original file that the image is linked to; you will still need it to edit or print the file from Illustrator.)

   Include Document Thumbnails to include a thumbnail of the file for previewing in the Open or Place dialog in Illustrator.

   Include CMYK PostScript in RGB Files to convert RGB objects in the EPS file to CMYK colors. This option makes it possible to print the file from programs that output only CMYK colors. Note: If you reopen the EPS file in Illustrator, RGB colors will still be in that original mode.

   Compatible Gradient and Gradient Mesh Printing to include instructions for older PostScript devices to print gradients and gradient meshes. Unless you have gotten a printing error when printing gradients or meshes in this particular file, leave this option unchecked.

8. Choose whichever **Adobe PostScript** option conforms to your printing device: LanguageLevel 2 or LanguageLevel 3. Choose LanguageLevel 3 if the file contains meshes and will be output to a Level 3 printer.

9. Click OK. If you didn't check Include Linked Files and your file contains placed, linked images, an alert dialog will appear (**C**, next page). Click Embed Files or Preserve Links.

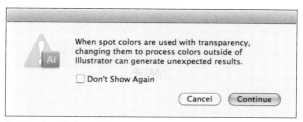

A *This alert dialog will appear if you save a file in the Illustrator EPS format and objects containing spot colors in the file are either semitransparent or are stacked below other semitransparent objects.*

EPS Options

Version: Illustrator CS5 EPS

Preview
Format: TIFF (8–bit Color)
● Transparent ○ Opaque

Transparency
Overprints: Preserve
Preset: [Medium Resolut...] [Custom...]

Fonts
☑ Embed Fonts (for other applications)

Options
☐ Include Linked Files
☐ Include Document Thumbnails
☑ Include CMYK PostScript in RGB Files
☐ Compatible Gradient and Gradient Mesh Printing
☑ Use Printer's Default Screen
Adobe PostScript®: LanguageLevel 2

Warnings
⚠ Only fonts with appropriate permission bits will be embedded.
⚠ The document contains artwork that requires flattening.

OK
Cancel

B *Choose preview, transparency, font, and other settings in the EPS Options dialog.*

SAVING ILLUSTRATOR FILES IN EARLIER EPS FORMATS

If you need to save a copy of a file in an earlier Illustrator EPS format, in step 3 on the preceding page, choose the desired Illustrator CS EPS option, and be sure to read the messages in the Warnings area at the bottom of the dialog. The CS EPS, CS2 EPS, CS3 EPS, and CS4 EPS formats preserve transparency, effects, and type features; the CS2 through CS4 formats also preserve live features, such as live blends and Live Paint. However, saving a file in any of these earlier formats may cause some loss of editability, as well as some changes to area type. Understandably, saving a file to a non-CS version of Illustrator will result in an even greater loss of editability.

Linked files will not be saved as a part of this document. Choose "Embed Files" if you want this document to be self-contained or you intend to open or print it from another application.

Embed Files   Cancel   Preserve Links

C *This alert dialog will appear if you didn't check Include Linked Files in the EPS Options dialog and your file contains placed, linked images. This is your second chance to include those placed files.*

Saving files in the Adobe PDF format

The versatile Adobe PDF (Portable Document Format) is a good choice for output to the Web and to other applications and platforms. It is also useful for showing Illustrator artwork to clients, as the only software a user needs in order to view a PDF file is Adobe Reader 7 or later (which is available as a free download) or, in Mac OS X, the Preview application; the viewer doesn't need Adobe Illustrator. Plus, your artwork will look as it was originally designed, because this format preserves all object attributes, groups, fonts, and type.

PDF files can also be viewed in Adobe Acrobat, in which edits and comments can be applied. Acrobat versions 5 and later support transparency; Acrobat versions 6, 7, and 8 also preserve layers; and Acrobat 8 offers support for 3D features. This format also supports document text search and navigation features.

Note: The following steps are long-winded (yawn). If you like, you can end your journey at the end of step 3, after choosing one of the default presets.

To save a file in the Adobe PDF format:

Save as PDF using a preset

1. With your file open in Illustrator, choose File > Save As or Save a Copy.

2. From the Format/Save as Type menu, choose **Adobe PDF (pdf)**, and choose a location for the file. To save each artboard as a separate page, click **All**; or to save only specific artboards as pages, click **Range** and enter a range. Click Save. The Save Adobe PDF dialog opens (**A**, next page).

3. From the **Adobe PDF Preset** menu, choose a preset that is best suited for the intended output medium (the default Acrobat version for the chosen preset will display on the Compatibility menu):

   ➤ You can read information about the currently chosen preset in the Description window.

   Illustrator Default creates a PDF file that can be reedited in Illustrator or placed into InDesign or QuarkXPress. Fonts are embedded, and bitmap images aren't downsampled or compressed.

   High Quality Print creates PDF files for desktop printing and proofing devices.

   PDF/X-1a: 2001, **PDF/X-3: 2002**, and **PDF/X-4: 2008** create Acrobat-compatible PDF files that are checked to ensure that they comply with specific printing standards, to help prevent printing errors. The PDF/X-1a and PDF/X-3 presets don't support transparency (files are flattened); the PDF/X-3 and PDF/X-4 presets support embedded color profiles and color-managed workflows; the PDF/X-4 preset also supports transparency (the artwork isn't flattened). If you need the file to remain fully editable in Illustrator, don't choose a PDF/X preset.

   Press Quality produces high-quality files for commercial printing. This preset embeds subsets of fonts automatically, uses JPEG compression at an image quality setting of Maximum, preserves CMYK colors, and converts RGB colors. To accommodate all this data, however, the resulting file size will be large.

   Smallest File Size creates compact, low-resolution PDF files for output to the Web, e-mail, etc. Fonts are embedded and colors are converted to RGB.

   If you're satisfied with the settings in the preset you have chosen, click Save PDF. Or if you need to choose custom settings, proceed with any or all of the remaining steps.

Save as PDF using custom settings

1. We recommend leaving the Standard setting alone. From the **Compatibility** menu, you can choose which version of Adobe Acrobat you want your file to be compatible with. Note that not all applications can read Acrobat 7 or 8 files.

   If you choose any nondefault settings for a preset, the word "(Modified)" appears next to the preset name on the Adobe PDF Preset menu.

2. In the General option set, under **Options**, check any of the following, if available:

   Preserve Illustrator Editing Capabilities to save all the Illustrator data in the PDF file. This option will enable the file to be reopened and edited in Illustrator but also will increase its size and limit how much it can be compressed.

   Embed Page Thumbnails to save a thumbnail of each artboard into the file for display in the Open and Place dialogs in Illustrator.

   Optimize for Fast Web View to enable parts of the file to display in a Web browser while the file is downloading.

View PDF After Saving to have your system's default PDF viewer (most likely Adobe Reader or Adobe Acrobat) launch automatically and display the file after you click Save PDF (in step 9). We like to keep this option checked.

If the chosen Compatibility option is Acrobat version 6, 7, or 8, check **Create Acrobat Layers from Top-Level Layers**. This will preserve the editability of top-level layers if the file is opened in one of those versions of Acrobat.

To choose even more custom options, follow the remaining steps in this task. Otherwise, click **Save PDF**.

3. For online (not print) output, click **Compression** in the list of option sets on the left side of the dialog, then choose options to control how bitmap images and raster effects are compressed

Continued on the following page

A *These are the [Illustrator Default] settings in the General option set of the Save Adobe PDF dialog.*

(downsampled) to reduce the file size. **A** From the menus under Color Bitmap Images, Grayscale Bitmap Images, and Monochrome Bitmap Images, choose an interpolation method to be used for downsampling:

Do Not Downsample preserves the size of any bitmap images.

Average Downsampling To divides the image into sample areas, averages the pixels in each area, and substitutes those average values for the original values.

Subsampling To replaces a sampled area with pixel data taken from the middle of that area. It produces a smaller file size but may also diminish the smoothness of continuous tones.

Bicubic Downsampling To replaces the sampled area with an average of the area's values and produces smoother continuous tones than the Average Downsampling option.

For each of the chosen interpolation methods, enter the desired **ppi** resolution and the minimum resolution threshold an image must have in order to be downsampled.

Also choose a compression type from each of the **Compression** menus: None for no compression, one of the JPEG options (which cause data loss), or ZIP (the ZIP option is usually lossless). To learn more about these options, enter "compression options for pdf" in the search field in Illustrator Help. If you choose an Automatic option, Illustrator will choose the appropriate compression settings for the artwork — Automatic (JPEG) for the widest compatibility, or Automatic (JPEG2000) for the best compression.

4. For information about the Marks and Bleeds option set, see pages 394–395.

A *Choose Compression options in the Save Adobe PDF dialog.*

5. The Output set contains options for controlling the color conversion. Unless you're knowledgeable about setting up a color-managed workflow, it's best to leave the Color and PDF/X menus on the default settings. For a detailed explanation of these options, enter "output options for pdf" in the search field in Illustrator Help. For Web output, if you chose Smallest File Size from the Adobe PDF Preset menu, the correct Output options were set automatically.

6. Click **Advanced** on the left side of the dialog to access font, overprint, and flattening options.

By default, the PDF presets automatically embed all the characters of every font that is being used in the document. If only a portion of the characters in those fonts is being used in your artwork, you can reduce the file size by embedding just those subsets. To do this, enter a percentage in the **Subset Fonts When Percentage of Characters Used Is Less Than** field. If you enter 50%, for example, the entire font will be embedded if more than 50% of the font's characters are being used in the file, and the subset will be embedded if fewer than 50% of those characters are being used.

Acrobat versions 5 through 8 preserve overprinting and transparency settings automatically. If Acrobat 4 (PDF 1.3) is chosen as the Compatibility option and the document contains overprints, choose whether you want Illustrator to Preserve or Discard Overprints. Similarly, if the artwork contains transparency, choose a transparency flattener preset or custom options (see pages 404–406).

7. Moving right along, click **Security** on the left side of the dialog if you want to restrict user access to the PDF. The following options are available only for non-PDF/X files (and some aren't available for early versions of Acrobat):

Check **Require a Password to Open the Document** to protect the file with a password, and type that password in the Document Open Password field.

➤ Since the password can't be recovered from the document, jot it down somewhere (yes, on paper!).

Check **Use a Password to Restrict Editing Security and Permissions Settings** if you want to maintain control over your viewers' use of the file. Type a password in the Permissions Password field, and choose any of the following Acrobat Permissions settings:

Choose an option from the **Printing Allowed** menu to control whether users can print the file: None, Low Resolution (150 dpi), or High Resolution. The Low Resolution option is only available for Acrobat versions 5 and higher.

Choose an option from the **Changes Allowed** menu to specify precisely which parts of the document users may copy.

Check **Enable Copying of Text, Images, and Other Content** to permit users to copy the document content.

Check **Enable Text Access of Screen Reader Devices for the Visually Impaired** to permit screen readers to view and read the file.

Check **Enable Plaintext Metadata** if you want the file metadata to be searchable by other applications (this is available only for Acrobat versions 6 through 8).

8. Click **Summary** on the left side of the dialog to view an expandable list of the settings you've chosen in each option set.

9. Click **Save PDF**, then give yourself a nice pat on the back.

SAVE YOUR SETTINGS AS A PRESET!

➤ Once you've chosen custom settings in the Save Adobe PDF dialog, you should save them as a user-created preset by clicking Save Preset in the lower left corner (enter a name for the preset in the dialog, then click OK). You can then choose your custom preset from the Adobe PDF Preset menu for any file.

➤ To edit a user-created preset, choose Edit > Adobe PDF Presets, click your user-created preset on the list of Presets, then click Edit.

Using the Export command

The Export dialog gives you access to other file formats besides EPS and PDF.

To export an Illustrator file:

1. With the file open, choose File > **Export**. The Export dialog opens.

2. *Optional:* Change the file name in the Save As/ File Name field. Illustrator will automatically append the proper file extension (e.g., .bmp, .psd, .tif) to the file name for the format you are going to choose in the next step.

3. Choose from the **Format/Save as Type** menu, **A–B** and choose a location for the new file.

   ➤ To create a new folder for the file in the Mac OS, choose a location, click New Folder, enter a name, then click Create. To do this in Windows, click Create New Folder, then enter a name.

4. If the Use Artboards options are available for the chosen format and you want to save multiple artboards in the document as separate files (labeled with the artboard name ★), check **Use Artboards**, then click All or click Range and enter a range. Or if you want to combine all the artboards into one file, uncheck Use Artboards.

5. Click Export/Save. Choose settings in any further dialog that opens, then click OK. A few file formats are discussed briefly on the facing page. Following that, the GIF, JPEG, and PSD formats are discussed in depth.

USING ILLUSTRATOR FILES IN FLASH PROFESSIONAL OR FLASH CATALYST

Adobe Flash Professional can be used for Web animations and interactive graphics. An easy way to get Illustrator objects into Flash Pro is simply by importing your Adobe Illustrator (.ai) file into that program. All paths, strokes, gradients, standard type (or type that is designated as dynamic text), masks, effects, and symbols are preserved. In the Import dialog in Flash Pro, you can specify whether layers are converted to individual Flash layers, Flash frames, or a single Flash layer.

➤ Another option is to import the Adobe Illustrator (.ai) file into the Adobe Flash Catalyst program. ★ Flash Catalyst will preserve the Illustrator layer hierarchy and let you control layer visibility. Artwork from each artboard is placed on an individual Flash Catalyst page. Flash Catalyst displays an Illustrator Import Options dialog, in which you can choose whether to keep vector objects editable, expand or flatten (rasterize) complex objects to preserve their appearance, or choose automatic conversion to let Catalyst determine how to convert the objects. You can also apply fills, gradients, and strokes to imported Illustrator objects directly in Catalyst, which can help to minimize import problems. For more about Flash Catalyst, enter "Flash Catalyst importing artwork" in the search field in Illustrator Help.

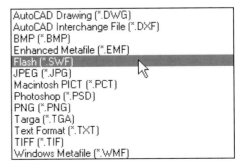

✓ PNG (png)
BMP (bmp)
AutoCAD Drawing (dwg)
AutoCAD Interchange File (dxf)
Enhanced Metafile (emf)
Flash (swf)
JPEG (jpg)
Macintosh PICT (pct)
Photoshop (psd)
TIFF (tif)
Targa (tga)
Text Format (txt)
Windows Metafile (wmf)

A *These choices are available on the Format menu in the Mac OS.*

AutoCAD Drawing (*.DWG)
AutoCAD Interchange File (*.DXF)
BMP (*.BMP)
Enhanced Metafile (*.EMF)
Flash (*.SWF)
JPEG (*.JPG)
Macintosh PICT (*.PCT)
Photoshop (*.PSD)
PNG (*.PNG)
Targa (*.TGA)
Text Format (*.TXT)
TIFF (*.TIF)
Windows Metafile (*.WMF)

B *These choices are available on the Save as Type menu in Windows.*

A few of the export formats, in brief

If you choose a raster (bitmap) file format in the Export dialog, such as BMP (bmp), the Rasterize Options dialog opens.**A** Choose a Color Model for the resulting file. For the file Resolution, choose Screen (72 dpi), Medium (150 dpi), or High (300 dpi), or enter a custom resolution next to Other. Choose an Anti-Aliasing option to control whether pixels will be added along curved edges to make them look smoother: None, Art Optimized (Supersampling) for artwork that doesn't contain much type, or Type Optimized (Hinted) for artwork that contains a lot of editable type. ★ Note: Settings chosen for type on the Anti-Aliasing menu on the Character panel (e.g., None, Sharp, Crisp, Strong) are honored only for the Type Optimized option.

BMP (bmp)

BMP is a standard bitmap image format on Windows computers. After choosing settings in the Rasterize Options dialog and clicking OK, the BMP Options dialog opens. Choose the Windows or OS/2 format as the target operating system, specify a bit (color) depth, and choose whether you want to enable RLE compression, if that option is available.

TIFF (tif)

TIFF, a bitmap image format, is supported by virtually all paint, image-editing, and page layout applications. It supports RGB, CMYK, and grayscale color, and offers LZW as a compression option. When you choose the TIFF (tif) file format in the Export dialog, the TIFF Options dialog opens.**B** Choose a

Color Model; choose a Resolution of Screen (72 dpi), Medium (150 dpi), or High (300 dpi) or enter a custom resolution; and choose an Anti-Aliasing option. Check LZW Compression if you need to compress the file; this lossless method won't discard or degrade image data. Choose your target platform in the Byte Order area, and check Embed ICC Profile if you have assigned such a profile to your file.

Enhanced Metafile (emf) and Windows Metafile (wmf)

Vector data is stored in a metafile as a list of commands for drawing objects such as straight lines, polygons, and text, and commands to control the style of the objects. Use these formats, when necessary, to export only simple artwork to the Windows platform. Windows Metafile (wmf) is a 16-bit metafile format; Enhanced Metafile (emf) is a 32-bit metafile format that can store a wider range of commands than WMF and is therefore the better choice of the two.

Microsoft Office

Choose File > Save for Microsoft Office to save your document in a PNG format that is readable by Microsoft Word, PowerPoint, and Excel. Transparent areas will become opaque. If you want to specify a resolution and background color, with an option to preserve transparency, use File > Export instead, and choose PNG (png) from the Format/Save as Type menu.

A *The Rasterize Options dialog opens if you choose a raster format in the Export dialog.*

B *Choose options in the TIFF Options dialog.*

Optimizing files for the Web

You can use Illustrator to create graphics for a Web page, such as a logo or an illustration, or perhaps some buttons, graphics, or text to be used as navigation devices. Before placing your artwork into a Web page creation program, such as Adobe Dreamweaver, you need to convert it from vector art into pixels, a process known as optimization.

Image size and compression

The length of time it takes for an image to load into a Web page is directly related to its file size. The file size, in turn, is governed by the dimensions of the image (in pixels) and the amount and kind of compression that is applied to it when it is optimized. Vector graphics, in particular, tend to compress well because they contain solid-color shapes. For your Web artwork, resist the urge to use patterns or gradients, which compress less than solid colors do. When choosing dimensions for an image, keep in mind that the Web page your graphics will be viewed on is smaller than the 1024 x 768-pixel area of a typical monitor.

The GIF and JPEG file formats

GIF and JPEG, the two file formats that are commonly used for optimizing graphics, are suitable for different types of graphics and use different compression schemes. Although those compression schemes cause a small reduction in image quality, it is a price that must be paid to enable the file to download more quickly on the Web.

GIF is an 8-bit format, meaning it can save a maximum of 256 colors. It's a good choice when color fidelity is a priority, such as for artwork that contains type or solid-color vector shapes. Graphics like these contain far fewer colors than continuous-tone (photographic) images, so the color restriction won't have an adverse impact. If your artwork contains transparency, you must choose this format, because it supports transparency, whereas the JPEG format does not. When you optimize an Illustrator file in the GIF format, the solid colors in your artwork translate into just a small portion of the maximum number of 256 possible colors. This set of colors is referred to as the file's color table. By reducing the number of colors in the color table, you can shrink the file size and enable the file to download more quickly.

If your Illustrator file contains continuous-tone images (e.g., raster images that you've imported into it, or gradients), the JPEG format, with its ability to save 24-bit color, will do a better job of preserving color fidelity than GIF. Another advantage to using the JPEG format is that its compression scheme is capable of shrinking an image significantly without lowering its quality. When saving an image in this format, you can choose a quality setting; the higher the quality setting, the larger the file size.

Unfortunately, the JPEG format, unlike GIF, doesn't preserve transparency or the sharp edges of vector objects. Furthermore, when you optimize an image as JPEG, some image data is lost; the greater the compression, the greater the loss.

Issues to address before optimizing a file

➤ Follow the instructions in "Creating pixel-perfect artwork for the Web" on page 82. For symbols, see "Aligning symbols to the pixel grid" in the sidebar on page 359.★

➤ The GIF and JPEG formats rasterize all vector objects at 72 pixels per inch. If you want to control both the resolution for rasterization and the kind of anti-aliasing applied to a particular vector object, apply the Object > Rasterize command to the object before optimizing the file (see page 206). This command is especially useful for rasterizing individual type objects.

Exporting type to the Web

All the options (except None) on the Anti-Aliasing menu ★ in the expanded Character panel add partially transparent pixels along the edges of the characters to make them look smoother: Sharp may produce inconsistent letterforms; Crisp preserves the weight and curvature of the original letterforms and is suitable for large point sizes; Strong increases the weight of the original letterforms and is suitable for type that has thin strokes. Choose None (no anti-aliasing) only for very small type. If you apply one of these options to type, you must set anti-aliasing to Type Optimized when using Object > Rasterize (see page 206), or when exporting a document to a raster format, such as BMP or TIFF (see the preceding page), or when exporting a document via the Save for Web & Devices dialog (see pages 422–423).

In the Save for Web & Devices dialog, you'll find all the controls you need to optimize your Illustrator graphics for the Web. Experiment with the multiple previews in this dialog first to test the effects of different optimization settings.

To use the preview controls in the Save for Web & Devices dialog:

1. Via the artboard navigation controls at the bottom of the document window or via the Artboards panel, display the artboard that you want to preview optimization settings for.

2. Choose File > **Save for Web & Devices** (Cmd-Option-Shift-S/Ctrl-Alt-Shift-S). The current artboard will display in the dialog.**A**

3. Do either of the following:

   Click the **4-Up** tab to display the original document and three optimization previews. Illustrator will use the current optimization options to generate the first preview (to the right of the original), then generate two other previews as variations of those optimization settings. You can click any preview and change the optimization settings (on the right side of the dialog) for just that preview. As you choose settings, note the change to the file size, which is listed below each preview.

   For a more definitive test preview at any time, click the **Preview in Default Browser** button at the bottom of the dialog. Your optimized image will open in the default Web browser application that is installed in your system. Or if you'd rather choose a different browser that's installed in your system, from the **Select Browser** menu, choose a browser name; or choose Other, then locate and open the preferred browser. Quit/exit the browser when you're done admiring your work.

Preview tabs   *Preview menu for choosing a download connection speed*   *Optimization options*

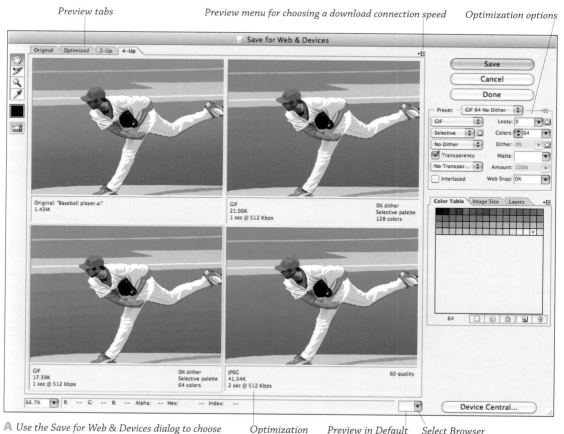

A Use the Save for Web & Devices dialog to choose and preview optimization settings for your document.

Optimization info   *Preview in Default Browser button*   *Select Browser menu*

We'll show you how to optimize files in the GIF format first, because it does a better job of optimizing vector objects and type than JPEG.

To optimize a file in the GIF format:

1. Save your file and display the artboard to be optimized.

2. Choose File > **Save for Web & Devices** (Cmd-Opt-Shift-S/Ctrl-Alt-Shift-S).

3. Click the **2-Up** tab at the top of the dialog to display both the original and optimized previews of the document.

4. Do either of the following:

   From the **Preset** menu, choose one of the **GIF** options. Leave the preset settings as is, then click Save. The Save Optimized As dialog opens. Keep the current name, choose a location for the file, and then click Save.

   Follow the remaining steps to choose custom optimization settings.

Choose GIF settings

1. From the Optimized File Format menu, choose **GIF**.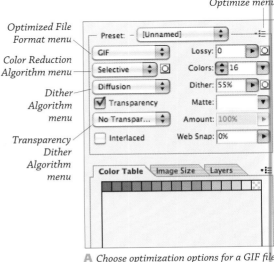

2. From the **Color Reduction Algorithm** menu, choose a method for reducing the number of colors in the image. We recommend using the Selective (default) option because it preserves both solid and Web-safe colors.

3. Next, to remove some colors from the document's color table to reduce the file size, choose 16 from the **Colors** menu. If it looks (in the optimized preview) as though some colors have been substituted, you can raise the Colors value to 32.

4. *Optional:* Dithering is a process by which Illustrator mixes dots of a few different colors to simulate a broader range of colors. This option increases the file size slightly but is helpful for artwork that contains gradients or soft-edged effects (e.g., drop shadows). Choose the Diffusion method from the Dither Algorithm menu, and on the right, choose a Dither value between 50% and 75%. (If you choose No Dither, the gradients may have noticeable bands.)

5. Check **Transparency** to preserve fully transparent pixels in the artwork. By default, the background becomes transparent. *Optional:* With Transparency checked, you have the option to define which colors in the artwork will become

transparent. To do this, choose the Eyedropper tool, click a color in the optimized preview area, then click the Map Selected Colors to Transparent button at the bottom of the Color table.

6. If the artwork contains any soft-edged effects (such as drop shadows) on top of transparent areas and you happen to know the background color of the target Web page, click the **Matte** swatch and choose that color via the Color Picker. This will help your artwork blend in with the background. If that color is unknown, set Matte to None; this option creates a hard, jagged edge.

   Another option is to choose Matte: None, and with Transparency checked, choose an option from the Transparency Dither Algorithm menu. With one of these options chosen, the art will look the same on any background.

7. Click the **Image Size** tab, then choose an **Anti-Aliasing** setting of None, Art Optimized, or Type Optimized. ★ Note: Settings chosen for type from the Anti-Aliasing menu on the Character panel are honored only for the Type Optimized option. Click Apply to preview the settings.

8. Click Save. In the Save Optimized As dialog, keep the current name, choose a location for the file, and then click Save.

➤ To save the current (Unnamed) options as a preset, see the tip on the next page.

Optimize menu

Optimized File Format menu

Color Reduction Algorithm menu

Dither Algorithm menu

Transparency Dither Algorithm menu

A *Choose optimization options for a GIF file in the Save for Web & Devices dialog.*

When a file is optimized in the JPEG format, its 24-bit color is preserved and can be seen and enjoyed by most of your viewers. If your artwork contains gradients, JPEG is a better choice than GIF. Two drawbacks to JPEG are that its compression method eliminates some image data and that it doesn't preserve transparency.

To optimize a file in the JPEG format:

1. Save your file and display the artboard to be optimized.

2. Choose File > **Save for Web & Devices** (Cmd-Opt-Shift-S/Ctrl-Alt-Shift-S). The Save for Web & Devices dialog opens.**A**

3. Click the **2-Up** tab at the top of the dialog to display both the original and optimized previews of the document.

4. Do either of the following:

   From the **Preset** menu, choose one of the **JPEG** options. Leave the preset settings as is, then click Save. The Save Optimized As dialog opens. Keep the current name, choose a location for the file, and then click Save.

   Follow the remaining steps to choose custom optimization settings.

Choose JPEG settings

1. From the Optimized File Format menu, choose **JPEG.**

2. Do either of the following:

   From the **Compression Quality** menu, choose a quality level for the optimized image.

   Move the **Quality** slider to the desired compression level.

   ➤ The higher the compression quality, the better the quality of the optimized file—and the larger the file size.

3. Increase the **Blur** value slightly to lessen the prominence of JPEG artifacts that may be created from the chosen JPEG compression method, and to reduce the file size. Be careful not to blur the artwork to the point that sharp vector shapes start looking too soft.

4. Choose a **Matte** color to be substituted for areas of transparency in the artwork (see step 6 on the preceding page). If you choose None from this menu, transparent areas will display as white.

   ➤ The JPEG format doesn't support transparency. To have the Matte color simulate

transparency, make it the same solid color as the background of the Web page (if you happen know what that color is).

5. Uncheck **Progressive** and **ICC Profile.**

6. *Optional:* Check Optimized to produce the smallest possible file size.

7. Click the **Image Size** tab, then choose an **Anti-Aliasing** setting of None, Art Optimized, or Type Optimized. ★ Note: Settings chosen for type from the Anti-Aliasing menu on the Character panel are honored only for the Type Optimized option. Click Apply to preview the settings.

8. Click Save. The Save Optimized As dialog opens. Leave the name as is, choose a location for the file, then click Save.

➤ To save the current (Unnamed) options as a preset, choose Save Settings from the Optimize menu, enter a name, then click Save. Your saved set is now available on the Preset menu in the Save for Web & Devices dialog for any file.

A *Choose optimization options for a JPEG file in the Save for Web & Devices dialog.*

Exporting Illustrator files to Adobe Photoshop

There are several ways to get an Adobe Illustrator file into Adobe Photoshop:

➤ For the greatest ease in future editing, we highly recommend using the Smart Object layer feature in Photoshop. A Smart Object layer is created automatically if you do any of the following: Place an Adobe Illustrator (.ai) file into a Photoshop document via the File > Place command in Photoshop or the File > Place > In Photoshop command in Bridge; or drag an object from an Illustrator document into a Photoshop document; or copy and paste an object from Illustrator into Photoshop, then choose Smart Object in the Paste dialog. When you double-click a Smart Object layer in Photoshop, the Illustrator artwork that you embedded into the Photoshop file opens as vectors in Illustrator. Edit and then save the embedded file, and the Smart Object layer updates in Photoshop — an easy round trip!

For print output, exporting Illustrator objects as Smart Objects has a major advantage over using the Photoshop (psd) export format. Photoshop will print vector objects or editable type layers in a Smart Object layer at the printer resolution, which on a high-resolution PostScript printer is usually higher than the Photoshop file resolution. Pixel layers (including converted Illustrator layers that are imported via the Photoshop .psd format), on the other hand, will print at the resolution of the Photoshop file, not of the printer.

➤ That said, if you want to export an Illustrator document in the Photoshop (psd) format, follow the steps at right.

➤ Copy and paste an object into Photoshop as pixels, as a path, or as a shape layer by choosing that option in the Paste dialog in Photoshop. To ensure that the Paste dialog displays in Photoshop, in Illustrator, go to Illustrator/Edit > Preferences > File Handling & Clipboard and check both of the PDF and AICB options. If you copy a compound path or compound shape from Illustrator, paste it into Photoshop, then click Shape Layer in the Paste dialog, it will arrive as multiple paths on a shape layer. The Foreground color in Photoshop will fill the shape.

➤ Drag and drop an Illustrator object as a plain, unstroked path into Photoshop by holding down Cmd/Ctrl as you drag. The path will be listed on the Paths panel in Photoshop.

To export an Illustrator file as pixels in the Photoshop (psd) format:

1. Choose File > **Export**. The Export dialog opens.

2. Type a name and choose a location for the file, then choose Format/Save as Type: **Photoshop (psd)**. To save multiple artboards as separate files (labeled with the artboard names ★), check **Use Artboards**, then click All, or click Range and enter a range. Or to combine all the artboards in one file, uncheck Use Artboards.

3. Click Export/Save. The Photoshop Export Options dialog opens.

4. Choose a **Color Model** that matches the current document color mode.

5. Click a preset **Resolution** value or enter a custom value.

6. In the Options area, do any of the following:

   To have all layers in the artwork import as one flattened layer in Photoshop, click **Flat Image**. Or to export the top-level layers to Photoshop, click **Write Layers** and check **Maximum Editability**. If the Illustrator file contains type that doesn't have a stroke or effects applied to it, you can check Preserve Text Editability to allow the text to remain editable in Photoshop.

   Note: Although the Write Layers option preserves the stacking appearance of objects that are nested within a layer, only top-level layers will become layers in Photoshop; hidden layers and empty artboards in the Illustrator file won't be included. If an Illustrator layer contains an object that Photoshop can't import in its current state (such as a stroke or an effect), that layer and any layers below it will be merged into one layer. A layer-level clipping set or an object-level clipping group will export as a rasterized layer, but the visual effect of the mask will be preserved.

   Check **Anti-Alias** to soften the edges of curved shapes in the artwork.

   Check **Embed ICC Profile** to embed the current color profile in the file, if one was assigned.

7. Click OK. Transparency and blending mode settings (if any) from Illustrator layers are preserved for each rasterized layer and are listed as editable options on the Layers panel in Photoshop. Compound shapes are converted to shape layers.

Appendix A: Artwork by Illustrator pros

Daniel Pelavin

Harry Campbell

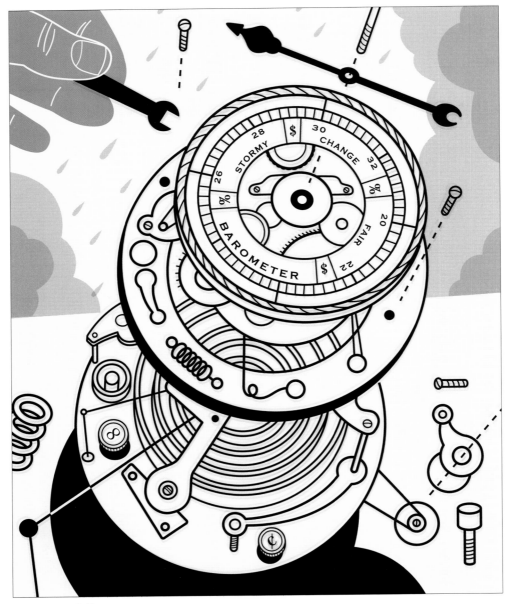

Harry Campbell

©Harry Campbell

Celia Johnson

Celia Johnson

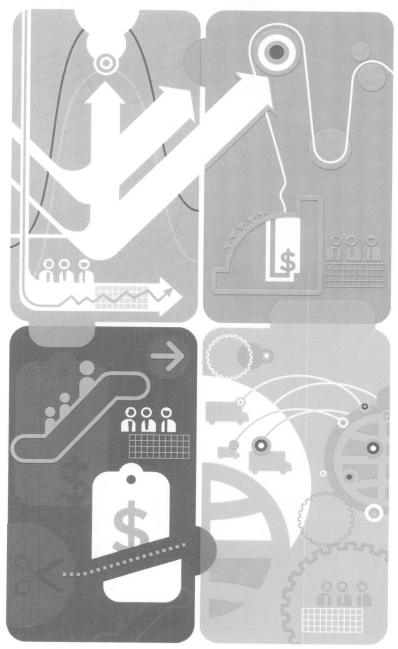

©Celia Johnson

Chris Lyons

©Chris Lyons

Chris Lyons

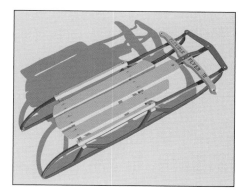

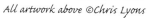

All artwork above ©Chris Lyons

Appendix B: Credits

Artists

Harry Campbell
Studio 410-371-0270
harry@harrycampbell.net
www.harrycampbell.net
Pages 426–427

Celia Johnson
Represented by Gerald & Cullen Rapp
Portfolio websites:
www.rappart.com/Celia_Johnson
www.illoz.com/celia
www.theispot.com/artist/johnson
Contact: celia@cprojex.com
Page 428–429

Chris Lyons
14 East Park Road
Pittsford, NY 14534
Studio 585-615-2781
www.chrislyonsillustration.com
Pages iv, x, 430–431

Daniel Pelavin
80 Varick Street, #3B
New York, NY 10013
Studio 212-941-7418
www.pelavin.com
Page 425

Vector art and photography

Shutterstock.com
Pages i, iii, v, 1, 6, 7, 10, 15, 23, 24, 26, 29, 30, 37, 38, 47, 55, 57, 60, 61, 75, 76, 77, 79, 80 (figure D), 81, 82, 83, 84*, 85*, 86, 87*, 89, 94*, 97*, 99, 100*, 111, 114*, 123, 133, 134, 135*, 137, 138, 139*, 140*, 144, 146*, 147, 150*, 151*, 153*, 154*, 156, 158*, 160*, 161*, 168, 169, 170, 189, 190*, 192, 196*, 197*, 198, 202, 203, 204, 205, 207, 209*, 213*, 216*, 217*, 219, 220, 233*, 235, 236, 239, 250, 253, 272, 273, 279, 280*, 282, 283*, 286*, 287*, 289, 297, 300, 301*, 302*, 304*, 306, 311, 315*, 317, 318, 323*, 324*, 327, 328*, 333*, 336*, 337*, 341, 342*, 349, 350*, 351*, 354*, 377*, 379, 380, 381, 385, 386, 387, 388, 390, 391, 402, 411, 421, 432

This artwork was modified by the authors.

All other artwork©Peter Lourekas and Elaine Weinmann

Unless noted otherwise, the entries in this index pertain to Illustrator.